mylabschool™

Where the classroom comes to life!

From watching actual classroom video footage of teachers and students interacting to building standards-based lessons and web-based portfolios . . . from a robust resource library of the "What Every Teacher Should Know About" series to complete instruction on writing an effective research paper . . . **MyLabSchool** brings together an amazing collection of resources for future teachers. This website gives you a wealth of videos, print and simulated cases, career advice, and much more.

Use **MyLabSchool** with this Allyn and Bacon Education text, and you will have everything you need to succeed in your course. Assignment IDs have also been incorporated into many Allyn and Bacon Education texts to link to the online material in **MyLabSchool** . . . connecting the teachers of tomorrow to the information they need today.

PEARSON
AB
and

VISIT **www.mylabschool.com** to learn more about this invaluable resource and Take a Tour!

Here's what you'll find in mylabschool™

Where the classroom comes to life!

VideoLab ▶

Access hundreds of video clips of actual classroom situations from a variety of grade levels and school settings. These 3- to 5-minute closed-captioned video clips illustrate real teacher–student interaction, and are organized both topically *and* by discipline. Students can test their knowledge of classroom concepts with integrated observation questions.

Becoming a Teacher

First year teacher Penny Brandenburg talks about why she became a teacher. Her philosophy of teaching is to encourage the students to take ownership of their learning.

00:22/4.53 sec

◀ Lesson & Portfolio Builder

This feature enables students to create, maintain, update, and share online portfolios and standards-based lesson plans. The Lesson Planner walks students, step-by-step, through the process of creating a complete lesson plan, including verifiable objectives, assessments, and related state standards. Upon completion, the lesson plan can be printed, saved, e-mailed, or uploaded to a website.

EDUCATIONAL RESEARCH

FIFTH EDITION

EDUCATIONAL RESEARCH

FUNDAMENTALS *for the* CONSUMER

James H. McMillan

Virginia Commonwealth University

Boston   New York   San Francisco
Mexico City   Montreal   Toronto   London   Madrid   Munich   Paris
Hong Kong   Singapore   Tokyo   Cape Town   Sydney

Senior Editor: Arnis E. Burvikovs
Series Editorial Assistant: Erin Reilly
Marketing Manager: Erica DeLuca
Editorial Production Service: Omegatype Typography, Inc.
Composition Buyer: Linda Cox
Manufacturing Manager: Megan Cochran
Electronic Composition: Omegatype Typography, Inc.
Cover Administrator: Kristina Mose-Libon

For related titles and support materials, visit our online catalog at www.ablongman.com.

Between the time website information is gathered and then published, it is not unusual for some sites to have closed. Also, the transcription of URLs can result in typographical errors. The publisher would appreciate notification where these errors occur so that they may be corrected in subsequent editions.

ISBN-10: 0-205-50830-8
ISBN-13: 978-0-205-50830-3

Library of Congress Cataloging-in-Publication Data

McMillan, James H.
    Educational research : fundamentals for the consumer / James H. McMillan. — 5th ed.
        p. cm.
    Includes bibliographical references and index.
    ISBN 0-205-50830-8
    1. Education—Research.   I. Title.
    LB1028.M365 2008
    370.7'2—dc22

                                                                        2006047972

Printed in the United States of America

10 9 8 7 6 5 4 3 2   RRD-VA   11   10   09   08   07

Credits appear on page 397, which constitutes a continuation of the copyright page.

To Janice, Jon, and Ryann

About the Author

 James H. McMillan is Professor of Education in the School of Education at Virginia Commonwealth University, Chair of the Department of Foundations of Education, and Director of the Metropolitan Educational Research Consortium. He obtained his doctorate from Northwestern University and masters from Michigan State University. Dr. McMillan has also published *Research in Education: Evidence-Based Inquiry*; *Understanding and Evaluating Educational Research*, and *Classroom Assessment: Principles and Practice for Effective Standards-Based Instruction* in addition to more than sixty journal articles. His current research interests include classroom assessment, grading, student motivation, and the impact of high-stakes testing on schools and students.

Contents

3 LOCATING *and* REVIEWING RELATED LITERATURE *54*

4 USING *the* INTERNET *for* EDUCATIONAL RESEARCH *82*

5 PARTICIPANTS, SUBJECTS, *and* SAMPLING *109*

6 FOUNDATIONS *of* EDUCATIONAL MEASUREMENT *130*

7 TYPES *of* EDUCATIONAL MEASURES *158*

8 NONEXPERIMENTAL QUANTITATIVE RESEARCH DESIGNS *185*

9 EXPERIMENTAL RESEARCH DESIGNS *217*

10 UNDERSTANDING STATISTICAL INFERENCES *251*

11 QUALITATIVE RESEARCH DESIGNS *and* ANALYSIS *270*

To the Instructor

This edition of *Educational Research: Fundamentals for the Consumer* is primarily for consumers of educational research and those involved in conducting action research. Consumers locate, read, understand, critique, and then use the results of research to become more effective professionally and to make sound educational decisions. The book is designed to enable students to become *intelligent* consumers of educational research and to introduce its basic principles to those who may eventually be involved in research in their work. The book is intended for a one-semester or one-term course in educational research. It is best suited for advanced undergraduate and beginning graduate students in education, and it is ideal for students enrolled in extended teacher preparation programs for initial certification, which emphasize research on effective teaching and action research (teacher researchers). The examples and excerpts from published studies are drawn largely from research that teachers and administrators will find interesting and informative. There are now excerpts from studies and different journals. The book is also appropriate for students in more traditional masters' programs, who will be consumers of educational research, and for students in related social sciences, who need to learn how to read and understand research.

The primary goal of this book is to educate students to be intelligent consumers. This is accomplished by promoting student understanding of the researcher's intent, the procedures, and the results. Students are then shown how to analyze and evaluate research, judging the usefulness of the findings for educational practice. More specifically, the book will help students to:

- apply the principles of scientific inquiry to everyday problem solving and decision making;
- develop a healthy skepticism about "studies" that purport to advance our knowledge;
- understand the process of conceptualizing and conducting educational research;
- understand strengths and weaknesses of different methodologies used in research;
- be able to read, understand, critique, and use published reports of research;

- understand the probabilistic, uncertain nature of knowledge about educational practice generated through research;
- keep a balanced perspective about the relative contributions of research and professional judgment; and
- understand how to conduct action research.

These goals are reached with a concise presentation of principles for conducting research and criteria for evaluating its overall credibility. The style of the book is informal, the language is nontechnical, and no prerequisite courses in measurement or statistics are needed. Numerous illustrations and excerpts from actual studies are highlighted as examples to familiarize students with the style and format of published articles, and to introduce students to the language of research.

The sequence of topics has remained unchanged from the fourth edition. The book covers fundamental principles in the sequence found in the research process, beginning with research problems and ending with conclusions. The emphasis is on teaching students that all aspects of conducting and reporting research are important in judging the overall credibility of the findings. The format of research articles is included in the first chapter to enable students to read published studies as early as possible in the course. My experience is that students need as much practice in reading and critiquing articles as possible.

Because good consumers know how to find helpful research, the chapter on reviewing literature includes skills in locating primary and secondary sources and in evaluating a review of literature section of an article. **New to this edition is an extensively revised chapter on reviewing literature consistent with the "new" ERIC, and an updated chapter on using the Internet to locate research.** This provides hints, sites, and procedures that will make it easy for students to use ERIC and navigate the Internet.

The chapters on measurement are fairly extensive because of its important role in educational research. **This edition includes a review of standards-based assessment.** Basic statistical principles are presented first to enhance understanding. For example, students must know about correlation to understand reliability and validity.

The emphasis in the discussion of each methodology—descriptive, comparative, correlational, survey, experimental, single-subject, qualitative, and mixed-method—is on what to look for in evaluating the credibility of the design and procedures. **The chapter on experimental designs has been expanded to reflect the increased emphasis on doing experiments initiated by the federal government, with a focus on quasi-experiments.**

The chapter on qualitative research has been expanded with added emphasis on data analysis. A conceptual introduction to inferential statistics is included to clarify the results sections of quantitative articles. **There is also a new chapter on mixed-method designs and action research.** This chapter provides a more extensive discussion of mixed-method strategies and analyses than the previous edition and provides students with essential skills to conduct action research.

As in the previous editions, the chapters include aids to facilitate learning essential skills and knowledge. Key research terms are highlighted in the margins to reinforce their importance, chapter summaries in the form of concept maps organize the material succinctly, and study questions allow students to check their knowledge. Throughout the book, special sections called Consumer Tips emphasize the skills needed to judge studies critically. Examples from over 90 published articles are included in the form of direct excerpts or examples from actual research, most of which are new and updated. **Pedagogical aids** include Chapter Road Maps, Internet Connections, Using Educational Research, and Author Reflections. Throughout the text there is an increased emphasis on use of the Internet.

In summary, the fifth edition has been strengthened with the following:

- Updates of all chapters, examples, and references
- Substantial revision of Chapter 3, Locating and Reviewing Related Literature, and Chapter 4, Using the Internet for Educational Research
- New chapter on mixed-method designs and action research
- Expansion of Chapter 11 to include more on qualitative data analysis
- New articles added to reach a total of 11
- Additional examples and excerpts from published studies in more than 50 different journals
- More emphasis on Internet (web-based) surveys
- New discussion of the nature of research consistent with *Scientific Research in Education*
- Expanded treatment of experimental and quasi-experimental designs
- Expanded treatment of effect size and limitations of statistical hypothesis testing
- Revised treatment of causal-comparative designs
- Special activities using **MyLabSchool** are also included at the end of every chapter. This powerful tool allows readers to investigate key concepts from the book using a collection of resources available online at **www.mylabschool.com,** including Research Navigator™, a collection of invaluable research databases.

SUPPLEMENTS

A full complement of supplements further enhance and strengthen the fifth edition.

- The newly revised **companion website, www.ablongman.com/ mcmillan5e,** can be accessed by both students and instructors to get additional help in understanding the content presented in the text.
- An **Instructor's Resource Manual,** including test questions and answers, additional exercises and activities, is available to adopters by contacting their local representative.
- A PowerPoint™ presentation is also available online to instructors by contacting their local representative.
- *Understanding Research: Student Activities for Educational Research: Fundamentals for the Consumer,* by Lisa M. Abrams and Richard Mohn of Virginia Commonwealth University, includes brief chapter overviews with key concepts, outlines designed to facilitate note taking, group and individual activities aligned with key concepts, web-based resources, and an answer key. This manual can be packaged with any new text by requesting a special package ISBN.

mylabschool is a collection of online tools for your success in this course, on your licensure exams, and in your teaching career. Visit www.mylabschool.com to access the following:

- Video footage of real-life classrooms, with opportunities for you to reflect on the videos and offer your own thoughts and suggestions for applying theory to practice
- An extensive archive of text and multimedia cases that provide valuable perspectives on real classrooms and real teaching challenges
- Allyn & Bacon's Lesson and Portfolio Builder application, which includes an integrated state standards correlation tool
- Research paper assistance using Research Navigator™, which provides access to three exclusive databases of credible and reliable source material: EBSCO's ContentSelect Academic Journal Database, The New York Times Search-by-Subject Archive, and "Best of the Web" Link Library
- Career Center with resources for Praxis exams and licensure preparation, professional portfolio development, and job search and interview techniques

ACKNOWLEDGMENTS

Numerous individuals have contributed much to this book. I am most grateful to my editor of the first two editions, Chris Jennison, for his support, encouragement, and needed recommendations; to my editor for the third edition, Art Pomponio; and to my current editor, Arnis Burvikovs. I am also indebted to many students who provided feedback to my approach and materials.

The following reviewers of previous editions contributed constructive suggestions: Jean Swenk, National University; Anthony Truog, University of Wisconsin-Whitewater; Judith Kennison, Ithaca College; Beatrice Baldwin, Southeastern Louisiana University; Kaia Skaggs, Eastern Michigan University; Ayers D'Costa, Ohio State University; Tamera Murdock, University of Missouri at Kansas City; Andy Katayama, West Virginia University; and John W. Sanders, Middle Tennessee State University. Lauren Miller and Wendy Balliet provided excellent reviews, suggestions, and editing. I also thank the reviewers of this edition: Anastasia Elder, Mississippi State University; Lisa Kirtman, California State University, Fullerton; William J. Murphy, Framingham State University; and Steven W. Neill, Emporia State University.

Finally, I am grateful to the staff at Allyn & Bacon, especially Erin Reilly, who have been exemplary in their editing and production of the book.

As this is being written, further ideas are germinating for possible changes in organization and content for the sixth edition. Please write with any suggestions. Your comments will be most helpful.

James H. McMillan
jmcmillan@vcu.edu

To the Student

It was not *too* long ago that I sat, somewhat nervously, in a university auditorium waiting for my first class in educational research. Perhaps you have had a similar experience. I distinctly remember thinking, given what I had heard about "research," that I needed to learn only enough to pass the course and would not have to worry about it again! It was another hurdle that I was forced to jump to graduate. I was not bad in mathematics, but my interest was in working with people, not numbers. I certainly never thought that I would someday teach and write about educational research. But something happened to me as I grudgingly struggled through the course. What I discovered was that research is a way of thinking, a tool that I could use to improve the work I do with other people and to enhance student learning. My hope is that this book can instill a similar disposition in you, providing knowledge, skills, and attitudes to improve your life and the welfare of others.

Although learning the content and skills needed to become an intelligent consumer of research is not easy, my experience in teaching hundreds of students is that you will improve yourself, professionally and otherwise, through your efforts. In the beginning, especially as you read published research articles, not everything will make sense. But as your experience in being an informed consumer increases, so will your understanding.

Good luck and best wishes, and please write to me or e-mail me if you have suggestions for improving the book or the updated Companion Website that accompanies it (www.ablongman.com/mcmillan5e).

James H. McMillan
jmcmillan@vcu.edu

Chapter 1

Introduction *to* Research *in* Education

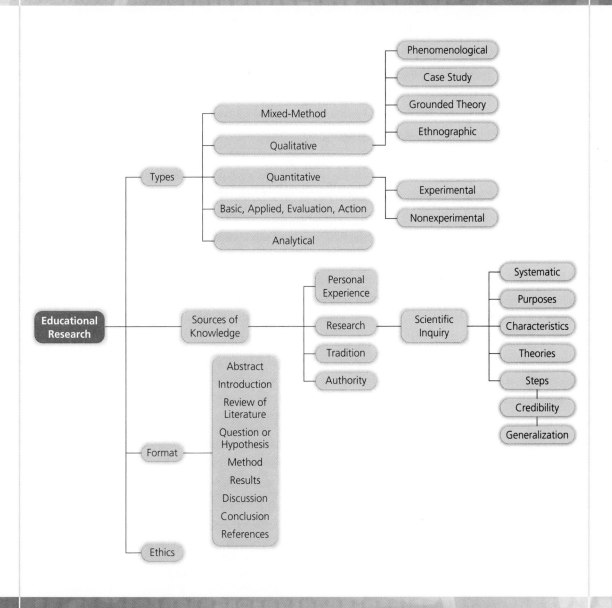

CHAPTER ROAD MAP

We begin our journey by considering different ways knowledge can be identified and constructed, with a special focus on how and why characteristics of scientific inquiry comprise the foundation for quality research. We then turn to overviews of different types of educational research and formats used with quantitative and qualitative studies, with two examples of published articles. As a result of studying this chapter, you will:

- Understand the unique contributions of scientific inquiry to our knowledge of effective educational practices
- Understand the steps used in scientific inquiry
- Understand the differences between experimental and nonexperimental research designs
- Become familiar with differences between quantitative and qualitative research
- Become familiar with the format of quantitative and qualitative studies as reported in published articles

WHY RESEARCH?

This book is about helping others to lead a richer, more satisfying life. That may seem like a strange beginning for a textbook, but I want to stress that there are good reasons for increasing your knowledge of research. It is clear that research in education has made, and will continue to make, important contributions to our understanding of teaching and learning at all levels. Educators, like other professionals, need to read and interpret research to keep abreast of these contributions. However, the quality of educational research varies greatly, so it is essential that we are able to make informed judgments about the credibility and usefulness of the studies. Because education is a complex, situation-specific endeavor, we must each make these judgments in our own context. This judgmental process can influence the lives of others positively. A proper, balanced perspective on research will strengthen the judgments we make constantly in educational settings, and in that way touch the lives of others.

Furthermore, teachers and administrators are increasingly involved in conducting research in their own classrooms, schools, and districts. They have found that even informal, small-scale studies can provide new knowledge and insights to help improve student learning.

Finally, there is a renewed interest at the national level to use "evidence-based" findings to evaluate programs and policy. The trend is to use research whenever possible to make decisions about effectiveness and to determine "what works" in schools. The intent is to better connect research with practice. In fact, the Elementary and Secondary Education Act, signed by President Bush in 2002, uses the phrase "scientifically based research" more than 100 times in the law.

SOURCES *of* KNOWLEDGE

Judgments are based on knowing. We "know" something when it is accepted as true or valid, when we can be fairly certain of its consequences. For example, good teachers seem to "know" when they are losing the students' interest and need to change the method of instruction, when students need a strong rebuke or a soft reprimand, and how to phrase questions to elicit involvement from most students. How do these teachers obtain such knowledge? There are several ways, identified here as sources of knowledge. Each is important, and by examining them we will be able to put research as a source of knowledge in perspective.

Personal Experience

It has been said that there is no substitute for experience, whether it is your own or someone else's. In education we rightfully depend a great deal on direct experience to know what works. Professionals become effective through practice, and teaching is no exception. But imagine if experience was the *only* way to obtain knowledge, or if you were confined to your own experiences and those of friends. Not only would it be difficult to know where to begin, but it would also be hard to know how to improve and how to handle new demands and situations. When research can be used to stimulate, inform, reinforce, challenge, and question our own experiences, the intuitive professional judgment that is absolutely essential for effective teaching and leadership is enhanced.

There are other limitations to using our personal experiences as sources of knowledge. Much of our knowledge from experience depends on what we have observed and how we have interpreted it. But as humans we can and do make mistakes in our observations. Sometimes, because we bring our own biases to a situation, we fail to see things that are clearly evident, and we make inaccurate observations and interpretations. Finally, because we are personally involved with our own interpretations, we have a natural inclination to protect our self-esteem and ego, and consequently we may not be totally objective.

Tradition

Many things seem to be done in certain ways simply because they have always been done that way. Advice, rules, approaches to handling problems, and "right" and "wrong" answers are passed from year to year, from one group to another, as accepted truths. Tradition eliminates the need to search for knowledge and understanding because we simply accept what has always been done as the best or right way. But reliance on tradition makes accepting new knowledge difficult and may mitigate our desire to question existing practices. For example, the tradition of a 180-day school year, with a summer vacation, in American public education makes it difficult to change to year-round schooling.

Authority

People we consider experts or authorities in a particular field are major sources of knowledge. An authority has experience or unique expertise in something and is able to provide insights and understanding that we are unable to see. We depend on such authorities, whether they are doctors, lawyers, professors, teachers, or plumbers, particularly in our specialized culture. But, like personal experience and tradition, authority can also hinder knowledge. Authorities can be wrong, and the public has a tendency to accept as fact what are actually opinions.

In fields such as education, where practice is heavily influenced by complex interactions among students, environments, and teachers, there is room for experts to disagree about what is known. Perhaps you have read one author who suggests one approach and another who suggests the opposite approach for the same situation or question. A good example is the research on computer-aided instruction (CAI). Some studies report that CAI is more effective than traditional instructional methods, but just as many studies fail to show that CAI is better or more effective than traditional methods. Thus, it is quite easy for experts to disagree about the effect of CAI on student learning. Also, the sheer number of authorities in education can be confusing. It is best to be able to analyze the suggestions of each authority and to make our own decisions.

Research

> **Research:** Systematic process of gathering and analyzing information.

In contrast to sources of knowledge that are primarily idiosyncratic, informal, and influenced heavily by subjective interpretations, **research** involves a systematic process of gathering, interpreting, and reporting information. Research is disciplined inquiry characterized by accepted principles to verify that a knowledge claim is reasonable. Defined in this way, research is not simply going to the library, gathering information on a topic, and doing a research paper. Rather, information is gathered directly from individuals, groups, documents, and other

> **Educational research:** Disciplined inquiry applied to educational problems.

sources. **Educational research,** then, is systematic, disciplined inquiry applied to educational problems and questions.

Two approaches to research have led to different methods of inquiry. These approaches, referred to today as *quantitative* and *qualitative*, are based on different assumptions about how to best understand and come to know what is true or what constitutes reality. We will briefly review these assumptions before looking at the contributions of science to educational research.

Positivism/Postpositivism. Positivism and postpositivism are based on the assumption that phenomena should be studied objectively with the goal of obtaining a single true reality, or at least reality within known probabilities. The researcher takes a neutral role, one that does not influence what is observed or recorded. Empiricism is emphasized through the use of numerical data. This approach has been widely adopted in the fields of psychology and education and has come to be known as a *quantitative* type of research.

Interpretive/Constructivist. The assumption guiding interpretive/constructivist research is that reality is socially constructed. Rather than a single objective reality, there are multiple realities, each related to the complexity of naturally occurring behavior, characterized by the perspectives of the participants. A less structured and more interactive mode of data collection is emphasized, and numerical data are used only to provide simple descriptions. The emphasis is on language to most closely reflect participant perspectives. Objectivity is replaced by confirmability. This approach is better known as a *qualitative* method of research.

CHARACTERISTICS *of* SCIENTIFIC INQUIRY

Research, whether based on the quantitative or qualitative approach, exhibits several characteristics that distinguish it from other sources of knowledge:

1. *Objectivity* in observation, data collection, and reporting of results
2. *Control of personal bias* so that a researcher's personal prejudices, beliefs, desires, and attitudes do not influence the research and conclusions
3. *Precision* to provide detailed, specific definitions and descriptions
4. *Parsimony* to provide the least complicated explanation
5. *Tentative conclusions* that are open to change
6. *Verification* of findings through replication
7. *Openness to scrutiny* by others
8. *Logic*, inductive and/or deductive, to provide meaning

These characteristics, taken together, are what makes research a systematic process that is guided by accepted procedures to establish credibility.

Many of these characteristics are similar to those of research in general; most are important for all types of research. The phenomena studied in education involve behaviors that are influenced by a large number of factors in complex social situations; hence the ideals of scientific inquiry may only be approximated. Obviously, rigid controls that may be possible with laboratory studies are usually not possible in schools. Measurement in educational research is often indirect and imprecise, and verifying findings by replicating studies may be difficult. Thus, scientific inquiry is one set of standards against which the adequacy of educational research may be judged, but most studies will not adhere rigidly to the characteristics.

The NATURE *of* SCIENTIFIC INQUIRY

We expect scientists to use the **scientific** approach. It is easy to understand the usefulness of this approach in fields such as agriculture, medicine, engineering, biology, and the like, but is education or teaching a science? Without debating this question, the important point is that the scientific approach is a logical method of inquiry, not a body of knowledge. It is not tied to particular fields of study, to laboratory situations, or to men and women in white coats developing complex theories. Consequently, we can study education in a *scientific manner*, even though education itself is not a science.

Scientific: Systematic, testable, and objective.

Purpose of Scientific Inquiry

The primary purpose of scientific inquiry is to explain natural phenomena and understand the underlying relationships and then, using this information, to predict and influence behavior. For example, we can use scientific inquiry to explain why some teachers appear to be more effective than others. The explanation leads to a knowledge base that novice teachers can use to become more effective.

Description provides fundamental knowledge about a phenomenon and is usually necessary before pursuing explanation and prediction. Accurate descriptions are essential to understanding explanations of events or people. For example, accurate descriptions of various teaching styles and student achievement are needed before the relationship between these two phenomena can be studied. Once these phenomena are adequately described, one may be predicted by knowledge of the other. This predictive power is very important because educators must constantly make predictive-type decisions (e.g., put Johnny in group A because he will do better with those children; admit a select group of students for a special program because they will benefit most; use cooperative teaching techniques because they will keep the students interested longer; advise against a particular occupation because the student will have difficulty passing the certification examination). Sometimes after describing phenomena, scientists control one to study its effect on the other. By controlling factors in experiments (discussed in detail in Chapter 9), researchers can determine whether one factor influences another.

In recent years, the idea that education can be studied "scientifically" has been strongly influenced by federal policy. Three significant developments include (1) the formation of the Institute of Education Sciences (IES) to provide leadership in expanding scientific knowledge and understanding of education; (2) formation of the What Works Clearinghouse to review studies for scientific rigor; and (3) publication of *Scientific Research in Education* (Sharelson & Towne, 2002). These influences have created unprecedented emphasis on the need for educational research to be "scientific" and policy and practice to be "evidence-based." This emphasis has focused researchers on what is meant by "scientific." Thus, the principles of scientific inquiry provide the foundation for conducting studies, regardless of the specific methodology used. These principles are in turn used in analyzing educational problems, making decisions, and designing, conducting, reporting, and evaluating studies.

Principles of Scientific Inquiry

Scientific inquiry, including educational research, is guided by six principles (National Research Council, 2002). While these principles are targeted to researchers, not consumers of research, they provide a set of guidelines that can be used to judge the quality and contribution of research. In concert with additional characteristics, these principles essentially constitute a set of norms that both researchers and consumers of research can employ to judge the quality of the research.

Scientific Principle 1: Pose Significant Questions That Can Be Investigated Empirically. This principle emphasizes two elements: (1) the need to identify important research questions that will have significant benefits once answered; and (2) to design empirical studies so that others can judge the quality of the methods and findings. Questions and designs are most significant when based on previous studies.

Scientific Principle 2: Link Research to Relevant Theory. In scientific research, generation and testing of theories is important for establishing a body of knowledge that will generalize widely. A **theory** can be defined as a set of propositions that explain the relationships among observed phenomena. Such general explanations of behavior can be used in many contexts and have more utility for a large number of people. For example, research on effective teaching has identified general teaching behaviors—such as close supervision, providing meaningful and timely feedback to students on their performance, and asking appropriate questions that keep students engaged—that are positively related to student achievement for most, if not all, teachers. It doesn't matter if the teacher has a fourth-grade class or a high school class, teaches French or science, or has honors or remedial students. The power of a theory to establish principles is what will advance our knowledge of effective teaching and educational interventions.

> **Theory:** Explains relationships among phenomena.

Scientific Principle 3: Use Methods That Permit Direct Investigation of the Question. An important principle in conducting educational research is that the method used in the study should be the best one for the research question. There is no single method that always provides the best answers. Rather, method must be matched to question. Method is also influenced by the situation in which the research is conducted and access to information. For example, whereas experiments are often thought to be the best method for determining whether an educational intervention is successful, it is difficult to design such studies in schools. Scientific claims are strengthened when multiple methods are used.

Scientific Principle 4: Provide a Coherent and Explicit Chain of Reasoning. Making scientific inferences, explanations, and conclusions requires a logical chain of reasoning that is coherent and persuasive. The chain includes links between the research question, pertinent literature, methods, findings, and conclusions. Inferences are strengthened when researchers identify limitations, uncertainty, possible bias, and errors. Descriptions of methods must include sufficient detail for others to review, critique, and analyze the study.

Scientific Principle 5: Replicate and Generalize Across Studies. Findings must be checked and validated, and subsequent studies need to determine if results generalize to a broader population and to other contexts.

Scientific Principle 6: Disclose Research to Encourage Professional Scrutiny and Critique. A hallmark of scientific inquiry is that studies are widely disseminated and subjected to review by peers. The information must be accessible and efforts must be made to publish results. This public, professional critique is needed so that the overall credibility of the findings is validated.

INTERNET CONNECTION

In 2001 the National Research Council released a report, "Scientific Inquiry in Education," which has caused much debate about whether educational research should be based on the scientific model of inquiry. Review this influential report at **www.nap.edu/books/catalog/10236.html**.

APPLYING SYSTEMATIC INQUIRY *to* EDUCATION

The purpose of research is to provide sound understanding and explanations that can become knowledge. The primary mode of inquiry, whether based on a positivist/postpositivist or interpretive/constructivist perspective, employs a systematic series of steps to conduct the investigation. These steps are associated with questions that help us judge the quality of the research and, hence, the credibility of the results. The researcher's goal is to obtain credible answers to research questions by designing, conducting, and reporting data that others will view as trustworthy, that is, as reasonable results that make sense.

In its most simple form, research involves four steps:

Question $\longrightarrow$ Method $\longrightarrow$ Results $\longrightarrow$ Conclusions

At the start is a question that needs to be answered, then there is some method of gathering and analyzing information. Based on the analysis and results, the researcher presents conclusions. For example, suppose you are interested in whether grading practices affect student motivation. The study could involve the four steps in the following manner:

Question $\longrightarrow$	Method $\longrightarrow$	Results $\longrightarrow$	Conclusions
What is the effect of grading practices on student motivation?	Teacher and student surveys	More frequent grades, greater student motivation	Training teachers to grade more frequently may increase student motivation

Once the question is established a method is selected. This involves identifying who will provide data, the instruments used to collect data, and procedures for gathering data and/or administering interventions. Results are determined by some kind of data analysis. Based on these results, the method, and previous studies, conclusions are drawn from interpretations of the results. This forms an

| FIGURE 1.1 | A framework for understanding the steps of scientific inquiry. |

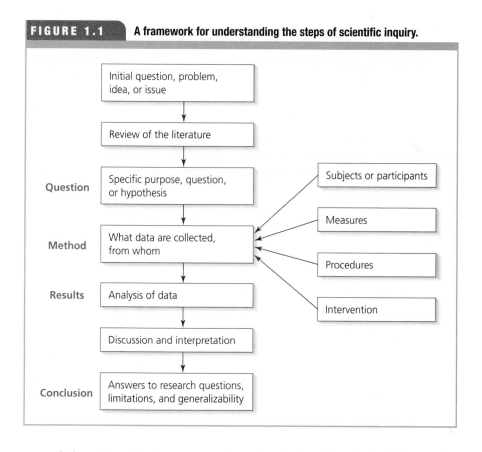

expanded version of the four steps to show that choice of method and data analyses can affect the conclusions (see Figure 1.1). That is, depending on the nature of the subjects who are studied, the instruments, and the procedures, different conclusions can be reached for the same question. So in the example above, how motivation is measured could make a big difference (e.g., is motivation based on student self-efficacy or level of interest, or both?). The conclusion is also limited to the nature of the sample (e.g., fourth- and fifth-graders).

The expanded number of steps in Figure 1.1 shows how researchers actually go about planning and then conducting research. Each step in the process is important and contributes to the overall credibility and usefulness of the research. This book is organized around these steps and questions to provide you with the knowledge and skills you will need to make sound overall judgments about the credibility and usefulness of various studies. We will elaborate the steps and questions introduced in later chapters, but it is helpful to understand the nature of the entire process from the beginning.

In the first step, the investigator faces an obstacle to effective decision making or understanding, or identifies a general idea or question that warrants further thought. The next step, reviewing previous research on the topic, involves finding relevant research, analyzing it, and relating it to the initial question.

Next, the researcher formulates a specific research hypothesis or question. The hypothesis is used with research that follows a positivist/postpositivist approach. It is an informed guess about the answer to the research question, a hunch based on related literature and professional judgment. A question is warranted when the nature of the original idea or problem does not lend itself to a hypothesis. In research that follows an interpretive/constructivist approach there may be only a general research problem or statement.

The design of the study is based on what will be an adequate test of the hypothesis or what will answer the question. It includes subjects, measures, procedures, and interventions. A carefully designed study is structured so that the explanation provided is the most credible one. Here the researcher must address "rival" explanations, often a result of faulty methodology, that may mitigate the credibility of the explanation offered. Examples of rival explanations include experimenter bias, differential loss of subjects in different groups or between a pretest and posttest, selection bias, and changes caused by factors that are not controlled.

Generalizability: Use of results in other situations with other individuals.

The credibility of the results builds on previous aspects of the study, focusing on the reasonableness of the results in light of previous research and the extent to which alternative explanations are eliminated. The evaluation of the conclusions, in turn, also builds on previous credible judgments. Finally, judgments are made on the **generalizability** of the research, that is, whether the findings and explanations are useful in other situations and with other subjects, times, procedures, and measures. In other words, can the conclusions be generalized to other people in other contexts? This is an important concern for educational research because educators are interested in applying the results to particular groups and circumstances. As we will see in later chapters, generalizability is defined differently depending on whether the research takes a positivist/postpositivist (quantitative) or interpretive/constructivist (qualitative) approach.

TYPES *of* EDUCATIONAL RESEARCH

Although all educational research is conducted using systematic inquiry, there are different types of educational research. Indeed, it is common to discuss educational research in the context of one of these types because framing the discussion this way provides further information about the purpose and nature of the study. That is, it means more to say "experimental research" or "applied correlational research" than it does to simply say "research." We consider the major types of educational research in this section.

Two Major Traditions of Research: Quantitative and Qualitative

Quantitative: Emphasizes numbers, measurements, deductive logic, control, and experiments.

Increasingly in recent years educational research has been described as either quantitative or qualitative (or sometimes both in the same study). These terms refer to two different research traditions, each with its own terminology, methods, and techniques. For many decades most educational research was based on the **quantitative** tradition, with what has already been described as a positivist/postpositivist approach. Until the mid-1970s the vast majority of studies in education were quantitative in nature. Today it is becoming more and more common to read studies that are qualitative, that have some qualitative features, or that use both approaches.

Qualitative research stresses a phenomenological model in which multiple realities are rooted in the subjects' perceptions. A focus on understanding and meaning is based on verbal narratives and observations rather than numbers. Qualitative research usually takes place in naturally occurring situations, as contrasted with quantitative research, in which behaviors and settings are controlled and manipulated.

> **Qualitative:** Emphasizes natural settings, understanding, verbal narratives, and flexible designs.

Table 1.1 summarizes the major features of these two traditions. Note the different terms that are used to refer to qualitative research. In the next section we examine different types of both quantitative and qualitative studies.

Quantitative Research. Research design refers to the plan for carrying out a study. For quantitative research a major distinction is made between nonexperimental and experimental designs. In **nonexperimental research,** the investigator has no direct influence on what has been selected to be studied, either because it has already occurred or because it cannot be influenced. In other words, the investigator is unable to manipulate or control any factors or phenomena that may influence the subjects' behavior or performance. This characteristic has important implications for the conclusions that are drawn. It usually means that the study can only describe something or uncover relationships between two or more factors.

> **Nonexperimental research:** No manipulation of factors that may influence subjects.

Nonexperimental quantitative studies can be classified as descriptive, comparative, correlational, or causal comparative. *Descriptive* research includes studies that provide simple information about the frequency or amount of something (e.g., How do high school counselors spend their time during the school day?). *Comparative* studies examine the differences between groups on a variable of interest (e.g., What is the difference between male and female self-concept scores? Do teachers in different grade levels have the same or different definitions of critical thinking?). *Correlational* studies investigate relationships among two or more variables (e.g., What is the relationship between physical conditioning and academic achievement? Is there a correlation between creativity and self-esteem?).

Causal-comparative research examines whether a naturally occurring "intervention" affects an outcome of interest, such as student performance. *Ex post facto* studies identify interventions that occurred in the past and subsequent responses in such a way that it may be possible to draw causal relationships between them (e.g., Do students who took typing in seventh grade have more positive attitudes in high school than students who did not take typing?).

In **experimental research,** the investigators have control over one or more factors (variables) in the study that may influence the subjects' behavior. That is, they can manipulate a factor and then see what happens to the subjects' responses as a result. The purpose of manipulating a factor is to investigate its causal relationship with another factor. For example, investigators may be interested in

> **Experimental research:** Manipulation of factors that may influence subjects.

TABLE 1.1	Characteristics of Quantitative and Qualitative Research	
	Quantitative	**Qualitative**
Other terms or phrases associated with the approach	Positivist Experimental Hard data Statistical	Naturalistic Field research Ethnographic Phenomenological Anthropological Ecological Case study Interpretive Constructivist
Key concepts	Variable Operationalized Controlled Statistically significant Replicated Hypothesized	Meaning Understanding Social construction Context
Academic affiliation	Agriculture Psychology Basic sciences	Anthropology History Sociology
Goals	Test theory Show relationships Predict Statistically describe	Develop understanding Describe multiple realities Capture naturally occurring behavior
Design	Structured Predetermined Specific	Evolving Flexible General

studying the causal relationship between the amount of time devoted to a given subject, such as math, and achievement. They manipulate the former by having one group of children spend a small amount of time on the subject and a second group a large amount of time. If the children who spend more time studying math show higher achievement than the other children, then time devoted to studying may be causally related to achievement.

There are several types of experimental research, depending on specific design characteristics. A *true experimental* design is one in which subjects have been randomly assigned to different groups. A *quasi-experimental* design does not have random assignment. *Single-subject* designs use the ideas of an experiment with a single person or a few individuals.

Qualitative Research. Unlike quantitative research, different types of qualitative research are not clearly distinguished by design characteristics. However, different purposes are identified with specific questions, data collection procedures, and analyses. The goal in a *phenomenological* study is to fully

TABLE 1.1	(Continued)	
	Quantitative	**Qualitative**
Sample	Large Random Stratified	Small Nonrepresentative Purposeful
Data	Measures/instruments Numbers Statistics	Verbal descriptions Field notes Observations Documents Photographs Narrative
Techniques or methods	Experiments Quasi-experiments Structured observations Structured interviews Surveys	Observation Open-ended interviewing Review of documents and artifacts
Role of researcher	Distant Short-term Detached Uninvolved	Close Involved Trusting
Data analysis	Deductive Statistical	Inductive Ongoing

Source: Adapted from Bogdan and Biklen, 2007.

understand the essence of some phenomenon (e.g., What is essential for students to view teachers as caring?). This is usually accomplished with long, intensive individual interviews. An *ethnography* is a description and interpretation of a cultural or social group system (e.g., What is the effect of high-stakes testing on the climate of the school? How has high-stakes testing influenced teacher-principal interaction?). Ethnographers spend extensive time in the setting being studied and use observations, interviews, and other analyses to understand the nature of the culture. *Grounded theory* studies are conducted to generate or discover a theory or schema that relates to a particular environment (e.g., How do students with learning disabilities adapt to being in regular classrooms?). As in an ethnographic study, many different modes of gathering information are used. *Case studies* concern in-depth study of a single or a few programs, events, activities, groups, or other entities defined in terms of time and place (e.g., examining the culture of a particular magnet school). Again, multiple methods of data collection are used, including observations, interviews, and analyses of documents and reports.

Analytical Research. While most educational research can be classified as quantitative or qualitative, there are some additional types that do not align well

Analytical research: Historical, legal, or concept anaylsis.

with either of these two classifications. These can be called *analytical* studies. **Analytical research** is a mode of inquiry in which events, ideas, concepts, or artifacts are investigated by analyzing documents, records, recordings, and other media. Like qualitative studies (some researchers classify analytical studies, as described here, as qualitative), contextual information is very important to accurate interpretation of the data. In *historical analysis* there is a systematic gathering and criticism of documents, records, and artifacts to provide a description and interpretation of past events or persons. Both qualitative and quantitative data may be used in historical studies. *Legal analysis* focuses on selected laws and court decisions to examine how legal precedents influence educational practice. *Concept analysis* is concerned with implications and applications of the meaning and usage of educational concepts (e.g., high-stakes testing, performance assessment, and mainstreaming).

Mixed-Method. Sometimes researchers use qualitative and/or analytical approaches and quantitative designs in the same study. This kind of research is called **mixed-method.** By using multiple methods in a single study the researcher is better able to match the approach to gathering and analyzing data with the research questions. The relative emphasis given to any particular method can vary widely. These studies can be primarily one method with a small contribution of another method, or can give the methods about the same weight. For example, it is typical in survey research to use sampling and closed-response type questions (quantitative) and also have some open-ended questions at the end that are analyzed qualitatively.

Mixed-method research: Combines quantitative and qualitative and/or analytical approaches.

Keeping these categories and examples in mind will help you understand important design characteristics of research. Use the decision tree in Figure 1.2 to identify different types of educational research. In the next section research is classified by the purpose or goal that is being pursued, regardless of methodology.

Author Reflection *Over the past two decades I have conducted many quantitative and qualitative studies. What have I learned about these methods as a result of these experiences? First, it is critical to match the reason for the research with the appropriate method. Method should always be determined by the purpose and the research question. Second, using each method well is a challenge. Either can be used without appropriate rigor, which diminishes the usefulness of findings. Third, on balance, it seems that my qualitative studies have had more impact. I think this shows the importance of depth of understanding, regardless of the design. It is really important to engage in your topic with sufficient depth. Superficiality at any stage in the research process leads to less helpful results.*

Basic, Applied, Evaluation, and Action Research

Basic research: Formulates and refines theories.

The purpose or goal of research is based on the use of the findings. The primary purpose of **basic research** (also called pure or fundamental research) is the

FIGURE 1.2 A decision tree of educational research.

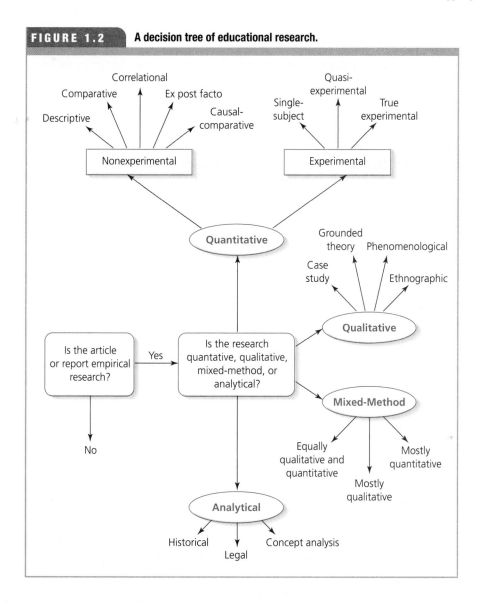

development of theories. The goal of basic research is to understand and explain, to provide broad generalizations about how phenomena are related. It is not concerned with immediate application of the results to practical situations. Examples include studies of how the memory system works, language development, and social development. Few educational studies would be classified as basic, although educational researchers do conduct and use basic research.

The purpose of **applied research** is to test theories and other ideas in the context of naturally occurring educational settings. It is usually focused on a

Applied research: Improves practice and solves practical problems.

problem that needs to be solved to improve the practice of education. The results are immediately and directly relevant to educational decision making. To the extent that general theories are tested, the results may be generalized to many different educational settings. For example, based on theories of human memory developed through basic research, a new curriculum may be tested for improved retention of science concepts. Other examples of applied research in education are studies that compare different teaching styles, identify characteristics of effective schools, or examine the effect of lengthening the school day on student achievement.

Action research:
Investigates specific classroom problems.

The goal of **action research** is to solve a specific classroom or school problem, improve practice, or help make a decision at a single local site. The intent is to improve practice immediately within one or a few classrooms or schools. Calhoun (1994) names three types of action research: individual teacher research, collaborative action research, and schoolwide action research. Teachers may act as researchers in action studies they have designed and carried out to improve practice in their classrooms. Administrators have used action research strategies for school renewal and other improvement efforts.

Evaluation research:
Judgments for decision making.

Evaluation research is directed toward making decisions about the effectiveness or desirability of a program. The goal is to make judgments about alternatives in decision-making situations. In most cases evaluation research is focused on a specific location or type of program and involves judgments about such questions as: Which reading curriculum should be implemented? Did the new program work? Should the district build two small schools or one large school? What is the impact of increased technology on student and teacher knowledge and attitudes? Often, such questions require research methods that are unique to each situation. A summary of the major types of educational research, with additional examples, is provided in Table 1.2.

Research Ethics

Before turning to the format of research articles there is a very important topic related to conducting studies that you need to be aware of—ethics. Within the context of gathering data from subjects or using data in which subjects are identified, ethics are concerned with what is right or wrong, good or bad, or proper or improper. There has been extensive discussion of the ethics of research, much of it by established research organizations, though it is only touched on here. Researchers should follow established ethical guidelines, and if you do want to do any kind of study, even something within your own work context, you need to be aware of these guidelines. Organizations such as the American Educational Research Association (AERA) and the American Psychological Association (APA) have formal ethical guidelines for conducting research with humans, and you can visit their Websites for details (**www.aera.net; www.apa.org**). The ten basic aspects of most ethical concern are:

TABLE 1.2	Major Types of Educational Research[a]	
Type	**Purpose**	**Example**
Quantitative	To describe phenomena numerically to answer specific questions or hypotheses.	The relationship between amount of homework and student achievement.
Qualitative	To provide rich narrative descriptions of phenomena that enhance understanding.	Observations of school renewal teams to understand the role of parents.
Nonexperimental	To describe, compare, and predict phenomena without actively manipulating factors that influence the phenomena.	Determine the relationship between socioeconomic status and student attitudes.
Experimental	To determine the causal relationship between two or more phenomena by direct manipulation of factors that influence the phenomena.	Determine which of two approaches to teaching science results in the highest student achievement.
Basic	To increase knowledge and understanding of phenomena.	Understand how feedback affects motivation or learning styles of adolescents.
Applied	To solve practical educational problems.	Determine the best approach for training teachers to use portfolios for classroom assessment.
Action	To improve practice in a school or classroom.	Determine which grouping procedure results in the highest achievement.
Evaluation	To make a decision about a program or activity.	Decide whether to keep or phase out a prekindergarten program.

[a]Note that some traits overlap among different types of research. For example, qualitative studies may contain numerical summaries of information.

1. The primary investigator of a study is responsible for the ethical standards to which the study adheres.
2. The investigator should inform subjects of all aspects of the research that might influence their willingness to participate.
3. The investigator should be as open and honest with subjects as possible, which usually requires full disclosure. Sometimes deception is necessary and not unethical, in which case participants are usually debriefed after the study.
4. Subjects must be protected from physical and mental discomfort, harm, and danger.
5. Often, informed consent must be obtained from the subjects prior to gathering data. In most studies of children, parental consent is required.
6. Subjects may discontinue participation at any time without penalty or risk.
7. Subjects should never be coerced to participate.
8. Unless otherwise agreed to, data should be held confidential.

9. For research conducted through an institution such as a university, approval for conducting the research should be obtained before data are collected. This often means obtaining permission from an internal review board (IRB) prior to data collection.
10. Potential benefits to a control group should be identified.

Universities have specific ethical guidelines for conducting research with human subjects. An internal review board (IRB) will need to approve studies in which there is interaction with or an intervention with humans. Often the process of obtaining IRB approval can be time-consuming. Student projects may require approval. Even if IRB approval is not required, all researchers have a professional obligation to conduct studies with appropriate attention to ethical and legal guidelines.

USING EDUCATIONAL RESEARCH

Applied research on the effect of class size on student achievement, which shows that smaller classes (<18) result in stronger student performance, led California to enact legislation that reduces grade K–3 class size. Evaluation research of the impact of the law on student achievement, teacher credentialing, and unintended effects is now being conducted. (Go to the CSR Research Consortium, **www.classize.org,** for more information and research findings on this initiative.)

EDUCATIONAL RESEARCH ARTICLE FORMAT

Every year millions of dollars are spent on educational research and millions more on related research in psychology, sociology, and other social sciences. Every year hundreds of articles are published. One of the primary objectives of this book is to help you become an intelligent reader of these articles. A research article sets forth the research problem, what the researcher has done to collect data, how the data are analyzed and interpreted, and the conclusions. In other words, the article is a summary of what was done, how it was done, why it was done, and what was discovered. Most articles, as well as research reports that are not articles, follow a standard format or organizational structure, as summarized in Figure 1.3, which show differences between quantitative and qualitative formats. These parts are discussed briefly and are then identified in published quantitative and qualitative articles.

Title and Author(s)

The research report typically begins with the title and name(s) of the author(s). The professional affiliation of the author(s) is provided in many reports, particularly published articles. This is the author's affiliation when the research was

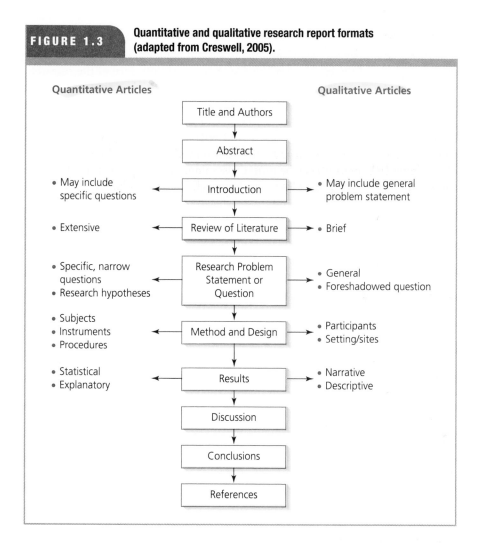

FIGURE 1.3   **Quantitative and qualitative research report formats (adapted from Creswell, 2005).**

Quantitative Articles   **Qualitative Articles**

Title and Authors

Abstract

- May include specific questions   ← Introduction →   • May include general problem statement

- Extensive   ← Review of Literature →   • Brief

- Specific, narrow questions
- Research hypotheses   ← Research Problem Statement or Question →   • General
• Foreshadowed question

- Subjects
- Instruments
- Procedures   ← Method and Design →   • Participants
• Setting/sites

- Statistical
- Explanatory   ← Results →   • Narrative
• Descriptive

Discussion

Conclusions

References

conducted, not necessarily his or her present affiliation. Good research report titles tell the reader something about the major variables and type of subjects that are studied in less than 15 words.

Abstract

In many reports, especially journal articles, title and author are followed by an abstract. The abstract in journal articles is typically 50 to 150 words long and is often set in smaller type than or a different font from the rest of the article. The abstract is a brief summary of the entire study, including the problem, methods used, and major findings. The abstract will usually provide enough details to allow the reader to decide whether to read the entire report.

Introduction

The introductory section is usually one to several paragraphs in length, including a statement of the context for the research, the significance of the research, and the general or specific research problem investigated. The context provides background information relating the study to broader areas. It also indicates briefly the development of the research problem. The significance of the research is contained in a statement about how the results will be useful. It can be thought of as a justification for conducting the research. Almost all introductions include a statement that indicates the research problem of the study. This statement can be broad or specific, and sometimes both a broad and a more specific problem are included. The problem indicates as concisely and clearly as possible the focus of the study. Most general problems are stated near the beginning of the report, and more specific research questions, if any, just before the review of literature, but the level of specificity or location across articles and reports is inconsistent. In qualitative articles you will find a foreshadowed problem rather than specific questions.

Review of Literature

Although the introductory section may include some references to other research or literature, a more formal review of literature begins after the research problem is introduced. The review, one to several paragraphs long, summarizes and analyzes previous research on the same problem. A good review critiques the studies and shows how the findings relate to the problem being investigated.

Specific Research Question or Hypothesis

Often, but not always, in quantitative studies specific research questions or hypotheses follow the review of literature. A hypothesis is an informed guess or prediction about the results; it indicates what the researcher thinks the results will be before the study is carried out. The hypothesis usually follows the review of literature because it is based on what other theories and previously completed related studies have found.

Method and Design

In this section the researchers indicate who was studied, how the information was obtained, and, in the case of an experiment, treatments or manipulations. The first part of the section usually describes the subjects (quantitative studies) or participants (qualitative studies). These are individuals the researcher observes or obtains information from to address the research problem. The report describes the characteristics of the subjects and indicates whether they have been selected from a larger group. The second section focuses on the instrumentation used to gather information from the subjects, including a description of the instruments and an evaluation of their reliability and validity. In some reports this section also describes how the instrument was administered; in others, this information is provided in the third section, procedures. The procedures section may also include a summary of how the data were collected and, in experimental studies, indicates how the manipulations were carried out. The researchers may also discuss the design of the study and materials used, and they may indicate what precautions were taken to reduce bias or otherwise improve objectivity.

Results

In this section researchers describe how they analyzed the data, and they present the results. Tables and graphs may be used to summarize large amounts of data succinctly. This section should be an objective reporting of what was found, without interpretation or discussion.

Discussion

This is the section in which the investigators explain their results. The data are interpreted in light of other research and possible weaknesses in the methodology of the study.

Conclusions

Conclusions are summary statements that reflect the overall answers to the research questions or whether or not the research hypotheses are supported. The conclusion is an inference derived from the results, weaknesses in the study, and the relationship of the results to previous studies. Conclusions should be limited to what is directly supported by the findings and what is reasonable, given other research. Implications and recommendations are often included in this section, although investigators should be careful not to overgeneralize.

References

This is a listing of the sources cited in the report. The style of listing references will vary, the most common being APA. A bibliography includes sources that are not cited in the report but are used by the authors.

ANATOMY *of a* RESEARCH ARTICLE

The best way to become familiar with educational research is to read published articles. Becoming comfortable with the format and language will allow you to critique and evaluate research. Don't be too concerned about understanding *everything* you read. You are not expected to be an expert researcher or statistician. But if you don't read the studies, it's hard to be an intelligent consumer.

Exhibit 1.1 is an example of a quantitative study, illustrates the format you will find and points out other features of a research article.

EXHIBIT 1.1   Format and features of a journal research article.

Gender, Achievement, and Perception Toward Science Activities[1]

Daniel P. Shepardson
Department of Curriculum & Instruction
Purdue University

Edward L. Pizzini
Science Education Center
The University of Iowa

Institutional affiliation when the study was conducted

The purpose of this study was to investigate the perception toward science activities and science achievement of boys and girls in middle school life science. Student perceptions toward science activities and achievement were measured in three different instructional treatments: textbook-worksheet, traditional laboratory, and Search, Solve, Create, Share (SSCS) problem solving. The results indicate no significant difference in student achievement by gender or science activities, and no significant difference in perception by gender. However, a significant difference (p < .05) was obtained for student perception by science activities. Follow-up comparisons suggested significant differences among SSCS problem solving and traditional laboratory and textbook- worksheet activities, with no difference between traditional laboratory and textbook-worksheet activities.

Abstract

The underrepresentation of women in scientific professions has become a national concern. This concern has resulted in a variety of studies designed to identify gender differences that may contribute to the dearth of females in the scientific pipeline (see Oakes, 1990). It has been proposed that the attitude of girls toward science is one factor that influences the decision of girls to participate in science, as well as their achievement in science. Important attributes of attitude formation, for girls, appear to be the perceived usefulness of the science being learned, confidence in learning and doing science, interest in people, and a liking of science (Oakes, 1990).

Introduction, background, and significance of the topic

Further, the learning situation can affect the attitude students develop toward science (Hofstein, Scherz, & Yager, 1986; Kulm, 1980; Talton & Simpson, 1987). Therefore, learning situations that are perceived positively by girls may contribute to their development of a positive attitude toward science, as well as improve achievement. The learning situation also influences the opportunity girls have to engage in learning science. Although there is evidence that boys benefit more from traditional instructional activities, whereas girls benefit more from cooperative and hands-on activities, the evidence is inconclusive (Oakes, 1990).

Review of literature to establish possible link between science class activities and attitudes

Kahle (1990) has stated that inquiry-oriented instruction has the potential of producing equitable outcomes in attitude and achievement, and Glaton (1981) has concluded that girls prefer inquiry-oriented instruction. Zimmerer and Bennett (1987) found that both eighth-grade boys and girls enjoy doing science experiments, but that boys were more enthusiastic than girls. Shymansky, Hedges, and Woodworth (1990) observed that inquiry-oriented instruction only improved the attitude of boys toward science, while Fleming and Malone (1983) found that boys had a more positive attitude

[1]Source: *School Science and Mathematics, 94* (4), April, 1994.

toward science than girls at the elementary level, but that girls had a more positive attitude toward science at the middle school level. Finally, the National Assessment of Educational Progress (NAEP) indicates that boys tend to have a more positive attitude toward science than girls and that this trend has changed little over time (Mullis & Jenkins, 1988).

Review of literature of gender differences in science achievement

From an achievement perspective, the NAEP results indicate no difference between boys and girls at the knowledge level (knows everyday science facts), but that boys perform at higher proficiency levels than girls in middle school/junior high, suggesting a relationship between attitude and achievement (Mullis & Jenkins, 1988; Mullis, Dossey, Foertsch, Jones, & Gentile, 1991). However, Steinkamp and Maehr (1983) concluded that there is insufficient evidence to link gender differences in attitude toward science to science achievement.

Because of the poor attitude toward science of both boys and girls, Yager and Penick (1986) have argued that science needs to be taught differently; that science needs to be taught dynamically, not as a static subject in textbooks. Exemplary science programs accentuate the dynamic teaching of science, emphasizing inquiry instruction, allowing students to pursue areas of personal interest (Reynolds et al., 1985). Exemplary science programs recognize that student attitude toward science arises from the success or failure students have with instructional materials (Penick & Krajcik, 1985).

Theoretical rationale for the study

Purpose

Major headings centered

Although studies have investigated student attitude toward science and achievement, few studies have attempted to investigate the underlying attributes of student attitude; that is, what it is about science that boys and girls like or dislike. The perception boys and girls have about science activities may contribute to the development of their attitude toward science, as well as influence achievement. Thus, the purpose of this study was to assess the perception toward science activities and science achievement of boys and girls in middle school life science. The specific questions of this study were:

Need for the study

Potential significance of the results

General research problem

1. Is there a difference in the perception boys and girls have of science activities?
2. Is there a difference in the science achievement of boys and girls exposed to different science activities?

Specific research questions

Method

The study involved a pretest/posttest design for student achievement and a posttest-only design for student perception toward science activities. Because students had different science experiences prior to the study, which colors their perception, and since we were only interested in their perception of the immediate science activities they were exposed to, the posttest-only design for student perception was considered appropriate. Gender was treated as an effect in both designs. The achievement pretest was administered 10 days prior to the study. The achievement posttest and perception questionnaire were administered immediately following the completion of the treatments, 20 days from the administration of the pretest.

Describes an experimental research design

Indicates procedure and time frame for data collection

(continued)

EXHIBIT 1.1   **(continued)**

as well as boys prefer inquiry-oriented instruction. Although this study was of a short duration, the results suggest that when science is taught dynamically, student attitude toward science may be enhanced through positive student perception of science activities.

| Restatement of conclusion |

References

Fleming, M.L. & Malone, M.R. (1983). The relationship of student characteristics and student performance in science as viewed by meta-analysis research. *Journal of Research in Science Teaching, 20,* 481–495.

Glaton, M. (1981). Differential treatment of boy and girl pupils during science lessons. In A. Kelly (Ed.), *The missing half.* Manchester, England: Manchester University Press.

Hofstein, A., Scherz, Z., & Yager, R.E. (1986). What students say about science teaching, science teachers and science classes in Israel and the U.S. *Science Education, 70,* 21–30.

Isaac, S. & Michael, W.B. (1987). *Handbook in research and evaluation.* San Diego, CA: Edits Publishers.

Kahle, J.B. (1990). Why girls don't know. In M.B. Rowe (Ed.), *What research says to the science teacher,* (Vol. 6). Washington, DC: National Science Teachers Association.

Kulm, G. (1980). Research on mathematics attitude. In R.J. Shumway (Ed.), *Research in mathematics education.* Reston, VA: National Council of Teachers of Mathematics.

Mullis, I.S. & Jenkins, L.B. (1988). *The science report card elements of risk and recovery.* Princeton, NJ: Educational Testing Service.

Mullis, I.S., Dossey, J., Foertsch, M., Jones, L., & Gentile, C. (1991). *Trends in academic progress.* Washington, DC: Office of Educational Research and Improvement, U.S. Department of Education.

| References in the American Psychological Association (APA) format |

Oakes, J. (1990). Opportunities, achievement, and choice: Women and minority students in science and mathematics. In C.B. Cazden (Ed.), *Review of Research in Education,* Washington, DC: American Educational Research Association.

Penick, J.E. & Krajcik, J. (1985). Middle school/junior high science: A synthesis and critique. In J. Penick & J. Krajcik (eds.), *Focus on excellence: Middle school/junior high science,* (Vol. 2, No. 2). Washington, DC: National Science Teachers Association.

| Chapter in a book |

Pizzini, E.L., Abell, S.K., & Shepardson, D.P. (1988). Rethinking thinking in the science classroom. *The Science Teacher, 55,* 22–25.

| Volume |

Pizzini, E.L., Shepardson, D.P., & Abell, S.K. (1989). A rationale for and the development of a problem solving model of instruction in science education. *Science Education, 73,* 523–534.

| Authors listed in order of relative contribution |

Pizzini, E.L., Shepardson, D.P., & Abell, S.K. (1991). The inquiry level of junior high activities: Implications to science teaching. *Journal of Research in Science Teaching, 28,* 111–121.

Reynolds, K.E., Pitotti, W.W., Rakow, S.J., Thompson, T., & Wohl, S.M. (1985). Excellence in middle/junior high school science. In J. Penick & J. Krajcik (Eds.), *Focus on excellence: Middle school/junior high science,* (Vol. 2, No. 2). Washington, DC: National Science Teachers Association.

| Publisher |

Shymansky, J.A., Hedges, L.V., & Woodworth, G. (1990). A reassessment of the effects of inquiry-based science curricula of the 60's on student performance. *Journal of Research in Science Teaching, 27,* 127–144.

Steinkamp, M. & Maehr, M. (1983). Affect, ability, and science achievement: A quantitative synthesis of correlational research. *Review of Educational Research, 53,* 369–396.

Talton, E.L. & Simpson, R.D. (1987). Relationships of attitude toward classroom environment with attitude toward and achievement in science among tenth-grade biology students. *Journal of Research in Science Teaching, 24,* 507–525.

Weiss, I.R., Nelson, B.H., Boyd, S.E., & Hudson, S.B. (1989). *Science and mathematics education briefing book 1989.* Chapel Hill, NC: Horizon Research, Inc.

Wilkinson, L. (1988). *SYSTAT: The system for statistics.* Evanston, IL: SYSTAT, Inc.

Yager, R.E. & Penick, J.E. (1986). Perceptions of four age groups toward science classes, teachers, and the value of science. *Science Education, 70,* 355–363.

Zimmerer, L.K. & Bennett, S.M. (1987). Gender differences on the California statewide assessment of attitudes and achievement in science. Paper presented at the annual meeting of the American Educational Research Association. Washington, DC.

Callouts in figure:
- Pages
- Journal titles all initial caps
- Title of article has first word capitalized, then lowercase
- Book title capitalize first word, then lowercase

STUDY QUESTIONS

1. What are some important ways in which educational knowledge is obtained? What are the strengths and weaknesses of different sources of knowledge?

2. How is a scientific approach to inquiry different from inquiry based on personal experience?

3. In what ways can explanation of educational phenomena improve teaching and learning?

4. In what ways can theories be useful in education? What are some limitations of theories?

5. What are the steps of scientific inquiry? Why are questions used as part of the overall framework?

6. What is necessary for a study to be judged credible?

7. What are the differences between qualitative and quantitative approaches to research?

8. How can research you have read be classified as basic, applied, evaluation, or action research? Is it experimental or nonexperimental?

9. What is the essential difference between experimental and nonexperimental research?

10. Read some research studies and identify the various sections, that is, introduction, review of literature, results, and so on.

@**WWW** SAMPLE TEST QUESTIONS

See this text's Companion Website at **www.ablongman.com/mcmillan5e** for sample test questions and answers.

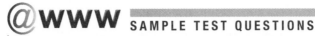 RESEARCH NAVIGATOR™ ACTIVITIES

1. On the Research Navigator™ home page, click on the second tab, Finding Sources. Compare these sources to those in Chapter 1. How are they different? How does technology affect sources of knowledge?
2. Use the Research Navigator™ Accession Number (AN 10755456; be sure to include a space between N and the first number) to obtain a journal article about the Education Sciences Act. From the point of view of this author, what is the political influence on designing educational research?

Chapter 2

Research Problems, Variables, *and* Hypotheses

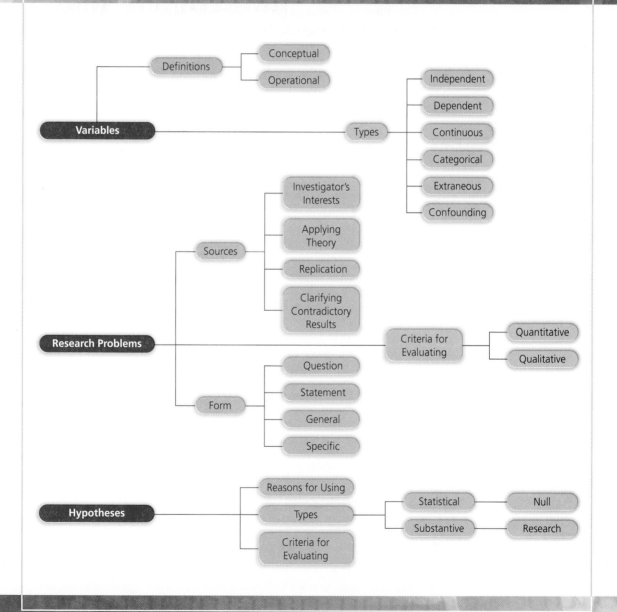

CHAPTER ROAD MAP

In this chapter we will discuss the first essential step in both conducting and understanding research: the research problem. We will see that all studies begin with a general research problem and that further refinement and specificity depend on whether it is quantitative or qualitative. We will also learn about variables and research hypotheses, important concepts in quantitative studies.

As a result of studying this chapter, you will understand:

- The difference between general and more specific research problems
- How researchers come up with research problems
- Different types of variables used in quantitative studies
- The difference between researchable and nonresearchable problems
- The nature and use of different types of hypotheses
- Criteria for evaluating quantitative research problems and hypotheses, and qualitative problems

RESEARCH PROBLEMS

The research problem comprises one or more sentences that indicate(s) the goal, purpose, or overall direction of the study. It is generally found in the first paragraph of an article, often at the end of the paragraph, to provide an orientation to the reader about the proposed investigation. The research problem implies the possibility of empirical investigation. Usually there is a need identified and the study's purpose is to collect and analyze data in a way that will meet this need. It provides a focus for the researcher and is an essential first step in the investigation. It also helps the reader decide quickly if the study is pertinent or interesting, and by providing an overview makes the research much easier to understand.

The research problem statement is typically rather general, with just enough information about the scope and purpose of the study to provide an initial understanding of the research. Often the problem is introduced using the following phrases, though there is no one correct or best way:

"The purpose of this study is to. . . ."
"The aim of the current investigation is to. . . ."
"In this study we investigated. . . ."
"The goal of the research was to. . . ."

Here are some examples of general research problems:

EXAMPLE | **Research Problem Statements**

The purpose of this research is to study adolescent loneliness.

This research will investigate the social integration of adults with physical disabilities.

This study investigates the relationship between school culture and student achievement.

This research was designed to determine student perceptions of their high school experiences.

The research problem can also be stated as a question. Like problem statements, these tend to be general. For example:

EXAMPLE | **Research Problem Questions**

What is the relationship between school culture and student achievement?

Is there a difference in motivation between homogeneously and heterogeneously grouped students?

Do preschool teachers have different instructional styles?

What explains the high rate of teacher absenteeism?

It is important to distinguish the general research problem from more specific, focused statements and questions that communicate the nature of the study in greater detail. It should be noted that some researchers may use the term *research problem* as synonymous with a specific problem statement or question. Thus, you will find some variety in the form as well as in the location of the research problem in an article or report. In some articles the problem may be stated at the beginning in a general sense, with more specific questions later, while in other articles the research problem may be communicated only by more specific questions or statements. The nature of these more specific statements and questions depends on whether they are for quantitative or qualitative research (quantitative are specific, qualitative are general).

Sources for Research Problems

How does a researcher begin to develop a good problem? Several sources are commonly used to begin the process of problem formulation, though coming up with a good research problem may be a rather arduous and time-consuming task. Ideas that seem promising initially typically need revision as literature related to the idea is analyzed and implications for research design are clarified. Many researchers begin to identify a topic by reading current books and journals in their area and by talking with knowledgeable professionals about current problems or issues. Once a broad area of interest is identified, further reading usually leads to a more specific research problem. Additional factors influence the feasibility of the proposed study, such as cost, the ability and training of the investigator, and the availability of subjects.

Although there is no single strategy for identifying research problems that works best for all investigators, several sources have been useful for many.

Investigator's Interests and Experiences. Some of the best sources of ideas come from the interests and practical experiences of the investigator. A teacher encounters many problems and questions daily that may lead to researchable problems: concerns about teaching methods, grouping, classroom management, tests, individualization, grades, standardized test data. Administrators may face problems in scheduling, communicating with teachers, providing instructional leadership, generating public support, or handling serious discipline. University professors may see that student teachers are encountering difficulties that need to be resolved. In addition to personal experiences, each of us has interests and knowledge about our profession that can be the source of good problems. It may be a topic that we are curious about or have read about, or it may be a long-standing interest in certain areas.

Applying Theory. A common source for research problems is a theory that has implications for educational practice. One approach is to take a theory in a related area, such as psychology or sociology, and develop a problem that extends it to an educational setting. A good example is research on leadership styles. Psychological research has established that there are clear differences among autocratic, participatory, and laissez-faire leadership styles in affecting the outcomes of small groups. Would the same be true of principal leadership on student achievement? Other examples would be using theories of reinforcement, attitude development, information processing, and communication to generate research problems. In each case the theories suggest implications that can be further researched in educational settings. Another way to apply theories is to directly test, revise, or clarify an existing educational theory. Here the intent is to develop and change the theory rather than to test its implications.

Replication. An excellent type of study is one that replicates previous research, that is, repeats a completed study with relatively minor changes. It may seem that replication would not add new knowledge, but in fact just the opposite is true. Progress in building a body of knowledge depends on a series of replications to verify and extend the initial findings. One of the weaknesses in educational research is that there have been too few replications. Gall, Gall, and Borg (2007) summarize five reasons for conducting replication studies:

1. *To check the findings of a major or milestone study.* Replications can confirm or disconfirm the validity of a study that produces new evidence or reports findings that challenge previous research or theory.

2. *To check the validity of research findings with different subjects.* Replications often use the same procedures but change the type of subjects used to see if the original findings hold for different subjects. For example, much of Kohlberg's initial research on moral development was with men. A good replication study would ascertain whether the findings hold for women as well. Studies that are originally limited in scope can justifiably be replicated to extend the findings to other people and conditions.

3. *To check trends or change over time.* Replications can be used effectively to see if initial findings hold over time. This type of replication is done with attitudes, values, achievement, and other areas where trend data are important. For instance, the National Assessment of Educational Progress (NAEP) has measured the performance of 9-, 13-, and 17-year-old school children in key subjects since 1969. Every two years the same questions are asked, which provides a useful assessment of changes in student performance over time.

4. *To check important findings using different methodologies.* It is possible that a research finding may be unduly influenced by the way a variable is measured. For example, there are many ways to measure critical thinking. A particular study may report a "significant" result using one way to measure critical thinking, but the result may be limited by the way it was measured. Thus, a useful replication would repeat the study but change the instrumentation. The same is true for procedures in a study. Research that replicates and changes what may be faulty methods, such as the way an intervention is administered or what the experimenter says to the subjects, may change the results. A related reason to replicate is to use different statistics to analyze the data.

5. *To develop more effective or efficient interventions.* With the recent emphasis on determining the success of educational interventions, designing research that fine-tunes an intervention is important to maximizing student achievement. Often interventions that have been investigated on a small scale or in laboratory settings are tested in less controlled settings.

Clarification of Contradictory Findings. There are seemingly contradictory findings on many topics in the literature. Some studies indicate one conclusion, and other studies investigating the same problem come to an opposite conclusion. These apparent contradictions present good sources for research problems. For instance, research on the effect of between-class ability grouping (tracking) on student achievement is mixed. Some studies indicate that it promotes higher overall achievement, whereas other studies conclude that it makes no difference in student achievement but has adverse attitudinal and social effects. Why are there contradictions? By examining the studies, discrepancies in methodology or populations may be found that suggest further research to explain the contradictions.

USING EDUCATIONAL RESEARCH

One effective way to identify research topics is to read the conclusion and discussion section of an empirical study. Often there are recommendations for further research that can be used to identify a research problem or question. Another place to look is in the last chapter of dissertations. There is almost always a list of recommended topics for further research.

QUANTITATIVE RESEARCH PROBLEM STATEMENTS *and* QUESTIONS

In quantitative research there is a need for clear, concise research problem statements and questions that unambiguously communicate what will be studied. One important aspect of the statement or question is to convey information about the *variables* that will be investigated. Understanding and using the term *variable* is fundamental to all quantitative studies. We will discuss variables in some detail now before turning to specific quantitative problem statements and questions.

Variables in Quantitative Research

One of the most commonly used terms in quantitative research is *variable*. A **variable** is a label or name that represents a concept or characteristic. Concepts are nouns that stand for a class of objects, such as *tree, house, desk, teacher,* and *school.* A characteristic is a trait we use to describe someone, such as *tall, male, creative,* or *average.* Researchers use *variable* rather than *concept* or *characteristic* because most of what is studied varies, that is, involves variations that can be described numerically or categorically. Thus, a variable is a type of concept or characteristic that can take on different values or be divided into categories. For example, intelligence, achievement, social class, and cognitive style each involves a range of values, which is often expressed numerically. However, many variables are better described as containing two or more categories, for example, male and female, cooperative versus individualized instruction, beginning teachers with or without student teaching experience.

> **Variable:** A concept or characteristic that involves variations.

Variables are composed of *attributes* or *levels.* An attribute is the value or category that makes up the variation. Thus, for example, the variable gender would have as attributes *female* and *male.* These categories may also be referred to as *levels.* For a variable such as learning style, the attributes or levels may be field dependent and field independent, or impulsive and reflective, depending on the conceptual definition. Here are some more examples of variables with corresponding attributes or levels:

Variable	Attributes or Levels
Socioeconomic Status	High, Middle, Low
Grade Level	Grades 7, 8, and 9; or Elementary, Middle, High School
SAT	Score from 200 to 800
Age	10–19, 20–29, 30+
Race	Caucasian, African American, Hispanic, Asian

Conceptual and Operational Definitions

A precise definition of each variable communicates clearly the researcher's intent and enhances the usefulness of the results. Vague definitions are difficult to interpret and usually lead to less meaningful results. Two types of definitions are commonly used in research, *conceptual* and *operational.* A **conceptual** (sometimes called constitutive) **definition** uses other words and concepts to describe the variable, as in a dictionary. For example, *attitude* may be defined conceptually as "a predisposition to respond favorably or unfavorably toward a person, object, or event," and *value* may be defined as "the degree to which an event is perceived to be positive or negative." Conceptual definitions are important in communicating what is being investigated, but they may not indicate precisely what the variables mean. Another type of description, called an *operational definition,* is needed to provide this more precise meaning.

> **Conceptual definition:** Uses words or concepts.

An **operational definition** indicates how the concept is measured or manipulated, that is, what "operations" are performed to measure or manipulate the

> **Operational definition:** Defines a concept by how it is measured or manipulated.

variable. It is essential to understand operational definitions because researchers will use different ways of measuring or manipulating the same variable. Hence the meaning of the results depends on understanding the operational definition, not simply the more generic meaning implied by the conceptual definition. Suppose you are interested in learning about the relationship between parenting styles and children's loneliness. There are many definitions and ways of measuring both variables, and you would need to examine the questions asked and the way the responses were scored to know what a particular researcher means. Or, consider the variable socioeconomic status (SES), in which the terms *high*, *middle*, and *low* often describe categories. These terms are meaningful only if you know the rules for classifying subjects as high, middle, or low. The same subject might be classified as high in one study and middle in another. Thus, to some extent, operational definitions are arbitrary and often are not explicitly stated. If you are interested in knowing whether cooperative or individualized methods of teaching are most effective in promoting student achievement, knowing simply that a study of these two methods showed cooperative methods to be better is not sufficient. You need to know how the terms *cooperative*, *individualized*, and *achievement* are determined or measured.

Following are some examples of variables, with corresponding conceptual and operational definitions:

Variable	Conceptual Definition	Operational Definition
Self-concept	Characteristics used to describe oneself	Scores on the Coopersmith Self-Esteem Inventory
Intelligence	Ability to think abstractly	Scores on the Stanford-Binet
Teacher with-it-ness	Awareness of student involvement and behavior	Results of the Robinson Scale of teacher with-it-ness

Types of Variables

There are several types of variables in educational research. We will consider the most important: independent and dependent, extraneous and confounding, and continuous and categorical.

Independent and Dependent Variables. In much research, one variable precedes another, either logically or in time. The variable that comes first and influences or predicts is called the **independent variable.** The second variable, the one that is affected or predicted by the independent variable, is the **dependent variable.** In an experiment, at least one independent variable is the presumed cause of differences between groups on the dependent variable. The independent variable is the antecedent (intervention), the dependent variable is the consequence (outcome). Predictions are made from independent variables to dependent variables. When we say, "If X then Y," X is the independent variable and Y is the dependent variable. When we control which students receive particular teaching methods (antecedent), we may see the effect on achievement (consequence). Teaching method is the independent variable; achievement is the dependent

Independent variable: Precedes, influences, or predicts the dependent variable.

Dependent variable: Affected or predicted by the independent variable.

variable. In educational research, teacher behavior, methods of instruction, curriculum, individual characteristics of students, socioeconomic status, and peer group behaviors are common independent variables, and achievement, attitudes, values, self-concept, and social development are common dependent variables (these may also be independent variables, depending on the study).

In nonexperimental research, the independent variable cannot be manipulated or controlled by the investigator. Such variables may still be considered independent if they clearly precede the dependent variable, if they are used to create categories for comparison or are explanatory. For example, a study of the effect of school size (independent variable) on achievement (dependent variable) may locate and use large, medium, and small schools, although it cannot manipulate or alter the size of a particular school. However, it is clear that school size precedes achievement. In correlational studies, several nonmanipulated variables may be considered independent because they precede the dependent variable. For example, a school administrator may need to predict teaching effectiveness to hire the best teachers. Several variables are available for each candidate, including grade point average, supervisor's comments about student teaching, and an interview. If these variables are used to predict the outcome (effectiveness as a teacher), they are independent variables.

In some nonexperimental research, it is difficult to label variables as independent or dependent, particularly when one variable does not clearly precede the other. For instance, a study of the relationship between critical thinking and creativity may be conducted to show they are distinct, unrelated concepts. In this case neither is an independent or dependent variable; there are simply two variables in the study.

Nonexperimental, descriptive research may compare groups of subjects, and often the variable used to classify the groups is considered independent. For example, a descriptive study of the attitudes of school principals toward school financing might divide the principals into groups depending on the size and location of each school. Here attitudes would be the dependent variable and size and location of schools the independent variables.

Extraneous variable: Source of error affecting the results.	***Extraneous Variables.*** An **extraneous variable** affects the dependent variable but is either unknown or not controlled by the researcher. Extraneous variables are conditions, events, features, or occurrences that influence the subjects in a particular group that are not part of the study and that may compromise the interpretation of the results. That is, they may provide an alternative explanation for the results—they "mess up" the study. Sometimes such factors are called *nuisance variables*.
Confounding variable: Varies systematically with the independent variable.	***Confounding Variables.*** A **confounding variable** is one that varies systematically with the independent variable. For instance, suppose you find a study comparing two methods of teaching reading, a totally phonics approach and a combined phonics/whole language approach. Two classrooms are used in the study, one classroom implementing each approach. However, because different teachers are in each class, "teachers" is a confounding variable because the style,

personality, and knowledge of each teacher is confounded with each approach to teaching and will affect reading scores (dependent variable). So if one group of students did score better than the other, you would not know if it was because of the method or the teacher. Think of confounding variables as having different values or degrees of influence in each group of subjects. Extraneous variables target a specific group. Throughout the rest of the book further types of extraneous and confounding variables will be identified, and examples will show how they affect the interpretation of research findings.

Continuous and Categorical Variables. A **continuous variable** (or *measured variable*) can theoretically take on an infinite number of values within a given range of scores. In other words, the value of a continuous variable could be any point on a continuum. The values are rank ordered, from small to large or low to high, to indicate the amount of some property or characteristic. Common continuous variables in educational research are achievement and aptitude test scores; self-concept; attitude and value measures; and height, weight, and age. A **categorical variable** is used to assign an object or person to a group (level) that is defined by having specified characteristics. The most simple type of category has two groups (dichotomous), such as male/female, high/low, white/black, and morning/afternoon. Other categorical variables can have three or many more groups, for example, grade level, nationality, occupation, and religious preference. It is also common to use continuous scores to create categories. For instance, socioeconomic status is generally used as a continuous variable, but the scores can be grouped into categories such as high, middle, and low SES. Thus, the designation of a continuous or categorical variable may depend on how the researcher uses the scores. The same variable can be continuous in one study and categorical in another. Also, although most dependent variables are continuous, both independent and dependent variables can be either continuous or categorical.

> **Continuous variable:** Infinite values within a range.

> **Categorical variable:** Groups defined by specific characteristics.

The relationship of independent, dependent, extraneous, and confounding variables is illustrated in Figure 2.1 in the context of an investigation on the effect of different science teaching methods on student achievement and attitudes.

Specific Quantitative Research Problem Statements and Questions

We have already discussed general research problems as statements or questions that provide some indication of the direction of the research, a preview of what is to come. With these statements and questions you have a general idea of what will be studied, but for quantitative studies these statements may lack clarity, may contain ambiguous terms, and may not provide sufficient information. They are fine as a beginning statement of purpose, but they eventually need to be more focused.

At the other end of the specificity continuum are statements that contain more detail and information than is necessary. As a result, they are difficult to understand. An extreme example would be the following:

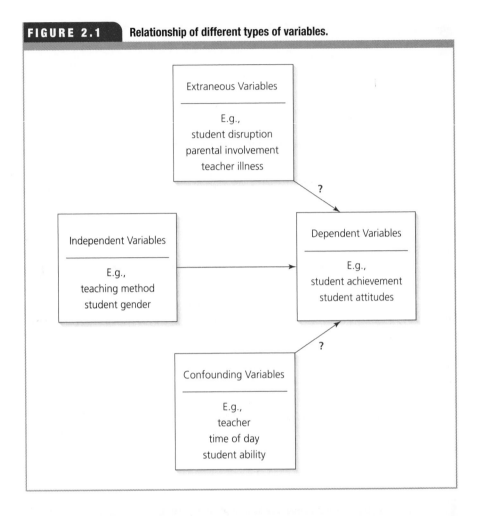

FIGURE 2.1　Relationship of different types of variables.

The purpose of this study is to investigate whether seventh- and eighth-grade male and female teachers who teach in a predominantly middle-class school in a western Michigan suburb who are identified by principal ratings and the Teacher Effectiveness Inventory, given in the fall semester by trained observers, will have students who, matched by ability when entering school in the fall, differ in the level of achievement in mathematics and language arts as measured by the Iowa Test of Basic Skills.

The majority of specific quantitative research problem statements are in the middle of the continuum. These statements contain sufficient detail and information in a sentence that is clear and succinct. The sentence may be in the form of a question or a statement. Following are examples from two published articles:

> **EXAMPLE** | **Published Research Problem Statements at Appropriate Levels of Specificity**
>
> "Does parental involvement affect the reading achievement (specifically comprehension) of sixth grade students?" (Hawes, C. A., & Plourd, L. A. (2005). Parental involvement and its influence on the reading achievement of 6th grade students, *Reading Improvement, 42*(1), p. 50)
>
> "In addition to the development of a knowledge test, the following questions were examined:
>
> 1. What are elementary teachers' beliefs about grade retention and do they differ by grade taught?
> 2. What factors influence teachers' decisions to retain students?" (Witmer, S. M., Hoffman, L. M., & Nottis, K. E. (2004), *Education, 125*, p. 178)

One of the reasons for using specific language in the research problem statement or question is to demonstrate that it is researchable. A researchable problem is one that can be answered with empirical procedures.

Table 2.1 includes quantitative research questions in both general and specific language to illustrate the difference between nonresearchable and researchable questions. The specific questions are good because they summarize several aspects of the study, including the type of research (experimental, relationship, or descriptive), independent and dependent variables, and characteristics of the subjects. Each of these will be considered in greater detail in discussing criteria for evaluating problem statements or questions.

TABLE 2.1   **Researchability of Quantitative Problems**

Nonresearchable	Researchable
Should we teach sex education in elementary schools?	What is the difference in knowledge and attitudes of fifth-graders taught sex education compared to fifth-graders who are not taught sex education?
Do teachers need to have courses in test construction?	Will the classroom testing procedures used by teachers who take a course in test construction differ from those of teachers who have not had the course?
Should the school day be longer?	What is the relationship between length of the school day and SAT scores of high school students?
Should learning-disabled students be mainstreamed in English as well as in physical education?	What is the effect of mainstreaming fourth-grade learning-disabled students into English classes on the self-concept, attitudes, and achievement of all students?

CONSUMER TIPS: *Criteria for Evaluating Quantitative Research Problems*

1. The problem should be researchable. A researchable problem is one that can be answered empirically by collecting and analyzing data. Problems that are concerned with value questions or philosophical ideas are not researchable in the sense that a specific question has a correct answer. There are many interesting questions in education that require value or ethical analyses, but to be able to conduct research, the question must lend itself to the systematic process of gathering and analyzing data.

2. The problem should be important. The results of research need to have theoretical or practical importance. Theoretical importance is determined by the contribution of the study to existing knowledge. Are the results meaningfully related to what is already known? Do the results add new knowledge or change the way we understand phenomena? Practical importance suggests that the results will have immediate use in day-to-day activities or decisions.

3. The problem should indicate the type of research. The language used in the research problem should indicate whether the study involves a simple description, a comparison, a relationship, or a difference. A simple description is implied from such problems as these: How many third-graders have computer experience? What criteria are most important in placing children with mental retardation? What are the social and personality characteristics of gifted children? How do children react when parents separate? A relationship study indicates how two or more variables may be related. For example, the following problems imply a relationship: What is the relationship between achievement and self-concept? Is there a relationship between effort in doing an assignment and attitudes about it? Can leadership potential be predicted from high school grades, recommendations, and participation in extracurricular activities?

Research that compares categories of one or more independent variables can also be nonexperimental. For example:

How do males and females differ in their attitudes toward freedom of the press?

Are elementary school teachers different from secondary school teachers in assertiveness?

What is the difference between sixth, seventh, and eighth graders' self-concept of ability?

Some research problems imply more than a simple relationship or comparison. They suggest that one variable causes a change in another one. Here the intent of the research is to test a cause-and-effect relationship between the independent and dependent variables. This includes all experimental research and some types of nonexperimental research. Typically, differences are emphasized in the problem statement, and often the word *effect* is used. (Unfortunately some relationship studies that are not causal still use the term *effect*, which may be misleading.) Here are some difference questions that imply cause-and-effect relationships:

Will method A result in higher achievement than method B?

Is there a difference in attitude between students having peer teaching compared to students who have traditional instruction?

What is the effect of small group instruction on the reading achievement of second graders?

4. The problem should specify the population. The population is simply the people that the researcher wants to investigate. A good research problem identifies, in a few words, the most important distinguishing characteristics of the population. Too much detail about the subjects will unnecessarily repeat the full description in the subjects section of the research report. Hence the description of the population in the research problem should be concise yet informative. Here is a problem in which the description of the population is too vague:

Do children who practice with calculators achieve more than those who do not practice with calculators?

Here is the same problem with a description that is too specific:

Do fourth-grade, low-SES, low-ability students from Carpenter Elementary School who practice with calculators achieve more than those who do not practice with calculators?

A good level of specificity would be this:

Do low-ability, low-SES fourth-graders who practice with calculators achieve more than those who do not practice with calculators?

5. The problem should specify the variables. A good problem statement of a relatively simple study will name the variables and how they may be related in a single sentence. Often these will be independent and dependent variables. Variables are described, like the population, with a moderate level of specificity. "A study of the effect of teacher workshops" is far too general; in fact there is no dependent variable at all. "A study of the effect of teacher workshops on teacher morale as measured by the Smith Morale and Attitude Scale" does provide a dependent variable, but provides more detail than necessary and still does not communicate much about the independent variable (workshop). Here the design of the study will contribute to the description of the independent variable. If two groups of teachers are being compared, one who attends the workshop and one who does not, a better, more informative problem would be: Is there a difference in the morale of teachers who attend a teacher workshop compared to teachers who do not attend? Here the independent variable is more than just named; it is described.

Research problems that are more complex because of having several independent and/or dependent variables may need to be stated in more than one sentence. The first sentence typically includes either the main variables or a general term to represent several variables. It is followed by one or more sentences that describe all the variables:

The aim of this study is to investigate the relationship between measures of aptitude and attitudes toward college among high school students. The measures of aptitude include scores from the SRA and SAT, high school grade point average, and class rank. Attitudes toward college are assessed by the Canadian College Attitude Scale, which reports four subscale scores: motivation, academic versus social climate, reputation, and expectations for success.

This study involves four independent and four dependent variables, and it would be cumbersome to try to include all of them in one sentence.

6. The problem should be clear. The importance of a clear, concise research problem statement cannot be overemphasized. One purpose of the research problem statement is to communicate the purpose of the study, ensuring that the reader's understanding of the purpose is consistent with the researcher's. Also, a clear research problem reflects clear thinking by the researcher. A clear problem does not include ambiguous terms. Ambiguity occurs when different people, reading the same thing, derive different meanings from what is read. If a term or phrase can mean several things, it is ambiguous. Terms such as *effect, effective, achievement, aptitude, methods, curriculum,* and *students,* by themselves, are ambiguous or vague. They should be replaced or modified so that the meaning is clear. A vague statement such as "What is the effect of sex education?" needs much more specificity. What is meant by "effect" and "sex education"? What grade level is being studied? What type of study is it? A successful problem indicates unambiguously the what, who, and how of the research by using declarative sentences such as "The purpose of this study is to . . ." or questions such as "What is the relationship between . . ."; "Is there a difference between . . ."; "How do . . ."; and "What is . . ." Either type of sentence is acceptable, and you will find both in the literature.

HYPOTHESES

Hypotheses: Tentative predictions or expectations.

Hypotheses are educated "guesses" or tentative expectations about a correct solution to a problem, descriptions, possible relationships, or differences. In research, a hypothesis is typically the investigator's prediction or expectation of what the results will show. It is a conjectural statement of the researcher's expectations about how the variables in the study are related. In short, a hypothesis is a prediction that is made prior to data collection. (As we will see, this kind of hypothesis is usually referred to as a "research hypothesis.")

Why Researchers Use Hypotheses

Researchers use hypotheses in some quantitative studies because they serve a number of important purposes:

1. The hypothesis provides a focus that integrates information. Researchers often have hunches about predictions, based on experience, previous research, and the opinions of others. By forming a hypothesis, the researcher synthesizes the information to make the most accurate prediction possible. Usually the researcher draws heavily on the related literature. If the hypothesis does not follow from or is not logically related to the previous literature, the importance or contribution of the research is questionable, and the overall credibility of the study is diminished.

2. The hypothesis is testable. It provides a statement of relationships that can be tested by gathering and analyzing data.

3. The hypothesis helps the investigator know what to do. The nature of the hypothesis directs the investigation by suggesting appropriate sampling, instrumentation, and procedures. It helps the researcher keep a focused, specific scope.

4. The hypothesis allows the investigator to confirm or disconfirm a theory. Hypotheses help advance knowledge by refuting, modifying, or supporting theories.

5. The hypothesis provides a framework for developing explanations that can be investigated scientifically. Explanations that are not contained in a hypothesis are metaphysical in nature and are not subject to scientific verification.

6. When supported, the hypothesis provides evidence of the predictive nature of the relationship between the variables. Knowledge of a tested, confirmed prediction is more powerful evidence than an unconfirmed, untested observation.

7. The hypothesis provides a useful framework for organizing and summarizing the results and conclusions of the research. It helps the reader understand the meaning and significance of the study.

Types of Hypotheses

There are two ways to classify hypotheses: whether the hypothesis is derived from inductive or deductive logic, and whether the hypothesis is stated as a *research* or *statistical* hypothesis. We will briefly consider both ways of classification.

An *inductive hypothesis* is formed from a researcher's observations of behavior. The observations are synthesized to form tentative explanations about how the behaviors are related to one another and to other variables such as teaching methods, curriculum materials, and teacher behavior. In fact, teachers provide a rich source for inductive hypotheses because they can use their experience and knowledge to formulate hypotheses that may explain observed relationships. A limitation of inductive hypotheses is that because they depend on local data and idiosyncratic observations, generalizations are often restricted and hard to relate to a broader theory or established body of applied research.

Deductive hypotheses are derived from theory, and thus testing them contributes to a better understanding of the theory or its application. The findings are integrated with existing facts and theories, which helps build a meaningful body of knowledge. For example, the theory of positive reinforcement suggests that teachers should reward desirable behavior. This principle has generated a great amount of research based on deductive hypotheses. From the general theory we have built a larger knowledge base that includes the effects of intrinsic and extrinsic reinforcement, praise, tokens, immediate and delayed reinforcement, and self-reinforcement.

Hypotheses are also classified as *research* or *statistical*. A **research hypothesis** is a conjectural, declarative statement of the results the investigator expects to find. Research hypotheses are sometimes referred to as working or substantive hypotheses. Most research hypotheses are directional, in which the nature of the expected difference or relationship is stated. That is, a specified group is expected to score higher or lower than other groups, or a relationship is positive or negative. For example, a research hypothesis for an experiment would be:

> Fifth-grade students participating in a computer-aided mathematics lesson will demonstrate higher achievement than students using a traditional paper-and-pencil lesson.

In a study of relationships the research hypothesis might be:

> There is a positive relationship between time on task and achievement.

A research hypothesis is used when the investigator anticipates the specific outcome of the study, for example, which group will score higher than the other, an increase or decrease in scores, a positive or negative relationship, more or less of something, and so forth. Here are some examples of research hypotheses from published studies:

Research hypothesis: Statement of expected results.

EXAMPLE | **Published Research Hypotheses**

"Study 1 tested the hypothesis that performance goals (approach or avoidance) relate highly to indices of anxiety and depression. Study 2 tested the hypothesis that performance-oriented students (approach or avoidance) are highly anxious prior to a stressful event to protect their self-worth." (Sideridis, G. D. (2005). Goal orientation, academic achievement, and depression: Evidence in favor of a revised goal theory framework. *Journal of Educational Psychology, 97*(3), p. 367)

"It is hypothesized that prior achievement will directly predict GPA because historically students' performance on standardized tests has been considered an optimal predictor of their subsequent success in school. Prior achievement is also expected to predict homework reports because high achieving high school students spend more time on their assignments than low achieving students. . . . In addition, high achieving students are hypothesized to form higher self-efficacy beliefs about their capability to learn on their own." (Zimmerman, B. J., & Kitsantas, A. (2005). Homework practices and academic achievement: The mediating role of self-efficacy and perceived responsibility beliefs. *Contemporary Educational Psychology, 30*, p. 400)

"The predicted relationships are as follows: Participants who respond 'never' to all items within each of the theft subgroups (low petty, high petty, burglary, and robbery) will have significantly higher P scores . . . than those who admit involvement, to any degree, in the respective behaviors." (Judy, B., & Nelson, E. S. (2000). Relationship between parents, peers, morality, and theft in an adolescent sample. *The High School Journal, 83*(3), p. 34)

Research hypotheses can also be nondirectional. The researcher believes there will be a difference or relationship, but is unsure about the nature of it; for example,

> There will be a difference in achievement when comparing individually tutored children to those receiving group tutoring.

Such nondirectional research hypotheses are not very common. Usually either previous research or the experiences and intuition of the investigator suggest a direction.

The **statistical hypothesis** is a statement of a relationship or difference that can be tested statistically. Statistical hypotheses are usually stated in what is called the "null" form. A **null hypothesis** is a statement that there are no statistically significant differences or relationships. The null hypothesis is tested, based on the findings from the study, and results in either rejecting or failing to reject the null. The acceptance or nonacceptance of the null hypothesis provides support or no support for the research hypothesis. The statistical procedures used to test the null hypothesis are discussed in greater detail in Chapter 10. At this point it is important to understand that we do not test the research hypothesis itself; we "accept" it when the null hypothesis is rejected. We do it in this way because researchers do not prove true an expected result. Rather, they can tentatively accept the research hypothesis when the statistical test shows that the null hypothesis, which is assumed to be true before the test, can be rejected.

Table 2.2 shows the relationship among research problems, research hypotheses, and null hypotheses. The investigator begins with a problem, forms a research hypothesis based on a review of literature and/or personal experiences, forms the null hypothesis, tests the null hypothesis, and accepts or rejects the research hypothesis. Often there will not be an explicit null hypothesis in an

Statistical hypothesis: Statistical statement of possible results.

Null hypothesis: Statistical statement that no significant difference or relationship exists.

TABLE 2.2 Relationship of Research Problems, Research Hypotheses, and Null Hypotheses

Research Problem	Research Hypothesis	Null Hypothesis
What is the effect of a mainstreaming workshop on the attitude of teachers toward mainstreaming?	Teachers' attitudes toward mainstreaming will improve as a result of attending a workshop on mainstreaming.	There is no difference in teachers' attitudes toward mainstreaming measured before a workshop on mainstreaming compared to their attitudes after the workshop.
Is there a relationship between teachers' attitudes toward the curriculum and student achievement?	There is a positive correlation between teachers' attitudes toward the curriculum and student achievement.	There is no correlation between teachers' attitudes toward the curriculum and student achievement.
Is there a difference in achievement between students who are given highly detailed written comments on their work compared to students who are given grades only?	Students receiving highly detailed written comments on their work will show higher achievement than students given grades only.	There is no difference in achievement between students receiving highly detailed written comments about their work compared to students receiving grades only.

article or report; rather, it is usually implied in the statistical test. In some articles the research hypothesis is also implied.

CONSUMER TIPS: *Criteria for Evaluating Research Hypotheses*

1. The research hypothesis should be stated in declarative form. Because the research hypothesis is a possible explanation, it must be written in the form of a declarative sentence. A hypothesis cannot be stated in the form of a question.

2. The research hypothesis should be consistent with known facts, previous research, and theory. The research hypothesis should follow from other studies and established theories. In general, it should not contradict previous research but rather should build on related literature; the results should contribute to the established body of knowledge. It is best for the research hypothesis to follow the review of literature. The reader should be able to understand why a particular hypothesis is put forth.

3. The research hypothesis should follow from the research problem. It is confusing to use variables in the hypothesis that have not been identified by the research problem. A general problem may include several variables, and thus several research hypotheses may be used to indicate all of the anticipated relationships.

4. The research hypothesis should state the expected relationship between two or more variables. A hypothesis must have at least two variables and must indicate how the variables are related. A study that analyzes the relationship by a correlation coefficient will use the terms *positive relationship* or *negative relationship*. In a study that analyzes differences between groups, the relationship may be expressed as a difference (more or less, higher or lower). In either case, an expected relationship is stated. Most research hypotheses conjecture the relationship between two variables. It can be awkward and confusing to include more than two variables in one sentence, with the exception of studies that have several dependent variables and one independent variable (e.g., Students in the cooperative class will show more positive attitudes toward learning, higher achievement, and more prosocial behavior than students in the individualized class).

5. The research hypothesis should be testable. As pointed out previously, being testable means being verifiable; that is, data can be obtained to determine whether the hypothesis can be supported. It is a matter of measuring the variables in such a way that the hypothesis can be confirmed or not confirmed. Thus the variables must be measurable, and the researcher must be able to obtain data that represent values of the variables. The researcher must therefore include operational definitions of the variables (not necessarily as part of the hypothesis statement, but perhaps following the hypothesis). Stated differently, the variables must be amenable to operational definitions that can be applied by using an instrument or observations to collect data. For example, the hypothesis "Children taking a unit on nutrition will be more healthy" is not testable because "more healthy" is difficult to operationalize and measure, and it would be almost impossible to attribute better health to the unit on nutrition.

6. **The research hypothesis should be clear.** Like the terminology used in research problems, words, phrases, and descriptions in the research hypothesis should be unambiguous. A clear hypothesis is easier for the reader to comprehend and easier for the researcher to test.

7. **The research hypothesis should be concise.** Consistent with criteria for research problems, hypotheses should be sufficiently detailed to communicate what is being tested and, at the same time, should be as succinct as possible. A concise hypothesis is easier to comprehend.

QUALITATIVE RESEARCH PROBLEM STATEMENTS *and* QUESTIONS

In qualitative studies, researchers tend to use only general problem statements or questions (see Table 2.3). From the beginning, the logic and purpose of the questions are different from those of quantitative problems. As illustrated in the examples provided, qualitative problems tend to be much more open-ended, less specific, evolving rather than static, and process oriented. These differences result in unique usage of terms and language. For example, it is common for qualitative problem statements to use words like *generate*, *understand*, and *explore*, rather than *relate*, *differ*, or *compare*. A qualitative question is neutral with respect to what will be learned through the study. There are no predictions or expected results.

The first step in writing a qualitative problem statement or question is to identify the central phenomenon that is being studied. The **central phenomenon** is an issue or process that is being investigated (Creswell, 2005). Issues would be such things as teenage alienation, teacher retention, or principal burnout. Processes could include the manner in which beginning teachers are inducted into the profession, how teachers integrate the demands of standardized high-stakes

Central phenomenon: Issue or process studied.

TABLE 2.3	Differences Between Quantitative and Qualitative Research Problems	
Quantitative	**Qualitative**
Specific	General
Closed	Open
Static	Evolving
Outcome oriented	Process oriented
Contains variables	Does not contain variables

testing into their teaching, and the manner in which mainstreamed children are integrated into the regular classroom. The general research problem statement or question includes a single central phenomenon. Two or more phenomena are not compared or related as would be done in a quantitative study (comparisons and relationships can emerge from the data, it's just that qualitative researchers don't go into the research with these already in mind). Here are some examples of general problem statements from published qualitative studies that have a clear central phenomenon.

EXAMPLE | **Qualitative Research Problem Statements and Questions**

"Our research was designed as a descriptive investigation of the joint effects of external and internal accountability on sustainable improvement and addressed the following general questions:

- How do schools adapt to external accountability standards?

- How do schools' structure and culture relate to their ability to make sense of and respond to external standards?

- How do perceived power relations affect local responses to state testing and accountability?"

(Louis, K. S., Febey, K., & Schroeder, R. (2005). *Educational Evaluation and Policy Analysis, 27* (2) p. 181)

"The study reported here was designed to address the issue [of] whether teacher education can make a difference in graduates' teaching competence. Specifically, we addressed the following research questions:

1. How does teaching competence develop over time?

2. What are the relative influences of teacher education programs and occupational socialization in schools on the development of teaching competence?

3. Which program characteristics are related to competence development?"

(Brouwer, N., & Korthagen, F. (2005). Can teacher education make a difference? *American Educational Research Journal, 42*(1), p. 154)

"This research study used grounded theory in an attempt to explain how 10th-grade public school students in average and advanced classes used strategies to learn material in their high school social studies classes. This study sought to understand the strategies that students used to learn information, the frequency of the strategy use, and the student's method of acquiring these strategies." (Martin, L. A. (2005). Use of cognitive strategies by high school social studies students. *Action in Teacher Education, 26*(4), p. 63)

"The research questions were (a) What factors do students perceive to be contributing to their anxiety in learning statistics? (b) What instructional strategies do students feel helpful to lessen their statistics anxiety and to learn statistics effectively?" (Pan, W., & Tang, M. (2005). Students' perceptions on factors of statistics anxiety and instructional strategies. *Journal of Instructional Psychology, 32*(3), p. 206)

It is important that the central phenomenon not be too general or too focused. If it is very general (e.g., a study on caring relationships or parental involvement), then it is not helpful in understanding the study. If it is too specific, as is acceptable for quantitative research questions, then the researchers may miss significant information because they are too narrowly focused.

It is common in qualitative studies to find that initial research problems are changed or that new research problems or questions are introduced as data are being collected. This flexibility is needed so that new ideas, based on data gathered, can be integrated and used to improve on initial problems or questions. There is essentially an interactive relationship between the problem and the data, each influencing the other. New research questions are often introduced *after* data have been gathered. The initial problems are often referred to as *foreshadowed*.

CONSUMER TIPS: *Criteria for Evaluating Qualitative Research Problems*

1. The problem should not be too general or too specific. Research problems that are too vague and general give the impression that the research is more like a fishing trip than systematic inquiry, while problems that are too narrow are inconsistent with the reason for doing qualitative research. A middle ground is needed so that what is being investigated is clear while at the same time not so specific that the researcher is unable to capture new and significant information when it arises.

2. The problem should be amenable to change as data are collected. It is important to write the initial problem so that it is somewhat open-ended and general. This allows for and encourages changes as the data are being collected. The continuing reformulation of a problem reflects the emergent design of the research. For example, beginning a study with a problem like "What are the perceptions of students about tests for graduation?" would be more amenable to change than something like "What do students say about whether graduation tests are fair?"

3. The problem should not be biased with researcher assumptions or desired findings. In qualitative research the investigator's assumptions and biases must be considered in designing the study and interpreting the findings, but it is important to keep the central question as neutral as possible. All too often researchers want to gather data to "prove" something to be true, and this threat to good research is easily manifest in qualitative studies. Notice how a statement like the following suggests an assumption about what will be found: "The purpose of this study is to explore reasons college faculty give to explain a lack of multicultural awareness in their teaching." A better statement would be: "The purpose of the study is to explore multicultural awareness as reflected in teaching."

4. The problem should be written with "how" and "what" to keep the focus on description of phenomena. The most important goal of qualitative research is to be able to provide an in-depth description of the phenomenon that is studied. This goal is best achieved if the researcher focuses on what occurs and how it occurs, rather than why. If the focus is on why, there tends to be an emphasis on causal conclusions and relationships, not descriptions.

5. The problem should include the central question as well as an indication of the participants and the site in which the study is being conducted. Good qualitative research problem statements contain three elements: the phenomenon being studied, the participants, and the research site or setting. Creswell (2005) suggests using the following script: "What is *(the central phenomenon)* for *(participants)* at *(research site)*?" (p. 137) An example would be "What is athletic participation like for seniors at James River High School?" This kind of statement is clear and concise and tells the reader quite a lot about what is being studied, who is being studied, and where the study takes place.

Author Reflection *Coming up with a good research problem statement or question is sometimes the hardest part of doing research. It requires time and energy to read literature and synthesize the information so that it is known whether the problem or question is needed. Sometimes there can be a series of psychological ups and downs if what seems at first to be a good idea, upon further reading and reflection, turns out to be not so good after all. The process can take months. It took me about a year to come up with my dissertation research questions and only a few months to complete the study.*

STUDY QUESTIONS

1. What is the difference between a research problem and a research problem statement?
2. How is it possible for a research problem to be too specific?
3. What is the major difference between qualitative and quantitative research problems?
4. Under what circumstances would it be helpful to use research hypotheses?
5. What is the difference between research and null hypotheses?
6. What are some "original" examples of continuous and categorical variables?
7. Why is it important to have operational definitions of variables?
8. What is the difference between independent, dependent, extraneous, and confounding variables? How are they related?
9. Under what circumstances would it be difficult to identify separate independent and dependent variables?
10. Why is it important to indicate the central idea, participants, and site or setting in a qualitative research problem statement?
11. Why are qualitative research problem statements and questions tentative rather than fixed?
12. How are qualitative and quantitative research problem statements or questions different? In what way are they the same?

@WWW   SAMPLE TEST QUESTIONS

See this text's Companion Website at www.ablongman.com/mcmillan5e for sample test questions and answers.

mylabschool   RESEARCH NAVIGATOR™ ACTIVITIES

1. Identify the research problem statements or questions, type of research indicated, and variables in the following articles found in the Research Navigator™:
   a. AN 12103384
   b. AN 12010631
   c. AN 11453638

Locating *and* Reviewing Related Literature

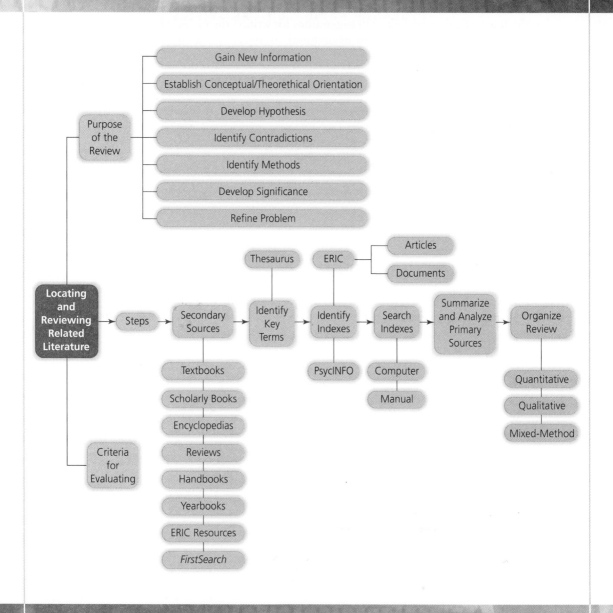

Chapter 3

CHAPTER ROAD MAP

Once a research problem or general question has been identified, a review of the literature is needed for several reasons. In this chapter we begin by summarizing these reasons. We then turn our attention to procedures for conducting reviews. This will include both primary and secondary sources, each of which is important. Major differences between qualitative and quantitative reviews of literature are included. Because use of the Internet is now essential in reviewing the literature, we will examine some Internet resources in this chapter (Chapter 4 will be entirely devoted to the Internet). We conclude with suggestions for writing the review of literature section of a manuscript, article, or report.

As a result of reading and studying this chapter, you will:

- Understand why reviews of literature are important for good research
- Understand the steps taken to conduct a review of literature
- Be able to distinguish between primary and secondary sources
- Become skilled at conducting computer searches of the literature
- Understand and use the ERIC system to identify and locate research reports and articles
- Understand the differences between quantitative, qualitative and mixed-method reviews of the literature
- Understand criteria for evaluating the review of literature section of a report or article

The PURPOSE *of* REVIEWING RELATED LITERATURE

The review of literature is the second major section of a research article. The review provides an important link between existing knowledge and the problem that is being investigated. A good review enhances the credibility of the research. Thus, it is important for you to be able to judge the quality of the review. As a professional in your field, it is important for you to be able to locate research that is related to a problem or issue.

Broadly stated, the purpose of the review is to relate previous research and theory to the problem under investigation. By showing how a current or proposed study compares to previous investigations, the research problem as well as the methodology can be placed in an appropriate context. Without a good review of literature, the researchers are less likely to use what have already been shown to be the most effective methods. From a consumer's viewpoint, knowing the purpose of the review will contribute to an overall evaluation of the credibility of the research, as well as indicate whether the nature of the review is closely targeted to the reader's needs. More specific purposes of reviewing literature include the following:

- Refining the research problem
- Establishing the conceptual or theoretical orientation
- Developing significance

- Identifying methodological limitations
- Identifying contradictory findings
- Developing research hypotheses
- Learning about new information

Refining the Research Problem

Initial research problems tend to be general and somewhat tentative. At this stage, the researcher thinks that the problem may be adequate but it needs to be more specific and more limited. By reviewing related studies and discussions of research in that area, the investigator learns how others have defined the general problem in more specific ways. Ideas and examples are found that help delimit the problem, and concepts and variables are clarified as the researcher finds operational definitions.

The process of refining a research problem can be frustrating. Typically, an initial problem that seems to have merit needs to be changed as the researcher reviews previous studies in the area. A new problem is formulated, and often it, too, needs revision as further literature is reviewed. This process can be repeated many times.

Establishing the Conceptual or Theoretical Orientation

It is important to place an individual study within the context of a pertinent conceptual framework or theoretical orientation. This includes statements that identify, delimit, and define relevant scholarship in which the study is grounded—that summarize the intellectual tradition on which it is based. It should be clear if a new theory is being proposed or tested, or whether existing theory is being used to frame the research problem. This part of the review also establishes a logical link between the research questions and methodology.

Developing Significance

It is important for research to be significant or meaningful if it is to make a contribution to existing knowledge or practice. Within the context of previous knowledge from existing research, a researcher should link the proposed study to accumulated knowledge to indicate specifically how it will add to, expand, and build on this base. Previous studies will also help the researcher identify new directions worth pursuing and avoid unnecessary duplication. Further, the researcher can interpret current results in terms of the findings from previous studies, making the conclusions more meaningful and enhancing the merit of the study. Without the foundation provided by the literature review, the results are less likely to be significant.

Identifying Methodological Limitations

By learning about the specific methods other researchers have employed to select subjects, measure variables, and implement procedures, investigators can identify approaches that may be useful for their studies. Both successful and unsuccessful methods are usually found, and both help investigators identify new ideas and avoid past mistakes or difficulties. Often, methodological weaknesses can suggest a need for research to be replicated with improvements in specific methods.

EXAMPLE | **Identifying Methodological Limitations**

"Why is there so little agreement on the short-term effects of retention? There are three methodological reasons why studies differ in their conclusions about the short-term achievements effects of retention: (a) the point at which researchers estimate achievement effects; (b) the comparability of test scores across grades; and (c) the ability of researchers to construct adequate comparison groups of retained and promoted children and account for their prior characteristics." (Roderick, M., & Nagaoka, J. (2005). Retention under Chicago's high-stakes testing program: Helpful, harmful or harmless? *Educational Evaluation and Policy Analysis, 27*(4), p. 311)

Identifying Contradictory Findings

A review of the literature may uncover studies or theories that contradict one another. Researchers find this a fruitful area in which to conduct subsequent studies. Possible reasons for the contradiction, such as the use of different types of subjects, measures, or procedures, can be identified, and research can be designed to resolve the contradiction. Such studies provide significant contributions to knowledge.

EXAMPLE | **Identifying Contradictory Findings**

"Results of research on the effects of immediate feedback on anxiety during testing have not been consistent. Some researchers have found immediate feedback to be associated with decreases in anxiety. . . . On the other hand, researchers have also frequently observed increases in anxiety . . . as well as reductions in test performance." (DiBattista, D., & Gosse, L. (2006). Test anxiety and the immediate feedback assessment technique. *Journal of Experimental Education, 74*(4), p. 313)

Developing Research Hypotheses

In quantitative research, a sound research hypothesis is usually based on a review of literature. Previous studies in related areas may suggest a specific result, and the hypothesis should be consistent with these studies. When there are few or no closely related studies, existing theories should be used to justify a particular hypothesis. Thus, the literature provides a basis for the hypothesis either by theory or by more specific facts established by previous studies. If educational studies or theories are not clearly related to the problem, the researcher should look to other fields of study, such as psychology, sociology, or communication. Often, theories in these fields can serve as the basis for the hypothesis.

Learning About New Information

A review of literature almost always leads to new information and knowledge, either in the topic of interest or in unrelated areas. Often, while searching the literature for one topic, you will come across interesting and useful research in other areas. In fact, it usually requires discipline to refrain from following a lead that is interesting and perhaps relevant in important ways but is not related to the problem or issue of initial interest. Through the review of literature, you will also learn about journals, books, and other sources, including recent publications with which you are unfamiliar.

STEPS *to* REVIEW RELATED LITERATURE

One of the best ways to become an informed consumer of research is to be able to conduct a review of existing studies and evaluate them, and use your interpretations in your work or to solve problems. You need to be able to find research before you can interpret and use it. By following a set of sequential steps, you will increase the quality of the research reviewed and be able to locate the most appropriate studies more quickly (see Figure 3.1).

Any search of literature should be preceded by complete familiarization with the library you will use. It is best to have someone orient you to the library, showing you where reference materials and journal indexes are located, and, perhaps most important, helping you understand the computer software that is used. If available, a librarian who is assigned to, or who knows about, educational literature will be especially helpful, and you should feel free to ask questions whenever necessary. Searching literature can be quite time-consuming, and a good librarian is there to help you. Many students, in fact, are surprised at how long it takes to do a review. For a new study in an area it would not be unusual to take 20 to 30 hours to complete a review. Also, do not be too discouraged if the library does not have a particular book or issue of a journal. Most libraries have an interlibrary loan procedure, which will allow you access to almost any source, including copies of journal articles. Computer resources are ubiquitous and change frequently, so you will need to become familiar with the procedures for using computers to search for literature.

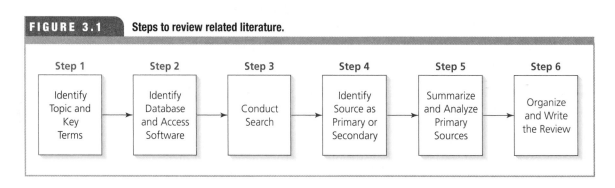

FIGURE 3.1   Steps to review related literature.

Step 1	Step 2	Step 3	Step 4	Step 5	Step 6
Identify Topic and Key Terms	Identify Database and Access Software	Conduct Search	Identify Source as Primary or Secondary	Summarize and Analyze Primary Sources	Organize and Write the Review

The sequence of steps for conducting an effective literature review has changed recently because of the ubiquitous presence of computers and ease of using the Internet. Where once I would have recommended using hard copy books and journals to begin a literature review, it is now more effective to use a computerized database.

Step One: Select a Topic and Key Terms

The first step in reviewing literature is to have some idea of the topic or subject in which you are interested. This could be rather general, like "what teaching methods are best for students with learning disabilities" or more specific, like the research questions and hypotheses discussed in Chapter 2. Identify the most important terms in the problem and then think about other terms that are closely related. You will then use these terms in computerized databases to find literature. For example, you may be interested in student motivation, and it would be wise to use related terms, such as *engagement, effort, persistence, intrinsic motivation,* and *self-efficacy.* All of these terms could be used, and different sources will be identified by each one.

Once you have identified terms, you may want to jump right into a computerized database and see what literature comes up, or you may want to begin by refining your search terms. For most searches of educational literature, it is best to use a special thesaurus to help select the most appropriate key terms. You will want to use either the ERIC *Thesaurus* or the *Thesaurus of Psychological Index Terms* (accessed in the PsycINFO database with definitions and uses that are somewhat different than the ERIC *Thesaurus*). ERIC, the Education Resources Information Center, is your best friend when it comes to educational literature. ERIC is a digital library of education-related resources. Although a hard copy of the *Thesaurus of ERIC Descriptors* could be used, the most recent and continually updated version is online (www.eric.ed.gov; other database vendors, such as EBSCO, use their own online format).

ERIC has a "controlled vocabulary" of terms called *descriptors*. Descriptors are used to organize and index database materials by subject. Each record is assigned several descriptors. The thesaurus also uses *keywords*. Keywords match words found in the indexed record, while descriptors locate records that may not contain the specific keyword. This means that if you use keywords for a search you will locate many more records. For example, the keyword *cognitive style* identifies over 15,000 records, while as a descriptor locates about 2,000 records.

You can search the ERIC *Thesaurus* by entering a specific term or phrase, or by browsing alphabetically or by category, to determine a match between how ERIC tends to define a term and your use of a term. A critical aspect of using terms is to understand that a given topic probably has general to narrow terms, as illustrated in Figure 3.2. When first beginning a search it is best to use more general rather than more specific terms (e.g., categories rather than keywords). You can get an idea of the specificity of a term by pulling up the thesaurus record on it, as illustrated in Figure 3.3. The record shows other broader and narrower terms, as well as related terms. Suppose your topic is "the effect of using alternative assessment on student achievement." You enter "alternative assessment" in the thesaurus and

FIGURE 3.2 Specificity of ERIC descriptors.

General → Measures

Tests

Objective Tests

Narrow → Multiple Choice Tests

FIGURE 3.3 Illustration of ERIC *Thesaurus* information.

Provides a definition or describes what the term covers.

Indicates the broad group of terms to which the descriptor belongs.

Suggests additional search terms that are less specific.

Suggests additional search terms that are more specific.

Suggests additional search terms that are conceptually related.

Indicates that the selected term should be used instead of the term.

Directs user to an active main term.

Directs user to a combination of terms

Indicates Status of a Term

- Main—term is a descriptor.
- Synonym—term is not a descriptor, see Use Term.
- USEAND—term is not a descriptor, use Use And.
- Dead—term is no longer used.

Alternative Assessment

Descriptor Details

Start an ERIC Search using **Alternative Assessment** as a search criteria

Record Type: Main
Scope Note: Appraising knowledge or skills by means other than traditionally employed, objective tests, especially standardized multiple-choice tests
Category: Measurement
Broader Terms: Evaluation;
Narrower Terms: Performance Based Assessment;
Related Terms: Educational Assessment; Evaluation Methods; Informal Assessment; Personnel Evaluation; Portfolio Assessment; Scoring Rubrics; Self Evaluation (Individuals); Standardized Tests; Student Evaluation; Writing Evaluation;
Used For: Alternative Evaluation (Individuals); Alternatives to Standardized Testing;
Use Term: n/a
Use And: n/a
Add Date: 09/15/2000

Shows when the term was added.

it shows as in Figure 3.2. The results give you the definition ERIC has used. It is in the measurement category, with "evaluation" as a broader term and "performance based assessment" as a narrower term. Interestingly, "authentic assessment" is not a related term. For many this would be a type of alternative assessment. However, when *authentic assessment* is used as a keyword for an ERIC search, over 1,000 records are identified. This illustrates an important point in using key terms for your search: You must spend considerable time trying different searches with different terms, and you cannot assume that the way you think about and define terms is the same as the ERIC personnel who maintain the database.

As an alternative to searching ERIC or PsycINFO with key terms, you may want to search a more traditional library card catalog or a database of a wide range of books that could be helpful in focusing your research problem and key terms (see step three for secondary sources).

Step Two: Identify Database and Access Software

Equipped with a fairly focused set of key terms you can use ERIC to identify articles and reports that can be reviewed in more detail to determine how helpful they will be for your literature review. ERIC is a database of resources sponsored by the federal government. It contains journal and nonjournal articles and reports obtained since 1966. ERIC is essentially a Web-based library for accessing historical and current resources. With the Education Sciences Reform Act of 2002, ERIC underwent significant changes and is continuing to adopt new procedures to further modernize the database, including the criteria for selecting resources and journals to be included.

There are several different ways to access ERIC, each involving different software. The most direct route is to go to the ERIC Website (www.eric.ed.gov). In addition, you may reach the ERIC database by using another server such as EBSCOhost, FirstSearch, or CSA Illumina (Cambridge Scientific Abstracts). Interestingly, enter "culture" as a descriptor for the year 2005, and the number of documents identified in each server is as follows:

ERIC (www.eric.ed.gov)	86
FirstSearch	83
CSA ILLUMINA	61
EBSCOhost	59

It has been my experience that using www.eric.ed.gov will usually give you more hits. It is not clear why there are differences. Simply keep this in mind and try more than one server. The convenient aspect of university library access points, such as EBSCO, is that more than one database can be searched, and it is easy to determine if an article or report is available online. You will be able to access library resources and databases from home and, of course, be able to go directly to www.eric.ed.gov.

The PsycINFO database contains documents, articles, dissertations, and books in psychology and related disciplines, including education. This database is accessible online and contains over 2 million records covering 2,000 journals

(98% are peer reviewed). All university libraries provide access to PsycINFO. Individuals can use PsycINFO at a cost determined by time or number of records used. There are also databases in sociology, business, medicine, and other fields related to education that will search sources that are not included in ERIC.

One additional database used by many libraries is InfoTrac Onefile. This database has access to over 50 million articles, about half of which are online and available to print from your computer. This file combines scholarly and popular journals and magazines in all fields.

Step Three: Conduct Search

The specific nature of the procedures to use to search ERIC depends on your server. Using the ERIC Website as an example, you begin by typing in words that describe your topic in the Search box. I strongly recommend that you click on Advanced Search and use that screen for your search. As illustrated in Figure 3.4, you have a number of options that can improve your search. The first decision with the Advanced Search screen is whether you want to limit your search to author, title, ERIC number, descriptor, journal name, or keywords (all fields), which is the default. These options appear when clicking on the box to the right with an arrow, along with some infrequently used options. You type the author, title, and so on

FIGURE 3.4   Advanced search.

in the box to the right. With Publication Date you can select documents appearing in specific years. It is often best to begin with the most recent five years. If you find too many documents, do another search limited to one year. If too few documents are identified, lengthen years to 10 or even more.

> **Author Reflection** *My experience in doing literature reviews is that the quality of studies has not changed appreciably for at least 20 years. Some topics were researched heavily many years ago with very good studies, so while it is important to use recent studies, don't ignore older research.*

The next decision has to do with Publication Type(s). You have a large number of choices here, though typically only a few are relevant. Obviously, Any Publication Type encompasses all documents (even those not formally published in an article). You can select specific types of documents by checking as many as apply down the rather long list. Book/Product Reviews is excellent for identifying secondary sources. If you check Journal Article, only CIJE documents will be shown. Often the best search of primary sources uses Journal Articles and Reports/Research. The Tests/Questionnaires choice works well to find sources that use a particular measure.

Most students find that they need to tailor their search until they can identify a reasonable number of sources that appear to be closely related to their research problem. The most common way of limiting a search is to use the connector "and." Using *and* will reduce the search because the computer will look for entries that are categorized by all the descriptors or keywords indicated. For example, a search of *teaching styles **and** elementary* would produce fewer hits than using only one of these terms (*teaching styles* by itself would include elementary, middle, and high schools, as well as colleges and universities). If a third descriptor, say *achievement*, is added, the search is further refined. This process of narrowing the search is illustrated in Figure 3.5, using Any Publication Type, Documents, and Publication Date years of 2000–2005. (Using Keywords rather than Descriptors resulted in 67 rather than 7 hits.) You can use either Sets (preferred) or Boolean logic (or, and) to construct a query. Put parentheses around sets, quotations around phrases, and commas between terms.

When a topic is searched with www.eric.ed.gov, the user is presented with a list of articles and documents, summary information, and an abstract. Clicking on the title of the document, or "more details," provides further specifics about the record, as illustrated in Figure 3.6. This entry resulted from a search of "student motivation." From Figure 3.6 you will note that there is an ERIC number assigned to the entry. This number is permanent and will be the same for all servers. If the number begins with EJ, it is a journal article; if it begins with ED, it is a nonjournal document. Most journal articles have some kind of peer review, which tends to result in better quality than what you will find with nonjournal documents. But there are exceptions! Many journal articles, even with peer review, are not very credible, and many nonjournal documents are excellent. One advantage of searching nonjournal documents is that conference presentations are often included. Some of these presentations eventually become articles, but

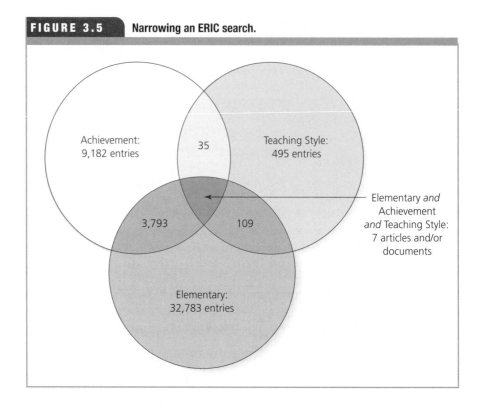

FIGURE 3.5 Narrowing an ERIC search.

Achievement: 9,182 entries

Teaching Style: 495 entries

35

Elementary *and* Achievement *and* Teaching Style: 7 articles and/or documents

3,793

109

Elementary: 32,783 entries

there may be a significant time lag between submission of a manuscript to a journal for publication and when the article appears in print.

With this format (Figure 3.7) there is sufficient information to determine if it would be useful to locate the full article or report. In the future, ERIC will

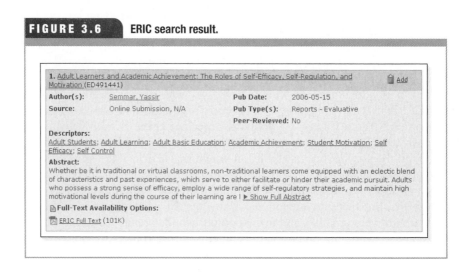

FIGURE 3.6 ERIC search result.

1. Adult Learners and Academic Achievement: The Roles of Self-Efficacy, Self-Regulation, and Motivation (ED491441)   Add

Author(s):	Semmar, Yassir	Pub Date:	2006-05-15
Source:	Online Submission, N/A	Pub Type(s):	Reports – Evaluative
		Peer-Reviewed:	No

Descriptors:
Adult Students; Adult Learning; Adult Basic Education; Academic Achievement; Student Motivation; Self Efficacy; Self Control

Abstract:
Whether be it in traditional or virtual classrooms, non-traditional learners come equipped with an eclectic blend of characteristics and past experiences, which serve to either facilitate or hinder their academic pursuit. Adults who possess a strong sense of efficacy, employ a wide range of self-regulatory strategies, and maintain high motivational levels during the course of their learning are l ▶ Show Full Abstract

Full-Text Availability Options:
ERIC Full Text (101K)

FIGURE 3.7   ERIC detailed search result.

ED491441 - Adult Learners and Academic Achievement: The Roles of Self-Efficacy, Self-Regulation, and Motivation

Result Details

📄 **Full-Text Availability Options:**

📄 ERIC Full Text (101K)

Click on any of the links below to perform a new search

ERIC #:	ED491441
Title:	Adult Learners and Academic Achievement: The Roles of Self-Efficacy, Self-Regulation, and Motivation
Authors:	Semmar, Yassir
Descriptors:	Adult Students; Adult Learning; Adult Basic Education; Academic Achievement; Student Motivation; Self Efficacy; Self Control
Journal/Source Name:	Online Submission
Journal Citation:	N/A
Peer-Reviewed:	No
Publisher:	N/A
Publication Date:	2006-05-15
Pages:	24
Pub Types:	Reports - Evaluative
Abstract:	Whether be it in traditional or virtual classrooms, non-traditional learners come equipped with an eclectic blend of characteristics and past experiences, which serve to either facilitate or hinder their academic pursuit. Adults who possess a strong sense of efficacy, employ a wide range of self-regulatory strategies, and maintain high motivational levels during the course of their learning are likely to be successful. In contrast, those who doubt their abilities, lack metacognitive activities, and exhibit low motivational levels tend to fail at accomplishing their goals. This paper sheds some light on the importance of self-efficacy, self-regulation, motivation, and their "synergistic" effect on adults' academic achievement. Implications for online educators are discussed.
Abstractor:	Author
Reference Count:	35
Note:	N/A
Identifiers:	N/A
Record Type:	Non-Journal
Level:	1 - Reproducible in paper and microfiche; and, since 1993, in electronic format; materials issued from January 1993 - July 2004 are now available at no cost through this Web site
Institutions:	N/A
Sponsors:	N/A
ISBN:	N/A
ISSN:	N/A
Audiences:	N/A
Languages:	English
Education Level:	Adult Education

provide what it calls "Structured Abstracts" that, with predefined headings, will provide more specific information about the study design.

Once you have limited your search to a reasonable number of documents, for instance between 5 and 20, you need to obtain the articles or reports to examine each one in greater detail to determine if they should be used in your review. Obtaining an actual article will depend on whether it is available online (increasingly journals are available on the Internet), or as hard copy in your library. You may need to use other libraries or use interlibrary loan.

The typical process, then, involves taking a large number of possible documents and reducing that number down to the relatively few appropriate to your review. For example, you might begin a study on science and mathematics teaching strategies with some 12,000 hits; reduce that number by restricting your search to a few years; reduce it again by accessing only journal articles; locate those articles; and then, finally, pick 8 articles from among the 22 you obtained.

Step Four: Identify the Source as Primary or Secondary

As you review literature you will come across many different types of articles and reports. This can seem confusing because there are hundreds of journals, agencies, and organizations publishing reports and sources on the Internet. A good first step is to identify sources as *primary* or *secondary*. A **primary source** is an original article or report in which researchers communicate directly to the reader the methods and results of their studies. These sources constitute empirical research, as described in Chapter 1 and illustrated in Figure 1.3. A **secondary source** is one that reviews, summarizes, or discusses primary research. The author(s) provide(s) information and analysis, but it is not a firsthand gathering of data.

In earlier editions of this book I recommended that students begin a literature review by searching for appropriate secondary sources. Secondary sources are good to begin with because they provide an overview of the topic, often citing relevant research studies and important primary sources. Some examples of secondary sources are textbooks, scholarly books devoted to a particular topic, reviews of research in books or journals, yearbooks, encyclopedias, and handbooks. When using secondary sources you should be aware that because they combine the information from other secondary sources and actual studies, it is possible that the author did not accurately report the research. Furthermore, the review may be selective to support a particular point of view, or the author may have failed to locate important studies.

Textbooks. Textbooks provide a nontechnical overview of several topics within a particular field of study. Hence, there are textbooks in most major fields of education, for example, educational psychology, reading, special education, measurement and evaluation, learning, early childhood education, counseling, and administration. These texts are located through the subject index of the appropriate catalog. The limitation of textbooks is that because they are written for students, they provide general overviews and may not have the necessary detail. Textbooks may also be out of date in the sense that the research cited may have been conducted several years before the book was available.

Primary source: Articles that report original research.

Secondary source: Summarizes, reviews, or discusses original research.

Scholarly Books. Scholarly books are written on many topics that you would find in a textbook. These books are intended for other researchers and professionals in the area and consequently contain more details about the research. Scholarly books can be located through the library's catalog, professors, publishers' advertisements, publishers' catalogs, journals, and conference proceedings.

Encyclopedias. Encyclopedias, with short summaries of many topics, are good sources during the initial stages of a review. Here is a partial list of available encyclopedias:

An Encyclopedia of Bilingual Education and Bilingualism
Encyclopedia of Adult Development
Encyclopedia of African American Education
Encyclopedia of American Education
Encyclopedia of Comparative Education and National Systems of Education
Encyclopedia of Early Childhood Education
Encyclopedia of Educational Evaluation
Encyclopedia of Educational Research
Encyclopedia of Higher Education
Encyclopedia of Special Education
Encyclopedia of School Administration and Supervision
Encyclopedia of School Psychology
International Encyclopedia of Education
International Encyclopedia of Teaching and Teacher Education

Reviews, Handbooks, and Yearbooks. A number of sources include comprehensive, up-to-date reviews on specific topics. Many of these reviews are in books or monographs that are published annually, although different subjects are reviewed each year. The following sources are examples of specific handbooks that are commonly used to locate reviews of educational literature.

EXAMPLE | **Handbooks**

Handbook of Reading Research (2000)
Handbook of Research on Educational Administration (1999)
Handbook of Research on Multicultural Education (2001)
Handbook of Research on Music Teaching and Learning (2002)
Handbook of Research on Teaching (2001)
Handbook of Research on Science Teaching and Learning (1994)
Handbook of Special Education (2006)
International Handbook of Early Childhood Education (1992)
International Handbook of Women's Education (1990)

When searching for reviews in journals you may come across what is called a **meta-analysis,** a review that quantitatively synthesizes previous studies. A meta-analysis is a procedure that uses statistical methods to systematically combine the results of a number of studies of the same problem. The studies are identified and

Meta-analysis:
A quantitative review of previous studies.

the results from all the studies are used to arrive at an overall conclusion. Most meta-analyses reported in reputable journals are characterized by a comprehensive search of the literature and sound statistical procedures. Because there are many different ways of identifying the studies that comprise a meta-analysis, as well as different approaches to statistically combine them, it necessary to examine the methodology to ensure credibility. However, because this type of review has only recently been published, there are some questions about its credibility. For example, what sense would it make if all studies, whether poorly conducted or well conducted, are included in the synthesis? (See the ERIC Digest *Meta-Analysis in Educational Research* for further information.)

EXAMPLE | **Meta-Analysis**

"Articles for this meta-analysis were identified using two methods. First, a computer literature search of PsycINFO and ERIC databases was conducted from 1980 to 2003. The descriptors included WM matched with dyslexia/reading disability/learning disability/LD. . . . The initial search yielded 75 studies . . . only 31 articles met the criteria for inclusion. . . . In the present meta-analysis 28 articles compared WM [Working Memory] performance of RD [Reading Disability] with that of skilled readers. . . . The 28 studies produced 208 effect sizes, for an average of 7 comparisons per study. The overall mean effect size across all studies was −0.81 ($SD = 0.92$). Based on Cohen's criteria, that is a large effect size that indicated that the overall mean performance of the RD group was almost one standard deviation below that of the normally achieving group." (Swanson, H. L. (2005). Memory and learning disabilities: Historical perspective, current status, and future trends. *Thalamus, 23*(2), pp. 37–38)

You may also come across an alternative to a meta-analysis that is called a **best-evidence synthesis.** In this type of review both qualitative and quantitative research can be included. Clear criteria are used by the researchers to determine which of the studies merit inclusion. An example of a best-evidence synthesis is provided in the following excerpt. Note that the term *narrative* is used to distinguish it from a meta-analysis.

Best-evidence synthesis: A review of quantitative and qualitative studies selected according to specified criteria.

EXAMPLE | **Best Evidence (Narrative) Synthesis Review of Literature**

"In this research synthesis, we sought to identify all high-quality research studies that analyzed implementation or reported outcomes of one-to-one initiatives from English-language journals and Web sites. We adopted a narrative, rather than meta-analytic approach to synthesizing findings, both because there were so few outcome studies and because the vast majority of studies reported on implementation processes that could better be summarized and synthesized using a narrative approach. In this section, we describe in detail our approach to identifying, selecting, and analyzing studies for the synthesis." (Penuel, W. R. (2006). Implementation and effects of one-to-one computing initiatives: A research synthesis. *Journal of Research on Technology in Education, 38*(3), p. 331)

Finally, with recent emphasis on "data-driven" educational practice there are many secondary sources that review empirical literature on a topic. A good example is *The Voice of Evidence in Reading Research* (McCardle & Chhabra, 2004).

ERIC Digests. For a number of years, ERIC produced what were called ERIC Digests. The digests are short reports that synthesize research ideas about contemporary educational issues. There are over 2,000 digests, and all are available online. To search the ERIC database for the digests, go to the Advanced Search screen, as illustrated in Figure 3.4, and select "ERIC Digests in Full Text" as the publication type.

USING EDUCATIONAL RESEARCH

There has been much debate in the educational literature about the impact of extrinsic reinforcement on students' intrinsic motivation. The spring 2001 issue of *Review of Educational Research* (volume 71, number 1) includes articles that debate the relative merit of different meta-analyses. It is an excellent source of information that shows the strengths and limitations of meta-analysis, and shows how researcher judgment is always an important influence in interpreting the data.

Primary sources are reported in a wide variety of journals. In fact there are hundreds of journals, which differ greatly in quality. To understand these differences, consider how articles get published. The most common procedure is for the author(s) to write a manuscript that will be submitted to a journal for publication. If the format and topic of the article are appropriate, the editor will usually send the manuscript to two or three reviewers and/or associate or assistant editors to be evaluated. The evaluation is structured so that the reviewers, who are experts on the topic investigated, comment on the significance of the problem, methodology, data analysis, contribution of the findings and conclusions, and other criteria. Usually the reviewers are asked to recommend that the manuscript be published as submitted, revised and resubmitted, or rejected. Rarely do they recommend to publish as submitted. The journal is said to be **refereed** if this procedure is followed. A **nonrefereed** journal does not use external reviewers to evaluate manuscripts.

Refereed: Sent to reviewers for an evaluation.

The strength of the refereed process is that helpful suggestions from reviewers improve the quality of the manuscript. Some journals use a blind review process to control for reviewer bias. A blind review is one in which the names of the authors of the manuscript are omitted. Clearly, a blind review process is desirable and is usually employed by journals that have a reputation for publishing high-quality articles. In the "publish or perish" culture of higher education it is more prestigious to be published in higher-quality journals. As a result, many more manuscripts are submitted than are actually accepted. Indeed, the rejection rate is often used, and justifiably so, as a barometer of quality.

Nonrefereed: Not reviewed by outside experts.

Remember that there are hundreds of journals, some of which are published primarily for financial reasons. Just because a study is published does not mean that it is good research, so you may want to learn which journals in your area are regarded as high-quality publications.

Step Five: Summarize and Analyze Primary Source Information

Once you locate your primary sources, you will need to read them and summarize the information they contain. It is useful to have a strategy for recording notes on the articles as you read them. An efficient approach is to record your notes on index cards (I find the 5×8 size best) because after you have reviewed all the articles the cards can be easily organized in different ways. Begin by reading the abstract of the article, if there is one, and the purpose or research problem. Then read the results and decide if it is worthwhile to read the article more carefully and take notes on it. Do not be too discouraged if some of the articles you locate are not useful. Part of the process of reviewing literature is to locate and read many more articles than you will eventually use.

INTERNET CONNECTION

See this Website for a very helpful summary of the roles of literature reviews, types of literature reviews, and carrying out a review: **www.scre.ac.uk/spotlight/spotlight71.html**.

After you decide to use the article, begin taking notes by writing or typing complete bibliographic information, preferably in the style you will use in writing; summarize the research problem as briefly as possible; and underline or circle the independent and dependent variables. Next, indicate in outline form the subjects, instruments, and procedures used and then summarize the results and conclusions. On the other side of the card, record interesting or insightful quotations; indicate any weaknesses or limitations in the methodology, analysis of the data, or conclusions; and indicate how the study may be related to your problem. You will find it useful to develop a code for indicating your overall judgment of the article. If you find it closely related to your problem and highly credible, you might give the article an A; if somewhat related and credible, a B; and so on. It will also help to develop a code that indicates the major focus of the study by topic or descriptor. For example, in reviewing studies on teacher awareness you may find that some studies examine the effect of awareness on student achievement, some focus on strategies to improve awareness, and others emphasize different approaches to awareness depending on the type of students in the classroom. Each of these could have a code or notation on the card, such as "effect on ach.," "improv. awareness," and "approaches" to denote how they are different.

Author Reflection *One of the best sources for new articles can be found in the reference section of a primary source that is closely related to your study. Read the titles of the articles and other documents that the author(s) used. Though these will* *obviously be older, they are likely to very helpful. Finding other studies as much like yours as possible is more important than obtaining more recent sources that are less like yours.*

Step Six: Organize and Write the Review

The nature of the written review of literature will depend on whether the study is quantitative or qualitative. Quantitative reviews are often very detailed and found in the beginning sections of an article. Qualitative reviews, in contrast, tend to be brief in the beginning but more integrated throughout the whole of the article. Most literature reviews, particularly those found in quantitative research, approach the review by summarizing and analyzing individual studies. Some reviews are *thematic*, in which a topic is identified and discussed, without a detailed analysis of individual studies. Most qualitative reviews are thematic. We will first examine the quantitative review.

Quantitative Reviews of Literature. Although reviews of literature can be organized in different ways, the most common approach is to group together studies that investigate similar topics or subtopics. This process is initiated by coding the studies as they are read; then the articles with the same code are put in one pile, those of another code in a second pile, and so forth. The different topics are then put in order, usually from articles related to the problem in a more general way first to articles specifically related to the problem. Within each topic it may be possible to organize the studies by date, with the most recent studies last. This arrangement gives you a sense of the development of the research over time. You should not organize your review by study or article, with each paragraph in the review dealing with a different study. Studies that are only generally related should be summarized briefly. If several of these studies have similar results they should be grouped together; for example, "Several studies have found that teacher expectations are related to student achievement (Smith, 1978; Tyler, 1985; Wylie, 1983)." Most reviews select representative general studies; there is no attempt to do an exhaustive review of all studies. However, exhaustive reviews may be necessary for theses, dissertations, and other major projects.

The following steps will be useful for studies that are closely related to the problem:

Step 1 Provide a brief summary of the articles.

Step 2 Analyze the studies. The analysis is important because it suggests that you are not simply accepting the studies as credible; you are examining the methodology of the studies critically to make better judgments about the contribution of the results.

Step 3 State explicitly how the reviewed studies are related to the present research. A critical examination enables you to show the relationship of the proposed or current study to previous literature. This step is essential for the results to contribute to our knowledge. It also generates many good ideas that will improve subsequent research.

For a few studies, then, those that are closely related to the problem, the review should include three elements: a *summary* of the study reviewed, an *analysis* of the study, and a summary of how the study *relates* to the research problem. Here are two examples from literature reviews of published articles that show how the current study differs from previous studies.

EXAMPLE | **Showing How Current Study Differs From Previous Research**

"Catanzano and Wilson (1977) compared the effects of three testing contingencies rather than the effects of the number of tests retaken, as did Smith (1987). Friedman (1987) addressed the effects of the number of tests retaken but reported on the final examination for a very select group—only those students who had earned an average grade of B on the unit tests. In the present study, we addressed those limitations of previous research by considering both the proximate and distal effects of optional retesting on academic achievement." (Juhler, S. M., Rech, J. F., From, S. G., & Brogan, M. M. (1998). The effect of optional retesting on college students' achievement in an individualized algebra course. *Journal of Experimental Education, 66*, p. 128)

"Although there are studies examining teacher efficacy after methods courses (Huinker & Madison, 1997) and after student teaching (Vinson, 1995), there is little research tracking the subject-matter-specific teacher efficacy of elementary preservice teachers throughout their preservice education (Tschannen-Moran et al., 1998)." (Utley, J., Bryant, R., & Moseley, C. (2005). Relationship between science and mathematics teaching efficacy of preservice elementary teachers. *School Science and Mathematics, 105*(2), p. 84)

"The current study differs from earlier studies in text comprehension and moral judgment development in several respects. . . . Previous research has focused on didactic stories such as fables, Bible stories, or folktales. . . . In this study, real-life, complex narratives were used with embedded moral reasoning at different stages of moral development. . . . Earlier studies in moral comprehension . . . have examined [the influence of moral schemas] directly by presenting moral reasoning in isolation and asking participants to paraphrase or recall it. . . . In this study moral arguments were presented in a stream of contextual detail. . . . This is the first time that the effects of moral judgment development on moral text comprehension have been examined." (Narvaez, D. (1998). The influence of moral schemas on the reconstruction of moral narratives in eighth graders and college students. *Journal of Educational Psychology, 90,* p. 16)

This part of the review should not contain long quotations or use the same wording in discussing each study, for example, "A study by Brown (1987) indicated that . . ."; "A study by Smith (2000) indicated that . . ."; "A study by Jones (2001) showed that. . . ." Quotations in general should be used sparingly and only when a special or critical meaning could not be indicated by your own words. The researcher should use short sentences as well as transition sentences so there is a logical progression of ideas and sections. Many of these parameters are illustrated in Exhibit 3.1, which is an excerpt of a review of literature from a quantitative article.

EXHIBIT 3.1   Review of the literature for quantitative research.

Cross and Frary (1996) and Cizek, Fitzgerald, Shawn, and Rachor (1996) report similar findings concerning the hodgepodge nature of assigning grades. Cizek et al. (1996) found that although almost all teachers used formal achievement measures in grading, other "achievement-related" factors such as attendance, ability, participation, demonstration of effort, and conduct were used by at least half of the teachers. Cross and Frary surveyed 310 middle and high school teachers of academic subjects in a single school district. A written survey was used to obtain descriptions of grading practices and opinions regarding assessment and grading. Consistent with Brookhart (1993), it was reported that 72% of the teachers raised the grades of low-ability students if they had demonstrated effort. One-fourth of the teachers indicated that they raised grades for high effort "fairly often." Almost 40% of the teachers indicated that student conduct and attitude were taken into consideration when assigning grades. Note that a very high percentage of teachers agreed that effort and conduct should be reported separately from achievement. More than half of the teachers reported that class participation was rated as having a moderate or strong influence on grades. In an earlier statewide study, Frary et al. (1993) used the same teacher survey that was used by Cross and Frary (1996), and obtained similar results. More than two-thirds of the teachers agreed or tended to agree that ability, effort, and improvement should be included in determining grades.

> Summary of previous research

Another recent study, by Truog and Friedman (1996), further confirms the notion of the hodgepodge nature of grading. In their study, the written grading policies of 53 high school teachers were analyzed in relation to grading practices recommended by measurement specialists. In addition, a focus group was conducted with eight teachers to find out more about their reasoning behind their grading practices. They found that the written policies were consistent with the findings from earlier studies of teacher beliefs and practices. Nine percent of the teachers included ability as a factor in determining grades, 17% included attitude, 9% included effort, 43% included attendance, and 32% included student behavior.

One of the limitations of current research on the grading practices of secondary teachers is that the studies do not differentiate grading practices by ability level of the classes. This may be important in examining such factors as effort and improvement, and may reveal patterns that exacerbate existing achievement differences among students with varying ability levels. For example, Alarso and Pigge (1993) reported that teachers believe essays provide better evidence of higher cognitive learning, and that students study harder for them. If it is demonstrated that higher-ability classes, such as honors and advanced placement classes, use more essays than basic classes, this may result in greater emphasis on thinking skills with higher-ability classes, while in lower-ability classes there would be more emphasis on rote memorization. Also, as with the research on assessment practices, most studies (e.g., Brookhart, 1991; Frary et al., 1993; Truog & Friedman, 1996) measure teacher beliefs, rather than actual practices or a reporting of what was actually used in a specific class.

> Analysis of previous research

Another limitation in the designs employed is that each of the factors used to assign grades has been considered separately. When put in the context of teaching, as pointed out by Stiggins, Frisbie, and Griswold (1989), it is more realistic to consider the joint effect of several factors. Only one study, Frary et al. (1993), reported an analysis of how factors were grouped into meaningful components for secondary teachers. In their study, teacher opinions about the desirability of different grading and assessment practices were examined together using a Likert scale. Their findings focused on teacher attitudes toward the desirability of certain practices, but did not investigate whether there were underlying dimensions associated with actual grading and assessment practices of teachers.

The present study used a large sample of secondary school teachers (grades 6–12) to describe assessment and grading practices in a way that addresses limitations cited from the previous research. The critical role of effort and other nonachievement factors in grading was examined, as was the way these different factors cluster together in describing teachers' practices. The study was designed to document differences in actual assessment and grading practices conducted for a specific class taught by each teacher across a range of classes representing different student ability levels. Four specific research questions were addressed:

> Relates previous research to current study

The length of the review depends on the type of study, whether or not it is published, and the topic that is researched. The review of literature for an exploratory study may not be very long, whereas an exhaustive review in a thesis or dissertation can be as long as 30 or 40 typed pages. A lengthy review requires structuring with major and minor headings and periodic summaries.

Qualitative Reviews of Literature. As with quantitative research, the review of literature in qualitative research is used to document the importance of the topic. Otherwise, the literature is used differently in qualitative studies. Rather than provide a detailed analysis of the literature prior to the methods section, the purpose of a qualitative review is to simply introduce the purpose and very general or broad questions. These questions provide a direction, but one that is purposefully general so that previous work does not limit, constrain, or predict what will be found. In this way, the review of literature is consistent with the discovery orientation and inductive approach of qualitative research. The statements or questions are often called **foreshadowed problems** or questions. The approach is to state a general purpose or question so that views of the participants will emerge. Thus, the initial review of literature in a qualitative study is *preliminary* rather than complete. It provides conceptual frameworks by citing appropriate areas of scholarship and thinking from different perspectives, such as psychological or sociological. Together, the foreshadowed problems and conceptual frameworks are used to justify the need for a qualitative approach. Some qualitative researchers will not conduct an extensive review of the literature because they don't want what others have said about something to influence the openness that is needed or their own perspectives.

Once the qualitative study is under way and data are being collected, the researcher continues to read broadly in the literature. The additional literature reviewed enables the researcher to better understand what has been observed. The literature may provide meaningful analogies, a scholarly language to synthesize descriptions, or additional conceptual or theoretical frameworks to better understand and organize the findings. It helps the researcher to understand the complexities of what is observed and to illuminate subtle meanings and interpretations. Like good quantitative studies, the literature is integrated with the discussion and conclusion section of the article or report. At this point, additional new literature may be introduced to better explain and interpret the findings.

In qualitative studies there may or may not be a separate "literature review" section. Because of the format required by some journals there may be a literature review header, but for a qualitative study the actual review will probably be different from what is provided for a quantitative study. Also, there are more and more **mixed-method** studies, which combine quantitative and qualitative approaches. These studies will probably have a more traditional review of literature. In actually reading research, then, be prepared for different formats and headings.

Exhibit 3.2 shows an example of the preliminary review of literature in a qualitative study.

Foreshadowed problems: Initial, general purpose of the study.

Mixed-method: Study that combines quantitative and qualitative approaches.

EXHIBIT 3.2 Example of a review of literature for a qualitative study.

Research into children's behavior in groups and their productivity was pioneered at the University of Iowa's Child Welfare Research Station toward the end of the 1930s. Working under the direction of Kurt Lewin, an acclaimed experimental psychologist, graduate students Ronald Lippitt and Ralph White undertook a series of experiments in 1938 to investigate how children worked together in groups (Marrow, 1965). Participants chosen for the studies were 20 children who met after school to make papier maché masks and to engage in other play activities. The children were divided into three groups, two of which were directed by an adult; each child was rotated through each of the three groups. The results of the experiments proved remarkable. Researchers found that children in an autocratically led group seemed discontented, often aggressive, and lacking in initiative. Youngsters in groups without a leader experienced similar problems: members appeared frustrated, and much of the work remained unfinished. In marked contrast, children in groups organized with a democratic leader—someone who allowed the group to set its own agendas and priorities—appeared far more productive, socially satisfied, and demonstrated greater originality and independence in the work they completed.

> *Provides historical background*

Although the Iowa studies excited the educational community, the advent of World War II—and its aftermath—greatly interrupted research into how children behaved and learned in groups. Scholarly attention did not again turn toward efforts to understand children's behavior and learning in groups until the 1970s (Slavin, 1991). Since that time, researchers have come to agree that cooperative and collaborative learning are valuable components of classroom learning (Blumenfeld, Marx, Soloway, & Krajcik, 1996; Gamson, 1994; Kohn, 1991; Webb, Troper, & Fall, 1995), and children are often instructed to "work together" at school (Gamson, 1994; Patrick, 1994; Wood & Jones, 1994). Slavin (1991, p. 71) stated that cooperative learning has been promoted as a solution to "an astonishing array of educational problems" and has been endorsed as a learning strategy by numerous researchers (Burron, James, & Ambrosio, 1993; Wood & Jones, 1994) who have investigated its effects on student achievement (Slavin), as well as on the contexts and ways in which children work together in classrooms (Keedy & Drmacich, 1994).

> *Summary of general literature*

Definitions for cooperative and collaborative learning, however, are contrary for different researchers and theorists. Vygotsky (1978), for example, viewed collaborative learning as part of a process leading to the social construction of knowledge. Other scholars (Kohn, 1992; Sapon-Shevin & Schniedewand, 1992) considered cooperative learning to be a form of critical pedagogy that moves classrooms and societies closer toward the ideal of social justice. Caplow and Kardash (1995) characterized collaborative learning as a process in which "knowledge is not transferred from expert to learner, but created and located in the learning environment" (p. 209). Others such as Burron, James, and Ambrosio (1993) and Ossont (1993) envisioned cooperative learning as a strategy to help students improve intellectual and social skills.

> *Shows different perspectives on collaborative learning*

Mixed-Method Reviews of Literature. In mixed-method studies the review of literature is usually presented in one section rather than having a separate review for the quantitative and qualitative sections. Though general reviews of literature in mixed-method studies are detailed and thorough, often a review reflects the quantitative or qualitative emphasis of the study. With an exploratory study the review tends to be like those found in qualitative research, while explanatory research uses a review like those in a quantitative study. Because mixed-method studies are much less standardized than either quantitative or qualitative research, the literature review section is also less standardized. This means that with these types of studies you will likely encounter quite different approaches to the review.

CONSUMER TIPS: *Criteria for Evaluating the Review of Literature*

You should consider several criteria when reading and evaluating the review of literature section of research studies or reports. First, identify which part of the article is the review of literature. Sometimes the review has a separate heading, but often it does not. Be sure to differentiate between an introduction, which provides a general overview or background, and the review, which should hone in on empirical studies that are clearly related to the research problem. Once identified, scan the review to get an idea of the general structure and organization. When reading, highlight dates of references, places where findings from other studies are summarized, and analyses of the studies. In the margins of a copy of the article you may find it helpful to write notes such as "sum" for summary and "an" for analysis, or even "+" to indicate places in the review that correspond to the criteria outlines on pages 76–80. Finally, determine how well the review corresponds to these criteria. This can be recorded so that when you review the overall credibility of the researcher and the study, the quality of the review can be a part of this summary judgment.

1. The review of literature should adequately cover previous research on the topic. In reading research in an area with which you are familiar, you will be able to judge the scope of the review. Were important studies ignored? Does the number of studies in the review reflect research activity in that area? Often you will realize that there is far more research in an area than the review indicates. Do the authors of the article cite mainly their own research? Although it is sometimes quite appropriate for authors to use their own work as a major part of the review, it may also indicate investigator bias. If the authors limit their review to their own studies and do not include other related research, the credibility of the study could justifiably be questioned. Overall, then, you will typically have some sense of whether the review is sufficiently comprehensive. Based on length, a one- or two-paragraph review on a much-studied topic for a quantitative study is probably too brief, while reviews that cover several journal pages are probably more than adequate.

EXAMPLE | **Relating Prior Research to Current Study**

"It would seem, however, that studies on the relationship between families and Black college students are more limited. The present study was designed to examine this gap in the literature on Blacks in higher education. The purpose of this study was to explore the role of family in the life of African American college students." (Herndon, M. K., & Hirt, J. B. (2004). Black students and their families: What leads to success in college. *Journal of Black Studies, 34*(4), p. 494)

---

2. The review of literature should cite actual findings from other studies. It is important for the review to be based on the empirical results of previous research, not on others' opinions about previous research or on the conclusions of previous research. To illustrate this point, consider the following example of a review of literature citing results:

EXAMPLE | **Summarizing Results from Previous Studies**

"The lack of evidence concerning the effectiveness of state early education programs has been at issue as well. A meta-evaluation of state prekindergarten programs highlighted substantial issues in research designs, measures, and analytical methods of the evaluations conducted prior to the review, and the lack of evidence about the implementations and outcomes of the state programs (Gilliam & Zigler, 2001). However, the body of research has grown since this meta-evaluation, and the research shows that state prekindergarten programs can produce positive effects on short-term measures (Gormley & Gayer, 2005; Gromley, Gayer, Phillips, & Dawson, 2005; Henry et al., 2003) and are associated with higher levels of achievement in later years (Grissmer, Flanagan, Kawata, & Williamson, 2000)." (Henry, G. T., Gordon, C. S., & Rickman, D. K. (2006). Early education policy alternatives: Comparing quality and outcomes of head start and state prekindergarten. *Educational Evaluation and Policy Analysis, 28*(1), p. 78)

Notice how the next example focuses on conclusions:

EXAMPLE | **Summarizing Conclusions from Previous Studies**

"The effects of parents' and students' expectations for educational attainment are important in science achievement expectations (Miller & Brown, 1992). Student expectations affect student involvement in classroom learning or the effort that students apply to studying and, thus, ultimately affect achievement (Pintrich & Schrauben, 1992). The effect of track and curriculum on achievement is well documented (Oakes, 1985)." (Brookhart, S. M. (1998). Determinants of student effort on schoolwork and school-based achievement. *Journal of Educational Research, 91*(2), p. 203)

---

3. The review of literature should be up-to-date. The studies reviewed should include the most recent research on the topic. This does not mean that older studies are not relevant. Sometimes the best and most relevant research was conducted decades ago. You also need to consider that it may take a year or more to publish a study after it has been accepted for publication. But if you read a study published in 1999 and most of the citations are from work in the 1980s, the review is probably out of date. A quick glance at the references at the end of the study will provide you with a good idea of how contemporary the review is.

4. The review of literature should analyze as well as summarize previous studies. As noted, a good review interprets the quality of previous research. This analysis may be a critique of methodology or inappropriate generalizations, an indication of limitations of the study (e.g., to certain populations, instruments, or procedures), or a discussion of conflicting results. In the following example, the authors comment on how a specific procedure used in two previous studies may be important in determining the results.

EXAMPLE | **Analysis of Previous Research**

"In general, they found that variability was most likely to occur when more than one feature of the target word was unstable in the child's phonological system. It should be noted, however, that only two productions of each target word were analyzed, only initial consonants were examined with regard to variability, and the target words were nonsense words developed specifically for the experiment." (Sosa, A. V., & Stoel-Gammon, C. (2006). Patterns of intra-word phonological variability during the second year of life. *Journal of Child Language, 33,* p. 35)

"In addition to these cases, there is a rich research literature on the effect of ability grouping on racial segregation within schools (e.g., Darling-Hammond, 1985; Larkins & Oldham, 1976; Lucas & Berends, 2002; Meier, Stewart, & England, 1989; Mickelson, 2001; Oakes, 1985; 1990; Oakes & Guiton, 1995). While this literature has been extremely useful in highlighting the costs of ability grouping at the secondary level, it has not focused on measuring trends and patterns in within-school segregation as such. Rather, much of the work focuses specifically on the disproportionate placement of black students in low track classes within small samples of high schools. There are some important exceptions. For example, Mickelson (2001) documents racial segregation in all Charlotte, North Carolina, high schools by counting the number of 'racially isolated classrooms,' defined as classrooms where the percentage black (or white) deviates by a nontrivial amount from the percentage at the school level. However, this article does not compare the overall racial contact within Charlotte schools to that occurring across schools and does not explore trends over time or variation across grades in within-school segregation." (Conger, D. (2005). Within-school segregation in an urban school district. *Educational Evaluation and Policy Analysis, 27*(3), p. 226)

5. The review of literature should be organized logically by topic, not by author. A review that devotes one paragraph to each study usually fails to integrate and synthesize previous research. A well-done review is organized by topic. Typically, several studies may be mentioned together in the same paragraph, or may be cited together. For example, rather than using a separate paragraph to summarize and analyze each study, a good review might be something like the following:

EXAMPLE | **Literature Review Organized by Topic**

Three studies were found that investigated the relationship between motivation and assessment techniques used in the classroom (Hager, 1995; Miller, 1997; and Smith, 1997). In each of the studies the frequency of different assessment techniques employed was measured by asking teachers to rate frequency on a 5-point Likert scale. While the findings from these studies suggested that students were more motivated by essay-type assessments, the increased motivation may be a result of simply having a different type of assessment since in all three studies the teachers used objective tests much more frequently than essays.

6. The review of literature should briefly summarize minor studies and discuss major studies in detail. Minor studies are those that are related to one or two aspects of the study, or those that provide a general overview. Major studies are directly relevant to most aspects of the study or have important implications. A good review concentrates on major studies. It may be informative to mention minor studies, but the focus of the review should be on an analysis of the most closely related studies.

7. The review of major studies should relate previous studies explicitly to the research problem or methods. It is important to emphasize how the major studies relate to or contribute to the research problem or the methods of the current study. For example, the author might say, "these findings suggest that it is important to include gender as an independent variable in the study" or "this study adopts the methodology successfully used by Smith and Jones (1998)." It should be clear to the reader why a particular analysis or finding is important or helpful to the current study.

The following example from a published study shows how the author effectively connected previous research to methodology:

EXAMPLE | **Explicitly Relating Previous Research to Methodology**

"These questions were included in the study because connecting prior knowledge to a learned topic enhances comprehension (McNamara, Kintsch, Songer, & Kintsch, 1996; Palincsar & Brown, 1984) and is an integral part of the reciprocal teaching method." (Alfassi, M. (1998). Reading for meaning: The efficacy of reciprocal teaching in fostering reading comprehension in high school students in a remedial reading class. *American Educational Research Journal, 35*(2), p. 316)

---

8. The review of literature should provide a logical basis for the hypothesis. If there is a hypothesis, it should be based on the review of literature. This provides evidence that the hypothesis is based on reasonable logic supported by others, rather than on the researcher's whim. If the review of literature is unclear or provides conflicting predictions, the researcher may still state a hypothesis, though justification should be provided. Overall, there should be clear connections among the problem, review, and hypothesis.

9. The review of literature should establish a theoretical or conceptual framework for the problem. For basic and most applied research the review should provide the theoretical context for the study. A good theoretical context enhances the significance of the study and shows that the researcher is aware of the theory and has used it in framing the questions and methodology. Often, the theoretical framework is provided as a foundation for reviewing specific studies.

Strengths and Weaknesses of Using the Internet for Educational Research

The amount of information that is readily and quickly available on the Internet is unprecedented. Your challenge is to sift through hundreds, even thousands, of Web addresses to find credible, helpful information. A careful consideration of the Internet's strengths and weaknesses will help you determine when and how to search the Internet for a specific topic. On the positive side, the Internet is particularly good at quickly delivering current and niche information. It is conveniently accessed from almost anywhere, at very little cost. However, the Internet does not serve as an exhaustive source for searching educational literature, nor does it make it easy to find journal articles. Primary studies usually are not available online, with the exception of articles in online journals and ERIC documents. Specific databases of literature are better sources for primary studies. In addition, the Internet is not designed and organized for the educational researcher, nor are there uniform standards for accuracy and quality of the information.

With the ERIC database you can search through the contents of full text articles and reports dating back to 1966 on a single Website. In comparison, when searching the Internet for educational journals, you must find each journal's Website and then browse through its archives. While many education journals now have their current issues available online (for a fee), few of them have archives that extend further than the previous 10 years.

One of the most difficult aspects of using the Internet for educational research is that, unlike databases such as ERIC, there is no standard controlled vocabulary that facilitates a search. In ERIC you can depend on the subject headings, descriptors, and keywords to target needed information. There is no comparable system in place for the Internet, and there is no universal thesaurus to consult to determine the best search terms. See Table 4.2 for a comparison of strengths and weaknesses of the Internet with ERIC.

Everything that you find in ERIC has been through some type of review process. Many journals in ERIC have an editorial staff of experts who judge the quality of the submissions. This does not mean that everything in ERIC is of high quality, but overall quality will be better than what is available from the Internet. Anyone (from a teenager to a respected scholar) can publish a Web page.

TABLE 4.2   **Comparison of ERIC Database and Internet Sources**

Source	Strengths	Weaknesses
ERIC	Controlled vocabulary 30+ year archive Reviewed for quality	Limited International coverage Abstracts instead of full text articles At least 6 months behind current articles
Internet	Current information Full text articles International coverage	No significant archive No search standards No quality control

While there is an appealing democratic beauty to the Internet, it is crucial to evaluate the quality of Internet sources (more on this later).

Even though ERIC offers a more comprehensive, better organized, and peer-reviewed set of information about educational research, the Internet does have advantages. If a journal has an online version, you will be able to browse the most recent issues, issues that might take many months to appear in ERIC. Also, online journals will often contain the full text of each article, while some ERIC articles and documents are limited to abstracts. ERIC covers educational research and issues in the United States very well; the Internet offers a wider access to educational research from other countries. You will also find useful information on the Internet beyond journal articles and research reports, such as statistics, e-mail links to experts, governmental information, data sets, and discussion forums (Table 4.3).

Fortunately, you are not limited in your research to either the Internet or journal databases like ERIC. In framing your research question, think about the type of information that each might offer. In turn, this will help with your searches in each source. For example, you would certainly want to know what the research on your topic has been for the past 10 years as well as in the past months. By combining the Internet with the research tools that were presented in Chapter 3, you can capture a well-rounded and diverse portrait for your topic.

The World Wide Web is an excellent medium for the expedient transmission of data and information because of the ease in publishing, accessing, and updating information. As this resource has developed, researchers have found more information available on the Internet and are therefore more willing to share information. Federal and state governments, as well as universities and colleges, are in the forefront in providing useful primary source information on the Web. This can include research information such as federally funded research projects, data sets from surveys and censuses, original journal articles, research reports, government legislation, online databases, and current news and newsletters. No matter what the researcher is looking for, it is always important to identify the type of material that is needed so the search can be refined before beginning. Otherwise the researcher runs the risk of browsing through the Web without any

TABLE 4.3	Examples of E-mail Discussion Lists for Educational Researchers
Discussion Lists	**Subscription Information and Archives**
American Educational Research Association	http://lists.asu.edu/archives/aera.html
Assessment in Higher Education	http://lsv.uky.edu/archives/assess.html
Distance Education Online Symposium	http://listserv.cac.psu.edu/archives/deos-l.html
Educational Research Forum on Minority Issues	http://listserv.unb.ca/archives/aera-mi.html
Qualitative Research for the Human Sciences	http://listserv.uga.edu/archives/qualrs-l.html

direction or purpose. In the following sections we will explore the similarities and differences between print and Internet research and then examine the basic elements of a Website.

ORGANIZATION *of* INFORMATION *on the* WORLD WIDE WEB

Similarities Between Online and Print Research Techniques

Research in the online environment is much like going to the library and using print resources. Researchers should try to employ many of the same techniques and methods of scholarly inquiry that are used for the literature review discussed in Chapter 3. Many of the steps will be the same. Researchers will identify key terms and subject headings in order to search online databases, and directories using search engines. Primary sources must be evaluated based on quality, depth, breadth, scope, and relevancy. Researchers use a wide range of materials and view much more information than they will use. Also, information will be recorded in a systematic fashion, by taking notes, saving printouts, or saving files on disks and hard drives. Incorporating information that is found by using the Internet is much the same as using print information, but there are also new and different challenges.

Differences Between Online and Print Research Techniques

Online research, like other types of computer-assisted work, can save the user countless hours of manual work. But searching the Web can be a time-consuming and frustrating experience for the novice user because it has developed with little systematic organization and no comprehensive directory to all Websites. The researcher often will not know where to start since this is such a formidable resource. The many layers of **hyperlinks** can often lead researchers from useful information into dead ends and get them hopelessly lost. In addition, it is often hard to determine the veracity of a document or even to determine the author or publication date. Also, unlike in a library, there is often little assistance available to the researcher. But the Internet does offer the most current and up-to-date information, and, unlike a library, searches can be done at all hours and from any location. Researchers need to start with a basic background in terminology and then develop the skills it will take to successfully conduct research on the Web. In the next section we will examine the basic elements of a Website and then proceed to basic search strategies that researchers can use to conduct online research.

> **Hyperlinks:** Highlighted words or phrases that access other sites.

Elements of Website Organization

The researcher needs to have a basic understanding of how information on the Internet is arranged and displayed. This is important because different search engines, directories, and databases will search Websites differently and return different results when searching the same topic. Just as you don't need to know how to print a book in order to use one, you don't need to know the programming languages and hidden hypertext tags that build Websites in order to understand their basic organizational elements. There are several major parts of a Website: *URL, title, meta-data, menu, body, images, hyperlinks,* and *author(s)*. By understanding how a Website is constructed, researchers can determine what techniques they need to employ to uncover pages using search engines and subject directories.

The **URL** is the Internet address for the Website. Where a Website is hosted gives you valuable clues about the site, including authenticity, value, and purpose. The type of host is indicated as a two- or three-letter extension to the Internet address. An address with *.gov* tells you it is a U.S. government-hosted site, *.edu* is a university, college or school Website, and *.com* is reserved for commercial Websites. These and other extensions are indicated in Table 4.4. Government sites are usually accurate, authoritative, and up-to-date. They focus on current news, policies and initiatives, and department information. Educational institution sites can be very research oriented and contain primary research, case studies, and original publications. Commercial sites may offer unique services and information but need to be critically evaluated because their primary purpose is profit, not facilitating research.

URL: Unique WWW address.

The *title* is the name that the author has given the Website. Most authors will attempt to give the site a relevant title because many search engines and directories will identify Websites whose title matches the search most closely. Authors also try to choose relevant titles because search engines and subject directories typically display only the title of a Web page in the results of a search.

Websites can also contain *meta-data*, hidden descriptions of the Website using terms that the author thinks are pertinent or synonymous with the site. Search engines select and rank more heavily those sites that have meta-data matching the search query.

Many Websites will include a *menu*. The menu is sometimes at the beginning of the document like a table of contents or sometimes in a separate frame on the

TABLE 4.4	Domain Name Extensions
Extension	**Domain Type**
.com	Commercial
.edu	Educational institution
.gov	Government
.net	A community- or organization-based free Internet provider
.org	Organization or association
Any two-digit extension	A site hosted at any country other than the United States. For example, <.uk> is United Kingdom, <.au> is Australia.

left-hand side. The menu is intended to be an outline of the Website, giving the researcher a quick guide to all its parts.

The *body* of the Website is the entire displayed page. It can include text, tables, and hyperlinks. Most search engines use full-text indexing of the body and will rank Websites according to the number of times that the search terms appear in the body.

Other important elements of a Website include *images*, *hyperlinks*, and the *author*. Some search engines and directories will also search for these elements and will return results ranked according to their appearance in the Website. Knowing how to search just these specific parts of the page can be important if you have already developed narrow search criteria. Examine a search engine or subject directory's help menus to determine whether searching these elements is possible.

It is important to remember the similarities and differences in searching print and online resources, and the elements of a Website, in order to develop your skills in retrieving information from the Internet. In the next section, we'll discuss the three major methods for identifying and retrieving relevant information.

INTERNET SEARCH STRATEGIES

Before you start typing words into the first search engine that comes along, it is important to have a focused search strategy with a number of key terms and subject headings. Based on that search strategy, choose from an assortment of secondary finding tools, including subject directories and search engines. Once you have identified appropriate Internet search tools, pay attention to the various search options that each one offers, and construct your computer search accordingly. Finally, evaluate the sources that you find for their quality and relevance to your research question.

Each Internet search company (like Yahoo! or Google) compiles its own database of Internet sites. When you "search the Internet," you are really searching these databases. That is, your search does not go out onto the Web and look at every page in existence. In choosing an Internet search tool, you want to peer beyond the search screen and get some idea of the quality, content, organization, and scope of the data behind the scenes. The three primary types of Internet search utilities are *subject directories*, *search engines*, and *metasearch engines*. Understanding the differences between these will improve your Internet searching considerably.

Subject Directories

Subject directory: Service that reviews and categorizes information.

Internet **subject directories** are the "yellow pages" of the Internet in which you are able to browse through lists of Internet resources by topic. Typically, each topic is located within a hierarchy of subjects. For example, in a subject directory there may be a choice for "Education," then numerous choices under that subject, such as "Universities, K–12, Government, History," and so on. Examples of subject directories include Yahoo!, WWW Virtual Library, and the Librarians' Index to the Internet. The advantage of subject directories is that the content has been reviewed and organized by a human! Subject directories rely on teams of editors who have knowledge of specific disciplines. Thus, under each category you will find a high degree of relevance and quality. Subject directories are often the quickest way to assemble a manageable list of Internet resources for a topic. Here are some research questions that would be especially good for a subject directory:

> Where can I find a list of educational associations?
> Where can I find the department of education from each state?
> Where can I find a listing of online education journals?

Two of the largest subject directories, Yahoo! and Google, index approximately 20 billion Web pages. Some subject directories have partnered with search engines in order to increase their coverage. For example, if you use the search box in Yahoo!, there will be options to run the same search in any number of search engines. By clicking over to a search engine from Yahoo!, you will search a bigger set of data but will not have the advantage of Yahoo!'s organization. Often the best search strategy in a subject directory is to steer clear of the search box and use the categories. The search function of a subject directory is most useful when you are not sure what category to choose for a particular subject. For example, in Yahoo! it is somewhat difficult to find Montessori education, especially if you choose the education category "K–12." If you search Yahoo! for "Montessori education" you will find that it is listed in the education category of "Theory and Methods."

Search Engines

Search engines are large searchable databases of Web pages. Whereas subject directories are assembled and organized by human editors, search engines are compiled in an automated fashion. Each search engine uses a "spider" or "robot" that trolls through the Web from hyperlink to hyperlink, capturing information from each page that it visits. Therefore, the content of each search engine is dependent on the characteristics of its spider:

Search engine: Service that categorizes by automated indexing of key terms.

- How many pages has it visited?
- How often does it visit each page?
- When it visits, how much of the Web page does it record?

In terms of "freshness," the addition of new pages or modifications to existing pages can take several months to appear in various search engines. Especially interesting is that there is not a consistent amount of overlap between search engines. This means that the Internet researcher is wise to try several search engines.

Despite the limitations of search engines, they do index billions of Web pages. Search engines offer a quick way to search for specific words that may appear in

Web pages. Here are some research questions that would be especially appropriate for a search engine:

Are there any Web pages that cover standardized testing in the state of California?

Are there any Web pages that deal with John Dewey's *Democracy in Education*?

Are there any Web pages with a biography of Paulo Freire?

In searching through a large set of data like a search engine, there are a number of strategies to keep in mind. The concepts discussed in Chapter 3 about computer searching, such as logical connectors, are relevant. Note that in all of the examples above, the search would be most effective when two or more concepts are combined. Your Internet search effectiveness can also be enhanced by paying attention to search language, special search features, and the most relevant search results.

Search Language. There is no standard search language that is consistent across all search engines. Some search engines understand logical connectors like "and," whereas others insist that you use a "+" before each word if you wish to limit your results to combined terms. Despite the lack of standards, there are several features that are common to most search engines. For example, even though some engines use "and" while others look for "+," the feature of combining more than one idea into a single search is available across all search engines. One of the best places to find out about each engine's search language is its online help page. It is advisable even for seasoned Internet searchers to revisit the help pages of their favorite search engine periodically. Google's searching tips are available at http://www.googleguide.com/. This site offers many tips to search more effectively and a guide that can be printed out from a PDF file (www.googleguide.com/print_gg.html). There is also a "cheat sheet," www.googleguide.com/cheatsheet.html, that offers examples for quick searches.

Special Search Features. Search engines continue to make advancements in the area of special search features. You will find these on the "advanced search" option within most search engines. Special search features help you construct very complex searches through the use of selecting various options from a menu. Special search features include the ability to limit your search by language, date, location, and media (such as audio or images).

Relevancy. In addition to search options, it is helpful to be familiar with the retrieval algorithms of various search engines. **Retrieval algorithms** determine both how many pages each search retrieves as well as how the results of each search are ordered. The search algorithm is a mathematical formula that determines how many times and where your search terms appear in each document. For example, if

Retrieval algorithms: Number and order of documents.

you were searching for "cooperative learning," the Web pages that appear at the top of your search results should be the most relevant. Perhaps these pages had both words as part of their title, whereas the Web pages that appear at the very end of your search results might simply have the word "cooperative" somewhere in their text. If your results start to look less and less relevant, don't keep looking through the same list. Move on to a new search or a new search engine.

Metasearch Engines

A **metasearch engine** submits your search to multiple search engines at the same time. Examples of metasearch engines include Dogpile, Clusty, Vivismo, and Fazzle. Metasearch engines can be especially useful since studies have shown that each search engine includes pages that others do not. On the other hand, no single metasearch engine includes all of the major search engines. Also, you cannot take advantage of the specific search language or features that are native to each search engine. For this reason, it is best to use search engines for your complex Internet searching, and rely on metasearch engines for searches that are very simple, having only one or two words. With metasearch engines it is especially important to pay attention to relevancy, as you have less control over how each search engine interprets your metasearch query. Examples of good questions for a metasearch engine are:

> Are there any Web pages that mention elementary school portfolio assessment?
> Are there any Web pages that mention Jonathan Kozol?

Metasearch engine: Searches many engines at once.

Blurring the Line Between Search Engine and Search Directory

The line between search engine and search directory is often difficult to discern. Advanced search technology that makes it easier to find the information you need can mask the type of tool that you are using. In search engines, there will often be an associated directory listing. For example, when you use Google, your search will also be matched against the Open Directory project for categories that may be relevant to your search. Likewise in Yahoo!, if there are no matches in that directory, your search will get expanded to a subset of Google's database. Although these types of partnerships can improve searching, they can change from day to day. Many of the search engines and subject directories are, in the final analysis, businesses that are trying to be commercially successful. A final search option that one sees is the "sponsored link" in which a company pays a search engine to link to its products or services if they are relevant to the search. Often, but not always, such results will be labeled.

Table 4.5 lists several subject directories and search engines that you will find useful in using the Internet to find educational research and other information on contemporary educational issues.

TABLE 4.5	Types and Examples of Internet Search Tools
Subject Directories	**Web Address**
The Internet Public Library	www.ipl.org
Librarian's Internet Index	www.lii.org
WWW Virtual Library	http://vlib.org
Yahoo!	www.yahoo.com
Education Subject Directories	
Education Index	www.educationindex.com
GEM: Gateway to Education Materials	http://thegateway.org
KidsClick	www.kidsclick.org
Search Engines	
AllTheWeb	www.alltheweb.com
AltaVista	www.altavista.com
Google	www.google.com
Wisenut	www.wisenut.com
Metasearch Engines	
Dogpile	www.dogpile.com
Fazzle	www.fazzle.com
Clusty	www.clusty.com
Vivisimo	http//.vivisimo.com

BEYOND WEB PAGES: SCHOLARLY COMMUNICATION STRATEGIES

Perhaps the most revolutionary aspect of the Internet is its ability to connect people with shared interests. This is especially powerful in highly technical and specific areas of study where geographical boundaries might otherwise hinder communication between a limited number of experts. For example, it might be hard to find a group of scholars in any one location who were all interested in the sociology of education. Through the Internet, however, scholars as well as practitioners are able to form groups and discuss various issues specific to their field of study. Through the use of e-mail, mailing lists, newsgroups, and conferencing, educational researchers have ready access to their peers and do not need to be isolated by location.

E-Mail

E-mail can be an especially valuable tool in conducting research. The speed and ease of e-mail communication allows you to find resources and "talk" to experts. Through e-mail it is possible to easily contact researchers, librarians, or institutions to get guidance on a specific research question. E-mail is also an excellent way to collaborate with colleagues on works in progress by sharing ideas, drafts, and files. You can locate experts on your topic by using Ask an Expert (www.askexpert.com) or the Directory of Educational Researchers, (ec.umich.edu/aera/) and by searching university departments and schools of education that list faculty members and their research interests. Simply type in the name of the college or university in a search engine, go to the Web page of the appropriate school or department, and peruse the list of faculty, which usually includes e-mail addresses.

Newsgroups, E-Mail Discussion Groups, and Listservs

On the Internet there are literally thousands of newsgroups, mailing lists, and listservs that cover every conceivable area of interest. Most Internet browsers, such as Netscape and Microsoft Internet Explorer, include a *news reader*, which allows you to read and post messages about various subjects to a newsgroup. A discussion group is similar to a newsgroup, except that the messages are transmitted as e-mail and are therefore available only to individuals who have subscribed to the mailing list. A listserv (registered trademark of www.Lsoft.com) is a specific type of software for managing e-mail lists.

There are many newsgroups and discussion groups that are very active in scholarly content and commentary. Through them, researchers can identify new viewpoints and new strategies for research as identified by others with similar interests. They are an excellent way to stay current in your area of interest. One of the major commercial resources for mailing lists is Topica, at www.topica.com, which offers a selection of many topics, including education.

Conferencing and Telecommunications

One of the fastest growing aspects of conducting business, either in the business world or at universities, is through Internet telecommunications and collaboration. Examples include chatting, video and audio conferencing, online data collection, and virtual shared workspaces. Free or fairly inexpensive software is available to help academics and researchers communicate in real time through these convenient and timesaving resources. New technology is continually being developed as the need arises and as the benefits and savings of its use for educational research are explored.

Using Known Locations

The third method for doing effective research on the Internet is to access known sources, authorities, and experts. A logical starting place when looking for any type of information in print is to go somewhere or ask someone you know has the answer. Since the library is where you start when using print resources, one good starting point for online research is a library Website. Many libraries have begun developing resource guides or directories of Websites classified by subject in order to make the Internet more accessible and better arranged for their users. Many colleges have resource guides for most academic subjects, usually including one specific to education (for example, www.library.vcu.edu/guides/education.html).

Researchers might investigate university and research center libraries that are known to be strong in the particular subject. Often the Websites for these organizations include unique information and resources. For example, the University of Illinois has a strong collection of children's literature, so if you were interested in that area it would make sense to contact the University of Illinois library to see what has been done there to organize the topic.

In addition to libraries, federal and state government Websites are excellent sources. A good starting place is the U.S. Department of Education's Website (discussed below). The department's page not only includes a great variety of primary data, but also hyperlinks to other government sites and related Websites. Other known sources of information include Websites for national associations and organizations, companies focusing on educational products, nonprofit organizations, newspapers, and online journals.

REVIEW *of* EDUCATION WEBSITES

This section briefly introduces and reviews several categories of Websites to show you the kind of information included at those locations.

Federal Government

The first place most education professionals will want to begin their research is at the U.S. Department of Education's Website, www.ed.gov. This site contains current news and headlines, announcements about new projects, initiatives, re-lated Websites, and listings of the department's educational priorities and na-tional objectives. It also includes budget information, information on legislation that affects education, and Websites for other departmental offices and contacts. In addition, excellent research can be found at the Website of the Institute for Ed-ucation Sciences (www.ed.gov/about/offices/list/ies) and the What Works Clear-inghouse (www.whatworks.ed.gov).

Valuable statistical information is available from the department's National Center for Education Statistics, http://nces.ed.gov. The center describes its stud-ies as covering "the entire educational spectrum, providing the facts and figures needed to help policymakers understand the condition of education in the nation today, to give researchers a foundation of data to build upon, and to help teach-ers and administrators decide on the best practices for their schools." Some of the most useful portions of the Website include survey results, issue briefs, and other data sets. The Website includes a list of frequently asked statistical questions, and the full statistical publications, *Digest of Education Statistics* and *Condition of Education*. Researchers can even use a site-specific search engine or browse a sub-ject index located on the "Education Statistics at a Glance" Website, http://nces.ed.gov/annuals.

State Government

All state governments have Websites, as do most state departments of educa-tion. The federal Department of Education maintains a page of links to state education agencies. In addition to current news and announcements and other typical reference information (i.e., phone numbers, office locations, etc.), state department Websites include lists of publications and usually a research (or data or statistics) Website. For example, the State of Virginia's Department of Education Website, www.pen.k12.va.us, has a section for "Data and Publica-tions." Once there, a researcher can find a great amount of information about education in the state, including, for example, the previous year's graduation and dropout rates for each county in the state. Virginia's departmental Website also includes the state Standards of Learning, job opportunity listings, and in-formation about the board of education and the superintendent of public in-struction. A comprehensive listing of state education agencies can be found at www.ed.gov/Programs/bastmp/SEA.htm.

National Research Centers

The United States Department of Education's Institute of Education Sciences has established five national institutes that are designed to address nationally signifi-cant problems and issues in education and support university-based national edu-cational research and development centers. There are currently 12 topic-specific centers. The current topics range from evaluation, standards, and testing to in-creasing the effectiveness of state and local education reform efforts. Researchers can find a variety of information at their Websites. For example, the Center for

TABLE 4.6	National Research Centers' Websites	

Center	URL
Center for Research on Education, Diversity, and Excellence (CREDE)	www.crede.berkeley.edu
Center for Research on Evaluation, Standards, and Student Testing (CRESST)	www.cse.ucla.edu
Center for Research on the Education of Students Placed at Risk (CRESPAR)	http://crespar.law.howard.edu/
Center for the Improvement of Early Reading Achievement (CIERA)	www.ciera.org
Center for the Study of Teaching and Policy (CTP)	http://depts.washington.edu/ctpmail
National Center for Early Development and Learning (NCEDL)	www.fpg.unc.edu/ncedl
National Center for Improving Student Learning and Achievement in Mathematics and Science	www.wcer.wisc.edu/NCISLA
National Center for Postsecondary Improvement (NCPI)	www.stanford.edu/group/ncpi
National Center for the Study of Adult Learning and Literacy (NCSALL)	www.ncsall.net
National Center on Increasing the Effectiveness of State and Local Education Reform Efforts	www.cpre.org/index_js.htm
National Research and Development Center on English Learning and Achievement (CELA)	http://cela.albany.edu/overview.htm
National Research Center on the Gifted and Talented	www.gifted.uconn.edu/nrcgt.html

Research on Education, Diversity, and Excellence, www.crede.berkeley.edu, contains a definition of the center, including its mission statement, as well as an explanation of the four project categories it hosts and links to the projects that are currently under way. The names and Web addresses of the National Centers are listed in Table 4.6.

Regional Educational Laboratories

Regional educational laboratories are educational research and development organizations supported by contracts from federal and state governments, foundations, and other organizations. The mission of each laboratory is to link the knowledge from research with the wisdom from practice to improve teaching and learning tailored to the specific needs of the geographic region served. In 2006, there were 10 regional laboratories, each offering different types of information on its Website (see Table 4.7).

Associations and Organizations

Many organizations and national associations have Websites and are providing quite a bit of primary information. Using subject directories or search engines,

TABLE 4.7	Regional Educational Laboratories
Laboratories	**URL**
Appalachia Regional Educational Laboratory	www.ael.org
Education Alliance at Brown University	www.alliance.brown.edu/
Far West Laboratory and Southwest Regional Laboratory	www.wested.org
Mid-Atlantic Regional Educational Laboratory	www.temple.edu/LSS
Mid-Continent Regional Educational Laboratory	www.mcrel.org
North Central Regional Educational Laboratory	www.ncrel.org
Northwest Regional Educational Laboratory	www.nwrel.org
Pacific Resources for Education and Learning	www.prel.org
Southeastern Regional Vision for Education	http://www.serve.org
Southwest Educational Development Laboratory	www.sedl.org

researchers can almost always find the pertinent association that matches their research. For example, the Web page of the Association of Teacher Educators, www.ate1.org, includes contact information, event schedules, and positions and resolutions, as well as links to related Websites. Table 4.8 lists several relevant education associations and organizations.

Online Journals, Reviews, and Abstracts

The following three Websites maintain extensive listings of online journals in education. Many indicate whether a title is free, scholarly, peer-reviewed, or full-text. Most university libraries also maintain institution-specific subscriptions to electronic journals. In addition to journal listings, Education Line hosts an archive of reports, conference papers, working papers, and preprints in the field of education and training.

1. Electronic journals in the field of education: aera-cr.ed.asu.edu/ejournals
2. Education journals and newsletters: www.scre.ac.uk/is/webjournals.html
3. Education Line: www.leeds.ac.uk/educol

Two Websites that index conference proceedings and other research reports are the Education Policy Analysis Archives at olam.ed.asu.edu/epaa and the Qualitative Report at www.nova.edu/ssss/QR. In addition to online bookstores that are common on the Internet, educational researchers may want to search the review articles of recently published books in education in the Arizona State University Book Review at www.ed.asu.edu/edrev. Examples of current online journals that contain research-oriented materials are listed in Table 4.9.

TABLE 4.8	Examples of Education Associations and Organizations

American Association for Health, Physical Education, Recreation, and Dance Research Consortium

www.aahperd.org/research

- Purpose is to further and promote research in health education, physical education, dance, athletics, exercise, and recreation.

American Association of School Administrators

www.aasa.org

- Focuses on improving the condition of children and youth, preparing schools and school systems for the 21st century, connecting schools and communities, and enhancing the quality and effectiveness of school leaders.

American Educational Research Association

www.aera.net

- Concerned with improving the educational process by encouraging scholarly inquiry related to education and by promoting the dissemination and practical application of research results.

American Federation of Teachers, Research Department

www.aft.org/research

- Features research-oriented publications such as salary surveys, legislative updates, newsletters, histories, research reports, position papers, and example forms.

Association for Supervision and Curriculum Development

www.ascd.org

- Includes everything from full-text articles published in *Educational Leadership* to descriptions of every ASCD professional institute. Also features new initiatives and programs, new distance learning opportunities at PD Online, and interactive forums.

Center for Data-Driven Reform

www.bestevidence.org

- Distills evidence from several different research groups on promising practices and interventions in education.

International Reading Association

www.reading.org

- Seeks to promote high levels of literacy for all by improving the quality of reading instruction through studying the reading processes and teaching techniques; serving as a clearinghouse for the dissemination of reading research through conferences, journals, and other publications; and actively encouraging the lifetime reading habit.

National Association for the Education of Young Children

www.naeyc.org

- Primary goals are improving professional practice and working conditions in early childhood education and building public understanding and support for high-quality early childhood programs.

National Association of Elementary School Principals

www.naesp.org

- Dedicated to ensuring that all children get the best education possible by serving the professional interests of elementary and middle school principals and promoting the highest professional standards.

National Association of Secondary School Principals

www.nassp.org

- Seeks to be at the forefront in establishing standards for exemplary schools and leaders by fostering a greater understanding of the global marketplace, the influence of technology, and the effects of the information age on teaching and learning.

National Council of Teachers of English

www.ncte.org

- Provides a forum for the profession, an array of opportunities for teachers to continue their professional growth throughout their careers, and a framework for cooperation to deal with issues that affect the teaching of English.

National Education Association

www.nea.org

- America's oldest and largest organization committed to advancing the cause of public educaton. Works on the local, state, and national levels to influence and set education policy.

National Middle School Association

www.nmsa.org

- The only educational association exclusively devoted to improving the educational experiences of young adolescents.

National Science Teachers Association

www.nsta.org

- Committed to promoting excellence and innovation in science teaching and learning for all.

Phi Delta Kappa International, Inc.

www.pdkintl.org

- Promotes quality education, with particular emphasis on publicly supported education, as essential to the development and maintenance of a democratic way of life.

TABLE 4.9	Examples of Research-Oriented Online Education Journals	
Title	**Subject**	**Address**
ALAN Review	Young adult literature	http://scholar.lib.vt.edu/ejournals/ALAN
American School and University	Educational administration	http://www.asumag.com
Chronicle of Higher Education	Higher education	http://chronicle.com
Education Next	School reform	www.educationnext.org
Education Policy Analysis Archives	Research and policy	http://epaa.asu.edu
Education Week	Current education news	www.edweek.com
Educational Theory	Educational theory	www.ed.uiuc.edu/eps/Educational-Theory/
Educause Quarterly	Educational technology	www.educause.edu/eq/eq
Effective Teaching	Higher education	www.uncw.edu/cte/ET
Exploring Adult Literacy	Adult education	http://literacy.kent.edu/cra
From Now On	Educational technology	www.fromnowon.org
Journal for Research in Mathematics Education	Educational research	www.nctm.org/jrme
Journal of Technology Education	Instructional technology	http://scholar.lib.vt.edu/ejournals/JTE
Journal on Excellence in College Teaching	Higher education	http://celt.muohio.edu/ject
OERI Bulletin	Educational research	www.ed.gov/bulletin
Rethinking Schools	Urban education	www.rethinkingschools.org
T. H. E. Journal	Instructional technology	www.thejournal.com
TESL-EJ	Teaching of English as a Second Language	www-writing.berkeley.edu/TESL-EJ

Statistics

The following lists and examples are just a few of the many statistical resources available to you on the Internet. Visiting these Websites should lead you to others. These resources may help you by containing information you need for a thesis or class project that has already been collected by experts willing to organize and share their findings with others in the educational community. In addition to archives of research reports and news, these sites may contain extensive data sets and data files that can be used in educational research.

- Inter-university Consortium for Political and Social Research: www.icpsr.umich.edu
- National Assessment of Educational Progress: http://nces.ed.gov/nationsreportcard/site/home.asp
- National Center for Education Statistics: http://nces.ed.gov
- National Library of Education: www.ed.gov/NLE
- Statistical Abstract of the U.S.: www.census.gov/compendia/statab/

Associations and University Web Pages

Almost all larger professional associations and universities have a substantial Web presence. At each of these sites you can find useful information, such as lists of faculty, publications, resolutions, and links to other Websites. By visiting these pages you can not only gain knowledge of educational research, but can also get a feel for the culture and activity of each organization.

Two national societies, the American Educational Studies Association at www3.uakron.edu/aesa and the American Education Research Association at www.aera.net, provide valuable information for the educational researcher. These Websites contain news, conference information, research reports, and other information relating to research in the field of education.

Another location at which to find educational research is universities and their departments of education. The following are the top ten graduate schools in education as rated by *U.S. News & World Report* in 2007. Each university's Website lists faculty and their research interests, research projects and partnerships, and other research material. Many include links to their university library's resources for education.

1. Harvard University Graduate School of Education: www.gse.harvard.edu
2. Columbia University Teacher's College: www.tc.columbia.edu
3. UCLA Department of Education: www.gseis.ucla.edu/ded.html
4. Stanford University School of Education: http://ed.stanford.edu/suse
5. Vanderbilt University Peabody College of Education: http://peabody.vanderbilt.edu/
6. University of California–Berkeley Graduate School of Education: http://www.gse.berkeley.edu/
7. University of Pennsylvania Graduate School of Education: www.gse.upenn.edu
8. University of Wisconsin–Madison Graduate School of Research and Education: www.wisc.edu/grad
9. University of Michigan School of Education: www.soe.umich.edu
10. Northwestern University School of Education and Social Policy: www.sesp.northwestern.edu

Author Reflection *Searching the Internet for educational research is now to the point where it actually makes sense to simply go online and try some things. There is so much out there that in all probability you will find something of value. It is especially helpful when searching for information on current issues and problems, even if much of what you find on these areas will be opinions, points of view, editorials, and positions, and not empirical studies. But to learn about contemporary topics quickly, the Internet is a great resource.*

Institute of Education Sciences

The Institute of Education Sciences (IES) (formerly the Office of Educational Research and Improvement [OERI]) is a particularly noteworthy part of the U.S. Department of Education. The institute maintains a leadership role in the field of educational research by conducting, collecting, and distributing research studies and statistics. The main Website for the institute includes current news in educational research, grant opportunities, statistics, and publications.

One of the keys to the IES research mission is the administration of the national institutes, research centers, and regional laboratories. The Institute hosts the National Center for Educational Research (NCER), the National Center for Educational Evaluation and Regional Assistance (NCEE), and the National Center for Education Statistics (NCES).

CONSUMER TIPS: *How to Cite Internet Resources in Your References*

As with any research, it is important to document your sources so that other researchers can visit the same sites you have found. In addition to the author, title, publication date, and address, most citation formats encourage you to list the date that you accessed the site. Most educational research is documented in either *Chicago Manual of Style*/Turabian style or APA format. You can find the APA's official guideline for citing electronic sources in the *APA Style Manual* and on the APA Web page at www.apastyle.org/elecref.html. The Chicago style formats can be accessed at www.aresearchguide.com/styleguides.html. Some examples of APA format follow.

EXAMPLE | **APA Citations of Online Articles and Documents**

Journal Article
VandenBos, G., Knapp, S., & Doe, J. (2001). Role of reference elements in the selection of resources by psychology undergraduates. *Journal of Bibliographic Research,* 117–123. Retrieved October 13, 2001, from **http://jbr.org/articles.html**

Multipage Document Created by Private Organization, No Date
Greater New Milford (Ct) Area Healthy Community 2000, Task Force on Teen and Adolescent Issues (n.d.). *Who has time for a family meal? You do!* Retrieved October 5, 2000, from **http://www.familymealtime.org**

Chapter or Section in an Internet Document
Benton Foundation. (1998, July 7). Barriers to closing the gap. In *Losing ground bit by bit: Low-income communities in the information age* (chap. 2). Retrieved from
http://www.benton.org/Library/Low-Income/two.html

Electronic Copy of an Abstract Obtained from a Secondary Database
Fournier, M., de Ridder, D., & Bensing, J. (1999). Optimism and adaptation to multiple sclerosis: What does optimism mean? *Journal of Behavioral Medicine, 22,* 303–326. Abstract retrieved October 23, 2000, from PsycINFO database.

Electronic Version of U.S. Government Report Available by Search from GPO Access Database (on the Web)
U.S. General Accounting Office. (1997, February). Telemedicine: *Federal strategy is needed to guide investments* (Publication No. GAO/NSAID/HEHS-97-67). Retrieved September 15, 2000, from General Accounting Office Reports Online via GPO Access:
http://www.access.gpo.gov/su_docs/aces/aces160.shtml?/gao/index.html

CONSUMER TIPS: *Evaluating Information on the Internet*

Information obtained from the Internet can be an excellent complement to print research, but it can also be low quality, even deceptive and misleading. Researchers using the Internet need to critically evaluate resources found online just as they would evaluate information found in a library, government office, center report, or journal. Remember that in most cases there is no peer review of information. As a result, the quality of the information varies considerably. Some of what you find may be of high quality and credible, while other information may be biased to present a particular point of view or simply be of low quality. Your evaluation of Internet material will be strengthened by asking the following questions:

- Who is the author or publisher of the information?
- What is the author's reputation and what are the author's qualifications in the subject covered?
- Is the information objective or is there a noticeable bias?
- Are the facts or statistics verifiable?
- Is there a bibliography?
- Is the information current?

It is common when searching for contemporary topics to find center and non-profit organization Websites. Many of these organizations have a clear agenda that is promoted, so it is advisable to understand these points of view so as to detect bias and opinion rather than a more balanced, scholarly perspective. The key to evaluating any type of research is to carefully read and analyze the content. It is also helpful to find a variety of sources so that you can compare and contrast them in order to get a fully informed view of any subject. If you are interested in learning more about evaluating sources on the Internet, visit the following Websites:

Evaluating Web Sites for Educational Uses: Bibliography and Checklist at www.unc.edu/cit/guides/irg-49.html

DESIRE Project. *Internet Detective.* Available at http://sosig.ac.uk/desire/internet-detective.html

Grassian, Esther. *Thinking Critically About World Wide Web Resources.* Available at www.library.ucla.edu/libraries/college/help/critical

Kirk, Elizabeth E. *Evaluating Information Found on the Internet.* Available at www.library.jhu.edu/researchhelp/general/evaluating

Ormondroyd, J., Engle, M., Cosgrave, T. *How to Critically Analyze Information Sources.* Available at www.library.cornell.edu/okuref/research/skill26.htm

Sheehy, Carolyn A., & Jagman, Heather A. *Internet Sources Quality Control.* Available at www.millikin.edu/ACI/internetQUALITY.html

USING EDUCATIONAL RESEARCH: INTERNET SEARCH SAMPLES

There are a number of strategies that can be used to enhance your Internet research. Let's see what happened when one of the authors conducted several quick searches on "student motivation" using large search engines, such as Yahoo! and Google. We will start with the basics. Both Yahoo! and Google provide users with an advanced Web search option that allows them to refine or narrow down the types of information. For example, if you are interested in researching "student motivation" and want to view only scholarly Websites that end in a certain domain (e.g., ".edu") and that have been updated within a certain time period, the advanced search option allows you to easily tailor your Website preferences. This option lets users specify and control the type of information or material they retrieve and helps filter out the inevitable junk that pops up when using a large search engine.

The author utilized both the Yahoo! and Google search engines to research "student motivation" using the advanced Web search option. In order to access the advanced Web search option in Yahoo!, click on Yahoo! Search at the top right of the Yahoo! homepage. On Google's homepage, the advanced search link is located to the right of the text box.

For Yahoo!, the author set the advanced Web search options to: (1) the words "student motivation," (2) only ".edu" domains, (3) Websites updated in the last year, (4) no filter, and (5) English language only. The search resulted in 61,900 hits on various nonjournal articles, different university organizations, course syllabi, and tips on how teachers can help motivate their students. At the top of the Yahoo! screen, the site offers users tips on how to rephrase a given topic in order to help vary or increase information received from a search.

Google has similar advanced Web search options. Under Google's advanced search option, the author specified search options comparable to the Yahoo! search. The search engine filter produced 128,000 hits that covered topics similar to the Yahoo! search, as well as Internet publications, newsletters, and Web postings.

A unique feature of Google is the option for a topic-specific search. Located at the bottom of Google's preferences page and under the heading of Topic-Specific Searches, users can choose to examine certain domains to refine their search options. To illustrate, the author chose "Google Scholar" to search for "student motivation" and was redirected to the Google Scholar page. After typing in "student motivation," the author clicked on "advanced scholar search" to refine the search. From there, the author narrowed the search to: (1) the exact phrase of "student motivation," (2) articles published in 2006, and (3) articles within the social sciences, arts, and humanities. The search produced 1 hit; however, after removing the quotation marks from the phrase "student motivation," a total of 28 hits in the form of various journal articles from their respective publisher sites appeared. As you can see, Google's topic-specific search allows for a very precise search that can be helpful for users who know exactly what type of information they are seeking. Yahoo! has a slightly similar Subscriptions option under its search options, but is limited to specific sites (e.g., the *Wall Street Journal*) rather than a specific topic.

Here is another example of an Internet search. The authors ran searches for the topic "charter schools" in August 2006. Starting with a large search engine, we searched for the words "charter schools and research." The results were varied, and included links to a number of pro-charter school Websites and think tanks. Note the millions of hits with Yahoo! and Google. Obviously, an advanced search procedure is needed to reduce these to more reasonable numbers.

Our search results also included a listserv message about charter schools, which alerted us to the existence of a charter school electronic mailing list and its searchable archive. One of the sites that stood out was the online journal called *Education Next: A Journal of Opinion and Research*. By repeating our search in a subject directory, we found the Charter School Research Project, which in turn led us to a current bibliography with links to charter school research. The subject directory also provided good lists of links to charter schools and charter school organizations.

In reviewing these results we noted that each search led us to unique material. Further, by following links from our results we found other sites that were not included in any of our original results. Therefore, it pays to search across a variety of sources. The wise researcher will also supplement the online research with the scholarly literature found through indexes like ERIC and PsycINFO. Figure 4.1 shows different results for "Charter Schools," depending on the search strategy.

FIGURE 4.1   Sample Internet search using multiple search tools.

Search Engine: Google
Advanced search limited to .gov
749,000 results
State of Charter Schools 2000
California, Texas, New Jersey...

Search Engine: AllTheWeb
+ "Charter Schools" + Reseach
5 million results
Center for Education Reform
Charter school listserv
Education Next: A Journal...

Known Location:
National Center for
Educational Statistics
Search: "Charter Schools"
839 results
Primarily statistics on number
of charter schools and
students served

Subject Directory: Yahoo
4.6 million results
Lists of charter schools
Charter school organizations
Charter School Research
The Center for Education Reform

Charter Schools

Beyond the Internet:
Indexes to scholarly literature
ERIC
Psychological Abstracts

Communication:
ERIC cites
Web guides

STUDY QUESTIONS

1. In what ways is searching the Internet different from searching a database such as ERIC?
2. Which parts of a Website are most helpful when conducting a review of research? Why?
3. What is the difference between using subject directories and search engines to locate information on the Web?
4. Why is the national Department of Education's Website a good one to use when beginning a search?
5. What could you expect to obtain from a regional educational laboratory that you could not obtain from a national research center?
6. Take a few minutes to try different search strategies to locate information on a topic. Which strategy was most helpful? Which one was easiest? What did you learn about using different strategies?

@WWW SAMPLE TEST QUESTIONS

See this text's Companion Website at www.ablongman.com/mcmillan5e
for sample test questions and answers.

mylabschool *Where the classroom comes to life!* RESEARCH NAVIGATOR™ ACTIVITIES

1. Click on Tab 2 of the Research Navigator™ and then click Using the
   Internet for Research. How is the strategy suggested for using the
   Internet different from what is presented in this chapter?
2. From this same source, what information do you find most helpful in
   searching the Internet for obtaining "literature"?

Chapter 5

Participants, Subjects, *and* Sampling

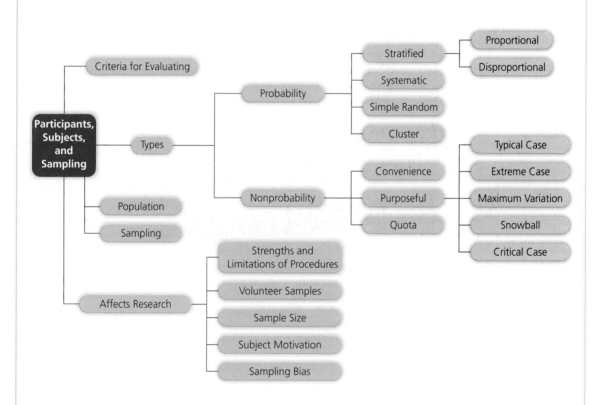

CHAPTER ROAD MAP

This chapter is divided into three major sections to help you understand the different ways researchers come up with participants and subjects from whom data are collected. We will first review the common approaches taken for quantitative studies and then look at some for qualitative studies. We will then examine how sampling affects research. As a result of studying this chapter, you will:

- Understand the difference between samples and populations
- Understand the differences between probability and nonprobability sampling
- Understand the different techniques for taking random samples
- Understand the different approaches for taking a purposeful sample
- Understand how the nature of the sample and sampling procedures may affect the outcome and quality of research

As noted in Chapter 1, the first subsection of the methodology section usually describes the participants from whom data are collected. The manner in which participants are selected and their traits and characteristics have important implications for identifying factors that affect participant performance and for generalizing the results. Hence, it is necessary to understand who the participants were and how they were selected.

WHAT IS *a* PARTICIPANT, *a* SUBJECT, *and a* SAMPLE?

Participant: Person from whom data are collected.

Simply put, a **participant** (subject), is someone from whom data are collected. In experiments, for example, each person who receives the intervention and whose behavior is measured is considered a subject. The term *participant subject* may also identify individuals whose behavior, past or present, is used as data, without their involvement in some type of treatment or intervention. For instance, a researcher might use last year's fourth-grade test scores as data, and each fourth-grader included is considered a participant. In some studies the term **subjects** may be used rather than participants, though the meaning of the term is the same. The term *subject* is gradually being replaced by *participant* and *source of data*. In qualitative research individuals are always identified as participants. Collectively, the group of subjects or participants from whom data are or have been collected is referred to as the *sample*.

Subject: Person from whom data are collected.

Sample: Group of subjects or participants from whom data are collected.

The **sample,** then, is the group of elements (e.g., persons), or a single element, from which data are or have been obtained. Although the phrase "the sample included . . ." is used to indicate the characteristics of the individuals or events in the sample, the nature of the sampling procedure is usually described by one or more adjectives, such as *random* sampling, *purposive* sampling, or *stratified random* sampling. These types of sampling procedures are defined, with illustrations from actual studies, in the following section.

It is important for the researcher to define as specifically as possible both the sampling procedure and the characteristics of the sample used in the study. Here are two examples of good descriptions of samples.

EXAMPLE | **Descriptions of Samples**

"Students come from four small towns, the largest with a population around 300, and the surrounding countryside. Socio-economically, the student population is drawn primarily from middle-class to lower middle-class families with some families at or near the poverty level. Over 50% of the student population qualify for free and reduced lunches. The eighth grade class in this study is representative of the school population. Ethnically the class is homogeneous with no minority students. The students also tend to be fairly homogeneous in terms of ability with no very low or very high ability students." (http://education.ucsc.edu/faculty/gwells/networks/journal/Vol.8(1).2005june/Morelock.html. Obtained June 27, 2006)

"Participants included 26 male and 14 female students enrolled in 3rd-grade classes at an urban elementary school and classified with a learning disability in mathematics (MLD). . . . Participants were drawn from a larger sample from which children diagnosed with either attention-deficit/hyperactivity disorder or reading difficulties were not selected. . . . Selection criteria for participants required that WISC-III scores and WRAT-R reading and spelling standard scores fall within normal limits." (Rosvic, G. M., Dihoff, R. E., Epstein, M. L., & Cook, M. L. (2006). Feedback facilitates the acquisition and retention of numerical fact series by elementary school students with mathematics learning disabilities. *The Psychological Record* *56*(1), p. 39)

"Students were enrolled in one of three kindergarten classes: 283 students (57.9%) attended half-day classes (157 half-day morning and 126 half-day afternoon) and 206 students (42.1%) attended full-day classes. Student ages ranged from 5 years 0 months to 6 years 6 months upon entering kindergarten; overall average age was 5 years 7 months. The total study included 208 girls (44.0%) and 265 boys (56.0%). The majority of students received no monetary assistance for lunch, which was based on parent income (89.0%, n = 424); 49 students (10.0%) received some assistance. Twenty-six students (5.3%) spoke a language at home other than English. The majority of students (90.5%, n = 428) were Caucasian; 31 students (6.3%) were Hispanic; and 14 students (2.8%) were African American, Native American, or Asian American. Those data reflect the community demographics within the school district." (Wolgemuth, J. R., Cobb, R. B., Winokur, M. A., Leech, N., & Ellerby, D. (2006). Comparing longitudinal academic achievement of full-day and half-day kindergarten students.

The Journal of Educational Research 99(5), p. 264)

TYPES *of* SAMPLING PROCEDURES
for QUANTITATIVE STUDIES

The purpose of sampling in quantitative studies is to obtain a group of participants who will be representative of a larger group of individuals or who will provide targeted responses. The degree of representativeness and the quality of the information obtained is based on the sampling technique employed. In this section we will review types of sampling procedures that are most commonly used in quantitative studies.

Probability Sampling

Population: A larger group to whom results can be generalized.

Many quantitative studies need to generalize results to a well-defined larger group of individuals. This larger group, whether individuals, objects, or events, is called the **population.** This group is also referred to as the *target population* or *universe.* The specification of the population begins with the research problem and review of literature, through which a population is described conceptually or in broad terms, for example, seventh-grade students, beginning teachers, principals, special education teachers, and so forth. A more specific definition is then needed, based on demographic characteristics. These characteristics are sometimes referred to as *delimiting* variables. For example, in a study of first-grade minority students, there are three delimiting characteristics: students, first grade (age), and minority.

It is important to distinguish the target population from the *survey population* or *sampling frame.* For example, in a study of beginning teachers, the target population may be beginning teachers across the United States, in all types of schools. The survey population may be a list of beginning public school teachers obtained from 40 states. Although the intent may be to generalize to all beginning teachers, the generalization in this case would be most accurately limited to beginning public school teachers in the 40 states.

When investigating a large population, it is often impractical and usually unnecessary to measure all the elements in the population of interest. Typically, a relatively small number of subjects or cases is selected from the larger population. The goal is to select a sample that will adequately represent the population, so that what is described in the sample will also be approximately true of the population. The best procedure for selecting such a sample is to use **probability sampling,** a method of sampling in which the subjects are selected randomly in such a way that the researcher knows the probability of selecting each member of the population (remember—random *selection* is a type of sampling; random *assignment* is used for some experimental designs).

Probability sampling: Known probability of selection from the population.

Random selection implies that each member of the population as a whole or of subgroups of the population has an equal chance of being selected. As long as the number of cases selected is large enough, it is likely that a small percentage of the population, represented by the sample, will provide an accurate description of the entire population. The steps taken in probability sampling are illustrated in Figures 5.1 and 5.2

Note, however, that there is always some degree of error in sampling, and that error must be considered in interpreting the results. In probability sampling, this calculation can be made precisely with some statistical procedures. Consider a population of 1,000 third-graders, from which you will randomly select 5%, or 50, to estimate the attitudes of all the third-graders toward school. If the attitude score was 75 for the sample of 50 subjects, 75 can be used to estimate the value for the entire population of third-graders. However, if another sample of 50 students is selected, their score might be a little different, say 73. Which one is more correct? Since not all 1,000 students have been tested to obtain the result, we do not know for sure, but the results can be used to estimate the error in sampling.

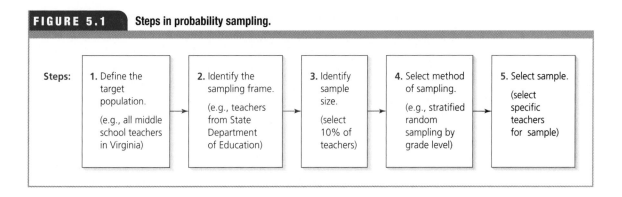

FIGURE 5.1 Steps in probability sampling.

Steps:

1. Define the target population.

   (e.g., all middle school teachers in Virginia)

2. Identify the sampling frame.

   (e.g., teachers from State Department of Education)

3. Identify sample size.

   (select 10% of teachers)

4. Select method of sampling.

   (e.g., stratified random sampling by grade level)

5. Select sample.

   (select specific teachers for sample)

FIGURE 5.2 Sampling and margin of error.

Target Population

Survey Population

Sample

Data Gathered from Sample

Margin of Error Included

This is basically the technique that political polls follow when it is reported that the vote is 45% ± 3%. The plus or minus 3 is the estimate of error in sampling. For example, it is common to report what is called a *margin of error* in polling. The **margin of error** indicates an interval within which the true population value lies. In polling there is typically a 95% probability that the population value is within the interval. So for 45% +/− 3, there is a 95% chance that when the entire population votes the result will be between 42 and 48.

There are many types of probability sampling procedures. You will most likely encounter four types in educational research: simple random, systematic, stratified, and cluster.

Simple Random Sampling. In **simple random sampling** every member of the population has an equal and independent chance of being selected for the sample. This method is often used with a population that has a small number of cases, for example, putting the names or numbers of all population members in a

Margin of error: Likely error in determining the result for the population.

Simple random sampling: Each member of the population has the same probability of being selected.

hat and drawing some out as the sample. If every member of the population can be assigned a number, a table of random numbers can identify the population members who will make up the sample. This approach is not convenient if the population is large and not numbered. The most common way of selecting a simple random sample from a large population is by computer. There are computer programs that will assign numbers to each element in the population, generate the sample numbers randomly, and then print out the names of the people corresponding to the numbers. In the following example simple random sampling was used to study the prevalence of all forms of child maltreatment in the United Kingdom within the context of social and cultural differences due to social class, ethnicity, and region.

EXAMPLE | **Simple Random Sampling**

"Two thousand eight hundred sixty-nine (2,869) young adults aged 18–24, obtained by random probability sampling throughout the UK, were interviewed face to face by trained interviewers." (May-Chahal, C., & Cawson, P. (2005). Measuring child maltreatment in the United Kingdom: A study of the prevalence of child abuse and neglect. *Child Abuse & Neglect: The International Journal, 29*(9), p. 969)

Systematic sampling: Every *n*th member of the population is selected.

Systematic Sampling. In **systematic sampling** every *n*th element is selected from a list of all elements in the population, beginning with a randomly selected element. Thus, in selecting 100 subjects from a population of 50,000, every *n*th element would correspond to every 500th subject. The first element is selected randomly. In this example that would be some number between 1 and 500. Suppose 240 was randomly selected as a starting point. The first subject chosen for the sample would be the 240th name on a list, the next subject would be the 740th, then the 1,240th, and so on until 100 subjects were selected.

There is a possible though uncommon weakness in systematic sampling if the list of cases in the population is arranged in a pattern so that only subjects with similar characteristics or who come from similar contexts are selected. For instance, if a list of fourth-graders in a school division is arranged by classroom and students in the classrooms are listed from high to low ability, there is a cyclical pattern in the list (referred to as *periodicity*). If every *n*th subject selected corresponds to the pattern, the sample would represent only a certain level of ability and would not be representative of the population. Alphabetical lists do not usually create periodicity and are suitable for choosing subjects systematically.

Stratified sampling: Subjects are selected from strata or groups of the population.

Stratified Sampling. **Stratified sampling** (*stratified random sampling*) is a modification of either simple random or systematic sampling in which the population is first divided into homogeneous subgroups. Next, subjects are selected from each subgroup, using simple random or systematic procedures, rather than from the population as a whole. The strata are the subgroups.

Stratified sampling is used primarily for two reasons. First, as long as the subgroups are identified by a variable related to the dependent variable in the research (e.g., socioeconomic status in a study of achievement) and results in more homogeneous groups, the same sized sample will be more representative of the population than if taken from the population as a whole. This result reduces error and allows a smaller sample to be chosen.

Second, stratified sampling is used to ensure that an adequate number of subjects is selected from different subgroups. For example, if a researcher is studying beginning elementary school teachers and believes that there may be important differences between male and female teachers, using simple random or systematic sampling would probably not result in a sufficient number of male teachers to study the differences. It would be necessary in this situation first to stratify the population of teachers into male and female teachers and then to select subjects from each subgroup.

The samples can be selected using one of two methods. A **proportional stratified sample,** or *proportional allocation,* is used when the number of subjects selected from each stratum is based on the percentage of subjects in the population that have the characteristic used to form the stratum. That is, each strata is represented in the sample in the same proportion as represented in the population. Thus, if 20% of the population of 200 elementary teachers is male, 20% of the sample would also be male teachers. In the following excerpt you will see that the researchers stratified on three different variables—population density, enrollment, and school level. This process would have resulted in 18 different groups from which proportional sampling was conducted.

> **Proportional stratified sample:** Reflects proportion of stratum in population.

EXAMPLE | Proportional Stratified Random Sampling

"A stratified random sample of schools was selected across population density (i.e., urban, suburban, and rural), enrollment (i.e., 0–599, 600–999, 1,000 and greater), and school levels (i.e., middle school and high school). Percentages of schools across population density and enrollment [and level] were established to maintain a sample consistent with the overall make-up of schools in Maryland." (Maccini, P., & Gagnon, J. C. (2002). Perceptions and application of NCTM standards by special and general education teachers. *Exceptional Children, 68*(3), p. 329)

Using proportional stratified sampling, however, does not always ensure that a sufficient number of subjects will be selected from each stratum. A second approach, referred to as **disproportional stratified sampling,** mitigates this problem by taking the same number of subjects from each stratum, regardless of the percentage of subjects from each stratum in the population. For instance, if only 10% of a population of 200 elementary teachers are male, a proportional sample of 40 would include only 4 male teachers. To study teacher gender, it would be better to include all 20 male teachers in the population for the sample

> **Disproportional stratified sample:** Number of subjects in each strata does not reflect proportion in population.

Convenience sample:
Nonprobability available
sample.

Convenience Sampling. A **convenience sample** is a group of subjects selected because of availability, for example, a class of a university professor who is conducting a study on college students, the classrooms of teachers who are enrolled in a graduate class, the schools of principals who are participating in a workshop, people who decide to go to the mall on Saturday, or people who respond to an advertisement for subjects. There is no precise way of generalizing from a convenience sample to a population. Also, the nature of the convenience sample may bias the results. For example, if the available sample for studying the impact of college is the group of alumni who return on alumni day, their responses would probably be quite different from those of all alumni. Similarly, research on effective teaching that depends on the participation of teachers in a particular geographic area, because they are available, may result in different findings than research done in other geographic areas.

Although we should be wary of convenience samples (sometimes these samples are negatively referred to as *accidental* or haphazard), often this is the only type of sampling possible, and the primary purpose of the research may not be to generalize but to better understand relationships that may exist. Suppose a researcher is investigating the relationship between creativity and intelligence, and the only available sample is a single elementary school. When the study is completed, the results indicate a moderate relationship: Children who have higher intelligence tend to be more creative than children with lower intelligence. Because there was no probability sampling, should we conclude that the results are not valid or credible? That decision seems extreme. It is more reasonable to interpret the results as valid for children similar to those studied. For example, if the children in the study are from a school that serves a low socioeconomic area, the results will be useful for children in similar schools but less useful for those from schools that serve a middle or high socioeconomic level. The decision is not to dismiss the findings but to limit them to the type of subjects in the sample. As more and more research accumulates with different convenience samples, the overall credibility of the results is enhanced.

Although it is uncommon for a researcher to state explicitly that a convenience sample was used, it will be obvious from the subjects subsection of the article. If some type of probability sampling procedure was used, it will be described. Thus, in the absence of such particulars you can assume that the sample was an available one. The following examples are typical.

EXAMPLE | **Convenience Samples**

"Thirty-six first-grade teachers in eight schools in a southeastern medium-sized school district were recruited to participate in this research, 12 to conduct first-grade PALS, 12 to conduct first-grade PALS and CAI, and 12 to provide a contrast group." (Mathes, P. G., Torgensen, J. K., & Allor, J. H. (2001). The effects of peer-assisted literacy strategies for first-grade readers with and without additional computer-assisted instruction in phonological awareness. *American Educational Research Journal, 38*(2), p. 377)

"Participants in this investigation were 482 undergraduate students. Student volunteers were solicited primarily from educational psychology and human developments courses at a large urban land-grant university in the mid-Atlantic United States." (Buehl, M. M., & Alexander, P. A. (2005). Motivation and performance differences in students' domain-specific epistemological beliefs profiles. *American Educational Research Journal, 42*(4), p. 704)

"Data were collected from a rural high school in northern California at which the researcher had previously worked as a resource teacher. . . . The sample (*N* = 355) consisted of the school's entire English learner population in the spring of 2002." (Callahan, R. M. (2005). Tracking and high school English learners: Limiting opportunity to learn. *American Educational Research Journal, 42*(2), pp. 312–313)

Quota Sampling. **Quota sampling** is used when the researcher is unable to take a probability sample but still wants a sample that is representative of the entire population. Different composite profiles of major groups in the population are identified, and then subjects are selected, nonrandomly, to represent each group. Thus, subjects are selected nonrandomly according to specific criteria. A type of quota sampling that is common in educational research is used to represent geographic areas or types of communities, such as urban, rural, and suburban. Typically, a state is divided into distinct geographic areas, and cases are selected to represent each area. As in availability and purposive sampling, there is a heavy reliance on the decisions of the researcher in selecting the sample, and appropriate caution should be used in interpreting the results.

> **Quota sampling:** Nonrandom sampling representative of a target population.

TYPES *of* SAMPLING PROCEDURES *for* QUALITATIVE STUDIES

In qualitative studies participants are selected purposefully. That is, there is a reason or justification for why the sample of individuals or sites will provide the best information to address the research question. In **purposeful sampling** (sometimes referred to as *purposive, judgment,* or *judgmental* sampling), the researcher selects particular individuals or cases because they will be particularly informative about the topic. Based on the researcher's knowledge of the population, a judgment is made to include those cases that will be information-rich. These few cases are studied in depth. For example, in research on effective teaching, it may be most informative to observe "expert" or "master" teachers rather than all teachers. To study effective schools, it may be most informative to interview key personnel, such as the principal and teachers who have been employed in successful schools for a number of years. A study on the resilience of students at risk of failure selected students to be interviewed on the basis of several characteristics, including grade level, why the student was considered at risk, gender, and current degree of success in school (McMillan & Reed, 1994). Sometimes researchers will be interested in *deviant* cases, selecting individuals who do not fit

> **Purposeful sampling:** Selection of particularly informative or useful subjects.

an established pattern. This approach can be used to establish a better understanding of more common traits.

There are a number of different purposeful sampling procedures that qualitative researchers use to obtain "information-rich" individuals and sites. The more common types are summarized here and in Table 5.1.

Typical Case Sampling

Typical case sampling: Selecting representative participants.

In **typical case sampling** (or model instance sampling) the researcher investigates a person, group, or site that is "typical" or "representative" of many. This kind of sampling requires sufficient knowledge about the important characteristics of the larger "population" of interest so that there is a reasonable definition of "typical." It is like sampling the "average" elementary teacher (one with several years of experience rather than a new teacher or one nearing retirement, and a woman). Note the criteria used to select the sample in the following study to identify the "typical" adult attending community college.

EXAMPLE | **Typical Case Sampling**

"Interviewees of these two community colleges were identified through a purposeful sampling strategy target to adults who (a) were at least 30 years of age, (b) were in good academic standing according to their institution's criteria, (c) were in a college transfer program, and (d) had completed at least 15 hours of academic coursework beyond developmental studies." (Kasworm, C. (2004). Adult student identity in an intergenerational community college classroom. *Adult Education Quarterly, 56*(1), pp. 6–7)

Extreme Case Sampling

Extreme case sampling: Selecting unique or atypical participants.

An extreme case is one that is unique or atypical, an outlier compared to most others in the category. In education, **extreme case sampling** is often used to identify unusually successful students or schools with the intent of studying them

TABLE 5.1	**Types of Purposeful Sampling Procedures**
Sampling Procedure	**Description**
Typical case	Choosing individuals or sites that are representative of most others.
Extreme case	Choosing individuals or sites that are unusual or atypical.
Maximum variation	Choosing individuals or sites that represent extreme values of the phenomenon being studied.
Snowball	Selecting individuals based on recommendations of participants.
Critical case	Choosing a dramatic illustration of the phenomenon being studied.

to learn why they perform so well. Another strategy is to identify a continuum of an important characteristic and then take samples at one end of that continuum. In the following example, extreme case sampling is based on the significant role played by homework. The sample is at one end of a continuum of the importance of homework.

EXAMPLE | **Extreme Case Sampling**

"This student body was selected because homework played a major role in the curriculum and because it would provide a definitive test of the effects of this academic experience." (Zimmerman, B. J., & Kitsantas, A. (2005). Homework practices and academic achievement: The mediating role of self-efficacy and perceived responsibility beliefs. *Contemporary Educational Psychology, 30*, p. 401)

Maximum Variation Sampling

In **maximum variation sampling** (or *maximum heterogenity sampling*) individuals, groups, or cases are selected to represent both ends of a continuum of values on a characteristic of interest. For example, if it is known that there are some teachers who never use zeros when grading and others who always use zeros, sampling from both extremes would provide for maximum variation. Or, suppose a researcher has a sample of schools differing on a measure of school climate. Schools scoring extremely high and schools scoring extremely low on school climate could be selected to understand how climate is formed and its impact on students.

Maximum variation sampling: Selecting participants to represent extreme cases.

Snowball Sampling

Occasionally qualitative researchers are in a situation in which the sampling is carried out as data are being collected. In **snowball sampling** (also called *network sampling*), the researcher begins with a few participants and then asks them to nominate or recommend others who are known to have the profile, attributes, or characteristics desired. For example, a researcher could begin interviewing a few elementary school counselors known for using play therapy and then ask them to nominate other elementary school counselors they know who also use play therapy. This kind of sampling is especially useful when the researcher has only a limited pool of initial participants. A related kind of selection of cases, *opportunistic sampling*, also occurs after the study is under way and takes advantage of including participants who are identified as being rich in the information needed.

Snowball sampling: Selecting participants from recommendations of other participants.

Critical Case Sampling

Sometimes the phenomenon of interest is illustrated by individuals, groups, or sites in unique and dramatic ways. **Critical case sampling** is used in these situations as an opportunity to learn and understand. For instance, suppose a researcher

Critical case sampling: Selecting the most important participants to understand phenomena being studied.

was interested in how the implementation of a particular technology initiative—say, laptop computers for all students—was impacting teaching and learning. If a single school district could be identified that had such an initiative it would be considered a critical case.

EXAMPLE | **Purposeful Sampling**

"The perceptions of the meaning of care as experienced by the participants in their interactions with one another was the primary focus. At each of the two sites, a teacher who was identified by the principal as being particularly caring was purposely selected." (Alder, N. (2002). Interpretations for the meaning of care: Creating caring relationships in urban middle school classrooms. *Urban Education, 37*(2), p. 249)

"In order to obtain a homogeneous sample for this grounded theory study (Creswell, 1998), the participants were limited to 40 social studies students (20 males and 20 female) and 2 teachers in a public school located in the southwestern United States. Because the students' academic performance in the class could affect their strategy use and I was interested in students who were academically successful in their social studies class, I only interviewed students who had an 'A' or 'B' average in their social studies classes." (Martin, L. A. (2004). Use of cognitive strategies by high school social studies students. *Action in Teacher Education, 26*(4), p. 65)

HOW PARTICIPANTS *and* SAMPLING AFFECT RESEARCH

In reading and interpreting research, you need to be conscious of how the sampling procedures might have affected the results, and how the characteristics of the subjects affect the usefulness and the generalizability of the results.

Knowledge of Sampling Procedures

To understand how sampling may affect research, it is essential to know the characteristics of different sampling procedures. This knowledge will help you interpret the sample that is used. You should first be able to identify the sampling procedure and then evaluate its adequacy in addressing the research problem and in supporting the conclusions. It will be helpful to know the strengths and weaknesses of each sampling procedure, as summarized in Table 5.2.

Volunteer Samples

A continuing problem in educational research, as well as in much social science research, is the use of volunteers as subjects. It is well documented that volunteers differ from nonvolunteers in important ways. Volunteers tend to be better educated, higher socioeconomically, more intelligent, more in need of social approval, more sociable, more unconventional, less authoritarian, and less conforming than nonvolunteers. Obviously, volunteer samples may respond differently than nonvolunteers because of these characteristics.

TABLE 5.2	Strengths and Weaknesses of Sampling Methods	
Method of Sampling	**Strengths**	**Weaknesses**
Probability		
Simple random	1. Usually representative of the population 2. Easy to analyze and interpret results 3. Easy to understand	1. Requires numbering each element in the population 2. Larger sampling error than in stratified sampling
Systematic	1. 1, 2, and 3 above 2. Simplicity of drawing sample	1. Periodicity in list of population elements
Proportional stratified	1. 1, 2, and 3 of simple random 2. Allows subgroup comparisons 3. Usually more representative than simple random or systematic 4. Fewer subjects needed 5. Results represent population without weighting	1. Requires subgroup identification of each population element 2. Requires knowledge of the proportion of each subgroup in the population 3. May be costly and difficult to prepare lists of population elements in each subgroup.
Disproportional stratified	1. 1, 2, 3, and 4 of proportional stratified 2. Ensures adequate numbers of elements in each subgroup	1. 1, 2, and 3 of proportional stratified 2. Requires proper weighting of subgroup to represent population 3. Less efficient for estimating population characteristics
Cluster	1. Low cost 2. Requires lists of elements 3. Efficient with large populations	1. Less accurate than simple random, systematic, or stratified 2. May be difficult to collect data from all elements in each cluster 3. Requires that each population element be assigned only one cluster
Nonprobability		
Convenience	1. Less costly 2. Less time-consuming 3. Ease of administration 4. Usually ensures high participation rate 5. Generalization possible to similar subjects	1. Difficult to generalize to other subjects 2. Less representative of an identified population 3. Results dependent on unique characteristics of the sample
Quota	1. 1, 2, 3, 4, and 5 of convenience 2. More representative of population than convenience or purposive	1. 1, 2, 3 of convenience 2. Usually more time-consuming than convenience or purposive
Purposeful	1. 1, 2, 3, 4, and 5 of convenience 2. Adds credibility to qualitative research 3. Assures receipt of needed information	1. 1, 2, and 3 of convenience

The potential weaknesses of using volunteers are illustrated in some survey research. When conducting a survey the investigator typically sends questionnaires to a sample of individuals and tabulates the responses of those who return them. Often the percentage of the sample returning the questionnaire will be 50% to 60% or even lower. In this circumstance the sample is said to be *biased* in that the results may not be representative of the population. Thus, the nature of the results depends on the types of persons who respond, and generalizability to the target population is compromised. The specific effect of a biased sample on the results depends on the nature of the study. For example, a study of the relationship between educational level and occupational success would be likely to show only a small relationship if only those who are most successful respond. Without some subjects who are not successful in the sample, success cannot be accurately related to level of education. If a survey of teachers is conducted to ascertain their general knowledge and reading and writing skills, the results would probably be higher than the true case because of the tendency of volunteers to be better educated.

Volunteers are commonly used in research because the availability of subjects is often limited by time and resources. There have been thousands of studies with teachers who volunteer their classes for research. Much research on school-age children requires written permission from parents, and this necessity can result in a biased sample. Suppose a researcher needed parents' permission to study their involvement in the education of their children. Chances are good that parents who are relatively involved would be most likely to agree to be in the study, affecting a description of the nature of parental involvement for "all" students.

Sample Size

An important consideration in judging the credibility of research is the size of the sample. In most studies there are restrictions that limit the number of subjects, although it is difficult to know when the sample is too small. Most researchers use general rules of thumb in their studies, such as having at least 30 subjects for correlational research, and at least 15 subjects in each group for experimental research. However, in many educational studies conducted in the field, higher numbers of subjects are needed. In surveys that sample a population, often a very small percentage of the population needs to be sampled, for example, less than 5% or even 1%. Of course, if the survey sample is too small, it is likely that the results obtained cannot characterize the population. Formal statistical techniques can be applied to determine the number of subjects needed, but in many educational studies these techniques are not used.

With purposeful sampling, the major criterion for using an adequate number of cases is the information provided. Since the purpose of the sampling is to provide in-depth information, sampling is considered complete when no new information is forthcoming from additional cases.

In educational research a major consideration with respect to sample size is the interpretation of findings that show no difference or relationships, particularly in studies that use small samples. For example, suppose you are studying the relationship between creativity and intelligence and, with a sample of 20 students, found that there was no relationship. Is it reasonable to conclude that in reality there is no relationship? Probably not, since a plausible reason for not finding a relationship is that such a small sample was used. In addition to the small number of subjects, it is likely that there may not be many differences in either creativity or intelligence, and without such differences it is impossible to find that the two variables are related. That is, with a larger sample that has different creativity and intelligence scores, a relationship may exist. This problem, interpreting results that show no difference or relationship with small samples, is subtle but very important in educational research since so many studies have small samples. As we will see in Chapter 10, it is possible to misinterpret what is reported as a "significant" difference or relationship with a very large sample. Also, a sample that is not properly drawn from the population is misleading, no matter what the size.

INTERNET CONNECTION

These sites show you how to determine sample size from populations of different sizes:
www.surveysystem.com/sscalc.htm
www.researchinfo.com/docs/calculators/samplesize.cfm

Subject Motivation

Sometimes subjects will be motivated to respond in certain ways. Clues for this phenomenon will be found in the description of how the subjects were selected. For example, if a researcher was interested in studying the effectiveness of computer simulations in teaching science, one approach would be to interview teachers who used computer simulations. The researcher might even want to select only those science teachers who had used the simulations for more than two years. It is not hard to understand that the selected teachers, because they had been using the simulations, would be motivated to respond favorably toward them. The response would be consistent with the teachers' decision to use simulations. Psychology students may be motivated to give inaccurate responses in studies conducted by their psychology professor if they do not like the professor, or they may respond more favorably if they want to help a professor they like.

Sampling Bias

In selecting a sample from a population there is always some degree of sampling error. This error (which is expected and precisely estimated as part of probability sampling) is the discrepancy between the true value of a variable for the population and the value that is calculated from the sample. A different type of error is due to **sampling bias,** a type of sampling error that is controlled or

Sampling bias: Sampling error caused by the researcher.

influenced by the researcher to result in misleading findings. Occasionally researchers will deliberately skew the sampling. The most obvious deliberate bias is selecting only those subjects who will respond in a particular way to support a point or result. For instance, if a researcher is measuring the values of college students and wants to show that the students are concerned about helping others and being involved in community service, bias would result if the researcher deliberately selected students in education or social work and ignored majors that might not be so altruistically oriented. Selecting friends or colleagues may also result in a biased sample. An even more flagrant type of bias occurs when a researcher discards some subjects because they have not responded as planned or keeps adding subjects until the desired result is obtained. Sampling bias also occurs nondeliberately, often because of inadequate knowledge of what is required to obtain an unbiased sample and the motivation to "prove" a desired result or point of view. In qualitative studies the researcher needs to be particularly careful about possible unintended bias if sampling changes during the study.

Bias can also result from selecting subjects from different populations and assigning them to different groups for an experiment or comparison. Suppose a researcher used graduate sociology students to receive a treatment in an experiment and graduate psychology students as a control group. Even if the samples were selected randomly from each population, differences in the populations, and consequently samples, in attitudes, values, knowledge, and other variables could explain why certain results were obtained.

Response Variability

An important goal in sampling in a quantitative study is to obtain subjects who will represent adequate variability on the measures that are used. Sufficient variability is needed so that differences and relationships can be detected. Thus, if you wanted to find a relationship between types of counseling techniques used and student depression, the sample would need to be selected so that there is a sufficient number of counselors using each type of technique, as well as students who have different degrees of depression.

USING EDUCATIONAL RESEARCH

Sometimes sampling can make all the difference when using educational research for policy. David Berliner, a noted educational psychologist, has recently argued that states emphasizing high-stakes testing fail to show gains on other measures of student achievement, such as on the SAT. Chester E. Finn, Jr., president of the Thomas B. Fordham Foundation, points out that the SAT is not taken by all students and therefore is not a good external measure, especially if state accountability efforts are focused on low-achieving schools. So the story may depend, in part, on the sample of students taking the test.

shaped like a cross-section of a bell. It tells us that the majority of scores tend to cluster around the middle, with the same number of scores above and below the middle point. Because the normal curve characterizes many naturally occurring phenomena and has standard properties, it is used extensively for research and statistical procedures. In a flat, or rectangular curve, the scores are widely spread out from the middle. Distributions that concentrate scores at the high or low end of the distribution are called *skewed*. In a **positively skewed** distribution, the scores are concentrated at the low end of the distribution; in a **negatively skewed** distribution, the majority of the scores are at the high end of the distribution. Actually, it is the mean that is either positively or negatively skewed, that is, either more positive or more negative than what is obtained with a normal curve.

Positively skewed: Large number of low scores; few very high scores.

For example, in a study of administrators' salaries, the distribution would be positively skewed if most of the salaries were relatively low and a few of the salaries were very high. Negatively skewed distributions are common in mastery testing, where, typically, most of the students score high and a few students score low. Bimodal distributions are those that have two modes, as discussed below.

Negatively skewed: Large number of high scores; few very low scores.

Frequency distributions are also important in identifying unusually high or low scores. Such scores, if they are very different from others, are *outliers*. **Outlier scores** are so atypical that their inclusion would distort the findings. Whenever researchers use quantitative data they must look carefully for outliers and decide how to handle them. Sometimes outliers are bad data, perhaps because of an entry error; sometimes they represent inaccurate responses. In both these cases it would probably be best to delete these scores. In the following example outlier scores were eliminated based on a specified set criterion.

Outlier scores: Scores that are very high or low in comparison to others.

> **EXAMPLE** | **Outlier Scores**
>
> "Preliminary analysis revealed five univariate outliers with z scores in excess of 3.20 (which Tabachnick & Fidell, 1996, indicates is a suitable threshold), and these cases were excluded from further analysis." (Nussbaum, E. M., & Kardash, C. M. (2005). The effects of goal instructions and text on the generation of counterarguments during writing. *Journal of Educational Psychology, 97* (2), p. 160)

Author Reflection *There was a time when I thought that you had to include all your obtained scores, that ethically it was expected. I've learned that what you really want are accurate data. So, you should never include bad data in a study! Outliers are indicators of possible bad data, as are specific patterns of subject responses. Look and check data carefully. Bad data make for bad results and bad conclusions.*

Measures of Central Tendency

Although it is useful to know the pattern of the scores as indicated by the frequency distribution, it is also important to be able to use a single score to characterize the set of scores. Measures of central tendency provide statistics that indicate the average or typical score in the distribution. There are three measures of central tendency: mode, median, and mean.

Mode: Score that occurs most frequently.

Mode. The **mode** is simply the score in the distribution that occurs most frequently. It is a crude index of central tendency and is seldom used in research. Sometimes distributions have more than one most frequent score. Such distributions are bimodal, trimodal, or multimodal. These terms also describe a distribution that may technically have only one mode; for example, two scores in different parts of the distribution clearly occur more frequently than the rest in a bimodal distribution. There is no mode in distributions in which each score occurs the same number of times.

Median: Score in the middle of the distribution.

Median. The **median** is the middle score of the distribution, the point that divides a rank-ordered distribution into halves containing an equal number of scores. Thus 50% of the scores lie below the median and 50% lie above the median. The median is unaffected by the values of the scores. This characteristic is an advantage when the distribution contains atypically large or small scores, such as measures of "average" income and the "average" cost of a new house. The median is symbolized by *Mdn* or *Md*.

In some studies the median score is used to split groups into two classifications or subgroups. In the following example, graduate students were divided into two groups based on an instrument that measured test anxiety.

EXAMPLE | **Median-Split Technique**

"The 61 students were allowed 10 minutes to complete the TAI (Spielberger, 1980) to assess their propensity toward test anxiety. TAI scores ranged from 28.0 to 49.0 with a median of 39.0 and a mean of 39.16. Using a median split, participants classified as high (i.e., above 39.0) or low (i.e., below 39.0) in text anxiety were assigned to either a high or low threat of evaluation section of the course." (Hancock, D. R. (2001). Effects of test anxiety and evaluative threat on students' achievement and motivation. *The Journal of Educational Research, 94*, p. 286)

Mean: Arithmetic average of all scores.

Mean. The **mean** is the arithmetic average of all the scores in the distribution. It is calculated by adding all the scores in the distribution and then dividing this sum by the number of scores. For example, if a distribution contains the scores 5, 7, 8, 10, 10, 12, 14, 15, 15, 17, the mean would be 11.3 (5 + 7 + 8 + 10 + 10 + 12 + 14 + 15 + 15 + 17 = 113; 113/10 = 11.3). or the distribution of critical thinking scores in Table 6.1, the mean is 21.92 (789/36). The mean is used extensively in research, usually symbolized by $\bar{x}$, or M for the sample mean and μ for the mean of the population. The mean may be misleading as a typical score in skewed distributions that contain extremely high or low scores because it is pulled toward the extreme scores. Thus, in a positively skewed distribution, such as personal income, the mean income is higher than the most typical income because some very high incomes are used in the calculation. In this case the median income is more typical. Conversely, in a negatively skewed distribution, the mean is lower than the median.

Measures of Variability

Although a measure of central tendency is an excellent statistic of the most typical score in a distribution, to obtain a full description of the scores we also need to know something about how they tend to cluster around the mean or median. Measures of variability show how spread out the distribution of scores is from the mean, or how much dispersion or scatter exists in the distribution. If there is a large degree of dispersion, that is, if the scores are very dissimilar, we say the distribution has a large or high variability, or variance. If the scores are very similar, there is a small degree of dispersion and a small variance.

The need for a measure of dispersion to describe a distribution is illustrated by comparing the different types of distributions in Figure 6.3. Distributions A and B would have the same mean but represent different distributions. It is necessary to add a measure of variability to the mean to provide a more complete description. We will discuss two measures of variability, the range and the standard deviation, which provide more specific statistics than such general terms as *small*, *large*, *great*, or *little*.

Range. The **range** is simply the numerical difference between the highest and lowest scores in the distribution. It is calculated by subtracting the lowest score from the highest score. The range is a crude measure of dispersion because it is based on only two scores in the distribution, and it does not tell us anything about the degree of cluster. The range is particularly misleading in highly skewed distributions.

Range: Difference between the highest and lowest scores.

Standard Deviation. The measure of variability used most often in research is the **standard deviation,** a statistic that indicates the average distance of the

Standard deviation: Average distance of the scores from the mean.

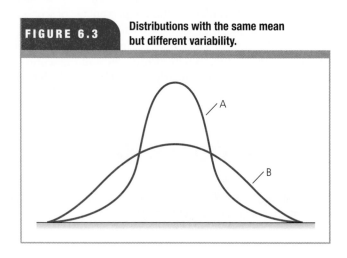

FIGURE 6.3 Distributions with the same mean but different variability.

scores from the mean of the distribution. It tells us, in other words, the "average" variability of the scores. It is determined by first calculating the distance of each score from the mean. These are the *deviation* scores, which tell us how much each score deviates, or differs, from the mean. Then the deviation scores are averaged to determine a number that is called the standard deviation. In one sense, then, the standard deviation can be thought of as the *average deviation*.

For any set of scores, the standard deviation will be unique to the distribution of the scores. Thus, the standard deviation of one distribution may be .72; for another distribution, 16; and for yet another, 35. Once the standard deviation is computed, it is reported by indicating that 1 standard deviation equals a number; for example, 1 SD = 12.7, or 1 SD = 3.25. (Two other symbols are also used for standard deviation: s, which indicates the sample standard deviation, and the lowercase Greek letter sigma, σ, which indicates the population standard deviation.)

The standard deviation is particularly useful because of its relationship to the normal distribution. In a normal distribution, a specific percentage of scores falls within each standard deviation from the mean. For example, if the mean of a distribution is 40 and the standard deviation is 10, we know that about 34% of the scores of the distribution fall between 40 and 50. Similarly, we know that about 34% of the scores fall between 30 and 40. Thus, in normal distributions, regardless of the values of the scores, we know that about 68% of the scores fall between -1 and $+1$ SD (see Figure 6.4). Furthermore, we know that about 14% of the scores fall between $+1$ and $+2$ SD and between -1 and -2 SD, and that about 2% of the scores fall between $+2$ and $+3$ SD and between -2 and -3 SD. These properties of the normal curve and standard deviation, illustrated in Figure 6.4, allow researchers to compare distributions by knowing the standard deviations. Two distributions may have similar means, but if one has a standard deviation of 36 and the other 8, the former is far more variable. The square of the standard deviation is called the *variance*, though this term is also used more generally to mean dispersion or spread of scores.

Standard deviation is related to another important term in measurement, *percentile rank*. The **percentile rank** indicates the percentage of scores at or below a particular score. For example, if 17 is at the 64th percentile, 64% of the scores in the distribution are the same or lower than 17. In a normal distribution, a score at $+1$ SD is at the 84th percentile. In other words, 84% of the scores in a normal distribution are at or below $+1$ SD. Similarly, -1 SD is at the 16th percentile, $+2$ SD is at the 98th percentile, and -2 SD is at the 2nd percentile (percentiles for the normal curve are indicated as cumulative percentages in Figure 6.4).

Percentile rank:
Percentage of scores at or below a specified score.

INTERNET CONNECTION

For more information about descriptive statistics, with some application problems presented in a very effective manner, go to the Websites **www.mste.uiuc.edu/hill/dstat/dstat.html** and **http://www.socialresearchmethods.net/kb/statdesc.htm.**

FIGURE 6.4	Normal probability curve.

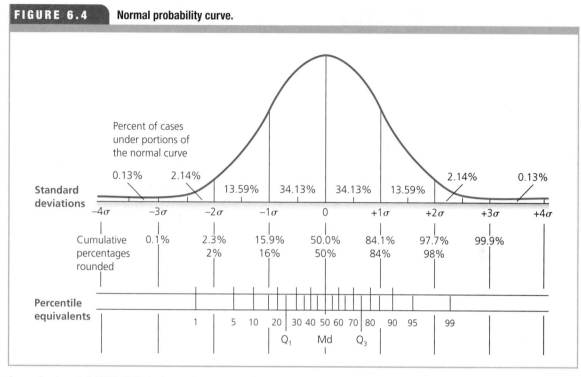

Correlation

Frequency distributions, measures of central tendency, and measures of variability are used to summarize characteristics of one variable. However, in many instances it is useful to know the degree to which the scores of two or more variables are related. A **correlation** is a measure of the relationship between two variables. A relationship means that the values of the variables vary together, that is, that the value of one variable can be predicted by knowing the value of the other. For example, we would expect that there is a relationship between age and weight, that by knowing a person's age we can predict, in general, the person's weight. Thus, we can predict that most 10-year-olds weigh more than most 3-year-olds. In this case we have a **positive correlation,** in which an increase in one variable is accompanied by an increase in the other variable. This is also called a *direct* relationship. A positive correlation is illustrated graphically in the form of a *scatterplot* for age and weight in Figure 6.5. The values of each variable are rank ordered, and the intersections of the two scores for each subject are plotted in the graph (see Figure 6.6). Scatterplots are useful in identifying scores that lie outside the overall pattern, such as point I in Figure 6.5, and indicate whether the relationship is linear or curvilinear. Correlation is indicated numerically by the

Correlation: Measure of relationship between two or more quantitative variables.

Positive correlation: Increases in one variable accompanied by increases in the other variable.

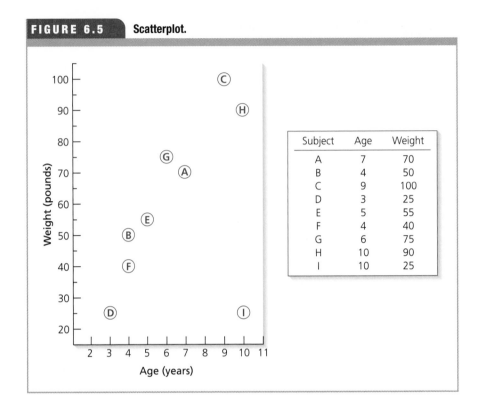

FIGURE 6.5   Scatterplot.

Subject	Age	Weight
A	7	70
B	4	50
C	9	100
D	3	25
E	5	55
F	4	40
G	6	75
H	10	90
I	10	25

correlation coefficient. Although there are several types of correlation coefficients, the one you will encounter most is the Pearson product moment coefficient. This type of correlation assumes a linear relationship between two interval or ordinal scale variables. Thus, if a scatterplot reveals that the correlation is curvilinear and the Pearson correlation coefficient is used, the calculated correlation will be less than the true relationship because of the assumption of linearity.

Correlation coefficient: Number between −1 and +1 that indicates the direction and strength of the relationship.

A **correlation coefficient,** or *bivariate* correlation, is a number between −1 and +1 that indicates the direction and strength of the relationship between two variables. The correlation coefficient is calculated by a formula and is reported as $r = .45$, $r = -.78$, $r = .03$, and so on. A positive correlation coefficient will have a positive value; for example, $r = .17$ or $r = .69$. The strength, or magnitude, of the relationship is the degree to which the variables are related. For a positive correlation the strength increases as the number increases. Hence a correlation of .85 is stronger than a correlation of .53, which is stronger than .37. In general, correlations between .10 and .30 are referred to as small or low positive relationships, .40 to .60 as moderate positive relationships, and .70 and above as high positive relationships.

Negative correlation: Increases in one variable accompanied by decreases in the other variable.

A **negative correlation** indicates that as one variable increases, the other variable decreases. This is also referred to as an *inverse* relationship. Examples of negative correlations include the relationship between absenteeism and achievement

FIGURE 6.6   Scatterplots of different correlations.

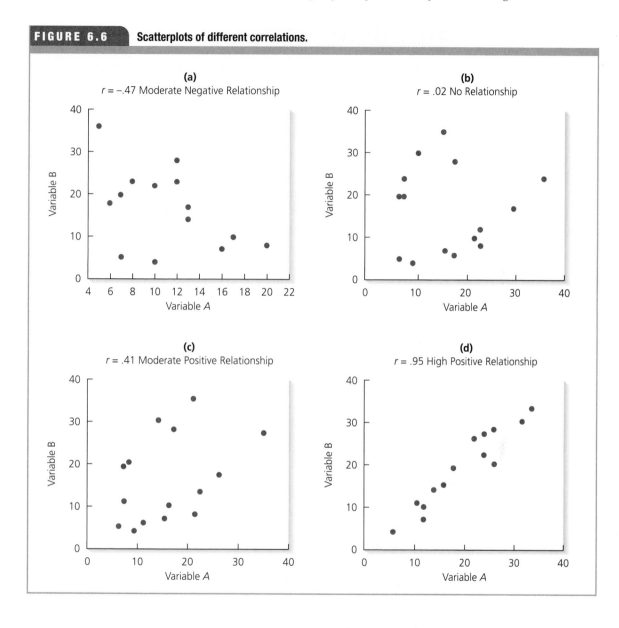

and between amount of practice and number of errors in tennis. A negative correlation coefficient always has a negative sign (–). The strength of a negative relationship increases as the absolute value of the correlation increases. Thus, a correlation of −.75 is a stronger relationship than −.52. In other words, the strength of any relationship is independent of its direction. A correlation of −.63 indicates a stronger relationship than .35. Correlations between −.10 and −.30 are considered small; between −.40 and −.60, moderate; and between −.70 and −1.0, high. Correlations between −.10 and .10 generally indicate no relationship.

Author Reflection   *The more I learn about statistics the more I realize that simple descriptive indices such as mean and standard deviation are really important in understanding what numerical data tell us about something. These simple statistics not only form the foundation for other statistical procedures, they give us the best direct measure. They are essential for appropriate interpretations, so learn them well and be able to apply them.*

VALIDITY *of* MEASUREMENT

It has been noted that the credibility of research depends on quality measurement. If the measurement is not sound, the results are not useful. In this section, we will discuss the first of two technical characteristics of measurement used to judge overall quality and appropriateness—validity. The second important characteristic, reliability, will be discussed in the next section.

What Is Validity?

Until recently, validity was defined as the degree to which an instrument measures what it says it measures or purports to measure. The emphasis was on judging the extent to which a test or questionnaire was valid. A more contemporary definition emphasizes the use of test results rather than the test itself: **Validity** is an overall evaluation of the extent to which theory and empirical evidence support interpretations that are implied in given uses of the scores. In other words, validity is a judgment of the appropriateness of a measure for the specific inferences or decisions that result from the scores generated by the measure. It is the *inference* that is valid or invalid, not the measure. The same instrument can be valid in one circumstance or for one use and invalid for another. For example, tests of beginning teacher competency may be valid for judging how much a prospective teacher knows and understands about classroom management, child development, learning, motivation, and curriculum, but it may be invalid as a predictor of teaching effectiveness. Similarly, most standardized achievement tests are not valid for evaluating the effectiveness of a specific curriculum in a specific school because the test was constructed to measure a broad range of curricula, not a specific one. Important characteristics of validity are summarized in Table 6.2.

Validity: The extent to which inferences are appropriate and meaningful.

TABLE 6.2	Characteristics of Validity

1. Validity refers to the *appropriateness* of the interpretation of the results, not to the procedure or measure itself. Saying "the validity of the test" is not as correct as saying "the validity of the inference."

2. Validity is a *matter of degree;* it does not exist on an all-or-none basis.

3. Validity is *specific* to some particular use or interpretation. No measure is valid for all uses or purposes. Each interpretation may have a different degree of validity.

4. Validity is a *unitary concept.* It is a single concept that is based on accumulating and integrating different types of evidence. There are not different types of validity.

5. Validity involves *an overall evaluative judgment.* Your professional judgment, given the evidence presented and the nature of the interpretation, is needed to determine the extent to which the inference is valid.

Source: Adapted from Linn & Miller (2005).

Sources of Validity Evidence

Validity is established by presenting evidence that the inferences are appropriate. There are five major sources of evidence, each based on a different kind of logic and data: test content, internal structure, relations to other variables, response processes, and consequences of testing. Each source represents a different type of evidence. Under ideal conditions the nature of evidence used is consistent with the use of the results to provide support for the intended interpretation of the scores. Establishing sound validity involves an integration of information from these different types of evidence to show that the intended interpretation of the scores is appropriate and reasonable. We will consider the first three types of evidence since they are most closely related to conducting and reporting research.

Evidence Based on Test Content. In general, **evidence based on test content** demonstrates the extent to which the sample of items or questions in the instrument is representative of some appropriate universe or domain of content or tasks. This type of evidence is usually accumulated by having experts examine the contents of the instrument and indicate the degree to which they measure predetermined criteria or objectives. Experts are also used to judge the relative criticality, or importance, of various parts of the instrument. For example, to gather evidence for a test of knowledge for prospective teachers, it is necessary to have experts examine the items and judge their representativeness (e.g., is a question about Piaget representative of what needs to be known about child development?) and whether the percentage of the test devoted to different topics is appropriate (e.g., 20% of the test is on classroom management, but maybe it should be 40%). Evidence based on test content is essential for achievement tests. Also, the domain or universe that is represented should be appropriate to the intended use of the results.

Evidence based on test content: Representative sample of larger domain.

Unfortunately, evidence based on test content for validity is often not reported in research articles, usually because there is no systematic effort to obtain such evidence for locally devised instruments; when standardized instruments are used, the reader must refer to previous research, reviews of the instrument, or technical manuals.

EXAMPLE | **Content-Related Evidence for Validity**

"Content-related evidence for validity for the initial draft of 47 items was strengthened by asking 15 teachers to review the items for clarity and completeness of covering most, if not all, assessment and grading practices used." (McMillan, J. H. (2001). Secondary teachers' classroom assessment and grading practices. *Educational Measurement: Issues and Practice, 20*(1), p. 23)

Evidence based on internal structure: Showing item relationships.

Evidence Based on Internal Structure. The *internal structure* of an instrument refers to how items are related to each other and how different parts of an instrument are related. **Evidence based on internal structure** is provided when the relationships between items and parts of the instrument are empirically consistent with the theory or intended use of the scores. Thus, if a measure of self-concept posits several "types" of self-concept (e.g., academic, social, athletic), then the items measuring the academic component should be strongly related to each other and not as highly related to the other components. In the following example the authors summarize data that support the internal structure of students' domain-specific (history and mathematics) epistemological beliefs (i.e., importance and certainty of knowledge). Data supported six distinct factors, and results were analyzed using these subscales.

EXAMPLE | **Evidence Based on Internal Structure**

"Confirmatory factor analyses of these data provided support for the domain specificity and multidimensionality of students' beliefs. . . . There were six distinct epistemological belief factors (three per domain) that represented students' beliefs with respect to the structure, stability, and source of knowledge of history and of mathematics." (Buehl, M. M., & Alexander, P. A. (2005). Motivation and performance differences in students' domain-specific epistemological belief profiles. *American Educational Research Journal, 42*(4), p. 705)

Evidence Based on Relations to Other Variables. The most common way that validity of interpretations is established is by showing how scores from a given measure relate to similar as well as different traits. There are several ways this can be done. When scores from one instrument correlate highly with scores from another measure of the same trait, we have what is called *convergent* evidence. Note in the following example how convergent data are used as evidence of "construct validity," a term you may encounter in reading research.

The term *construct validity* was used prior to the current categories of validity evidence. In this example, scores from the Test of Early Reading Ability were correlated to another measure of reading ability.

Discriminant evidence exists when the scores do not correlate highly with scores from an instrument that measures something different. Thus, we would expect that scores from a measure of self-concept would correlate highly with other measures of self-concept and show less correlation to related but different traits such as anxiety and academic performance.

EXAMPLE | **Evidence Based on Relations to Other Variables**

"The authors reported adequate construct validity including significant correlations (.61) with performance on the Basic Skills Inventory-Diagnostic Reading Subtest." (Sacks, C. H., & Mergendoller, J. R. (1997). The relationship between teachers' theoretical orientation toward reading and student outcomes in kindergarten children with different initial reading abilities. *American Educational Research Journal, 34*(4), p. 725)

Another approach to gathering **evidence based on relations to other variables** pertains to the extent to which the test scores or measures predict performance on a criterion measure (test-criterion relationships). Two approaches are used to obtain test-criterion evidence: predictive and concurrent. With predictive evidence, the criterion is measured at a time in the future, after the instrument has been administered. The evidence pertains to how well the earlier measure can predict the criterion behavior or performance. For instance, in gathering evidence on a new measure to select applicants for leadership positions, the scores on the instrument would be correlated with future leadership behavior. If persons who scored low on the test turned out to be poor leaders and those who scored high were good leaders, predictive test-criterion evidence would be obtained. With concurrent evidence, the instrument and the criterion are given at about the same time. Criterion-related evidence is often reported in research by indicating that a measure correlates with criteria that assess the same thing. For example, in the following excerpt from a published study on the mediating role of self-efficacy in the relationship between homework practices and achievement, the authors correlated student self-reports of self-efficacy with teacher ratings of self-regulation gathered several weeks after the student self-reports.

> **Evidence based on relations to other variables:** Showing relationships to external variables.

EXAMPLE | **Predictive Evidence Based on Relations to Other Variables**

"To assess the predictive validity of the SELF [Self-Efficacy for Learning Form] . . . the English teacher for each grade level . . . was asked to rate each student's self-regulation of learning by a 12-point scale. . . . The teacher ratings were recorded at a later point during the semester after homework and self-belief measures were administered . . . the correlation between this teacher rating measure of self-regulation and the student self-efficacy for learning measure was .72, indicating a significant degree of predictive validity for the self-efficacy scale." (Zimmerman, B. J., & Kitsantas, A. (2005). Homework practices and academic achievement: The mediating role of self-efficacy and perceived responsibility beliefs. *Contemporary Educational Psychology, 30*(4), p. 404)

Often researchers use several types of evidence for validity, which provides a stronger result than what is indicated with a single approach. Note how this is illustrated in the following study of resourcefulness and persistence in adult autonomous learning.

EXAMPLE | **Use of Several Types of Evidence for Validity**

"Carr and Derrick's respective arguments supporting the validity of their respective instruments were based on the development of items with specific theoretical foundations (i.e., construct validity), a review by researchers whose work was pivotal to the development of these theories (i.e., face validity), and the results of principal components analyses performed to support the factor structure of each subscale (i.e., content validity)." (Ponton, M. K., Derrick, M. G., & Carr, P. B. (2005). The relationship between resourcefulness and persistence in adult autonomous learning. *Adult Education Quarterly, 55*(2), p. 119)

Effect of Validity on Research

Since validity implies proper use of the information that is gathered through measurement, it is necessary for both the investigators and consumers of the research to judge the degree of validity that is present, based on available evidence. In this sense, validity is a matter of degree and is not an all-or-none proposition. The investigators need to show that for the specific inferences they made in their study, there is evidence that validity exists. Consumers, however, may have their own uses in mind, and therefore need to base their own judgments on how they intend to use the results.

Does this suggest that evidence for validity must be established for each research situation and possible use? Such a requirement would add a considerable amount of data collection and analysis to each study. In practice, it is necessary to generalize from other studies and research that the intended interpretation and use are valid. This is one reason why established instruments, for which some evidence on validity has probably accumulated, usually provide more credible measurement. Some researchers mistakenly believe, however, that because an instrument is established, it is valid.

Locally devised instruments, with little or no history of use or reviews by others, need to be evaluated with more care. Typically, when researchers use new instruments, greater attention is paid to gathering evidence for validity, and this evidence is reported as part of the research. Consumers should be especially wary of research in which new instruments are used and evidence for validity is not presented. If an instrument has specific procedures for administration—for example, qualifications of the person who administers it, directions, and time frame—the results are valid only if these procedures have been followed. For instance, some instruments are appropriate for certain ages, but use with other ages would be invalid.

Validity should be established before the data to be analyzed in the research are collected. This is a major reason for a pilot test of the instrument and procedures for administering it. The evidence should be consistent with the use of the results. For example, if the results will be used to determine which students have mastered a body of knowledge, evidence based on test content is necessary. If a theory related to the development of cognitive style is being examined, evidence based on relations with other variables is needed.

Although validity is a key concept in research, you will find a great deal of variability in the amount of information given in articles and research reports. It is not uncommon to find that there is no mention of validity. However, the most credible and usable research is reported by investigators who understand the importance of validity, and explicitly address it.

INTERNET CONNECTION

For more complete coverage of validity and reliability, see the recently revised *Standards for Educational and Psychological Testing.* A description with information about how to order a copy can be found at **www.aera.net/publications/?id=1407.**

RELIABILITY *of* MEASUREMENT

An essential concept in understanding research is knowing that there is never a perfect indication of the trait, skill, knowledge, attitude, or whatever is being assessed. There is always error in measurement, and this error must be taken into consideration. It is not a question of whether error exists, only what type and how much. **Reliability** is the extent to which participant and/or rater scores are free from error. If a measure has high reliability, there is relatively little error in the scores, and if there is low reliability, there is a great amount of error.

Reliability: Consistency of scores.

Many factors contribute to the imperfect nature of measurement. Questions may be ambiguous, or students may not be trying hard, may be fatigued or sick, may be unfamiliar with the types of questions asked, or may simply guess incorrectly on many items. Sources of measurement error are listed in Table 6.3. Whatever the reasons, students will answer somewhat differently on one occasion than on another or on questions designed to measure the same thing. If possible, the researcher needs to indicate in specific, quantifiable terms the degree of error that exists.

TABLE 6.3	Sources of Measurement Error
Sources Associated with Test Construction and Administration	**Sources Associated with the Subject**
Observer differences	Test anxiety
Changes in scoring	Reactions to specific items
Changes in directions	Illness
Interrupted testing session	Motivation
Race of test administrator	Mood
When the test is taken	Fatigue
Sampling of items	Luck
Ambiguity in wording	Attitudes
Misunderstood directions	Test-taking skills (test wiseness)
Effect of heat, lighting, ventilation of room	Reading ability

Types of Reliability

An estimate of the amount of error in measurement is determined empirically through several types of procedures. As with validity, different types of evidence are used to indicate the error. These are called estimates of reliability. Each estimate measures certain kinds of errors. The estimates are reported in the form of a reliability coefficient, which is a correlation statistic that ranges between .00 and .99. If the correlation coefficient is high, say .78 or .85, the reliability is said to be high or good. Correlation coefficients below .60 generally indicate inadequate or at least weak reliability.

A more recent trend in estimating reliability, called *generalizability theory*, may be used. In this approach both systematic and random errors are included to give a more realistic estimate. Using the more traditional types, such as those found in most research articles, the tendency is to underestimate the amount of error. Regardless of the approach, error always refers to the scores received. Like validity, reliability is not a characteristic of a test or other instrument. Rather than saying "the reliability of the instrument was adequate," it would be more accurate to say, "the reliability of the scores was adequate."

We will consider five specific estimates of reliability: stability, equivalence, equivalence and stability, internal consistency, and agreement.

Stability: Measured by giving the same instrument twice.

Stability. A **stability** estimate of reliability is obtained by administering one measure to one group of individuals, waiting a specified period of time, and then readministering the same instrument to the same group. The correlation of the two sets of scores is then calculated. This type of estimate is also called *test-retest* reliability. What is being measured is the consistency of the subjects' performance over time. If the trait or skill that is being measured changes between the first and second administration, the correlation, and the reliability, will be low. Consequently, stability estimates should not be used with unstable traits such as mood, and when it is used, any changes that may have occurred between the administrations should be noted. The value of the correlation will also vary with the length of time between administrations. Other things being equal, a longer time interval will result in a lower correlation. It is therefore best to report the time interval with the correlation coefficient. On the other hand, if the interval is too short, subjects may remember their answers and simply reproduce them, making the reliability higher than it should be.

Stability estimates are used for many aptitude tests, tests in the psychomotor domain, and some achievement tests. As illustrated in the following examples, stability estimates are written in a straightforward manner, so they are easy to identify.

EXAMPLE | **Stability Estimate of Reliability**

"Test-retest reliability was examined using alternate forms on a sample of 49 7-, 8-, and 9-year-olds. The obtained correlation was .79." (Sacks, C. H., & Mergendoller, J. R. (1997). The relationship between teachers' theoretical orientation toward reading and student outcomes in kindergarten children with different initial reading abilities. *American Educational Research Journal, 34*(4), p. 725)

Equivalence. A measure of **equivalence** is obtained by administering two forms of the same test to one group of individuals and then correlating the scores from the two administrations. Each form of the test should be equivalent in content, mean, and standard deviation, although the specific questions are different. This type of reliability estimate is often used in research on achievement when both a pretest, given before a treatment, and a posttest, given after a treatment, are administered to show how much the achievement of the subjects changed. Rather than giving the same test twice, the researcher gives alternate but equal tests.

> Equivalence: Correlation of two forms of the same test.

Equivalence and Stability. An **equivalence and stability** estimate is obtained by administering one form of an instrument and then a second form after a time interval to the same group of individuals. This method combines equivalence (alternate forms) with stability (time interval). Although this is the most stringent type of reliability estimate, it is seldom employed. It is especially useful when researchers are concerned with long-range prediction (the strength of stability) and need to generalize to a large domain of knowledge or aptitude (the strength of equivalence).

> Equivalence and stability: Two forms given at different times.

Internal consistency: Correlation of items measuring the same trait.

Internal Consistency. **Internal consistency,** the most widely used estimate of reliability, indicates the degree to which subjects' answers to items measuring the same trait are consistent. Unlike the other estimates, only one form of an instrument is given once to one group of individuals. There are three common types of internal consistency estimates: *split-half, Kuder-Richardson,* and *Coefficient Alpha (Cronbach Alpha).* In split-half reliability the items in a test are divided into equal halves, and the scores of each person on the two halves are correlated for the reliability coefficient. The Kuder-Richardson method is used in tests for which there is a right and wrong answer to each item. It avoids problems of the split-half technique, such as deciding how to divide the test into equal halves, by calculating the average of all the correlations that could be obtained from all possible split-half estimates. This method is usually indicated as KR20 or KR21. The Coefficient Alpha method is similar to the KR20 but is used with instruments that contain a range of possible answers for each item, such as agree-disagree, that constitute a scale rather than right/wrong scoring.

Internal consistency is used when the purpose of an instrument is to measure a single trait. To allow calculation of the correlation, several items must measure the same thing. Thus, in some instruments, it seems as if the same questions are being asked over and over. To have internal consistency, a general rule of thumb is that there must be at least five questions about the same thing. In instruments in which there are subscales or subtests, a separate measure of internal consistency should be reported for each subscale. Of all the estimates, internal consistency is easiest to obtain and usually gives the highest reliability.

As shown in the following examples, the accepted convention in reporting internal consistency is simply to state the type of method used and to indicate the correlations.

EXAMPLE | **Internal Consistency Estimate of Reliability**

"A three-part pre-tested instrument with 43 items was used to collect the research data. Section A with seven (7) items collected demographic data. This part of the instrument was designed by the researchers. Section B with 16 items consisted of a 6-point Likert-type attitude toward inclusive education scale (1SD, 2D, 3 Somewhat disagree, 4 Somewhat Agree, 5A, 6SA). This instrument was adopted from Wilczenski (1992). The alpha reliability for this scale was .86. . . . Section C contained the 21-item 4-point Likert-type concerns about inclusive education scale (1—Not at all concerned, 2—A little concerned, 3—Very concerned, 4—Extremely concerned). The scale's alpha reliability was 0.88." (Bradshaw, L., & Mundia, L. (2006). Attitudes to and concerns about inclusive education: Bruneian inservice and preservice teachers. *International Journal of Special Education, 21*(1), p. 37)

"Internal consistency coefficient for the scales in the instrument were as follows (Cronbach's alpha): Technology Integration Scale = .95; Exploration subscale = .84; Experimentation subscale = .93, Adoption subscale = .95, Integration subscale = .92, Barriers scale = .85, and Effectiveness scale = .91." (Kotrlik, J. W., & Redmann, D. H. (2005). Extent of technology integration in instruction by adult basic education teachers. *Adult Education Quarterly, 55*(3), p. 209)

Agreement. There are three situations in which there is some type of *coefficient of agreement*, expressed as either a correlation or as a percentage of agreement. The first situation concerns establishing the reliability of ratings. The usual procedure is to assess the extent to which different raters agree on what they observe or score. That is, when two or more raters independently observe the same behavior, will they record it in the same way? Will two raters scoring an essay give the same score? Typically, raters are trained until they reach a desired level of agreement. A statistic termed *kappa* is used to report the results, rather than a bivariate correlation.

EXAMPLE | **Interrater Reliability**

"There were four observers. They were all experienced researchers who were familiar with working in schools and able to explain the research and put teachers and pupils at their ease. The basic aim was to avoid passing judgments and to use the schedule as intended. All observers had initial training in which they were provided with an observation manual of categories, conventions, and procedures, as well as tips acquired during previous use. Conventions were discussed, and there was work on videotapes, accompanied by periodic checks of accuracy and understanding of how to use categories. This was followed by at least a day's observation in a class not involved in the study and then a follow-up training session to discuss field visits and iron out difficulties. . . . Reliability coefficients for the main sets of mutually exclusive categories were high. Setting; subject; teacher-child social setting, child role, teacher content; and child-to-teacher child contribution, child content, and not interaction all had reliability coefficients (kappas) greater than 0.80. Kappa for child-child content was 0.77." (Blatchford, P., Bassett, P., & Brown, P. (2005). Teachers' and pupils' behavior in large and small classes: A systematic observation study of pupils aged 10 and 11 years. *Journal of Educational Psychology, 97*(3), p. 459)

"Observers were trained for approximately 6 weeks using videotaped samples of instruction . . . data collectors' scores were compared with a master file for each videotape, and observers were required to obtain at least a .80 agreement estimate across codes for three consecutive sessions before beginning live practice observations. . . . Interobserver agreement was assessed during 19% of the sessions. Percentage scores were calculated by dividing total agreements by agreements plus disagreements multiplied by 100. The interobserver agreement estimate across all variables was 82.4%." (Sutherland, K. S., & Wehby, J. H. (2001). The effect of self evaluation on teaching behavior in classrooms for students with emotional and behavioral disorders. *The Journal of Special Education, 35,* pp. 163, 165)

The second situation involves an insufficient number of items on an instrument measuring a single trait to compute an internal consistency estimate. In this circumstance, the researcher can use a method similar to stability by giving the instrument to the same group of individuals twice. If there are only a few persons, say 15 to 20, the researcher can compute the percentage of responses that are the same rather than a correlation coefficient. This alternative is common in studies in which a new instrument has been developed and there has not been an opportunity to use a large number of individuals in a pilot test.

EXAMPLE | **Agreement Estimate for Reliability**

"Reliability was initially assessed by asking the teachers in the second pilot test to retake the questionnaire after a 4-week interval. Coefficients of agreement were calculated by examining the percentage of matches of the items. Items that showed an exact match of less than 60% were deleted or combined with other items. . . . The average exact match for the items was 48% of the teachers; 89% of the matches were within 1 point on the 6-point scale." (McMillan, J. H. (2001). Secondary teachers' classroom assessment and grading practices. *Educational Measurement: Issues and Practice, 20,* p. 23)

"Interrater agreement for the coding of the transcripts . . . was calculated by dividing the total number of agreements by the total number of agreements plus disagreements, and multiplying by 100, as well as by using Cohen's (1960) kappa value. The interrater agreement across the 19 categories was 88% (median = 86%, range = 67%–96%), Cohen's kappa was .86 (median = .84, range = .66–.95). . . . According to Fleiss's (1981) general benchmark, a kappa value between .40 and .75 can be interpreted as intermediate to good, and a value above .75 can be considered excellent." (Veenman, S., Denessen, E., van den Akker, A., & vander Rijt, J. (2005). Effects of a cooperative learning program on the elaborations of students during help seeking and help giving. *American Educational Research Journal, 42*(1), p. 128–129)

Third, many achievement tests result in a skewed distribution of scores (e.g., criterion-referenced tests, discussed in Chapter 7). With highly skewed distributions it is difficult to obtain a high correlation, and thus, most estimates of reliability would be low. With these types of tests, a percentage of agreement is often used to show the number of individuals who would be classified in the same way on a second test as they were on the first. Generally, it is the consistency of the decision that would be made as a result of the test rather than the scores themselves that is used to estimate reliability.

These five methods for estimating reliability are compared in Table 6.4 according to three criteria—the number of forms of the instrument, when the instruments are administered to gather the evidence, and the type of statistic used to report reliability. For internal consistency only one form is given once; for stability the same form is given twice. Agreement estimates are done at one time but involve two or more raters.

Effect of Reliability on Research

As with validity, reliability is best be established *before* the research is undertaken, and also reported for subject scores from the study. The type of reliability should

TABLE 6.4	Procedures for Estimating Reliability[1]		
	Time 1	**Time 2**	**Statistic**
Stability	A	A	Bivariate correlation
Equivalence	A B		Bivariate correlation
Equivalence and Stability	A	B	Bivariate correlation
Internal Consistency	A		Bivariate correlation
Agreement	R1 R2		Percentage agreement, kappa

[1]A and B refer to different forms of the same test; R1 and R2 refer to rater 1 and rater 2.

be consistent with the use of the results. If you wish to use the results for prediction or selection for special programs, stability estimates of reliability are necessary. If you are interested in programs to change attitudes or values, internal consistency estimates are needed. Reliability should also be established with individuals who are similar to the subjects in the research. If previous studies report good reliability with middle school students and you intend to use the results with elementary school students, the reliability may not be adequate. Usually, reliability is reported with the subjects used in the study.

You will read some research in which reliability is not addressed, yet the results of the research show what are called "significant differences." This is an interesting situation in research because it is more difficult to find differences between groups with instruments that have low reliability. It is as if the differences were observed despite what may have been low reliability. Of course it is possible that the scores were reliable, even though no reliability estimates were reported. This situation is likely to occur in research in which the subjects are responding to questions so straightforward and simple that reliability is assumed. In much research, the subjects report information such as age, sex, income, time spent studying, occupation, and other questions that are relatively straightforward. For these types of data, statistical estimates of reliability are generally not needed.

Several conditions affect reliability. One is the length of a test or questionnaire: A longer test is more reliable than a shorter one. Reliability is also a function of the heterogeneity of the group. It is greater for groups that are more heterogeneous on the trait that is being measured. Conversely, the more homogeneous the subjects, the lower the reliability. Reliability is also a function of the nature of the trait that is being measured. Some variables, such as most measures of achievement, have high reliabilities, whereas measures of personality have lower reliabilities. Consequently, a reliability of .80 or above is generally expected for achievement variables, whereas estimates of .65 are usually acceptable for measuring personality traits. By comparison, then, a personality instrument reporting a reliability coefficient of .90 would be judged excellent, and an achievement test with a reliability of .70 would be seen as weak. A much higher reliability is needed if the results will be used to make decisions about individuals. Studies of groups can tolerate a lower reliability, sometimes as low as .50 in exploratory research. Measures of young children are usually less reliable than those of older subjects.

To enhance reliability, it is best to establish standard conditions of data collection. All subjects should be given the same directions, have the same time frame in which to answer questions at the same time during the day, and so on. Error is often increased if different individuals administer the instruments. It is important to know if there are any unusual circumstances during data collection since these may affect reliability. The instrument needs to be appropriate in reading level and language to be reliable, and subjects must be properly motivated to answer the questions. In some research, it is difficult to get subjects to be serious, for instance, when students are asked to take achievement tests that have no implications for them. Reliability can also suffer when subjects are asked to complete several instruments over a long period of time. Usually an hour is about all any of us can tolerate, and for younger children less than half an hour is the maximum. If several instruments are given at the same time, the order of their administration should not be the same for all subjects. Some subjects should answer one instrument first, and other subjects should answer the same instrument last. This is called *counterbalancing* the instruments.

Finally, reliability is a necessary condition for validity. That is, scores cannot be valid unless they are reliable. However, a reliable score is not necessarily valid. You can obtain a very reliable score of the length of your big toe, but that would not be valid as an estimate of your intelligence!

STUDY QUESTIONS

1. How is measurement different from evaluation and assessment?
2. Why is measurement important in determining the quality of educational research?
3. What is the purpose of different scales of measurement?
4. What is the difference between nominal and interval scales of measurement?
5. In what ways are descriptive statistics useful in research?
6. Give some examples of different types of frequency distributions.
7. What are the common shapes of frequency distributions?
8. What are the special properties of a normal distribution?
9. In what ways are the mode, median, and mean different?
10. Explain the concept of standard deviation. Why is it important for research?
11. What is the relationship between the standard deviation and percentile rank?
12. Why is a scatterplot important in examining relationships?
13. Give some examples of positive and negative correlations.
14. Define validity and reliability. How are they related?
15. What types of evidence are used for validity?
16. Describe some factors that should be considered when evaluating validity.

17. What are the types of reliability?

18. How is error in measurement related to reliability correlation coefficients?

19. In what ways can different factors affect reliability?

 SAMPLE TEST QUESTIONS

See this text's Companion Website at **www.ablongman.com/mcmillan5e** for sample test questions and answers.

---

mylabschool *Where the classroom comes to life!* **RESEARCH NAVIGATOR™ ACTIVITIES**

1. In a study that describes the teaching styles of instructors providing distance education (AN 12920076), take the frequency distribution data and construct a histogram. Does the histogram suggest a skewed distribution? From the data presented in Table 2, construct a scatterplot of the standard deviations and sample sizes. What does this suggest about the relationship between standard deviation and size of the sample?

2. Accession Number 22065346 will take you to an article that investigates the effects of an intervention of students' self-esteem. An established measure of self-esteem is used, the Coopersmith Self-Esteem Inventory. Evaluate the evidence for both reliability and validity presented in the article. Is it sufficient for the use of the instrument for this specific population and context? What additional information would strengthen the evidence?

Chapter 7

Types *of* Educational Measures

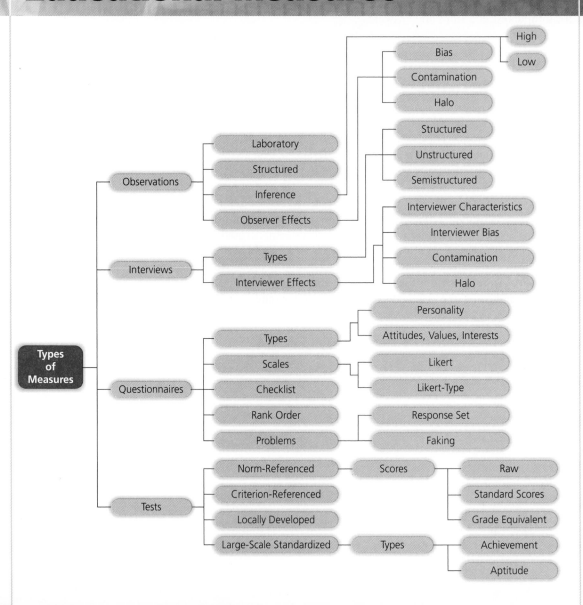

CHAPTER ROAD MAP

Researchers select from a large number of educational measures/instruments to gather data. The measure selected depends on the research problem, the advantages and disadvantages of each type of measure, and practical constraints. As a consumer of research, it is important for you to understand the strengths and weaknesses of different approaches to measurement, how the results of different kinds of instruments should be interpreted, and how the nature of measurement influences results and conclusions. This chapter reviews the most common types of educational measures with an emphasis on the interpretation and use of scores. Each technique has unique characteristics that affect the way validity and reliability are established and evaluated.

As a result of studying this chapter, you will:

- Understand the different kinds of educational tests that are used for research
- Understand the difference between norm-referenced and criterion-referenced test interpretations
- Understand how questionnaires are designed and used to measure attitudes, values, and interests
- Understand how observations are used to record behavior
- Understand how interviews are used to gather information
- Learn how to locate and evaluate existing measures

CLASSIFYING EDUCATIONAL MEASURES

Educational measures can be classified in three ways. One major distinction is between *cognitive* and *noncognitive* measures. Cognitive measures focus on what a person knows or is able to do mentally. They include achievement and aptitude tests, measures of critical and creative thinking, and cognitive style. Noncognitive measures include personality, attitude, value, and interest inventories. These instruments require some degree of cognitive processing, but the emphasis is on affective, or emotional, "feelings" and intuitions.

A second major factor in distinguishing educational measures is whether the instrument is commercially developed (often referred to as "off the shelf") or developed locally by the researcher ("home grown"). Most commercially prepared instruments will have more extensive use, information on reliability and validity, and specific directions for administration and scoring. Locally developed instruments are often better suited to applied research but may lack technical qualities. Both cognitive and noncognitive instruments may be either commercially prepared or locally developed.

A third important difference in educational measures is whether the subject is answering questions directly or the information is gathered without direct interaction with the subjects. Most tests, questionnaires, and interviews rely on information provided by the subjects. They are often called "self-report" instruments.

Other measures, such as many observational ones, do not require subjects' responses to specific questions.

The first type of measure we'll examine is cognitive tests. Given the current emphasis on accountability and high-stakes testing of student performance, beginning here is appropriate. It seems that studies that include such tests as dependent variables are becoming ubiquitous.

TESTS

Test: Standard questions of cognitive knowledge or skills.

A **test** is an instrument that requires subjects to complete a cognitive task by responding to a standard set of questions. The answers to the questions are summarized to obtain a numerical value that represents a cognitive characteristic of the subjects. All tests measure performance at the time the test is given. Tests differ in how the results are used, in their development, and in the types of validity and reliability that are established. The major differentiating characteristics are whether tests have norm- or criterion-referenced interpretations, whether they are measuring achievement or aptitude, and whether they are standardized or locally developed.

Norm- and Criterion-Referenced Interpretations

A critical aspect of testing is the interpretation of the results. When a score is obtained, what does it convey? How do you interpret it? What does it mean, for example, when the average score is 70% correct? Measurement specialists have identified two approaches to interpretation to derive accurate meaning from the scores.

Norm-referenced: Interpretations that compare subjects with others.

In **norm-referenced** interpretation, individual scores are compared to the scores of a well-defined norm (reference group) of others who have taken the same test. Typically the norm or reference group has the same characteristics, such as age and grade level, as the subjects in the study. Performance is described as relative position (e.g., percentile rank). There is less emphasis on the absolute amount of knowledge or skill demonstrated. What matters most is the comparison group and the test's ability to distinguish between individuals on the trait being measured.

Because the purpose of a norm-referenced test is to differentiate between individuals, it is desirable to obtain a group distribution of scores that shows a high variance. It would be hard to say much about relative standing if the scores were all about the same. To achieve high variability, the test items are often moderately difficult. For instance, in many standardized achievement tests it is not uncommon for students around the middle of the distribution to answer only about 60% of the items correctly. Easy items, ones that most know the answer to, and very hard items, ones that few can answer correctly, are used sparingly. The emphasis on items with moderate difficulty may affect what is covered on the test, which, in turn, would affect the interpretation of the results.

High variability is good when the researcher is looking for relationships between the test results and other variables. In fact, correlations are stronger if each variable has a large variation in the results. Many studies investigating relationships with achievement use norm-referenced tests because these types of tests are most likely to provide data that will show a large variance.

It is also necessary to attend carefully to the nature of the norm or reference group in interpreting the results. Proper interpretation requires knowing what the scores are being compared against. It is like being in a class with an instructor who grades on a curve (each student's grade depends on how others in the class did on the test). If the class contains mostly very bright, motivated students, you can learn a lot and still look bad by comparison! On the other hand, if you are in a class with students who have low ability and are unmotivated, you can look good even though you have not learned much. National standardized tests usually report national norms, so that the score is compared to students across the nation. However, there are different ways of obtaining a "national" sample. Often, for instance, the norm group will contain a greater percentage of minority students than is actually present in the population to make sure each minority group is represented adequately. An accurate interpretation can be made only if the characteristics of the norm group are understood. Also, evidence of reliability and validity established with the norm group may be inappropriate for individuals not represented in the norm group.

The purpose of a **criterion-referenced** or "standards-based" interpretation is to show how an individual compares to some established level of performance or skill. Here the score is interpreted by comparison to a standard or criterion rather than to the scores of others. The result is usually reported either as a percentage of items answered correctly or as pass/fail. Examples of criterion-referenced measurement include grading scales, such as 95 to 100 = A, 88 to 94 = B, and so on, and competency tests, in which the emphasis is on making sure that students know certain concepts and principles and have certain skills. An important characteristic of most tests with criterion-referenced interpretations is that the results show a highly negatively skewed distribution. This characteristic lessens variability, which may make it difficult to find relationships between the test results and other variables. Another feature of criterion-referenced interpretations is that when pass/fail or some other mastery decision is made, professional judgment is used to set the passing or mastery score. There are many ways to make these professional judgments, with quite different results. A related term, *domain-referenced* testing, indicates the degree to which a larger domain of knowledge is demonstrated by those being tested.

> **Criterion-referenced:** Interpretations that compare subjects with a standard of performance.

The differences between norm- and criterion-referenced (standards-based) interpretations are summarized in Table 7.1.

Large-Scale Standardized Tests

A **standardized test** has uniform procedures for administration and scoring. Directions specify the procedures for giving the test, such as qualifications of the person administering the test, time allowed to answer the questions, materials that can be used by the subjects, and other conditions. The scoring of responses is usually objective, with specific instructions for how to score that do not involve the tester's personal judgments. Scoring is typically a count of the number of items

> **Standardized test:** A test with uniform procedures for administration and scoring.

TABLE 7.1	Characteristics of Criterion- and Norm-Referenced Interpretation	
	Criterion-Referenced (Standards-Based)	**Norm-Referenced**
Purpose	To describe learning tasks that can and cannot be performed.	To discriminate between individuals; indicate relative standing.
Content Tested	A delimited domain tested by a relatively large number of items.	Typically a large domain of tasks tested with relatively few items testing each task.
Item Difficulty	Items are matched to learning tasks; tend to be relatively easy.	Items are moderately difficult; omits very easy or hard items.
Interpretation	Describes performance in relation to a clearly defined learning task.	Describes performance in relation to a clearly defined group.

Source: Adapted from Linn & Gronlund, 2000.

correct. Most standardized tests have been administered to a norming group, which is helpful in interpreting the results, and most are prepared commercially by experts in measurement. This means that careful attention has been given to technical aspects such as cultural bias, reliability, validity, clarity, and item analysis.

Large-scale standardized tests are intended to be used in a wide variety of settings; obviously commercial test publishers want to sell as many tests as possible. The traits and skills measured are usually defined in broad, general terms. Consequently, the test may not be specific enough for use in a particular setting. For example, suppose a teacher is investigating the effect of different instructional methods on 11th-grade students' achievement in English. A standardized test of English may be available but may not be consistent with the specific reading materials this teacher intends to use. In this case the standardized test would probably not be sensitive enough to the different materials to show positive results. Thus, there is a trade-off in using standardized tests for classroom-oriented research. Although there may be established technical qualities, the test may not focus directly on what is being studied.

Standards-Based Tests. In recent years there has been a trend toward accountability testing that is based on learning standards for students. These measures are often called **standards-based tests.** They are standardized achievement tests with criterion-referenced interpretations. As such, they are influenced both by what students learn in school and by what students learn at home and in the community. Students are typically judged to be "proficient" or "not proficient" on the basis of their scores on the tests. These tests are domain-referenced. A sample of content and skills is selected from a larger domain of standards. Because standards-based tests are very visible for both students and schools, there is now a tendency to use them in evaluating school programs and methods of instruction. This may be appropriate as long as inferences are limited to the domain that is tested, and as long as the influence of home and community is recognized.

Standards-based tests: Criterion-referenced test interpretation based on established standards.

These tests also have high stakes, often determining whether a student can be promoted to the next grade or can graduate from high school, and whether schools can be accredited. We know that in a high-stakes environment test score increases may, in part, reflect increased testwiseness by students rather than an increase in student knowledge and skills. Like other standardized tests, what is measured tends to be broad and general and may not be the best measure when research has targeted more specific dependent variables. For example, it would not be appropriate to use a high school end-of-course science test (one that covers the entire year) when an intervention in an experiment consists of a specific four-week unit.

Standardized Achievement Tests. A **standardized achievement test** is large-scale. It is commercially prepared, with the characteristics previously indicated, and measures present knowledge and skills of a sample of relevant content. The emphasis is on recent school learning—what has been learned by the student—measuring proficiency in one or more areas of knowledge.

> **Standardized achievement test:** Tests content area knowledge or skill.

There are several types of standardized achievement tests. Some, diagnostic in nature, identify specific strengths and weaknesses in a particular discipline or area. Some measure achievement in a single subject, such as reading or mathematics. Survey batteries are achievement tests that survey a number of different subjects. Most standardized achievement tests are norm-referenced, although some are criterion-referenced. Some focus on recall and recognition of specific facts, concepts, and principles, and others measure skills and application of knowledge.

The type of achievement test selected (diagnostic, survey battery, etc.) depends on the purpose of the study. If the investigation is concerned with a single topic, a test that measures only that area would be preferable to a comprehensive battery of many topics. If the purpose is to compare schools on achievement, a norm-referenced achievement test would be best. Evaluations of overall school performance are best assessed with survey batteries. It is also important to select a test that has an appropriate degree of difficulty for the students. A test that is either too easy or too hard will not have the variability needed to show relationships with other variables.

It is critical to evaluate evidence based on test content to establish validity when using an achievement test. This assessment should include judgments about the relevance of the test content to the selected curriculum. These judgments can be made by determining the degree of match between the test items and the curriculum being taught.

When existing standardized achievement tests do not match well with the purpose of the research, a locally developed test is needed. These are often called teacher-made, or informal, tests for examining classroom learning. There are important differences between large-scale standardized and locally developed achievement tests, as summarized in Table 7.2.

Standardized Aptitude Tests. A **standardized aptitude test** is a commercially prepared measure of knowledge or skills that is used to predict future performance. The difference between an achievement and an aptitude test is in the way the results are applied. The actual items can be very similar, especially in

> **Standardized aptitude test:** Predicts future performance.

TABLE 7.2	**Characteristics of Large-Scale Standardized Tests and Informal, Locally Developed Tests[1]**	
	Large-Scale	
	Standardized Tests	**Informal, Local Tests**
Relevance to research	Low	High
Technical quality	High	Low
Quality of test items	High	Low
Administration and scoring	Specific instructions	Flexible
Score interpretation	Compared to national norms	Limited to local context
Content tested	General	Specific to local context

[1]This table shows general trends. Some locally developed tests, for example, have high-quality items, and some standardized tests are highly relevant to the research.

tests for young children. Often the terms *intelligence* and *ability* are used interchangeably with *aptitude*. Actually, *aptitude* is a more general term that refers to the predictive nature of the instrument. Intelligence tests measure a particular type of aptitude, which is defined by the content of each specific test. Intelligence usually means some indication of an individual's capacity to understand, process, and apply knowledge and skills in thinking or problem solving. It involves many different aptitudes.

Because of the negative connotation of intelligence tests, many publishers today use the terms *ability* or *academic aptitude* in naming the tests, for example, the Otis-Lennon School Ability Test and the Cognitive Abilities Test. The basic structure and content of these tests is much the same as when they were referred to as intelligence tests. Such tests are widely used in education and are useful in predicting performance on many tasks. Some tests, such as those just mentioned, are given to large groups of students; others, such as the Stanford-Binet and the Wechsler Scales, are given on an individual basis. For research, both individual and group tests are common, and, for both types, it is important that the person administering the test be properly qualified.

There are also a large number of aptitude tests that measure specific kinds of aptitudes, such as vocational, clerical, mechanical, critical thinking, and creative thinking skills, and the skills that are needed to be successful in law or medical school. A few aptitude tests are batteries that assess many aptitudes at once. For example, the Differential Aptitude Tests (DAT) measure eight aptitudes: verbal reasoning, numerical ability, abstract reasoning, clerical speed and accuracy, mechanical reasoning, spatial relations, spelling, and language use. These tests have been useful in predicting both scholastic and vocational success.

Because aptitude tests are concerned with predicting future behavior, it is important to establish predictive criterion-related evidence for validity. It is also best to have a stability estimate of reliability. These technical qualities are important in tests that are used to select individuals for special programs that attract a large pool of applicants. Almost all aptitude tests are standardized.

Scores from Norm-Referenced Interpretations

A characteristic of norm-referenced interpretation is that different types of scores are reported and used in research, each having unique characteristics. Two of the most common are *standard scores* and *grade equivalents.*

Standard Scores. Most publishers of standardized, norm-referenced tests report at least two types of scores. One is the actual number of items correct, the raw score, and another is calculated from these raw scores, the standard score. **Standard scores** are transformed raw scores that have a distribution in the same shape as the raw score distribution but with a different mean and standard deviation. The most basic standard score is called a linear z score. A z score has a mean of 0 and a standard deviation of 1. The formula is

> **Standard scores:** Raw scores transformed to a standard scale.

$$z = \frac{\text{raw score} - \text{mean}}{\text{standard deviation}}$$

Every raw score can be transformed to a z score with known percentile ranks, as illustrated in Figure 7.1.

Many other derived standard scores are then calculated from z scores, such as SAT and IQ scores. When interpreting these types of standard scores, consider two important points. First, the unit of standard deviation is determined arbitrarily and does not reflect "real" differences between subjects. For instance, the SAT has a standard score mean of about 1,040 and a standard deviation equal to about 200. One subject may score 850 and another 890, but the 40-point difference is only in standard score units. In fact, the 40 points may represent a difference of only a few correct answers. Second, in small distributions, and in any raw score

FIGURE 7.1 *z* scores and percentile ranks.

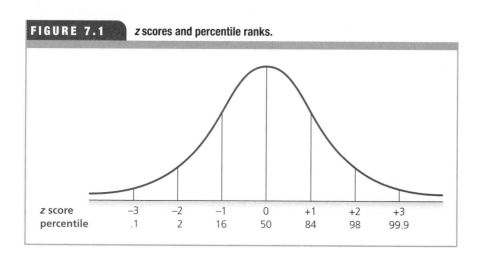

z score	−3	−2	−1	0	+1	+2	+3
percentile	.1	2	16	50	84	98	99.9

distribution that is not normal, scores are sometimes "normalized," that is, forced into a normal distribution and reported as standard scores. This practice may distort the meaning of the scores. Despite these limitations, standard scores are often used in research because the data are in a form that can be used in statistical analyses of the results. Also, with standard scores, it is easier to compare groups who have taken different tests.

Grade Equivalents. Grade equivalents (GEs) are a popular type of score for reporting achievement, even if they are often misinterpreted. A **grade equivalent** score indicates how an individual compares with others in a normative group in terms of grade level. For example, a student who scores 5.0 has achieved the median score for all beginning fifth-graders in the norm group. The score 3.2 is equivalent to the average score of third-graders in November. One limitation of GEs is in interpreting these in-between scores, 5.6, 2.3, and so on, since they are calculated as approximate, not exact, scores. Estimates are also made for grade levels beyond the norming group, although GEs are generally not used beyond the ninth grade because not all students take all subjects. Perhaps the most serious misinterpretation is the belief that a student who scores, say, 6.0, should be in the sixth grade, or knows as much as a sixth-grader. Grade determination is based on local school policy and the level of achievement of students in a particular school, whereas the GE is based on a national norm.

Grade equivalent:
Norm-referenced
grade-level performance.

> ### USING EDUCATIONAL RESEARCH
>
> Over the last two decades qualitative research has surged. Now, with the reauthorization of the Elementary and Secondary Education Act, there is a clear trend toward more objective standardized testing to determine the effectiveness of educational programs. This emphasis on large-scale, objective testing will influence the nature of dependent variables for many studies. What will be important is to recognize that any single approach to documenting student learning has limitations, and that no important decisions should be made on the basis of a single score. Standardized tests do provide important information, but there are other schooling outcomes that also are very important. It will be necessary, therefore, for researchers to be careful not to be enticed too much by easily obtained, visible instruments, when other measures would be more appropriate. Schooling is too complex to be narrowly evaluated by one set of measures.

QUESTIONNAIRES

The questionnaire is a widely used type of measure in educational research. A **questionnaire** is a written document containing statements or questions that are used to obtain subject perceptions, attitudes, beliefs, values, perspectives, and other traits. Questionnaires are used extensively because they provide an efficient

Questionnaire: Solicits
subject responses to written
items.

way to obtain information about a wide range of research problems, from surveys of large populations to reactions of students to different instructional methods. Questionnaires can be used to assess different kinds of traits and can take several formats.

Personality Assessment

Personality assessment is tied to two traditions. One is closely linked to psychology and is used by trained counselors and clinicians. The other is used by teachers and researchers who may not have extensive psychological training and who are typically interested in different aspects of personality.

Psychologists have been concerned with measuring personality for many decades. Although there are different definitions of personality, a common theme is that it involves the total individual—noncognitive, affective traits as well as cognitive characteristics. This holistic emphasis is evident in personality instruments that assess general adjustment, such as the Minnesota Multiphasic Personality Inventory (MMPI). The MMPI is a self-report questionnaire for adults aged 16 and above. Fourteen scales are reported, including paranoia, hysteria, social introversion, schizophrenia, and depression. The objective is to identify thinking and behavior that are not "normal," that may be psychopathic. Interpretation of the results of the MMPI, which is complex and difficult to understand, requires a highly trained, skilled clinician. Other self-report personality instruments are the Adjustment Inventory, California Psychological Inventory, and Psychological Inventory.

Questionnaires that are used by teachers and educational researchers are not typically intended to identify psychopathology. Rather, they measure important individual traits related to learning and motivation, such as self-concept, cognitive style, and locus of control. The instruments are designed so that educators without clinical training can understand and use the results.

One personality trait that is studied extensively in educational research is self-concept. Self-concept, or self-image, can be defined as the way one characterizes oneself. It is a description formed by self-perceptions and beliefs. Although it is possible to measure a single, global self-concept, most questionnaires are designed to assess many different self-concepts, such as descriptions about the physical, social, academic, moral, and personal self. The items in the instruments require self-report perceptions.

Typically, short statements are presented that describe various aspects of self-concept. The subjects answer each item by indicating whether it is true for them, or whether they agree or disagree that the statement is like them. For example, subjects would be directed to answer yes or no or true or false to the following statements:

1. I have few friends.
2. I have happy parents.
3. I have a nice looking body.
4. I am good at schoolwork.
5. I make friends easily.

6. I get good grades.
7. I am happy in school.
8. I like my teachers.
9. I am confident of my athletic ability.

Often the scoring of the instruments indicates a positive or negative self-concept, an interpretation that has an evaluative component termed self-esteem. It has to do with how subjects *feel about* their self-concepts. In the literature *self-concept* and *self-esteem* may be used interchangeably, so it is necessary to examine the nature of the items to understand what is being measured.

Attitude, Value, and Interest Questionnaires

Attitudes, values, and interests are generally thought of as noncognitive or affective traits that indicate some degree of preference toward something. Attitudes are defined as predispositions to respond favorably or unfavorably to an object, group, or place. They reflect likes and dislikes and generally predict behavior. Like attitudes, interests are concerned with preferences. Both are related to favorable or unfavorable responses toward something. Interests, however, are feelings and beliefs about an activity rather than an object, concept, or person. Like attitudes and interests, values can be defined in a number of ways, so it is necessary to examine items in a value survey to know what is being measured. Established instruments that measure values, such as Rokeach's Value Survey, Study of Values, and Gordon's Surveys of Values, tend to assess personal and social values that may not relate well to educational outcomes.

Preferences are important in education because they influence motivation and goals, which in turn affect achievement. The most common measure of these preferences in educational research is through self-report questionnaires, in which students answer questions to indicate how they feel about something, what their beliefs are, or their self-perceived capability to perform well (self-efficacy).

When reading research that investigates attitudes, values, and interests, you will note that different types of items are used. We will consider three major types of items commonly used in questionnaires: scales, checklists, and ranked items.

Scale: Series of gradations.

Types of Scales. A **scale** is a series of gradations that describes something. The most typical format for a scaled item is following a question or statement with a scale of potential responses. Subjects indicate their attitudes or values by checking the place on the scale that best reflects their feelings and beliefs about the statement. The **Likert scale** is the most widely used example. In a true Likert scale the statement includes a value or positive or negative direction, and the subject indicates agreement or disagreement with the statement:

Likert scale: Measures level of agreement to a statement.

It is very important to go to college.

strongly agree   agree   neither agree   disagree   strongly disagree
nor disagree

Likert-*type* rating scales, which have a different form, begin with a neutral statement, and the direction or gradation is provided in the response options:

Mrs. Stadler's classroom management is:

outstanding   excellent   good   fair   poor

Likert-type scales are useful for measuring traits, other than attitudes. Such measures are usually referred to as rating scales. Statements and response options can be selected for a wide variety of needs, as indicated in the following examples.

EXAMPLE | **Likert-Type Scales**

How often does your principal visit your classroom?

| every day | two or three days a week | once a week | once every two weeks | once a month |

How often does your teacher give praise?

| always | most of time | sometimes | rarely | never |

How did you feel about your performance on the exam?

| very satisfied | somewhat satisfied | somewhat dissatisfied | very dissatisfied |

Note that the number of possible responses on a Likert-type scale is not always the same. There is usually a minimum of four options, and there can be as many as seven or eight. Some questions will have a middle option, and others will have an even number of options to "force" the subject to one side of the scale or the other. However, if a neutral or middle choice is not provided and this is the real attitude or belief of the subject, the subject will be forced to give an inaccurate response (or may choose not to respond at all).

A good example of a study in which I have participated used Likert-type items to survey teachers about their grading and classroom assessment practices for a specific class and students about their motivation to be engaged in the class and to work for high grades. The purpose of the study was to determine relationships between teacher practices and student motivation. Some of the items for both the teacher and student surveys are illustrated in the following examples. Both of the questionnaires used a 5-point scale. Sometimes a 3-point or 7-point scale is used, though rarely more than 7.

Another type of scale is the **semantic differential,** which has adjective pairs that provide a series of scales. Each adjective acts as an end anchor, and the subject checks a point between each end anchor of each scale to indicate attitudes toward some person, concept, or idea. Although the true semantic differential uses the same set of adjective pairs in the three clusters, changing the object or concept that is being studied and changing the adjective pairs as appropriate are common in educational research.

Semantic differential: A 7-point scale with adjective pairs as end points.

EXAMPLE | **Likert-Type Items**

To what extent did you use the following grading and assessment practices *in the class you are currently teaching?*	Not at All	Minimally	Some	Quite a Bit	Extensively
19. feedback (written or verbal) on performance that was given privately to each student	1	2	3	4	5
20. specific, individualized feedback (written or verbal)	1	2	3	4	5
21. feedback (written or verbal) that contained suggestions for further learning	1	2	3	4	5
22. checklists to evaluate student work (**not** rubrics)	1	2	3	4	5
23. formative assessments (i.e., assessment given during instruction to check student learning; anecdotal or structured)	1	2	3	4	5
24. retakes of tests	1	2	3	4	5
25. assessments that measured student deep understanding (e.g., exploration, inquiry, and problem solving)	1	2	3	4	5
26. tests and other assessments of moderate difficulty	1	2	3	4	5

Directions: Carefully read each sentence and then rate *how true* each one is for you *in this class.* Circle the number next to each sentence that matches your answer. The number (1) stands for *not at all true for me,* (3) stands for *somewhat true for me,* and (5) stands for *very true for me.*

	Not at All True for Me		Somewhat True for Me		Very True for Me
11. I'm certain I can understand the ideas taught in this class.	1	2	3	4	5
12. It's important to me that I learn a lot in this class.	1	2	3	4	5
13. It's important to me that other students in my class think I am good at my class work.	1	2	3	4	5
14. I **don't** want my teacher to think I know less than other students in class.	1	2	3	4	5
15. One of my goals is to gain a lot of new skills in this class.	1	2	3	4	5

Checklist: Provides a list of choices.

Checklists. A **checklist** provides the respondent with a number of options from which to choose. The checklist can require a choice of one of several alternatives, for example, Check one: The research topic I enjoy most is _____ measurement, _____ qualitative designs, _____ quantitative designs, _____ reviewing literature. Or, respondents can check as many as apply:

Check as many as apply. The topics in research that I find very useful are:

_____ measurement
_____ qualitative designs
_____ quantitative designs
_____ reviewing literature

Checklists are also used when asking participants to answer yes or no, or to check the category to which they belong. For example:

Are you married?

_____ Yes
_____ No

Check the appropriate category:

_____ single, never married
_____ married
_____ separated
_____ divorced
_____ widowed

Ranked Items. In a **rank-ordered** item the respondent is asked to place a limited number of categories into sequential order. The sequence could be based on importance, liking, degree of experience, or some other dimension. Asking subjects to rank order may provide different results from those provided by a Likert item or semantic differential. For example, if a researcher is interested in determining the importance of different staff development topics, a Likert-type item format could be used. For each topic the teachers check or circle "critical," "very important," "important," or "not important." If most of the teachers check or circle "critical" for each topic, then there is limited information about which of the topics should be given priority. However, if the teachers rank order the topics by importance from 5 for most important to 1 for least important, an average rating can be found that will more likely identify which topic should be given priority.

Rank-ordered: Sequenced categories.

Problems in Measuring Noncognitive Traits

Compared to cognitive measures, such as achievement and aptitude tests, noncognitive instruments such as questionnaires generally have lower reliability and less evidence for validity. One difficulty with noncognitive measurement is clearly defining what is being assessed. There are different definitions of terms such as *attitude, belief, value,* and *personality*. Thus, the same labels can be used, but what is being measured can be different. An "attitude" toward mathematics can mean one thing in one study and something different in another study. Consequently, when reading research that uses noncognitive instruments, it is important to examine the *operational* definition of the trait that is being measured, which is best accomplished by reading the actual items in the scale. The results are most meaningful in regard to the way in which the attitude or personality trait is measured, not by how the researcher labels or communicates the findings in titles or conclusions.

Most noncognitive measures are susceptible to two sources of error: response set and faking. **Response set** is the tendency of the subject to respond in the same way, regardless of the content of the items, for example, always selecting the neutral category or the "strongly agree" category in a Likert scale or marking the favorable adjectives on a semantic differential. An especially troublesome type of response set is *social desirability*. This is the tendency to respond to the items in a way that is socially acceptable or desirable, regardless of the true or real attitudes or beliefs of the individual. For example, if a question asks students about their alcohol consumption, the responses may be influenced by what the students think is socially accepted. Or students may indicate an interest in attending college because that is more desirable socially than not attending college. Response set tends to be more prevalent on Likert-type inventories, with ambiguous items, and in situations in which the subjects are not motivated to give honest answers. In evaluating noncognitive instrumentation it is best to look for techniques that lessen response set, such as forced-choice responses, short inventories, an approximately equal number of positively and negatively worded items, alternating positive and negative adjectives in the same column on a semantic differential, ensurance of anonymity, and motivation of subjects.

Faking occurs when subjects give deliberately inaccurate indications of their attitudes, personality, or interests. Faking is usually dependent on the purpose of the test and the consequences of the results. Sometimes it occurs if the researcher indicates that certain results will have positive consequences; sometimes subjects fake responses simply to please the researcher (which is why someone other than the researcher probably should administer the instrument). In other situations faking occurs because the results have important consequences for the individual, for example, to determine admission to college or selection for a management training program. Occasionally, subjects will fake to provide a more negative picture. Faking can be controlled by establishing good rapport with the subjects and proper motivation, by disguising the purpose of the instrument and research, and using a forced-choice format. There are also techniques to detect faking. Whatever the approach, it is best for the instrument to be pilot-tested with similar subjects to ensure that problems such as response set and faking are controlled as much as possible. If little or no attention is given to these problems, it is more likely that the responses will be invalid.

Response set: Tendency to respond in the same way.

Faking: Deliberately inaccurate responses by subjects.

Observations

Tests and questionnaires are similar in that they rely on subjects' self-reports. Although self-reports are relatively economical and easy to obtain, they have limitations that may bias the results, such as response set, subject motivation, and faking. A second major type of data collection, which does not rely on self-reports, is the observational method. Although observational techniques also have limitations, they are more direct than self-reports. The observation of behavior as it occurs yields firsthand data without the contamination that may arise from tests, inventories, or other self-report instruments. Moreover, observation allows the description of behavior as it occurs naturally. Any kind of self-report introduces artificiality into the research. Observation of behavior in natural settings also allows the researcher to take into account important contextual factors that may influence the interpretation and use of the results. This is essential for qualitative studies.

There are several types of observational data-gathering techniques. Some observations are made in natural settings and others in controlled, laboratory settings. Some observations may be guided by a general problem and there may be flexibility about what and who to observe, whereas other observations may be specific and highly structured. Observers may be detached from the subjects, even unknown, or they may essentially become subjects themselves. Quantitative observations are more controlled and systematic and rely on numbers to summarize what has been observed. Qualitative approaches are much less controlled, allowing observers' hunches and judgments to determine the content and sequence of what is recorded. Either or both types of observations are used in some mixed-method studies. In this chapter we will focus on the more controlled, quantitative types of observation. Qualitative observations will be discussed in Chapter 11.

Inference

A major factor in observational research is the extent to which the person who is observing and recording the behavior makes inferences, or judgments, about what is seen or heard. Although there will always be some degree of inference, the amount can vary considerably. At one extreme, the observer may record specific, easily identified behaviors, such as "asks a question" or "wrote objectives on the board." These are called **low-inference** observations because the observer does not have to interpret what is seen. Either the behaviors are present or not, and the observer makes no judgment about their meaning. The recorded behaviors are then summarized and interpreted by someone else; the inference is made after all the data have been gathered. At the other extreme are observations that require the observer to make and record a judgment or interpretation. This approach, referred to as **high-inference** observation, requires the observer both to see relevant behaviors and to make inferences about their meaning. A common example of high-inference observation is that of a principal who, on the basis of a few visits to a classroom, rates a teacher as excellent, good, adequate, or poor on dimensions of teaching such as "classroom management" or "asking questions."

With low-inference observation the reliability is usually high, but in order to understand the results, you need to understand how the recorded behavior is translated. Translation can be a complex process and will involve some degree of arbitrary judgment, for example, how many times a teacher needs to give praise to be judged competent in praising students or how many student questions during a class period indicates acceptable student involvement. Critics of low-inference

Low-inference: Involves little interpretation or judgment.

High-inference: Involves recording interpretations of judgments.

systems also point out that teaching and learning may not be understood by recording specific behaviors without putting them into context.

In high-inference observations the competency of the observer in making correct judgments is critical. Training high-inference observers is more difficult, and reliability is often lower, as compared to low-inference observation. With high-inference results, greater trust in the observer is needed. Thus, you should look for any factors that may bias a high-inference observer, such as the researcher also acting as the observer or observers knowing about the expected results of the study.

Some observations are in between the low- and high-inference extremes. One such approach is to make high-inference ratings and indicate the specific behaviors and contextual factors that led to the inference implied in the judgment.

Laboratory Observation

The most controlled observational techniques are found in laboratory studies. A specified environment is created by the researcher and the observations are recorded during the study. A well-structured form or procedure is used to record specific behaviors that have been identified before the study begins. Low-inference observations are made, and methods of summarizing and analyzing the observations are specified in advance. The emphasis is on objectivity and standardization; usually the study is an experiment.

Subjects in laboratory observation may give biased responses because they know that they are in an experiment and are being observed. They may respond according to their interpretation of how they "should" respond, given the treatment they experience, or they may give answers they believe the researcher wants. These are called *demand characteristics*. Deception, in which the subjects are not told the real purpose of the study, is commonly used to reduce the effects of demand characteristics, but there are serious ethical problems with lying to subjects, even if they are debriefed after the study.

Structured Field Observations

Most observational studies in education take place in the field, in schools and classrooms where behavior occurs naturally. The typical approach is to define the behaviors to be observed, identify a system of coding and recording them, train observers to use the system, and go to the school or other setting and make the observations. The intent is to measure the frequency and/or duration of predetermined behaviors.

The behaviors can be recorded in several ways. The most common approach is to indicate the number of times a behavior occurs during a specified time period. The observer has a list of behaviors that may be observed, and every time a behavior is seen a tally is placed next to that behavior. Sometimes the observer will observe for a short time, such as one to three minutes, then record all the behaviors seen in that time; and sometimes the recording is done continuously. With high-inference instruments, the observer may not record anything for an hour or more.

EXAMPLE | **Structured Field Observations**

"Observers distributed the ESF forms during the last 5 minutes of mathematics class. Each of the selected students completed a form on each of 4 days in the fall and 4 days in the winter, within a 2-week period each season, resulting in a possible return of 336 response forms. Although the standard use of the Experience Sampling Method is to electronically 'beep' students randomly during the day and ask that they complete an ESF questionnaire describing their thoughts and feelings at that specific time, we did not want to disrupt mathematics classes by distributing ESFs in the middle of activities. Therefore, we asked students to generalize about the entire class experience. Students' involvement might ebb and flow during class (e.g., Reed, Hagen, Wicker, & Schallert, 1996), but there was rarely more than one class activity per day, and we measured the overall assessment rather than involvement during any one activity." (Schweinle, A., Meyer, D. K., & Turner, J. C. (2006). Striking the right balance: students' motivation and affect in elementary mathematics. *The Journal of Educational Research, 99*(5) p. 275)

Observer Effects

The observer is the key to observational research, and the quality of the results depends to a great extent on how the observer and the procedures for observing affect the subjects. In reading observational research you should be aware of the following potential limitations.

Observer Bias. Bias is a type of error that occurs because of the background, expectations, or frame of reference of the observer. For example, if an observer of classroom management techniques has a predetermined idea that a particular approach is best, and the teacher who is observed does not use this style, the observer may have a tendency to bias the observations in a negative direction. On the other hand, bias in a positive direction may occur when observers record the behavior of a style of management they believe to be most effective.

You should look for one of several procedures to reduce potential observer bias. First, there should be evidence that the observer has been trained and will provide reliable results. The evidence for training should be based on research done before the actual study is implemented. Second, if possible, two or more observers should independently observe at least some of the same behavior. Third, bias can also result because of prejudice toward certain races; toward one gender or the other; and toward other characteristics such as physical attractiveness, social class, and exceptionalities. In the following excerpt the researcher demonstrates her understanding of possible bias, using interobserver reliability to lessen this potentially problematic issue.

EXAMPLE | **Accounting for Observer Bias**

"I was aware that researcher bias would be a potential difficulty in my study and monitored flexibility and openness in the analysis of material . . . in addition, my research supervisor re-coded some of the videos so that 36% of the total sample was reviewed to ensure reliability. Inter-observer reliability . . . was calculated using kappa, with high agreement (> 0.90) between observers." (Anderson, C. (2006). Early communication strategies: Using video analysis to support teachers working with preverbal pupils. *British Journal of Special Education, 33*(3), p. 116)

Contamination: Knowledge of the study influences observer or interviewer.

Contamination. **Contamination** occurs when the observer has knowledge of one or more aspects of the study and this knowledge affects subsequent observations. One type of contamination results from knowledge of the study's hypothesis. If the observer knows which group is "expected" to do best, for example, he or she may unconsciously favor that group. Contamination also occurs if the same observer is assigned to more than one type of group. For example, if an observer begins with a group of "expert" teachers and then observes "poor" teachers, the second group will probably receive lower ratings than they deserve because of the comparison. Contamination is less likely to occur when specific behaviors are targeted for observation, when observers are trained, when the observers do not know about expected outcomes, and are not told which groups are experimental and control.

Halo effect: Specific ratings affected by initial impression.

Halo Effect. The **halo effect** occurs when an observer allows an initial impression about a person or group to influence subsequent observations. For example, an initial positive impression about a teacher, based on the way the teacher begins a class, may create an overall positive "halo" so that ratings of subsequent behaviors, such as questioning or monitoring of classroom activities, are higher than they should be. The halo effect is an inappropriate generalization about all aspects of the observation. It is suspected in ratings of different behaviors when all the ratings are the same, which results in a positive relationship between unrelated scales. The halo effect, like other sources of errors in observation, is reduced with adequate training.

INTERVIEWS

Interview: Oral questions and answers.

The **interview** is a form of data collection in which questions are asked orally and subjects' responses are recorded, either verbatim or summarized. There is direct verbal interaction between the interviewer and the respondent, which has both advantages and disadvantages compared to self-report tests, inventories, and questionnaires. By establishing a proper rapport with the subject, a skilled interviewer can enhance motivation and obtain information that might not otherwise have been offered. More accurate responses are obtained as the interviewer clarifies questions that the subject may have and follows up leads (probing).

The interview allows for greater depth and richness of information. In face-to-face interviews, the interviewer can observe nonverbal responses and behaviors, which may indicate the need for further questioning to clarify verbal answers. The interview can be used with many types of persons, such as those who are illiterate or too young to read or write. The presence of an interviewer tends to reduce the number of "no answers" or neutral responses, and the interviewer can press for more complete answers when necessary. Compared to questionnaires, interviews usually achieve higher return rates; often as many as 90 or 95% of the subjects will agree to be interviewed.

One disadvantage of interviews is that because they are expensive and time-consuming compared with other methods of data collection, the sample size is often small. With small samples a high response rate is needed to avoid bias in the nature of the sample. The number of refusals to be interviewed, if greater than 20%, may seriously bias the results. The advantages of flexibility and the opportunity for probing and clarification allow for a certain degree of subjectivity in summarizing what is heard. This subjectivity may lead to biased interpretation of responses. These effects will be discussed in greater detail following a brief summary of different types of interview questions.

Like observations, interviews are used for quantitative, qualitative, and mixed-method studies. Here we will be primarily concerned with interviews for quantitative and some mixed-method studies. More detail on qualitative interviewing will be covered in Chapter 11.

Types of Interview Questions

There are three types of interview questions: structured, semistructured, and unstructured. **Structured questions** give the subject choices from which an answer is selected. For example, in a study of student attitudes, the interviewer may ask, "How important is it to you to obtain high grades in school? Is it critical, very important, important, or not very important?" Structured questions are often used in telephone interviews, which for some purposes can provide data comparable to those obtained through personal interviews at about half the cost.

Structured questions: Subject chooses from responses provided.

Semistructured questions do not have predetermined, structured choices. Rather, the question is open-ended yet specific in intent, allowing individual responses. For instance, an interviewer may ask, "What are some things that teachers you like do best?" The question is reasonably objective, yet it allows for probing, follow-up, and clarification. It is the most common type of interview question in educational research.

Semistructured questions: Specific questions without predetermined response options.

Unstructured questions are open-ended and broad. The interviewer has a general goal in mind and asks questions relevant to this goal. Thus, there is some latitude in what is asked, and often somewhat different questions are used with each subject. The unstructured interview is difficult to conduct. It is highly subjective and requires considerable training and experience. Thus, in research that has employed unstructured questions, look carefully for evidence that the interviewer has the appropriate expertise to conduct the interview and then interpret the results.

Unstructured questions: Open-ended, general questions.

Regardless of the type of interview, it is important that the questions are worded so that the subject is not led to a particular answer. A **leading question** biases the results by encouraging one answer from all the subjects. For example, if the interviewer asks, "Wouldn't you agree that Mrs. Jones is an excellent teacher?" the subjects are led toward a yes response.

Interviewer Effects

The ideal role of the interviewer is to act as a neutral medium through which information is transmitted. The interviewer should not have an effect on the results, except to make it possible for the subject to reveal information that otherwise would not have been known. However, because of the one-on-one nature of the interview there are several potential sources of error. Like observers, interviewers must be careful that preexisting bias does not influence what they hear or record, which is a possibility if they harbor stereotypes about certain types of subjects. Contamination can also occur if the interviewers have knowledge of facets of the study. They should not be aware of which subjects are receiving special interventions or whether certain results will have positive benefits. The halo effect can also occur with interviewers. Obviously, they need to be trained so that many of these potential sources of error will not arise. Interviewers also need to be trained to establish positive rapport with subjects.

There is some evidence that certain interviewer characteristics may influence the results of in-person interviews. For example, matching interviewers and subjects on demographic variables such as age, socioeconomic status, race, and gender may result in more valid results. Generally, most inhibition in responding occurs with persons of the same age but different gender. Interviewers should dress according to existing norms or in a fashion familiar to the respondents, not in such a way that the subjects sense that particular responses are desirable.

Additional error may occur from the way the in-person interview is conducted. It is important for the interviewer to be pleasant, friendly, and relaxed in establishing a relationship with the subject that is conducive to honest interchange and little inhibition. This result is often accomplished by beginning the interview with "small talk." Probing should be anticipated and planned for in the training of the interviewers, and specific types of probes should be identified for certain situations.

The manner in which the interviewer records responses may affect the results. At one extreme, a tape recorder can provide a verbatim record of the answers. The tapes can then be analyzed by different individuals to increase validity. This method is most useful with unstructured questions, which lend themselves to greater subjectivity on the part of the interviewer. However, the mere presence of a tape recorder may inhibit some subjects. Consequently, if a tape recorder was used in research, you need to look for assurance that subjects were not affected by its presence. At the other extreme, the interviewer can wait until the interview is over and then write notes that summarize the results. This procedure is more prone to error because it is easier for interview bias to affect what is remembered and recorded. To reduce this source of error, most interviewers take some notes during the interview. Rarely can interviewers write out the exact response of the subject. More typically, they write brief notes for each question during the interview that can be expanded after the interview is over. One way to increase reliability is to send a copy of the interviewer's notes to each subject and give them an opportunity to add or revise as necessary to increase accuracy.

A summary of problems faced by researchers using questionnaires, observations, and interviews for obtaining noncognitive information is provided in Table 7.3. Look for these problems when determining the quality of the measurement.

Author Reflection *Which method of collecting data is best? I have used all of the approaches in this chapter and have found that the richest, most relevant data comes through well-done interviews. There is simply no substitute for engaging another person in a face-to-face setting. Yes, it is time-consuming, but the advantage of being able to probe and observe nonverbal communication is invaluable. There is something about direct personal interaction that is unique, even when determining what someone knows and can do from an achievement standpoint.*

My experience after being involved in many studies in which interviews were used to collect data is that respondents are very honest. This has been my experience with adults, children, and adolescents, whether tape-recorded or not. Generally people want to be helpful, especially most education professionals. As long as you have the resources, interviewing is a great way to obtain great data.

TABLE 7.3	**Problems for Researchers Measuring Noncognitive Traits**

Questionnaire

Multiple sources of error, especially over time.
Unclear definitions of the trait.
Response set, especially social desirability.
Faking; subject motivation to respond seriously and honestly.

Observation

High inference depends on quality of observers to make judgments; may be less reliable.
Low inference reliable but often too artificial.
Observer bias.
Contamination, especially if observer knows which group is experimental and which is control.
Halo effect.

Interview

Depends on skills of the interviewer.
Low sample size.
Contamination.
Expensive and time-consuming.
No anonymity for subjects.
Halo effect.
Interviewer characteristics may influence subjects.
Procedure for recording responses may not be accurate or may influence subjects.

LOCATING *and* EVALUATING EDUCATIONAL MEASURES

Literally thousands of instruments have been used in educational research over the past 50 years. When you read research you will encounter many different measures. How will you know if they are providing valid and reliable information? As noted earlier, research is only as good as the measurement on which it is based. Consequently, it is best to be able to evaluate the instruments that were used by studying

TABLE 7.4	Sources of Information about Available Instruments
Source	**Information Provided**
Index to Tests Used in Educational Dissertations (Fabiano, 1989)	Describes tests and test populations used in dissertations from 1938 to 1980; keyed by title and selected descriptors.
ERIC	The ERIC database can be used to locate instruments in two ways. One approach is to find research articles and reports that include a measure of a construct that can be used as a keyword or descriptor in the search. Another good strategy is to go to the Advanced Search Web page, enter your keyword or descriptor, and then go to the Publication Type pull-down menu and click on "Tests/Questionnaires." For example, in July 2006, I used the term "science attitude" as both a descriptor and keyword, and limited the search to 2000–2006 and "tests/questionnaires." For the keyword search I obtained 40 hits; for the descriptor search there were 16 hits.
Test Link	Test Link is a database that contains descriptions of over 25,000 previously administered tests, surveys, and assessment tools that are contained in the ETS (Educational Testing Service) Test Collection. This library contains instruments collected from the early 1900s to the present, and it is the largest such compilation in the world. The database can be searched by author, title, topic, or date. A search of "self-efficacy" in July 2006 resulted in 86 instruments. Each record contains information about the test, including an abstract. Once identified, a test can be ordered from ETS in two ways: (1) Tests in Microfiche (over 1,300) for a small fee; or (2) Tests on Demand (over 1,000) for a larger fee. Ordering information about tests that are only available from publishers or from individual researchers is also provided. The collection also includes materials that accompany tests, such as administration guidelines, scoring procedures, and psychometric information.
Tests: A Comprehensive Reference for Assessments in Psychology, Education, and Business, 4th ed. (Maddox, 2002)	Provides a description of over 3,100 published tests, including purpose, cost, scoring, and publisher.
Test Critiques, Vols. 1–10 (Keyser & Sweetland, 1984)	Gives evaluations for widely used, newly published, and recently revised instruments in psychology, education, and business. Contains "user-oriented" information, including practical applications and uses, as well as technical aspects and a critique by a measurement specialist. The companion, *Test Critiques Compendium,* reviews major tests from *Test Critiques* in one volume.
Mental Measurements Yearbooks (MMYs) Buros Institute of Mental Measurements	Provides critical reviews of commercially available tests in several different areas, including character and personality, achievement, and intelligence. References for most of the tests facilitate further research. The MMYs have been published periodically for 65 years. The *Sixteenth MMY* was published in 2006. Each new MMY edition provides reviews of only new or revised tests. The MMY contains descriptions of newly released or revised instruments. Thus, if a test has not been revised recently, information could be obtained by consulting an earlier edition. The MMY evaluations are available on Test Reviews Online, also sponsored by the Buros Institute. Test Reviews Online is a subscription service that allows searching by title, purpose, publisher, acronym, author, and scores. The database contains nearly 4,000 commercially available tests.

TABLE 7.4	(Continued)

Source	Information Provided
Tests in Print (TIP)	Also published periodically by the Buros Institute (most recently published in 2002 as *Tests in Print VI*). TIP provides a comprehensive index to the MMY by including brief descriptions of over 4,000 commercially available instruments, intended uses, and a reference list of professional literature about each instrument.
A Consumer's Guide to Tests in Print, 2d ed. (Hammill, Brown, & Bryant, 1992)	Provides brief evaluative summaries of 250 tests and 2,000 test scores, based on reliability and validity.
Tests and Measurements in Child Development: Handbook I and II (Johnson, 1976)	Two volumes describe about 900 unpublished tests and instruments for children through age 18.
Evaluating Classroom Instruction: A Sourcebook of Instruments (Borich & Madden, 1977)	Reviews instruments that can be used in the classroom to evaluate teacher and student behavior. Observation schedules are included.
A Sourcebook of Mental Health Measures (Comrey, Backer, & Glaser, 1973)	This reference describes about 1,100 instruments related to mental health, including juvenile delinquency, personality, and alcoholism.
Measures for Psychological Assessment: A Guide to 3,000 Original Sources and Their Applications (Chun, Cobb, & French, 1974)	A list of tests used in research reported in 26 different psychological journals.
Measures of Social Psychological Attitudes (Robinson & Shaver, 1973)	Describes hundreds of attitude instruments used in psychological and sociological research.
Mirrors for Behavior III: An Anthology of Observation Instruments (Simon & Boyer, 1974)	About 100 observation instruments are described in various fields, including medicine, business, and anthropology, as well as education.
Socioemotional Measures for Preschool and Kindergarten Children: A Handbook (Walker, 1973)	Describes instruments to measure attitudes, personality, self-concept, and social skills of young children.
Handbook for Measurement and Evaluation in Early Childhood Education (Goodwin & Driscoll, 1980)	A comprehensive review of affective, cognitive, and psychomotor measures for young children.
Handbook of Research Design and Social Measurement, 6th ed. (Miller & Salkind, 2002)	Reviews and critiques popular social science measures.
Directory of Unpublished Experimental Mental Measures, Vol. 7 (Goldman & Mitchell, 1997)	Describes nearly 1,700 experimental mental measures that are not commercially available. Includes references, source, and purpose on topics ranging from educational adjustment and motivation to personality and perception.

the information provided by the researchers in a report or article. Often, however, there is insufficient information in the article to make an informed judgment. In this case, a number of sources can be used to both identify and evaluate existing educational measures (see Table 7.4). Some of the sources summarize the instruments; others provide a critique as well.

In addition to these sources, an excellent way to obtain information about an instrument is to contact its developer. The developer may be able to send you a technical manual and may know about other researchers who have used the instrument. Technical manuals are almost always available for published tests.

Finally, you may want to try a computer search of journal articles that have up-to-date information on critical evaluations of validity and reliability and other studies that have used the instrument. In the ERIC database a proximity search is one alternative. In a proximity search terms that make up the name of the instrument, or related terms, are used to locate relevant articles. The database for *Psychological Abstracts*, PsycINFO, indexes major instruments by name.

CONSUMER TIPS: *Criteria for Evaluating Instrumentation*

1. Evidence for validity should be stated clearly. The researchers should address validity by explicitly indicating the type of evidence that is presented, the results of analyses that establish validity, and how the evidence supports the inferences that are made. For evidence that does not match well with the subjects or situation of the investigation, the researcher should indicate why it is reasonable to believe that the results are appropriate and useful. References should cite previous research that supports the validity of the inferences. It is best to collect evidence for validity in a pretest or pilot test.

2. Evidence for reliability should be stated clearly. The researchers should clearly indicate the reliability of all scores. The type of reliability estimate used should be indicated, and it should be consistent with the use of the results. Reliability should be established in a pretest or pilot test with subjects similar to those used in the research. High reliability is especially important for results that show no difference or no relationship.

3. The instruments should be clearly described. Sufficient information about the instrument should be given to enable the reader to understand how the subjects gave their responses. This information includes some idea of the type of item, which is often accomplished by providing examples. It is also necessary to indicate how the instrument is scored.

4. The procedures for administering the instrument should be clearly described. The reader needs to know when the instrument was given and the conditions of its administration. Who gave the instrument to the subjects? What did they know about the study? What were the subjects told before they answered the questions? Did anything unusual happen during the administration? Did the subjects understand the directions for completing the instrument? These questions are especially critical for standardized tests.

5. Norms should be specified for norm-referenced interpretations. The norms used to determine the results need to be clearly indicated. What is the nature of the norm group? Is it appropriate to the type of inferences that are made?

6. Procedures for setting standards should be indicated for criterion-referenced interpretations. It is necessary to know how the standards used to judge the results are set. Were experts consulted to verify the credibility of the standard? What is the difficulty level of the items in relation to the standard?

7. The scores used in reporting results should be meaningful. Often standard scores or some type of derived scores are used in reporting the results. Whatever the scores, they should not distort the actual differences or relationships, either by inflating or deflating the apparent differences or relationships.

8. Measures of noncognitive traits should avoid problems of response set and faking. Researchers need to indicate how response set and faking are controlled for when measuring personality, attitudes, values, and interests. Special attention should be given to the manner in which the subjects are motivated.

9. Observers and interviewers should be trained. Researchers must show that the observers and interviewers in studies have been trained to avoid such problems as bias, contamination, and halo effect. Interviewers need to know how not to ask leading questions and how to probe effectively. Interobserver reliability should be indicated.

10. In high-inference observations the qualifications of the observers to make sound professional judgments should be indicated. With low-inference observations reliability is usually high, but if high-inference observations are used, the characteristics and training of the observer are more important and should be specified.

11. The effect of the interviewer or observer should be minimal. Examine the characteristics of the interviewers. Could these traits create any error in the nature of the responses obtained? Were appropriate steps taken to establish a proper rapport with the subjects? Any possible effects of the interviewer or observer on the subjects should be noted.

STUDY QUESTIONS

1. What are some ways of classifying educational measures?
2. What is the difference between "off-the-shelf" and "locally developed" tests?
3. What is the difference between criterion-referenced and norm-referenced interpretations?
4. Why are changes in scores and differences between groups difficult to obtain with many standardized tests?
5. What is the difference between standardized achievement tests and standardized aptitude tests?
6. Why are standard scores difficult to interpret?
7. Give some examples of different ways of measuring self-concept and attitudes.
8. What is the difference between Likert and Likert-type scales?

9. Identify factors that affect the measurement of noncognitive traits. How does each one affect the results?
10. What are the advantages of observations over self-reports?
11. Under what circumstances would it be better to use high-inference rather than low-inference observation?
12. In what ways are observer and interviewer effects the same?
13. Compare the interview with the questionnaire. What are the advantages and disadvantages of each?
14. Identify criteria for evaluating instrumentation. What would you look for when reading the instrumentation section of a research article?

@WWW SAMPLE TEST QUESTIONS

See this text's Companion Website at **www.ablongman.com/mcmillan5e** for sample test questions and answers.

 RESEARCH NAVIGATOR™ ACTIVITIES

1. Examine the method used to measure reading attitudes and interest in reading in a study of adolescents who had experienced repeated failure (Research Navigator AN 22557955). What are the strengths and weaknesses of the measure that was used? What alternative approach to measuring attitudes might have been better?
2. As pointed out in this chapter, evidence for the validity of test scores is based on the inferences from and uses of the scores. In a recent study that is reprinted in the Research Navigator (AN 21701255), investigators examined the usefulness of standardized test scores for teachers in improving their teaching. What kind of standardized test is used in the study? Are the uses of the scores appropriate?

Chapter 8

Nonexperimental Quantitative Research Designs

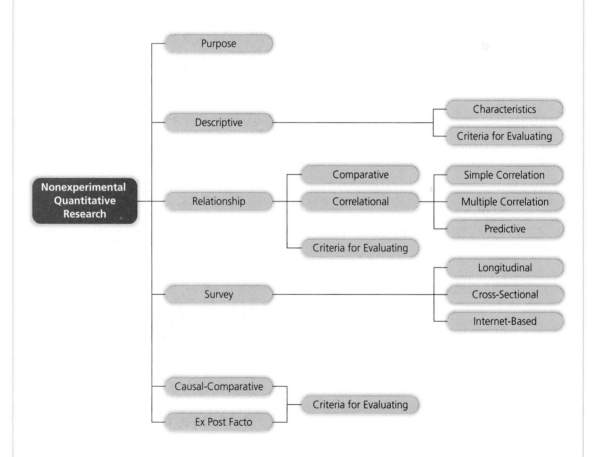

CHAPTER ROAD MAP

Research design: How
information is obtained.

We now turn our attention to commonly employed quantitative research designs. **Research design** refers to the way information is gathered from subjects and, in the case of experimental research, the nature of the interventions. In this chapter we will consider four types of *nonexperimental* research designs: descriptive, comparative, correlational, and ex post facto. Identifying and understanding these designs will enable you to know what to look for and what to ask about research weaknesses, limitations, and mistakes.

As a result of reading and studying this chapter, you will:

- Understand different types of nonexperimental quantitative designs
- Understand how relationships are examined by comparative and correlational studies
- Understand how the criteria for forming groups affect results
- Learn why causation cannot be inferred from most nonexperimental designs
- Understand how to interpret a correlation matrix
- Understand how predictive studies differ from correlational studies
- Know limitations in interpreting correlational findings
- Understand the purpose and design of causal-comparative studies
- Understand how to design and conduct survey studies
- Learn about the advantages and disadvantages of conducting Web-based surveys
- Learn how to read, understand, and critique nonexperimental quantitative studies

The PURPOSE *of* NONEXPERIMENTAL RESEARCH

Whereas experimental research seeks to understand causal relationships by manipulating an intervention, nonexperimental research essentially describes participants, traits, scores, and other characteristics without an intervention. In this sense, nonexperimental studies investigate the current status of something—a report of the way things are or the way things were. We'll begin with the most basic, and often most important, nonexperimental designs—descriptive ones. Description is the fundamental building block of all quantitative research.

DESCRIPTIVE STUDIES

Characteristics of Descriptive Studies

A descriptive study simply describes a phenomenon. The description is usually in the form of statistics such as frequencies or percentages, averages, and sometimes variability. Often graphs and other visual images of the results are used. Descriptive research is particularly valuable when an area is first investigated. For example, there has been much research on the nature of classroom climate and its relationship to student attitudes and learning. A first step in this research was to describe adequately what is meant by "classroom climate," initially by a clear constitutive definition, then operationally with measures. Climate surveys, which assess characteristics such as how students talk and act toward one another, how they feel about the teacher and learning, and feelings of openness, acceptance, trust, respect, rejection, hostility, and cooperation, are used to understand classroom atmosphere. Once this understanding is achieved, various dimensions of climate can be related to student learning and teacher satisfaction, and ultimately climate can be controlled to examine the causal relationship between them.

Suppose you read a study on the relationship between principals' leadership styles and teachers' attitudes. You should first look for an adequate description of *leadership styles* of principals and *attitudes* of teachers, since the usefulness of the results depends on credible descriptions. Much of the current emphasis on accountability in our schools is based on descriptive research, examining student outcomes such as current levels of proficiency or dropout rates. The following questions are the types investigated with descriptive research designs:

What do teachers think about magnet schools?
How often do students write papers?
What is the nature of the papers students are required to write?
What percentage of students score above 1100 on the SAT?
What forms of communication are used in the school district?
How often are higher-order questions used in the classroom?
What type of reinforcement does the teacher use?

A good example of a descriptive study investigated parental involvement with homework. Middle school students completed homework with parents and then answered questions about how much they enjoyed working with parents and whether they believed they did better in school if they worked with their parents. The results were analyzed by showing the number of students who gave different answers.

EXAMPLE | **Descriptive Research**

"Answers to Question 3 found that a significant number of students (40) perceived they do better in school if their parent(s) help them with homework. . . . Twenty-two students reported that they believe they sometimes do better in school when their parents help them with homework. Three students reported that parental involvement with homework does not help them do better in school." (Balli, S. J. (1998). When mom and dad help: Student reflections on parent involvement with homework. *Journal of Research and Development in Education, 31*(3), pp. 143–144)

CONSUMER TIPS: *Criteria for Evaluating Descriptive Studies*

1. Conclusions about relationships should be made with caution. An important limitation of descriptive studies is that relationship conclusions generally

FIGURE 8.2 Diagram of a relationship study examining group differences.

Sample of Students

Students with Learning Style A → Average Reading Achievement

Students with Learning Style B → Average Reading Achievement

Students with Learning Style C → Average Reading Achievement

Students with Learning Style D → Average Reading Achievement

Differences between groups are compared to study the relationship between learning styles and reading achievement

provides a measure of the differences among the groups, which represent a relationship between learning style and achievement. In this case we must be careful not to conclude that the learning styles *caused* differences in achievement. At best, we can predict that students with a particular type of learning style will have higher or lower achievement. Learning style may affect or influence achievement, but our relationship study does not give us a good measure of cause and effect. This hypothetical study is diagrammed in Figure 8.2.

In the examples that follow, the first is a comparative study that determines the differences between men's and women's perceptions of bullying. In the second example, the study examines whether graduate students from a CACREP program have stronger counselor self-efficacy than graduates of non-CACREP programs (CACREP is an accrediting agency for school counseling programs).

EXAMPLE | **Comparative Research Designs**

"Do male and female teachers perceive bullying differently? To begin to answer this question, we compared the mean scores of men and women teachers on our measures of bullying. There were no significant differences between men (n = 40) and women (n = 53) on the two measures. For student bullying, men had a mean of 3.36 and women had a mean of 3.69 ($t = -.15$, ns) and for teacher protection, men had a mean of 3.62 and women 3.79 ($t = -.76$, ns)." (Smith, P. A., & Hoy, W. K. (2004). Teachers' perceptions of student bullying: A conceptual and empirical analysis. *Journal of School Leadership, 14*, p. 308)

"This study was designed to investigate counseling self-efficacy of graduate students in counselor education programs to determine whether Bandura's (1986) self-efficacy theory applies. Specifically, we investigated the relationship between the training background of graduate students and counselor self-efficacy. . . . In other words, we examined whether students from CACREP-accredited and non-CACREP-accredited counselor training programs would demonstrate differences in counseling self-efficacy." (Tang, M., Addison, K. D., LaSure-Bryant, D., Norman, R., O'Connell, W., & Stewart-Sicking, J. A. (2004). Factors that influence self-efficacy of counseling students: An exploratory study. *Counselor Education and Supervision, 44*, p. 73)

CONSUMER TIPS: *Criteria for Evaluating Comparative Studies*

1. **Subjects, instrumentation, and procedures should be well described.** As in descriptive studies, it is important for the researcher to clearly and completely describe the subjects, instruments used, and procedures for gathering the data. In comparative studies it is also important to know if subjects who are in different groups have unique characteristics that could better explain differences on the dependent variable than could be explained by the independent variable. For example, suppose a researcher drew a sample of first-grade students from one school and compared the students to second-graders from a different school on attitudes toward reading. Even if more positive attitudes were found for the second-graders, this result may have been because of differences between the student populations (e.g., one school serving a higher socioeconomic level, or one school being private, the other public) rather than grade level.

2. **Identify the criteria for establishing different groups.** It is important to know how the researcher formed the different groups that are compared. In some studies the criterion or procedure for forming the groups is self-evident, such as studies that compare males to females, but there are many studies in which the procedure is important to interpretation of the results. For example, suppose a study is designed to compare participation in athletics of low-ability students and high-ability students. How the researcher identifies "high ability" and "low ability" is important. What measure, if any, was used to assess ability? How were the groups formed? One approach would be to take all the students and divide them into two ability groups on the basis of the median ability score of the group as a whole. Or, the researcher could take the highest and lowest third or quartile of students. Another approach would be to establish groups by how the students compared with the national norms, rather than just themselves. You can see that several approaches are possible, and none of them are necessarily better or more correct than others.

3. **Do not infer causation from comparative research designs.** It is important not to infer that a causal relationship exists in a comparative study. The best that you can conclude with a comparative design is that a relationship exists or that there are significant differences between the groups, but it is not a *causal* relationship. This principle is easy to overlook because some comparative

studies seem to logically establish a causal connection between the independent and dependent variables. For instance, suppose it is reported that students from private schools outscore students from public schools on measures of achievement. It is tempting to conclude that the reason, or cause, of the difference is the nature of the school (private or public). However, there are many other possible explanations, such as differences in parental involvement, socioeconomic status of students, curriculum used, and quality of teachers.

4. Graphic presentations should not distort the results. Since graphs are used frequently to present comparative results, you need to be careful in interpreting the resulting "picture." Graphs, whether histograms, pie charts, or frequency polygons, show an image of the results, and you are more likely to remember the image than the numbers that correspond to it. This is fine when the image is a reasonable representation of the numbers, but numbers can be manipulated in a graph to present different images. One type of distortion to look for is in the vertical dimensions of the graph. The size of the interval between different scores is set by the researcher, and this size greatly affects the resulting image. In fact, a crafty researcher can make fairly substantial differences appear quite small by decreasing the size of the intervals between scores or other measurement units. The researcher can also make small differences look large. For example, look at the two graphic presentations in Figure 8.3. Although each graph has summarized the same information about expenditures per pupil, the visual results

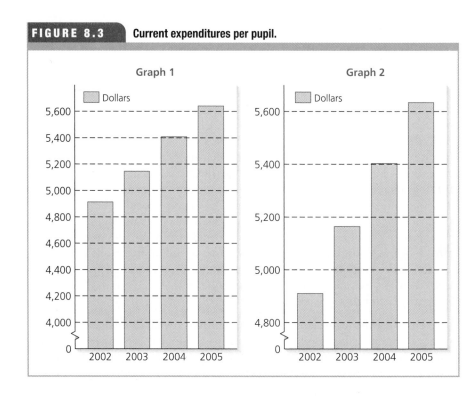

FIGURE 8.3   **Current expenditures per pupil.**

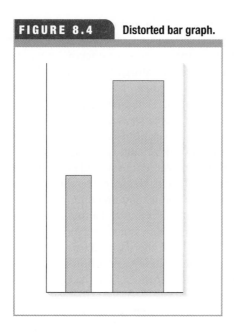

FIGURE 8.4   Distorted bar graph.

are different because the size of the interval between each amount is much smaller in one graph than in the other. In Figure 8.4 you can see that, by changing the width of the bars, one bar can look more than twice as large as the other bar.

> **Author Reflection**   *Over the years I have seen many students conduct seemingly simple descriptive, comparative, or correlational studies and then become overwhelmed by the number of analyses, tables, and variables. It is easy to include many variables and just "a few more" questions on a survey. Often these variables or questions are "interesting" but not directly related to the main purpose of the research. Researchers learn more by focusing on a few variables or questions in depth than by measuring many variables with many questions and then spending arduous hours reporting and interpreting the results.*

CORRELATIONAL STUDIES

Characteristics of Correlational Studies

In a correlational design two or more variables are related with the use of one or more correlation coefficients. Relationships are indicated by obtaining at least two scores from each subject. The pairs of scores are used to produce a scattergram and to calculate a correlation coefficient. Each score represents a variable in the study. For example, variables such as self-concept, cognitive style, previous achievement, time on task, and amount of homework completed can be related to achievement, attitudes, self-concept, and motivation. Grades in student teaching can be related to principals' ratings of effective teaching. In each case a correlation coefficient expresses the nature of the relationship between the variables.

When reading correlational research you should examine carefully the selection of instruments and subjects. The first aspect of instrumentation to examine is reliability. When highly reliable scores are used, correlations are stronger. Conversely, if reliability is low, correlations are weak. Consequently, the researcher should demonstrate evidence of reliability for the types of subjects in the study. It is also important for the instrument to provide a range of responses from a sufficient number of subjects. That is, the scores on the measures need to show good dispersion. If the scores are about the same on a variable, it is difficult to relate the variable to anything else. For example, if a study examines the relationship between ratings of teacher effectiveness and teaching style and all the teachers in the sample are rated as excellent, there would be no chance of finding a relationship. Similarly, it is difficult to find relationships between achievement of gifted students and other variables because of the lack of variability of achievement among these students.

Lack of variability can result when an instrument fails to differentiate along a continuum, or when the subjects are too homogeneous on one of the traits being measured. In either case, you will need to be careful in your interpretation of relationship studies that fail to find significant relationships. If there is a lack of variability, you will not know whether there really is no relationship or, because of a small range of responses, a particular study was unable to show the relationship.

There is also a limitation on finding significant relationships in a study that has a very large number of subjects and/or variables. Some researchers, using what is sometimes called the "shotgun" approach, measure a large number of variables with the hope that at least some of the many correlations that are calculated will be significant. However, in such studies some of the correlations will be statistically significant by chance alone, and without a theoretical or practical reason for inclusion, the results will be difficult to interpret. When thousands of subjects are used it is also possible to calculate statistically significant correlations that are actually quite small. Consequently, the relationship that is reported may be very small and of little value. We will discuss this limitation later in this chapter. Correlations studies strive to have at least 30 subjects.

The following example shows how several simple correlations were reported in the form of a *correlation matrix*. Can you follow the narrative in this example? The statements come directly from the correlations in the table.

Prediction Studies

In a prediction study, correlation coefficients show how one variable can predict another. Whereas in a simple relationship study, both variables are measured at about the same time, a predictive study shows how one variable can predict what the value of a second variable will be at a later time. Predictions are made constantly in education. Teachers predict students' behavior. Principals predict teachers' behavior.

EXAMPLE | **Correlation Matrix**

Descriptive Statistics

Eighth grade. The overall classroom social environment construct was correlated positively with social efficacy with teachers ($r = .44$, $p < .001$), social efficacy with peers ($r = .18$, $p < .01$), academic efficacy ($r = .30$, $p < .001$), and self-regulated learning ($r = .20$, $p < .01$), and related negatively to disruptive behavior ($r = -.43$, $p < .001$). Means, standard deviations, and correlations among the four dimensions of the classroom social environment and the motivation and engagement indices measured in eighth grade are presented in Table 8.1. An expected pattern of correlations was found. Teacher support, promoting interaction, and promoting mutual respect were related positively to social efficacy with teachers and peers, academic efficacy, and self-regulated learning, and related negatively to disruptive behavior. Promoting performance goals was related negatively to social efficacy with teachers and peers, academic efficacy, and self-regulated learning, and related positively to disruptive behavior.

Table 8.1 Means, Standard Deviations, and Correlations Among Perceived Classroom Social Environment Variables and Student Motivation and Engagement In Eighth Grade, Gender, Race, and Prior Achievement

	1	2	3	4	5	6	7	8	9	10	11	12
1. Teacher support	—											
2. Promote interaction	.49	—										
3. Promote mutual respect	.60	.40	—									
4. Promote performance goals	−.41	−.14	−.39	—								
5. Social efficacy: teacher	.71	.47	.49	−.45	—							
6. Social efficacy: peers	.17	.15	.20	−.17	.30	—						
7. Academic efficacy	.35	.14	.46	−.29	.47	.42	—					
8. Disruptive behavior	−.41	−.16	−.35	.45	−.35	.04	−.18	—				
9. Self-regulated learning	.44	.25	.50	−.22	.41	.20	.50	−.38	—			
10. Gender[a]	.07	.15	.10	−.18	.11	.13	−.02	−.21	−.01	—		
11. Race[b]	.01	−.16	.16	−.05	−.05	.09	.31	−.02	.10	.06	—	
12. Prior achievement[c]	.21	.05	.06	−.31	.20	.11	.11	−.21	.00	.09	−.17	—
Mean	3.22	3.22	3.52	2.15	3.60	4.16	3.86	2.54	3.27	0.57	0.44	6.72
Standard deviation	1.05	1.07	1.11	0.97	1.01	0.77	0.92	1.14	0.82			3.56

Note: Correlations about .13 are significant at the $p < .05$ lavel.
[a]Gender is coded 0 = *male* and 1 = *female*.
[b]Race is coded 0 = *European American* and 1 = *African American*.
[c]Prior achievement is seventh grade math grades 0 = *F* through 13 = *A+*).

Source: Ryan, A. M., & Patrick, H. (2001). The classroom social environment and changes in adolescents' motivation and engagement during middle school. *American Educational Research Journal 38*(2), pp. 448–449. Copyright © 2001 by the American Educational Research Association. Reprinted with permission of the publisher.

Students are selected for special programs because they are expected to do well or to do better than others. Coaches predict the performance of their players. Students are counseled to attend particular colleges or to pursue certain occupations.

CONSUMER TIPS: *Criteria for Evaluating Correlational Studies*

1. Causation should not be inferred from correlation. The most important principle in evaluating correlational research is not to infer causation. This is not as easy as it sounds, for many relationships based on correlations seem as if they *do* infer causation. For example, if you find a positive predictive relationship between time on task and achievement, it is easy to conclude that increasing time on task will increase achievement. Although this *may* be true, it cannot be concluded from a correlational finding for two reasons. First, the direction of possible causation is not clear. That is, it may be that higher previous achievement causes students to be on task more. Second, other variables associated with time on task that are not included in the study may affect the relationship and may, in fact, be causally related. For instance, perhaps students who spend more time on task have a higher aptitude for learning, better motivation for learning, and more parental support than students who spend less time on task. Perhaps teachers interact differently with students who are on task compared with students who tend to be off task.

This principle is illustrated more clearly in a relationship between student achievement and per-pupil expenditures. Although a positive relationship exists, it would be a mistake to think that achievement can be affected simply by spending more money because many other variables also related to per-pupil expenditure, such as family background, are causes of student achievement.

As a final example of this important principle, consider the following "true" statement: There is a positive relationship between students' weight and reading achievement. Unbelievable, you think? Examine Figure 8.5. There is a positive relationship between the two factors because a third variable, age, is related to weight. Obviously, there is a positive relationship between age and reading achievement. If you were puzzled by the first conclusion, you were implying causation, which would lead to the conclusion that achievement could be improved by fattening up the students!

2. The *reported* correlation should not be higher or lower than the *actual* relationship. You need to be aware of factors that may spuriously increase or decrease a correlation. One factor is the nature of the sample from which the correlation is calculated. If the sample is more homogeneous on one of the variables than the population, the correlation will be lower than for the population as a whole. Conversely, if a sample is more heterogeneous on the variable than the population, the correlation will be higher than would be true for the population as a whole.

A second factor is the range of scores on the variables that are correlated. If the variability of scores on one variable is small, the correlation will be low. This is sometimes referred to as **restriction in range.** If the range is restricted, the variability is reduced, and without adequate variability the correlation will be low. Thus, in some research in which the range is restricted, the actual relationship is higher than that reported.

A third factor relates to the reliability of the scores obtained of the correlated variables. As noted, correlations are directly related to reliability—the lower the

Restriction in range:
A small range of variability.

FIGURE 8.5   Relationship between weight and reading achievement.

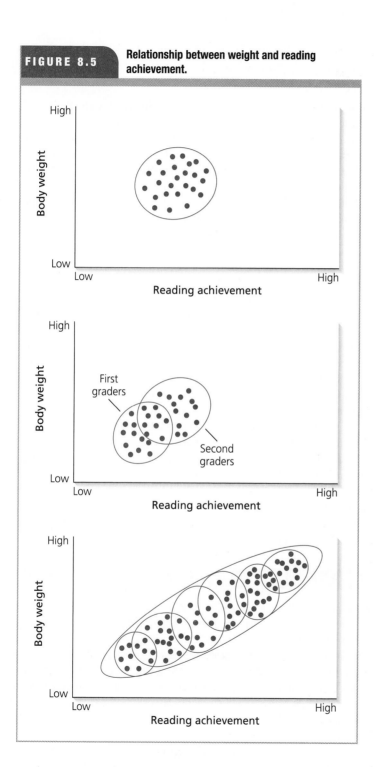

Attenuation: Lowering of correlation because of unreliable measures.

reliability, the lower the correlation. A lowering of the correlation because of unreliability is called **attenuation** and is sometimes "corrected" statistically to show what the correlation would be if the measures were more reliable.

3. Practical significance should not be confused with statistical significance. Researchers use the word *significant* in two ways. In one sense, it refers to a statistical inference, which means the coefficient that is calculated is probably different from zero, that is, no relationship (Chapter 10 discusses this concept in greater detail). Thus, a researcher may report that "a correlation of .30 is significant." This type of phrase is associated *only* with the *statistical* meaning of significance. Another meaning of significance implies importance or meaningfulness of the practical value of the correlation. This is a more subjective judgment, one that should be made by the reader of the research as well as by the researcher. One important principle of correlation needs to be considered in making this judgment. Because correlations are expressed as decimals, it is easy to confuse the coefficient with a percentage. However, the correlation coefficient is not an indication of the percentage of "sameness" between two variables. The extent to which the variables share common properties or characteristics is actually indicated by the square of the correlation coefficient. This is called the **coefficient of determination,** and it is a much better indicator of practical or meaningful significance than the correlation coefficient. For example, a correlation of .50, squared, indicates that the variables have 25% in common, or 25% "explained" of what can be accounted for, which leaves 75% unexplained. Thus, if the correlation between achievement and some other variable is .70, which is regarded as a "high" correlation, about 50% of what can vary with respect to achievement is not predicted or accounted for by the correlation.

Coefficient of determination: The square of the correlation coefficient.

In the following example use of the phrase "percentage of variance predicted" is used to interpret the results of correlations between school readiness (preschool and kindergarten academic/cognitive and social/behavioral assessments) and similar measures after the first and second grades. The authors use the term "effect size" in their discussion, which is a common term when addressing practical significance. In this case effect size is synonymous with coefficient of determination.

EXAMPLE | **Interpretation of Correlation Coefficients**

"The moderate estimates of effect size found for the academic/cognitive domain indicate that, on average, 25% of variance in early school academic/cognitive performance is predicted from preschool or kindergarten academic/cognitive status. . . . In contrast, social/behavioral assessments at preschool or kindergarten age account for 10% or less of the variance in social/behavioral measures in kindergarten, first grade, or second grade." (LaParo, K. M., & Pianta, R. C. (2000). Predicting children's competence in the early school years: A meta-analytic review. *Review of Educational Research, 70*, p. 474)

---

4. The size of the correlation should be sufficient for the use of the results. Much larger correlations are needed for predictions with individuals than with groups. Crude group predictions can be made with correlations as low as .40 to .60, whereas correlations above .75 are usually needed to make predictions for individuals. In exploratory studies low correlations (e.g., .25 to .40) may indicate a need for further study, but higher correlations are needed for research to confirm theories or test hypotheses. In studies using regression analysis, correlations between .20 and .40 are common and usually indicate some practical significance.

5. Prediction studies should report accuracy of prediction for new subjects. To use the results of prediction research, consumers must know the accuracy of the predicted relationship. This figure is found by testing a presumed predictive relationship with a new, different group of persons.

6. Procedures for collecting data should be clearly indicated. It is important for researchers to indicate, in detail, the procedures used to collect the data with which correlations are calculated because the procedures affect reliability. As previously noted, correlation coefficients are directly related to the reliability of the measures and the sampling of subjects.

CAUSAL-COMPARATIVE *and* EX POST FACTO STUDIES

We have seen how correlations and differences between groups can be analyzed to examine relationships between variables. Although most nonexperimental, quantitative research designs explore simple or predictive relationships, some nonexperimental designs do investigate cause-and-effect relationships. We will look at types of these designs: causal-comparative and ex post facto.

USING EDUCATIONAL RESEARCH

With the growing importance of high-stakes testing for student promotion and graduation there has been a renewed interest in the relationship between teaching and student performance. One approach in studying this relationship is to use multiple regression analysis to determine if aspects of teaching, such as style or approach, correlate with student performance. Regression can use previous measures of student ability in the analysis to "control" for the effect of student differences prior to their classroom experiences. It would not make much sense, for example, to correlate teaching style with student achievement without accounting for student ability, socioeconomic status, absenteeism, and other variables that are related to performance.

INTERNET CONNECTION

See Trochim's Website for a summary of correlational designs, terms, and limitations. **(http://trochim.human.cornell.edu/kb/index.htm).**

Causal-Comparative Designs

In many educational situations, after a program or project is implemented, questions of cause arise. While it is not possible for researchers to control the intervention, it is possible to monitor what occurs and measure outcomes that compare the intervention group with the control group. Suppose you were interested in determining the impact of attending preschool on first-grade performance. The intervention, preschool, is the independent variable. You can't really control the intervention, but you can measure the extent to which it is implemented. A comparison group of children not attending preschool could be used in this design to investigate whether preschool results in greater first-grade achievement (dependent variable). The quality of the design depends on how well the comparison group is matched to the intervention group, and how well you can understand how the intervention may have caused an increase in achievement.

Causal-comparative: Nonexperimental studies designed to determine cause and effect.

There are many types of "interventions" that can be studied using **causal-comparative** designs. For example, different approaches to mentoring beginning teachers, different curricula, staff development, different ways that principals evaluate teachers, group counseling compared to individual counseling, and inclusion of students with disabilities would lend themselves to investigation using a causal-comparative design because the researcher cannot control (manipulate) the program or strategy.

The obvious weakness of a causal-comparative study is lack of control. The researcher cannot control the independent variable or extraneous/confounding variables. If random assignment is possible, many of the extraneous/confounding variables can be accounted for, but there is still lack of control over the intervention and what occurs within in each group as the intervention is experienced. It is very important in these designs to choose comparison subjects who are as similar as possible in the intervention group. This is typically accomplished by matching or using homogeneous groups, and there are some statistical adjustments that can be used as well.

Ex Post Facto Studies

Ex post facto: Presumed cause that occurred in the past.

In **ex post facto** research the investigators decide whether one or more preexisting conditions have caused subsequent differences when subjects who experienced one type of condition are compared to subjects who experienced a different condition (the phrase *ex post facto* means "after the fact").

Ex post facto designs are very much like causal-comparative designs. As in a causal-comparative study, there is typically an "intervention" and/or "comparison" group, and the results are analyzed with the same statistical procedures. Of course, in ex post facto research, there is no active manipulation of the independent variable because it has already occurred, but the comparison of group differences on the dependent variable is the same. In an ex post facto study, then, the researcher investigates an intervention that has already occurred, while in a causal-comparative design the researcher is able to monitor and observe the intervention as it occurs.

In conducting an ex post facto study the researcher selects subjects who are as similar as possible except for the independent variable that is being investigated.

For example, in a study of the effect of class size on achievement, the researcher needs to locate groups of subjects who are similar in all respects except whether they attended large or small classes. In making the final selection of the groups of subjects, the researcher must be aware of possible extraneous variables that make causal conclusions problematic. Thus, in a study of class size the only difference between students who attend small classes and those who attend large classes should be the size of the class, not such factors as socioeconomic status, quality of teachers, teaching methods, curriculum, student ability, and student motivation. That is, if the students in all the small classes had more ability, better teachers, or higher motivation, these factors could affect achievement in addition to, or in spite of, class size.

CONSUMER TIPS: *Criteria for Evaluating Causal-Comparative and Ex Post Facto Studies*

1. **The primary purpose of the research should be to investigate causal relationships when an experiment is not possible.** The experiment is the best method for studying cause-and-effect relationships, so causal-comparative studies should only be used when it is not possible or feasible to conduct an experiment. There should be sufficient evidence in prior research to indicate that relationships exist between the variables and that it is appropriate to study causal relationships. Without existing empirical evidence of relationships, a strong theoretical rationale is needed.

2. **The presumed causal condition should have already occurred in an ex post facto study.** It is essential for the condition represented by the independent variable to have occurred before data are collected on or recorded for the dependent variable. The "intervention" must have already taken place for a study to be classified as causal-comparative.

3. **Potential extraneous variables should be recognized and considered.** It is crucial for the researcher to show the reader that potential extraneous variables have been considered. Because existing groups are usually used in the comparison, these variables usually consist of differences in characteristics of the subjects, but other factors may also be related. It is incumbent on the researcher to present evidence that the groups being compared differ only on the dependent variable. Failure to do so suggests that the groups have not been carefully selected to avoid the influence of extraneous variables.

4. **Differences between groups being compared should be controlled.** When it is clear that there are measurable differences between groups being compared, researchers must use appropriate procedures to control their effect. Matching subjects is one procedure; statistical techniques can also be used.

5. **Causal conclusions should be made with caution.** Even when all potential extraneous variables have been controlled, which is rare, it is best to accept *with caution* results that seem to suggest a causal relationship. Researchers

should indicate possible limitations and frame the finding as "suggesting" a causal relationship. In almost all causal-comparative studies, there will be sufficient reason to be tentative in concluding cause-and-effect relationships.

USING SURVEYS *in* NONEXPERIMENTAL RESEARCH

Survey research has evolved over the years to become a popular method of collecting data for nonexperimental designs. In a survey, the investigator selects a group of respondents, collects information, and then analyzes the information to answer the research questions. The group of subjects is usually selected from a larger population through some type of probability sampling, which allows accurate inferences about a large population from a small sample. In other surveys an entire population is included. Most surveys describe the incidence, frequency, and distribution of characteristics of the population, such as demographic facts.

Surveys are used frequently in business, government, public health, politics, psychology, sociology, and transportation, as well as in education. In addition to being descriptive, surveys are also used to investigate relationships between variables, with a comparative or correlational design.

Survey research is popular because of versatility, efficiency, and generalizability. Surveys are versatile in being able to address a wide range of problems or questions, especially when the purpose is to describe the attitudes, perspectives, and beliefs of the respondents, and can be conducted with written questionnaires or with interviews. Relative to interviews, written surveys are less costly than phone interviews or personal interviews when there is a large number of respondents. An important value of survey research is that sampling from a population can be used to result in fairly accurate generalizable conclusions about the larger population. National polls of political preference or voting intentions, which may include 1,200–1,500 adults, are accurate indicators of the nation or state as a whole.

In designing a survey the researcher should complete the following steps:

1. **Define the purpose and objectives.** List each pertinent objective or research question that will be addressed and only collect information that has a direct bearing on the objectives or questions. Researchers should refrain from asking questions that "would be nice or interesting to know about," or questions whose results are analyzed before identifying how the data will be used.

2. **Identify resources needed and target population.** It is necessary to calculate the cost of preparing, printing, mailing, and analyzing surveys, and to know the nature of the target population. These parameters will help in knowing whether the survey is too long and the size of the sample.

3. **Choose an appropriate survey method.** Surveys are either paper- or Web-based written questionnaires, telephone interviews, or personal interviews. Each method has advantages and disadvantages. The most important advantages of the written survey are that many questions can be asked, respondents can be assured of anonymity, lower cost, and the ability to reach a fairly large sample.

Interviews are used when there is a need to have a very high response rate, when there is a need to probe, particularly with nonverbal feedback, when there are many open-ended questions, and when there are just a few questions.

4. Word questions carefully. Questions should be clear, understandable, and unbiased. To accomplish these goals the questions should:

- Use everyday, common terms and avoid jargon
- Be short and simple
- Be grammatically correct
- Not be biased or leading (e.g., "How satisfied are you with the timely response of school administrators?")
- Use the same scale for all questions if possible
- Use consistent wording and leading phrases (e.g., "To what extent was your grading based on:
  - Homework
  - Quizzes
  - Papers
  - Exams")
- Not be double barreled (e.g., "The principal is accessible and responsive.")

5. Design the survey. A well-designed format will use at least a 10-point typeface on paper and have sufficient white space so that different sections and questions can be clearly differentiated by the respondents. Cramming a lot of questions on a page to save paper is not recommended.

6. Develop directions. It is important to have clear instructions so that there is no ambiguity about how and where to respond and what to do when completing the survey.

7. Develop a letter of transmittal. The letter of transmittal is crucial to obtaining a high response rate. The letter should be brief and professional in appearance. The credibility of the researcher and the benefits of the research should be included.

8. Pilot test. A critical step in survey research is to pilot-test a draft of the letter of transmittal and survey. This is typically accomplished with a sample of 15–20 individuals who are from the population to be sampled. In the pilot test the respondents should read the directions and complete the survey. When finished, they can comment on the clarity and format of the survey. The pilot helps the researcher know how long it will take to complete the survey. Often two pilots are conducted to be sure that there will not be surface problems or costly mistakes.

INTERNET CONNECTION

Go to **www.pareonline.net/pdf/v10n12.pdf** for an excellent article on how to best format a paper-based survey.

One of the most serious limitations of survey research is a low response rate. The smaller the response rate the more likely the results will be biased. Response rates around 70% are considered adequate. If possible, nonrespondents should be analyzed to determine if they are different from the respondents. Response rate can be increased by doing the following:

- Use a well-designed, professional, attractive, and easy-to-complete survey.
- Use several contacts with the sample, including a prenotification card, reminder postcards, and remailings of the survey.
- Use at least first-class mail; certified mail and express mail are best for long surveys.
- Include return postage and a return envelope.
- Use a transmittal letter that clearly indicates the benefits of the survey.
- Use telephone follow-up.
- Use financial or other incentives.

Surveys are either given to one or more samples or populations at one time or are given more than once to the same or similar subjects over a specified length of time. These differences have important implications for interpreting results and are discussed next as cross-sectional and longitudinal methods.

Cross-Sectional Surveys

Cross-sectional survey: Given at one time.

In a **cross-sectional survey,** information is collected from one or more samples or populations at one time. There are two types of cross-sectional surveys. One type simply studies a phenomenon as it occurs at one time, for example, political surveys and surveys that study an attitude or characteristic of a group. A good illustration is the Annual Gallup Poll of the Public's Attitudes Toward the Public Schools, published in *Phi Delta Kappan.* The purpose of this poll is to estimate the attitudes of the adult civilian population in the United States toward many aspects of schooling, including the perceived biggest problems facing public schools, inner-city schools, part-time work by high school students, length of the school year and day, and parental choice.

Another type of cross-sectional survey is intended to compare different age categories of subjects to investigate possible developmental differences or relationships. For example, if researchers are interested in changes in students' self-concepts between 6th and 12th grades and factors that may affect self-concept at various ages, a cross-sectional survey could be designed in which samples of current 6th- through 12th-grade students are selected and questioned. All subjects are asked the questions at about the same time (e.g., October 1990).

Cross-sectional surveys are convenient and allow some tentative conclusions about how individuals may change over time. However, caution is advised for two primary reasons. First, there may be important differences between the subjects who are sampled in each grade or in each age category. For instance, if the sampling is done within a school, an assumption is that the type of students attending the school has not changed. If current 6th-graders are different in important ways, besides age, from 12th-graders, conclusions about changes over time are affected. Second, because the data are obtained at one time, what may show as a "difference" from 6th to 12th grade may not represent a change. It could be that 12th-graders did not, when in 6th grade, have the same responses of current 6th-graders.

Longitudinal Surveys

In a **longitudinal survey,** the same group of subjects is studied over a specified length of time. Thus, a longitudinal study of self-concept might begin in 1990 with 6th-graders and continue until 2002 for the same subjects. Data are collected at different times, often over several years. There are variations of longitudinal surveys, depending on the subjects who are sampled or used to make up the "same group." In what is called a *trend* study, a general population is studied over time, although the subjects are sampled from the population each year or time of data collection. Thus, the population changes somewhat over time. In a *cohort* longitudinal study, a specific population, such as the freshman class of 1995, is studied over time. A *panel* sample is a cohort study in which the same individuals are surveyed each time data are collected.

> **Longitudinal survey:** Same or similar subjects surveyed over time.

A longitudinal survey is typically much stronger than a cross-sectional one. However, a serious disadvantage may be loss of subjects, which occurs with studies that extend over a long period of time and with populations that are difficult to track (e.g., following high school or college graduates). Not only will the sample size sometimes become too small for adequate generalizations, but also there may be a systematic loss of certain types of subjects. For example, a longitudinal study of attitudes of high school students should consider the fact that some of the sample will drop out, leaving mainly those who in all probability have more positive attitudes.

It should be noted that the terms *longitudinal* and *cross-sectional* are also used to describe research that would not be thought of as a survey. The differences between longitudinal and cross-sectional studies are illustrated in Figure 8.6.

USING EDUCATIONAL RESEARCH

Recent federal legislation has mandated that states use test scores to show that "adequate yearly progress" is being made by students. One way to approach this is longitudinal, examining the same students each year as they progress in school. Another approach is to compare the scores of one grade for different years. That is, what is the score of 5th-graders in 2004 compared to 5th-graders in 2005 and 2006? This approach introduces the *cohort effect*, because differences from year to year for the same grade will be related to the nature of the group of students each year. Controlling for these differences represents a challenge for both researchers and policymakers.

| FIGURE 8.6 | Cross-sectional and longitudinal designs. |

			May 2006
Cross-Sectional			Samples of 4th-, 5th-, and 6th-grade students taken.
Longitudinal	May 2004	May 2005	May 2006
	Sample of 4th-grade students taken.	Sample of 5th-grade students taken.	Sample of 6th-grade students taken.

Internet-Based Surveys

The Internet has led to a dramatic increase in the number of electronic surveys. They are now commonplace, and are called e-surveys, e-mail surveys, Internet surveys, or Web-based surveys. Their common feature is that the Internet is used to send questions and usually to receive responses.

Types of Internet-Based Surveys. There are essentially two types of Internet-based surveys: e-mail and Web-based. An e-mail survey is usually sent as an attachment, and it typically looks much like a paper survey. The Web-based survey, which is the most common type, directs the respondent to a specific Website that contains the survey. Web-based surveys take full advantage of the electronic flexibility that is possible. The surveys are usually very attractive, using graphics and sometimes multimedia resources. Respondents often answer only one or two questions on each page, and then simply "click" to the next page. They are very easy to complete.

Advantages and Disadvantages. The advantages of electronic surveys are obvious: reduced cost and time, easy access, quick responses, and ease of entering responses into a database. It can be used effectively as a follow-up to a written survey. Electronic surveys are most effective with targeted professional groups, with "in-house" groups, when they are short and simple, and when a password can be used to ensure anonymity. Disadvantages are also obvious. Samples are limited to those with access to the technology, both hardware and software, which may lead to bias. For example, there are large disparities by race and socioeconomic status with respect to Internet access. Even when there is access, the respondents need to feel comfortable with the procedures and Internet tools that are utilized. Perhaps the most serious limitation is that respondents may not believe that their answers will be confidential. Confidentiality and privacy issues are very important; many will be reluctant to be honest because, even with the use of passwords and assurances from the researcher, there is a lingering feeling that any electronic response can be traced to the individual. These advantages and disadvantages are summarized in Table 8.2.

TABLE 8.2	Advantages and Disadvantages of Internet-Based Surveys

Advantages	Disadvantages
Costs less	Low response rate
Fast response	Response bias
Takes less time to distribute	Lack of confidentiality and privacy
Respondents enter answers directly for each question	Confidence that participant and not someone else answered the questions
Provides enhanced presentation through color and graphics (especially for children)	Potential information overload, such as too many questions
Immediate database construction	Participants must be skilled in computer usage
Convenient	Hardware compatibility
Increased accuracy of responses	Hard to inform participants about their ethical rights
Easy follow-up	Hard to provide incentives
Easy access to geographically diverse samples	Sampling limited to those with access to computers

It is clear that electronic surveys will be used with greater frequency. When the respondents are almost all Internet savvy (such as teachers, principals, college faculties and staff, and children and adolescents) and the nature of the topic is not personal, electronic surveys are excellent for conducting research.

Internet-Based Survey Design. Many of the suggestions about effective questionnaire and survey design previously summarized is applicable to Web-based surveys. There are some additional considerations related to technology. Essentially, a simple, clear layout with no clutter is needed for easy navigation. Some further suggestions include:

- Show one or at most only a few questions on each screen.
- Show both question and response categories on the same screen.
- Avoid excess scrolling.
- Limit the use of matrix format questions.
- Direct respondents to simply click on their response to closed-end questions.
- Use error messages that refer to the specific location that needs attention.
- Use graphics, hypertext, and colors, especially for children.
- Password protect Web-based surveys.
- Indicate progress toward completing the survey.

Consumer-friendly software for constructing Internet-based surveys, such as SurveyMonkey and Inquisite, allow most anyone to construct and use these types of surveys (including children, most of whom are very comfortable with computers). There is typically an editor to help develop the survey and many different attractive formats so that answers are easy to record. In addition, the responses are automatically stored in a database and can be used to produce tables and graphs (including real-time compilations).

INTERNET CONNECTION

For information about online surveys visit the Rand Corporation Website: **www.rand.org/pubs/monograph_reports/MR1480/MR1480/ch5.pdf**.

ANATOMY *of a* NONEXPERIMENTAL QUANTITATIVE RESEARCH STUDY

The following example of a published nonexperimental quantitative study is included to show you how such an investigation is designed and reported, and how it should be interpreted. This particular nonexperimental study is an example of comparative research.

EXHIBIT 8.1

Causal Beliefs of Public School Students about Success and Failure in Music

Roy M. Legette
Shorter College

Student motivation and achievement in relation to Attribution Theory were examined in this study. Public school students (N = 1,114) were asked to respond to items on Asmus's Music Attribution Orientation Scale, indicating those causes that they attributed most to succeeding or failing in music. Results showed that, collectively, students placed more importance on ability and effort as causal attributions. Gender, school level, and school system were found to have significant effects on student response. Implications for teaching and future research are discussed.

General research problem statement

Music educators have long been concerned with motivating students toward greater musical achievement. Although many studies involving this complex area have been conducted in educational psychology and related fields, few have specifically addressed issues in music education. In the present study, principles of Attribution Theory were applied to examine the causes that elementary and secondary public school students attribute most to succeeding or failing in music. According to Attribution Theory, motivation and achievement are influenced by students' beliefs about the causes of success or failure at given tasks, and future approaches to the same or similar tasks are influenced by these causal attributions (Weiner, 1972, 1972a). Four attributions commonly associated with this theory are ability, effort, task difficulty, and luck. These causal attributions are considered to be either internal (originating from the student) or external (not originating from the student). They are also viewed as stable (not perceived by the student to change with subsequent trials) or unstable (perceived by the student to change with repeated attempts). Thus, causal attributions of ability and effort are considered to be internal-stable and internal-unstable respectively, while task difficulty is considered external-stable and luck, external-unstable.

Causal attributions have also been used to gain insight into affective reactions of students regarding future success or failure situations (Bar-Tal, 1978; Nicholls, 1976; Weiner, 1972). When students are successful and the reason is internal (e.g., ability, effort), they feel a sense of pride and accomplishment. Conversely, feelings of deep shame are experienced if students are unsuccessful. The external attributions of task difficulty and luck appear to produce considerably less pride. Whether students perceive an attribution as stable or unstable is important, because this perception affects their level of expectancy for accomplishing the same or similar tasks in the future. If students attribute the cause of success for a particular task to ability (internal-stable), there is a high probability that they will expect to be successful at this task in the future. Alternately, if students cite ability as a cause for being unsuccessful at a task, they will often expect to fail in future attempts. Should students attribute success or failure to effort (internal-unstable), varying results are often expected in subsequent trials.

As a result of extensive research conducted by Weiner (1972a, 1972b) demonstrating the importance of causal attributions in understanding student motivation and achievement, a substantial body of research has emerged. Much of it has to do with attributions made by students about their own successes and failures, and how these attributions influence future expectancies, affect, and subsequent achievement strivings.

Medway and Lowe (1980) asked 122 children participating in crossage tutoring programs to cite causes they thought would influence successful or unsuccessful learning in a tutorial program. Whether attributions were measured prior to, during, or after tutoring, both tutors and tutees felt that tutorial learning was more dependent on effort than ability. Moreover, the tutees tended to attribute positive learning outcomes to their partners while attributing negative learning outcomes to themselves.

With the help of 176 students attending a junior high/high school for academically advanced students, Ames and Archer (1988) studied how motivation is related to mastery and performance goals in a classroom setting. Students were asked to respond to a questionnaire designed to ascertain their perceptions of classroom goals. Students who perceived an emphasis on mastery goals (e.g., students are given a chance to correct mistakes) in the classroom were reported as using their time more strategically, preferring challenging tasks, having a more positive attitude toward the class, and having a strong belief that success follows one's effort. Students who perceived an emphasis on performance goals (e.g., students feel bad when they do not do as well as others) tended to focus more on ability, attributing failure to the lack thereof. These findings suggest that causal attributions cited by students for success or failure affect how they approach various tasks in the classroom and that causal attributions are affected by students' perceptions of the classroom goals.

[Literature review continues.]

In music education, Asmus (1986a) studied 143 undergraduate and graduate students enrolled in music education or music therapy programs. Attribution Theory was used to determine whether there was a relationship between students' perceived causes of success and failure when talking about themselves and their perceived causes of success and failure when talking about others. Results showed that success or failure was strongly attributed to task difficulty when students talked about themselves and to effort when they talked about others. Asmus (1985) also examined the views of sixth-grade general music students to gain a better understanding of why students think they succeed and fail in music. Again, principles of Attribution Theory were applied. Findings revealed that the majority of students selected the internal-stable attribution of ability and the internal-unstable attribution of effort as the major causes of their success or failure in music. Asmus (1986b) expanded the previous study by adding junior and high school students, greatly increasing the sample size. Students were asked to give free responses as to why some students are successful in music and others are unsuccessful. The major finding of this study was that 80% of reasons cited had to do with effort and ability. In addition, students tended to change their causal attributions with grade level. As the music students advanced in grade level, there was a gradual shift from effort attributions to ability attributions.

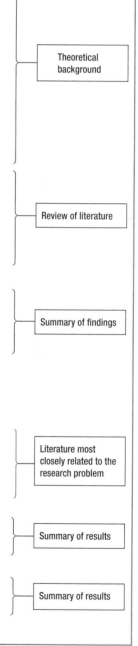

Theoretical background

Review of literature

Summary of findings

Literature most closely related to the research problem

Summary of results

Summary of results

(continued)

EXHIBIT 8.1 (continued)

Independent variable with two levels (dichotomous)

Dependent variables

Inferential statistic

TABLE 2 Comparisons of Causal Attributions Between Students Attending City Schools and Those Attending County Schools

Variable	City Students (n = 558)		County Students (n = 556)		Inferential statistic
	M	SD	M	SD	t
Effort	4.13	0.85	3.94	0.92	3.54*
Background	2.77	0.91	2.86	0.97	1.59
Class environment	3.72	0.74	3.99	0.73	6.07*
Musical ability	4.24	0.79	3.99	0.92	4.77*
Affect for music	3.62	0.83	3.68	0.91	1.13

*$p < .002$.

Findings shown in Table 2 reveal that subject responses within the two school systems differed significantly ($p < .002$) on three of the subscales, with students attending city schools placing more importance on effort and musical ability, and those attending county schools perceiving class environment as a more important causal attribution.

ANOVA is an inferential statistical procedure

One-way analyses of variance (ANOVAs) were used to compare cited causal attributions among the three different school levels. There were significant differences among the three school levels ($p < .002$) for the variables of effort, background, musical ability, and affect for music. No significant difference ($p > .002$) was found for class environment. Descriptive statistics are provided in Table 3.

Table 3 Means and Standard Deviations of Causal Attributions by School Level

School level independent variable with three levels

Dependent variables

Variable	Elementary (n = 596)		Middle (n = 318)		High (n = 199)		F	p
	M	SD	M	SD	M	SD		
Effort	3.83	0.95	4.16	0.82	4.43	0.59	43.24	.000*
Background	2.95	1.01	2.62	0.85	2.71	0.79	15.00	.000*
Class environment	3.90	0.77	3.79	0.74	3.83	0.67	2.39	.092
Musical ability	3.91	0.95	4.26	0.79	4.49	0.53	41.89	.000*
Affect for music	3.62	0.92	3.63	0.34	4.14	0.53	42.64	.000*

*$p < .002$

As shown in Table 3, music ability and effort were again listed as leading causal attributions with both variables increasing at each succeeding school level. Post-hoc means analysis using a Newman-Keuls multiple comparison procedure revealed that the mean responses by school level for the variables of effort, musical ability, and affect for music were significantly different from each other. As regards the background variable, scores were not significantly different between elementary and middle school students but were significantly different between high school students and the two remaining levels.

DISCUSSION

Summary of results

The results of this study indicate that students tend to place more importance on ability and effort as causal attributions for success or failure in music. This result is consistent with the findings of previous research (Asmus, 1988; Austin, 1991; Chandler, Chiarella, & Auria, 1988; Legette, 1993). In light of the fact that ability is often perceived by students as an internal-stable factor (Anderson & Dennis, 1978; Weiner, 1972), it is encouraging to see that students also place a great amount of importance on effort—a perceived internal-unstable causal attribution.

Results showed that females perceived ability and effort as being more important than did males. This finding contradicts previous research, which has shown that females have a tendency to be more external—often attributing success or failure to task difficulty or luck (Bar-Tal, 1978).

> Relationship to previous research

The school system attended (city versus county) significantly influenced how students responded on three of the attribution subscales: effort, class environment, and musical ability. Students in the city schools tended to place more importance on ability and effort, whereas students in the county schools perceived class environment as more important. The two school systems involved in the study were quite dissimilar in terms of ethnic makeup. Perhaps race was a contributing factor to the results.

> Possible explanation for differences, between city and county

There were significant differences in attributed causes due to school level. It was interesting to note that not only were ability and effort the leading attributions cited, but they tended to increase as the school level increased. Previous research conducted by Asmus has shown that younger students tend to use more effort-related attributions and shift to ability-related attributions as they grow older. The results of this study are inconsistent with these findings and seem to indicate that younger students use more ability-related attributions and that both ability and effort attributions tend to increase concurrently as students move through school.

> Relationship to previous research

The fact that most subjects placed more importance on ability and effort as causal attributions for success and failure in music should be of interest to music educators. Attribution Theory states that student beliefs about the causes of their success or failure at a particular task will influence how they approach that task in the future. Success due to ability promotes a sense of pride, whereas failure due to ability promotes a sense of shame. It seems that ability as a causal attribution might constitute a double-edged sword. That is, if students who are successful attribute their success to ability, it is quite probable they will expect the same results in the future. However, should students fail and perceive ability as the cause, they might continually expect to fail in the future. Since effort has been shown to be perceived by students as a changeable attribution, students might believe that a subsequent attempt at the same task will yield a totally different outcome. For this reason, music educators might consider giving effort more (or at least the same) attention than they do ability. It appears that student perception, motivation and achievement are inextricably linked as the student progresses through the educational system. Obviously, much more research is warranted.

REFERENCES

Ames, C., & Archer, J. (1988). Achievement goals in the classroom: Students' learning strategies and motivation processes. *Journal of Educational Psychology, 80* (3), 260–267.

Anderson, C., & Jennings. D. (1980). When experiences of failure promote expectations of success: The impact of attributing-failure to ineffective strategies. *Journal of Personality, 48* (3), 293–407.

Asmus, E. (1985). Sixth graders' achievement motivation: Their views of success and failure in music. *Bulletin of the Council for Research in Music Education,* no. 85, 1–13.

STUDY QUESTIONS

1. What do researchers accomplish with nonexperimental studies?
2. In what ways can the characteristics of subjects affect the interpretation of descriptive and correlational studies?
3. How can graphs be used appropriately and inappropriately to summarize descriptive data?
4. Why should causation not be inferred from comparative or correlational designs?
5. Why is it important to examine the size of correlations as well as narrative conclusions about relationships?

6. What criteria would support a credible prediction study?
7. Give some examples of studies that would be classified as ex post facto and causal-comparative. What are some possible limitations in the designs?
8. What is the difference between cross-sectional and longitudinal surveys?
9. What are the advantages and disadvantages of using a cross-sectional rather than a longitudinal survey?
10. What are the advantages and disadvantages of using a written survey rather than a face-to-face interview?
11. Why is a pilot test an important step in designing a survey?
12. What are the advantages and disadvantages of using an electronic survey?

@WWW   SAMPLE TEST QUESTIONS

See this text's Companion Website at www.ablongman.com/mcmillan5e for sample test questions and answers.

 RESEARCH NAVIGATOR™ ACTIVITIES

1. A nonexperimental study is illustrated in Research Navigator™ AN 18752820. This study of 138 fifth- and sixth-graders' learning preferences used both correlational and comparative methods. Which research questions were investigated with the comparative data? Which were investigated with correlational methods? Why would it have been helpful to include a scatterplot in addition to the correlation coefficients? Would a different approach to determining criteria for group membership be better?
2. In the Research Navigator™ Finding Sources page, click the Education subject, then use the words *internet survey* for a search. You will find about fifty sources. Identify one or two of these that give you more information about how to make Internet surveys more effective.

Chapter 9

Experimental Research Designs

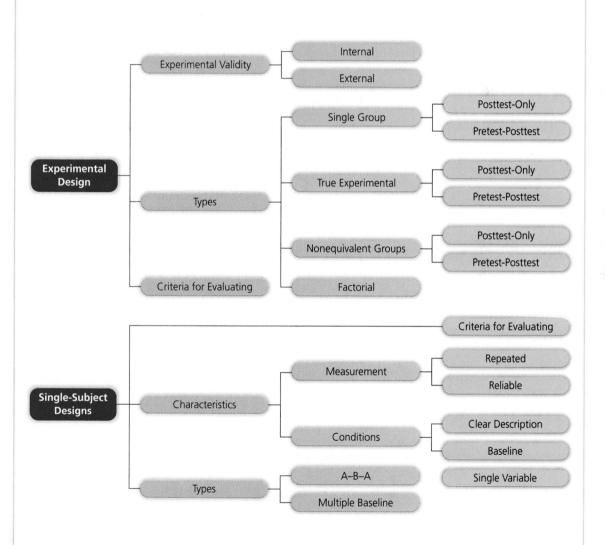

CHAPTER ROAD MAP

In descriptive, comparative, correlational, ex post facto, and causal-comparative designs, the researcher has no control over what has happened or what will happen to the subjects that may affect their responses to the dependent variable. We now turn to designs in which the researcher does have such control. These designs, experimental and single-subject, are the best approaches to investigating cause-and-effect relationships. However, experiments are rather difficult to carry out in educational settings in ways that permit definitive conclusions. Because of the applied nature of most educational experiments, many factors affect the credibility of the research.

As a result of reading and studying this chapter, you will:

- Know the characteristics of experimental designs
- Understand experimental validity
- Know and understand threats to the internal validity of experiments
- Know and understand threats to the external validity of experiments
- Understand true and quasi-experimental designs
- Understand factorial experimental designs and the concept of interaction
- Know and understand criteria for conducting credible experiments
- Know and understand how single-subject studies are conducted and evaluated
- Understand and critique articles with experimental designs

CHARACTERISTICS *of* EXPERIMENTAL RESEARCH

There is one essential characteristic of all experimental research: direct control (manipulation) of the independent variable. Direct manipulation of the independent variable means that the investigator determines when the subjects receive the intervention (treatment) and how much of it each subject receives. Most educational experiments compare subjects who have received different interventions. There must be some type of difference in the independent variable, and the researcher must be able to "manipulate" the time during which these different interventions are received or experienced by the subjects. One simple treatment, for instance, is to give feedback to one group of subjects and compare their progress with subjects who received no feedback. The difference in the independent variable is receiving or not receiving feedback, and the researcher determines when the "experimental" subjects take it. In educational research, the method of instruction, type of rewards given to students, curricula, type of grouping, amount of learning time, and assignments are common independent variables that are manipulated in experiments.

A second ubiquitous characteristic of experiments is control of extraneous and confounding variables. In an experiment, the researcher seeks to keep all conditions, events, and procedures the same, except the independent variable. Keeping such factors constant eliminates them as explanations for the cause-and-effect relationship. In other words, the effect, which is measured by differences on the dependent variable, should be produced only by variations in the independent variable. Control of extraneous variables is necessary to conclude that the intervention is causally related to the outcome. Though such control is relatively easy in contrived laboratory experiments, it is difficult in educational research.

Control is established by either eliminating a possible extraneous or confounding variable or keeping the effect of such variables constant for all groups. Some extraneous and confounding variables cannot be eliminated. For example, in an experiment designed to investigate which of two methods of instruction is most effective, teachers may be assigned to a particular method. To eliminate experimenter bias, a potential extraneous variable, the teachers should not be told about the experiment, or at least not informed of the research hypothesis. Control is more commonly achieved by keeping the effect of an extraneous variable constant for all groups of subjects. For instance, in a study of teaching methods, student aptitude will be related to the dependent variable, achievement, and this factor can be controlled by having the same overall level of aptitude in each group of subjects.

Author Reflection *I should point out that sometimes there is confusion about what an "experiment" is because of how science is taught. In some science "experiments" there is simply observation following an intervention or influence, such as mixing two chemicals. Other science "experiments" have a control or comparison group, more like educational experiments. Also, some sources on social science experiments maintain that there must be random assignment of subjects in an experiment. My take is that as long as there is control of the intervention, and you measure change, that qualifies as an experiment. There are different types of experiments, one of which includes random assignment.*

INTERNET CONNECTION

For an excellent, nontechnical summary of all aspects of experimental design, including different types, see **www.socialresearchmethods.net**. This Website also has information on most aspects of research.

EXPERIMENTAL VALIDITY

The purpose of a research design is to provide answers to research questions that are credible, that reflect reality. In the language and jargon of experimental research, two concepts are used to describe the level of credibility that results from the studies, *internal validity* and *external validity*. We will consider internal validity first since the primary purpose of experiments relates most closely to this concept.

Internal Validity

Internal validity: Control of
extraneous variables.

Internal validity is the sine qua non of experiments. It refers to the extent to which the independent variable, and not extraneous or confounding variables, produced the observed effect. A study is said to be strong in internal validity if most *plausible* extraneous and confounding variables have been controlled, and weak if one or more of these variables may have differentially affected the dependent variable. That is, if something other than the intervention as defined was responsible for the effect, the study has weak internal validity. As we will see, there are many ways to design experiments, and each design controls for different extraneous/confounding variables. Therefore, some designs are relatively strong in internal validity, whereas other designs are comparatively weak.

Most possible extraneous/confounding variables fall into one of several major categories. These categories, often referred to as "threats" to internal validity, comprise factors that may weaken the argument that the independent variable was solely responsible for the observed effects. We will discuss these threats briefly and then consider them within the context of different experimental designs. These factors represent the most important aspects of an experiment in interpreting the overall credibility of the research. When you read an experimental study you should keep each threat in mind and ask: Is this a *plausible* threat to the internal validity of the study? The word *plausible* is key. To be a plausible threat to internal validity two conditions must be met: (1) the factor must influence the dependent variable, and (2) the factor must be different in amount or intensity across levels of the independent variable. Thus, if a factor is present to the same extent at all levels of the independent variable it is not a threat to internal validity, even if it does affect the dependent variable. Just because a potential threat is not "controlled," it is not automatically a threat to internal validity.

Keep in mind that the names of these various threats to internal validity should not be interpreted literally. Often the names have a broader meaning than the term may suggest at first. While some of the names are unique to this book, most were established many years ago by Campbell and Stanley (1963). Since that time some of the factors identified for both internal and external validity have been applied to nonexperimental studies as well.

History. In an experiment, some amount of time elapses between the onset of the intervention and the measurement of the dependent variable. Although this time is necessary for the independent variable to take effect and influence the subjects, it allows for other events to occur that may also affect the dependent variable.

History: Threat from
uncontrolled events that
affect the dependent
variable.

History is the category of uncontrolled events that influence the dependent variable. If some event does occur during the study that is plausibly related to the dependent variable, it is difficult to know if the independent variable, the event, or some combination of the two produced the result. In this sense the event is confounded with the independent variable; the two cannot be separated.

History can occur "within" the study as subjects are affected by something that happens during the intervention (internal history), or "outside" of the experimental setting (external history). For example, suppose a class is studying the Far East and the researchers are trying to determine what effect this unit has on multicultural attitudes. During the unit a major crisis occurs in China. If the students are affected by the crisis, which in turn influences the way they respond to a multicultural attitude questionnaire, this event, external to the experimental setting, constitutes a plausible history threat to the internal validity of the study.

History threats can also occur within an experimental setting. For example, a series of unexpected announcements that distracts a class receiving one method of instruction could adversely affect the influence of the lesson. Students in this class might score lower than other classes, but the researcher does not know if this result is caused by the distraction or the method of instruction.

History also includes confounding variables that are associated with levels of the independent variable. For example, suppose an experiment compares two methods of instruction. One treatment is in the morning and the other is in the afternoon. A confounding variable, time of day, would constitute a threat to the internal validity of the study. Similarly, history is the category of threat in studies where different teachers are responsible for implementing each treatment.

Selection. In most experiments two or more groups of subjects are compared. One group receives one level of the independent variable, and the other groups receive other levels of the independent variable. In some experiments the subjects are randomly assigned to levels of the independent variable. This procedure ensures that the different groups of subjects are comparable on such characteristics as ability, socioeconomic status, motivation, attitudes, and interests. However, in some experiments the subjects are not randomly assigned, and sometimes only a few subjects are randomly assigned. In these circumstances it is possible that there will be systematic differences between the groups on characteristics of the subjects. If these differences are related to the dependent variable, there is a threat of **selection** to internal validity (sometimes called *differential selection*). For example, suppose one class is assigned to receive the blue health curriculum and another class receives the red health curriculum. The students are not randomly assigned to the classes; in fact, the students who have the blue curriculum are more capable academically than the students in the other class. At the end of the experiment the students who had the blue curriculum did better on a test of health concepts than the other class. Surprised? Obviously the result is related to the initial differences between the classes, and the study would be judged to have very weak internal validity.

Selection: Threat from the characteristics of subjects.

Selection is also a threat when the subjects are selected in a way that affects the results. As previously discussed, volunteers may respond in ways that nonvolunteers would not. Or suppose one group of subjects had a choice in the "treatment" experienced and another group had no choice. In such circumstances it is likely that the selection process will affect the findings.

Maturation. As stated earlier, there is some passage of time in an experiment. Just as events extraneous to the subjects may affect the results (history), changes that may occur *within* the subjects over time may also alter the results. These changes are called threats of **maturation.** People develop in naturally occurring ways that, over a sufficient period of time, can influence the dependent variable independent of a treatment condition. This can include physical, social, and mental development. For example, in an experiment on the effect of a new orientation

Maturation: Threat from changes in subjects over time.

course on the adjustment of college freshmen, the researcher may measure adjustment before college begins and then again at the end of the first year, after an orientation class. Although it would be desirable to attribute positive changes in adjustment to the orientation course, the researcher needs to consider the natural maturation process of 18- and 19-year-olds and how much adjustment will be influenced by this process.

Maturation also includes relatively short-term changes in people as they become tired, bored, hungry, or discouraged. Imagine that a researcher who needs to measure the attitudes of third graders toward science, mathematics, reading, and art asks the children to answer questions for an hour to complete the questionnaire. What do you suppose the children are doing after the first 20 minutes or so?

Pretesting. A *pretest* is a measure of the dependent variable given before the treatment begins. When it is used in an experiment it is possible for the subjects to act differently because they took the pretest. For example, if two groups are given a pretest measuring self-concept, the subjects may be sensitized to issues concerning the development of self-concept because they took the pretest. While one group may receive an intervention to improve self-concept, subjects in another group may become motivated to do some outside reading that they otherwise would not have done; this reading would probably affect changes in their self-concept and the results of the study. This threat is termed **pretesting** or *testing*. Pretesting is also a threat when one group of subjects is given a pretest that improves performance on the posttest. This effect is most likely in short studies of a single group on measures of factual material.

Instrumentation. The nature of the measurement used for the dependent variable can affect the results of research in several ways. **Instrumentation** refers to threats to internal validity because of changes or unreliability in measurement. Instrumentation also refers to changes in the measures or procedures for obtaining data. For example, if a researcher in an observational study has one set of observers for one group of subjects and a second set of observers for another group, any differences between the groups may be due to the different sets of observers. Observers or interviewers can also become bored or tired or change in other ways that affect the results.

Treatment Replications. In an experiment the intervention (treatment) is supposed to be repeated so that each member of one group receives the same intervention separately and independently of the other members of the group. If the researcher is testing a new method of instruction with a class of subjects, there is really only one replication of the intervention; that is, the intervention is conducted once. Each class is a subject, so several classes are needed to do the experiment properly. **Treatment replication** is a threat to internal validity to the extent that the reported number of subjects in the study is not the same as the number of replications of the treatment.

Pretesting: Threat from the effect of taking the pretest.

Instrumentation: Threat from unreliability or changes in measurement.

Treatment replication: Threat from insufficient replications of treatments.

Subject Attrition. **Subject attrition** (some researchers refer to this threat as *mortality*) occurs when subjects systematically drop out of or are lost from the study and their absence affects the results. This is most likely to be a problem in longitudinal research that extends over a long period of time, but it can also be a threat to short experiments if one of the treatments causes subjects to drop out. For example, if a study indicates that college seniors as a group are better critical thinkers than college freshmen, subject attrition is a possible extraneous variable since it is likely that students who are not good critical thinkers have dropped out of college and are not included in the senior sample. You should consider this threat in an experiment if a substantial number of subjects are lost in the groups that are compared.

> **Subject attrition:** Threat from loss of subjects.

Statistical Regression. **Statistical regression** (sometimes called *regression to the mean* or *regression artifact*) refers to the tendency of subjects who score extremely high or low on a pretest to score closer to the mean of both groups on the posttest, regardless of the effects of the treatments. That is, very low pretest scores are likely to be higher on the posttest and very high pretest scores are likely to be lower on the posttest (see Figure 9.1). Statistical regression is a result of measurement error and a function of mathematical probability. It is a threat when subjects are selected for research *because* they have high or low scores. For example, in studies

> **Statistical regression:** Threat from change of extreme scores to those closer to the mean.

FIGURE 9.1   **Illustration of statistical regression.**

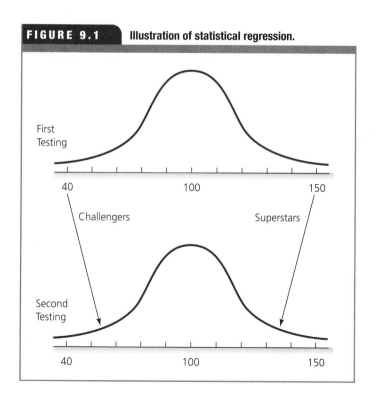

TABLE 9.1	Summary of Threats to Internal Validity	
Threat	**Description**	**Example**
History	Unplanned events that occur during the research	Fire drill occurs in the middle of a study on the effect of a computerized lesson.
Selection	Different characteristics of subjects in different groups	Students from a private school, who have strong parental support, are compared to students from a public school, who have weak parental support.
Maturation	Maturational or other natural changes in the subjects	Change in critical thinking of college students is attributed to a rigorous curriculum.
Pretesting	Taking a pretest affects subsequent behavior	Students take a pretest on their opinion toward creationism, read and discuss a book, then are posttested.
Instrumentation	Differences in results due to unreliability or changes in instruments, raters, or observers	One rater graded all the intervention group tests and a second rater graded all the control group tests.
Treatment Replications	Only a small number of independent, repeated treatments	A new method of instruction, using games, is administered in three classes.
Subject Attrition	Loss of subjects	More subjects drop out of the study from the intervention group, which was required to have strenuous exercise, than control subjects.
Statistical Regression	Scores of extreme groups of subjects moving closer to the mean on a second test	Students with the worst free throw–made percentage are used to test a new strategy for improving the accuracy of free throws.
Diffusion of Treatment	Treatment effects impact control or comparison groups	Fifth-grade students not able to participate in a new book club (control group) are resentful of the intervention group.
Experimenter Effects	Deliberate or unintended effects of the researcher	A teacher unconsciously helps experimental students get higher test scores.
Subject Effects	Changes in behavior generated by the subject by virtue of being in a study	Students give the professor high evaluations since they know he is up for tenure and their evaluations are key evidence.

procedures, and settings. Factors to consider in making appropriate generalizations are summarized in Table 9.2. To be able to make appropriate generalizations, you will need to attend carefully to the specific procedures for implementing an intervention, just as you need to know about the subjects' age, gender, socioeconomic status, and other characteristics to generalize appropriately to other individuals or groups. Like internal validity, external validity is described as weak or strong, depending on the specifics of the study's design. It is quite possible for a study to be strong in internal validity and weak in external validity. In fact, since

TABLE 9.2	Factors Affecting Generalizability
Factor	**Description**
Subjects	Characteristics of subjects such as socioeconomic status, age, gender, race, and ability. Whether and how subjects are selected from a larger population; conclusions based on group averages may be inappropriately assumed true for individuals or subgroups within the sample; subjects' awareness of the research.
Situation	Characteristics of the setting in which the information is collected, e.g., naturally occurring or contrived; time of day; surroundings.
Time	Some explanations change over time, e.g., years or decades.
Interventions (treatments)	Characteristics of the way in which an experimental treatment is conceptualized and administered.
Measures	Nature and type of measures used to collect information.

the primary purpose of experiments is to control extraneous variables, external validity is often weak with these types of designs.

Usually external validity refers to generalizing *from* a sample *to* a population or other individuals. It may also be inappropriate to make generalizations *within* the sample. Generalizing within the sample means that the researcher attributes the effects to subgroups of individuals in the sample rather than to the sample as a whole. For example, if a class of sixth graders was used in an experiment and the class as a whole showed a positive gain in achievement, it may not be accurate to generalize the findings to subgroups such as the males or high-aptitude students, unless there is a specific analysis of these groups. In other words, what may be true for the class as a whole may not be true for a subgroup.

TYPES *of* EXPERIMENTAL DESIGNS

We now turn our attention to experimental designs used to investigate cause-and-effect relationships. We will consider six types of designs, although there are many others. These six designs will illustrate how some threats to internal validity are controlled by specific features of the design and how other threats are not controlled.

Aspects of experimental designs include interventions manipulated by the researcher, pretests and posttests, the number of groups in the study, and the presence or absence of random assignment. These aspects of the study will be represented in this chapter through the following notation system:

R	Random assignment
X	Intervention(s) (subscripts indicating different interventions)
O	Observation (pretest or posttest)
A, B, C, D	Groups of subjects

Single-Group Posttest-Only Design

This design and the next two are often called *preexperimental* because they usually have inadequate control of extraneous variables. In some circumstances one of these three designs can provide good information, but as we will see, this occurs only in special conditions.

In the single-group posttest-only design, the researcher identifies a group of subjects, administers an intervention, and then makes a posttest observation of the dependent variable. It can be represented as follows:

$$\begin{array}{ccc} \text{Group} & \text{Intervention} & \text{Posttest} \\ A \longrightarrow & X \longrightarrow & O \end{array}$$

This is the weakest experimental design because without a pretest or another group of subjects, there is nothing with which to compare the posttest result. Without such a comparison, there is no way to know if the treatment effected a change in the subjects. This design is useful only when the researcher can be sure of the knowledge, skill, or attitude that will be changed before the treatment is implemented, and when there are no extraneous events occurring at the same time as the treatment that could affect the results. For example, suppose your research class instructor conducted an "experiment" by having you read this book and then giving you a posttest of your knowledge of threats to internal validity. It may be reasonable to assume that you had little knowledge about these concepts if this is your first research course, and it is unlikely that there would be any extraneous events or experiences that would also affect your knowledge of the concepts. In this circumstance the single-group posttest-only design would be appropriate.

Single-Group Pretest-Posttest Design

This design differs from the single-group posttest-only design by the addition of a pretest:

$$\begin{array}{cccc} \text{Group} & \text{Pretest} & \text{Intervention} & \text{Posttest} \\ A \longrightarrow & O \longrightarrow & X \longrightarrow & O \end{array}$$

A single group of subjects is given a pretest, then the intervention, then the posttest. The results are determined by comparing the pretest score to the posttest score. Although a change from pretest to posttest could be due to the intervention, there are many possible extraneous factors to be considered. Suppose an experiment is conducted to examine the effect of an in-service workshop on teachers' attitudes toward gifted education. An instrument measuring these attitudes is given to all teachers in a school division before two-day workshops are conducted and again after the workshops (one workshop for each school). What are some possible threats to the internal validity of this study?

First, because there are no control or comparison subjects, we cannot be certain that extraneous events have not occurred, in addition to the workshop, that would change attitudes. Perhaps an article that appeared in the local paper during the two days of the workshop changed some attitudes, or maybe some of the teachers in some groups gave moving testimonials. Second, if the teachers began with negative attitudes for some reason, regression would be a threat. Third, pretesting is a significant threat in this study because awareness due to completing the pretest questionnaire may affect attitudes. Fourth, attrition would be a problem if a significant number of teachers who do not like the workshop fail to show up for the posttest. Fifth, maturation is a potential threat if the teachers are tired at the end of the second day. Finally, experimenter and subject effects are definitely threats in this type of study since the teachers would probably want to please the person conducting the workshop. With this number of plausible threats the study would be weak in internal validity.

The single-group pretest-posttest design will have more potential threats to internal validity as the time between the pretest and posttest increases and as the experimental situation becomes less controlled and contrived. The design can be good for studies in which subject effects will not influence the results, such as achievement tests, and when history threats can be reasonably dismissed. The design is strengthened if several pretest observations are possible, thereby providing an indication of the stability of the trait. If there is a sufficient number of both pretests and posttests, the study may be called an *abbreviated time series* design. In this design it is necessary to use multiple pretests and/or posttests with the same or very similar subjects.

Suppose you want to study a new technique for increasing attendance. It involves having teachers make targeted phone calls to the parents of students who tend to be absent. All teachers in the school participate. Attendance is taken each week for four weeks prior to initiating the calls. After a week of calling, attendance is taken again. The study could be diagrammed as follows:

Group	Pretests (attendance)	Intervention (phone calls)	Posttest (attendance)
A $\longrightarrow$	$OOOO \longrightarrow$	$X \longrightarrow$	O

By having several "pretests" a stable pattern of attendance can be established so that it would be unlikely that a particularly "good" or "bad" week as a pretest would influence the results.

Nonequivalent-Groups Posttest-Only Design

The third preexperimental design has a comparison or control group but no pretest:

Group	Intervention	Posttest
A $\longrightarrow$	$X \longrightarrow$	O
B	$\longrightarrow$	O

One group of subjects (A) receives the treatment, while the other group (B) acts as a control, receiving no treatment. In some nonequivalent-groups posttest-only designs two or more groups receive different treatments:

Group	Intervention	Posttest
A $\longrightarrow$	X_1 $\longrightarrow$	O
B $\longrightarrow$	X_2 $\longrightarrow$	O
C $\longrightarrow$	X_3 $\longrightarrow$	O

The crucial feature of this design is that the subjects in each group may be different in ways that will differentially affect the dependent variable. That is, one group may be brighter, more motivated, better prepared, or in some other way different from the other groups on a trait that affects the dependent variable. Thus, selection is the most serious threat to the internal validity of this design. Without a pretest it is difficult to control for such selection differences. For example, if teachers in one school received one type of form that will be used to evaluate their teaching during the year, and teachers in another school used a different type of evaluation form, you might conclude that if teachers in the first school were judged to be more effective, the forms were causally related to this difference in effectiveness. However, it may be that the teachers in the first school were *already* more effective! It is also possible that extraneous events in one school affected the results. This design is best employed when groups of subjects are comparable and can be assumed to be about the same on the trait being measured before the treatments are given to the subjects.

Nonequivalent-Groups Pretest-Posttest Design

This design, which is often referred to as a *quasi-experimental* design (some contend that all experiments without random assignment are quasi-experimental) because it closely approximates the most desirable experimental designs, is commonly used in educational research. It is the same as the nonequivalent-groups posttest-only design, with the addition of a pretest:

Group	Pretest	Intervention	Posttest
A $\longrightarrow$	O $\longrightarrow$	X $\longrightarrow$	O
B $\longrightarrow$	O $\longrightarrow\!$		O

In this diagram there are two groups of subjects (A and B). One group (A) takes the pretest *(O)*, receives the intervention *(X)*, and then takes the posttest *(O)*; the other group (B) takes the pretest, receives no intervention, and takes the posttest. In this diagram group B is considered a "control" group because it does not receive any type of intervention. In other nonequivalent designs two or more different interventions may be compared, as indicated in the following diagram:

Group	Pretest	Intervention	Posttest
A $\longrightarrow$	O $\longrightarrow$	X_1 $\longrightarrow$	O
B $\longrightarrow$	O $\longrightarrow$	X_2 $\longrightarrow$	O

As a hypothetical illustration of this design, suppose Mr. Jones, a social studies teacher, wants to see if a new way of praising students is more effective than the method he uses now. Because it would be awkward to use different approaches in the same classroom, Mr. Jones decides to use the new type of praise in his morning class and to use an afternoon class as a comparison group. At the beginning of the same new unit on the Civil War, Mr. Jones gives his students a pretest of their knowledge. He then uses the new approach to praising students in the morning class and continues to use the same approach he has been using with his afternoon class. Both classes take the unit posttest at the same time.

The most serious threat to the internal validity of this design is selection. For example, Mr. Jones may find that students do better with the new type of praise, but this may be because the students in the morning class are brighter or more motivated than those in the afternoon class. Even though there is a pretest, which helps to reduce the threat of selection, differences in the subjects must be addressed. Often researchers will use measures of other characteristics of the subjects to show that even though the groups are not "equal," there are probably no significant differences between them.

The nonequivalent-groups pretest-posttest design is often used when subjects are available in existing, or "intact," groups such as classes. In the example with Mr. Jones, two intact classes were used. This procedure, using intact groups, creates problems other than selection. If the classes meet at different times of the day, as did Mr. Jones's classes, time of day is a confounding variable. In this example the same teacher conducted both interventions. Although in one respect this is a good method—because if different teachers were in each class, teachers would be an extraneous variable—it also increases the potential for experimenter effects. Perhaps the most serious limitation is that the "treatment" is given only once to each class. In effect, there is only one replication of the treatment, so that other extraneous events associated with that one replication may affect the results. Thus, treatment replication is a potential threat to internal validity. Even though a pretest is used in this design, pretesting is not likely to be an extraneous variable since its effect is probably the same for both groups.

The following example shows how to summarize a nonequivalent-groups pretest-posttest design. This study investigated the effect of a cooperative learning intervention on student achievement. Two versions of a math test were given to students, one version as the pretest and the other version as the posttest.

EXAMPLE | **Nonequivalent-Groups Pretest-Posttest Design**

"The present study followed a nonequivalent pretest-posttest control group design involving three instructional conditions: (a) a treatment group with 12 sixth-grade dyads from four primary schools using CL [Cooperative Learning] instruction and practices based on a 2-year staff development CL program . . . (b) a control group with 6 sixth-grade dyads from two primary schools using CL instruction and practices based on a 1-year staff development CL program, . . . and (c) a control group with 6 sixth grade dyads from one primary school not using CL." (Veenman, S., Denessen, E., van den Akker, A., & vander Rijt, J. (2005). Effects of a cooperative learning program on the elaborations of students during help seeking and help giving. *American Educational Research Journal, 42*(1), p. 120)

A strong indicator that groups are not significantly different, even though there is no random assignment, occurs when the groups are essentially equal on a pretest. That does not rule out other factors, but it does help in reducing the chance that selection is a plausible threat to internal validity. In the following excerpt the researchers compare pretest scores of two groups.

EXAMPLE | **Comparing Pretest Scores of Participants in Nonequivalent Groups**

"Our results indicated that prior to the beginning of the study no significant differences existed [between groups] in prior problem solving of procedural tasks between the two instructional approaches." (Kramarski, B., & Gutman, M. (2006). How can self-regulated learning be supported in mathematical E-learning environments? *Journal of Computer Assisted Learning, 22*(1), p. 27)

Randomized-to-Groups Posttest-Only Design

This design and the one that follows are termed *true* (pure) experimental designs because they include comparison groups that have been randomly assigned to different interventions or to an intervention and control condition. In the randomized-groups posttest-only design, subjects are first randomly assigned to the different intervention or control conditions, given the intervention (or no intervention if control), and then given the posttest. The design, with a control group, is represented by the following diagram:

$$
\begin{array}{ccccc}
\text{Random} & & & & \\
\text{Assignment} & \text{Groups} & \text{Intervention} & \text{Posttest} \\
 & A & \longrightarrow & X & \longrightarrow & O \\
R < & & & & \\
 & B & \longrightarrow\!\longrightarrow & O \\
\end{array}
$$

If a comparison group is included, rather than a control group, the design looks like this:

$$
\begin{array}{ccccc}
\text{Random} & & & & \\
\text{Assignment} & \text{Groups} & \text{Intervention} & \text{Posttest} \\
 & A & \longrightarrow & X_1 & \longrightarrow & O \\
R < & & & & \\
 & B & \longrightarrow & X_2 & \longrightarrow & O \\
\end{array}
$$

In most educational experiments there is a comparison group rather than a control group because of limited resources and time to work with students. In reading studies, therefore, you will usually find methods or approaches compared to one another.

Random assignment means that each subject has the same probability of being in either the treatment or comparison or control group. The purpose of random assignment is to equalize the characteristics of the subjects in each group. This equalization can be assumed when a sufficient number of subjects is randomly assigned to each group (generally 15 or more). The obvious strength of random assignment is the control of selection as a threat to internal validity. It is assumed that the subjects in each group are essentially "equal" on any characteristics that may affect the dependent variable. Other threats, however, need to be considered that are not controlled by random assignment, including diffusion of treatment, experimenter effects, subject effects, treatment replication, and extraneous events within a group of subjects.

In one example of a study with a randomized-groups posttest-only design, researchers investigated the effect of traditional and modified models of collaboration on participation and productivity outcomes. According to the authors, "The design in this study was a posttest-only, true experimental design. . . . Students were randomly assigned to participate in one of three types of work groups: traditional, modified, or control" (Wilcox, Williams, & Reutzel, 1997, pp. 344–345). The design of the study can be diagrammed as follows:

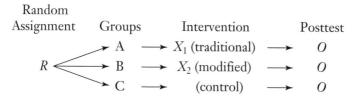

Random Assignment	Groups	Intervention	Posttest
	A →	X_1 (traditional) →	O
R ←	B →	X_2 (modified) →	O
	C →	(control) →	O

> **EXAMPLE** | **Randomized-to-Groups Posttest-Only Design with a Single Independent Variable**
>
> "Study 1 analyzed the effects of achievement feedback in a mathematical task on self-perceived verbal competence. Participants worked on a series of mathematical problems, after which they were given social comparison feedback information indicating that they had performed either better or worse than a comparison sample . . . participants were randomly assigned to conditions in a one-way design, with achievement feedback as the independent variable." (Moller, J., & Koller, O. (2001). Dimensional comparisons: An experimental approach to the internal/external frame of reference model. *Journal of Educational Psychology, 93*, pp. 827–828)
>
> "Participants were randomly assigned to one of three conditions; there were 35 participants in the control condition and 36 each in the reason and counterargue/rebut conditions." (Borman, G. D., & Dowling, N. M. (2006). Longitudinal achievement effects of multi-year summer school. *Educational Evaluation and Policy Analysis, 28*(1), pp. 25–48)

Careful attention needs to be paid to how "randomization" is carried out. If a researcher includes individual subject scores in the analysis, the "unit" of the analysis is the individual. As long as the randomization was done so that each subject could be assigned to each group, and there was independent replication of the intervention for each subject, then it is a randomized-to-groups design. In contrast, a study in which there are four existing classes of students, two of which are randomly assigned to the treatment and two to the control condition, is not a randomized-to-groups design. In this case randomly assigning only two cases to each group is not sufficient to be defined as a true experiment.

Randomized-to-Groups Pretest-Posttest Design

This true experiment has both a pretest and a posttest. Otherwise it is the same as the randomized-to-groups posttest-only design. A pretest is used to further equalize the groups statistically, in addition to what random assignment provides. Researchers use a pretest with random assignment when there may be small, subtle effects of different treatments, when differential subject attrition is possible, and when there is a need to analyze subgroups who differ on the pretest. Subjects can be randomly assigned before or after the pretest. In some studies the pretest scores are used to match subjects, and then one subject from each pair is randomly assigned to each group. The following describes a randomized two-group pretest-posttest experiment:

> **EXAMPLE** | **Randomized-to-Groups Pretest-Posttest Design**
>
> "Participants were 65 (boys and girls) ninth-grade students who were assigned randomly to two EL environments: EL+IMP and EL. Students in both environments studied the linear function unit for 5 weeks. . . . The study utilized two measures for the pre-test and post-test: mathematical test and SRL questionnaire." (Kramarski, B., & Gutman, M. (2006). How can self-regulated learning be supported in mathematical E-learning environments? *Journal of Computer Assisted Learning, 22*(1), p. 27)

This study can be diagrammed as follows:

Random Assignment	Groups	Pretest	Intervention	Posttest
20 schools R	A (10 schools) →	O (questionnaire) →	X_1 (new curriculum) →	O (questionnaire)
	B (10 schools) →	O (questionnaire) →	X_2 (textbook) →	O (questionnaire)

Table 9.3 summarizes threats to internal validity of the six designs. Although the "scoreboard" will give you a good start in evaluating the credibility of an experiment, each study must be judged individually. Overall, credibility is determined not so much by the particular design but by how well the researcher understands and controls for possible threats.

Factorial Designs

Factorial designs:
Containing two or more independent variables.

All of the designs we have considered in this chapter have one independent variable. Many experiments, as well as nonexperimental studies, will have two or more independent variables and employ what are called **factorial designs.** Factorial experimental designs are extensions of the designs summarized in this chapter that study more than one independent variable, or factor, and the interaction between independent variables. There are two primary purposes for using factorial designs. One is to see if the effects of a treatment are consistent across

| TABLE 9.3 | Internal Validity Scoreboard |

Threats to Internal Validity

Design	History	Selection	Maturation	Pretesting	Instrumentation
Single-Group Posttest-Only	–	–	–	NA	?
Single-Group Pretest-Posttest	?	?	–	–	?
Nonequivalent-Groups Posttest-Only	?	–	?	NA	?
Nonequivalent-Groups Pretest-Posttest	?	?	?	?	?
Randomized-to-Groups Posttest-Only	?	+	+	NA	?
Randomized-to-Groups Pretest-Posttest	?	+	+	?	?

Threats to Internal Validity

Design	Treatment Replications	Subject Attrition	Statistical Regression	Diffusion of Treatment	Experimenter Effects	Subject Effects
Single-Group Posttest-Only	?	?	–	NA	?	?
Single-Group Pretest-Posttest	?	?	–	NA	?	?
Nonequivalent-Groups Posttest-Only	?	?	?	NA	?	?
Nonequivalent-Groups Pretest-Posttest	?	?	+	?	?	?
Randomized-to-Groups Posttest-Only	?	?	+	?	?	?
Randomized-to-Groups Pretest-Posttest	?	?	+	?	?	?

In this table a minus sign indicates a definite weakness, a plus sign means that the threat is controlled, a question mark indicates a possible source of invalidity, and NA means that the threat is not applicable to the design.

subject characteristics, such as age, gender, or aptitude. The second is to examine interactions, which are relationships that can only be investigated with factorial designs. If a study is testing the effect of two methods of instruction, for example, computerized compared to traditional, it might be desirable to know if the effectiveness of the methods was the same for males as for females. Thus, such a study would have two independent variables, each with two levels. The study may be diagrammed in different ways, as illustrated in Figure 9.2. Figure 9.3b and c show

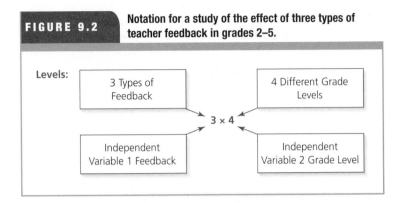

FIGURE 9.2 Notation for a study of the effect of three types of teacher feedback in grades 2–5.

that the students were first divided into groups of males and females and then randomly assigned to the two instructional methods. There is a numerical notation system used with factorial designs that tells you about the number of independent variables and the number of levels within each independent variable. In the previous example, the notation would be 2 × 2. Each number indicates a single independent variable with two levels. If a study has one independent variable with three levels and one with four levels, it would be designated as 3 × 4 (see Figure 9.2). If a third variable is added, with two levels, it would be 2 × 3 × 4.

Interactions are very important since much of what we do in education is based on the assumption that we should match student characteristics with appropriate teacher feedback or instructional methods. What may work well for one student may not work well for other students. Factorial designs allow us to test these assumptions. **Interactions** occur when the effect of one variable differs across the levels of the other variable. In other words, the effect of a variable is not consistent across all levels of the other variable. Applying this definition to the example in Figure 9.3, we would have an interaction if the difference between males and females for computerized instruction was not the same as the difference between males and females for traditional instruction. This result would show that the effect of the method of instruction depends on whether we are studying males or females. In a sense, method and sex are operating together. An important aspect to consider in interpreting results is that because of possible interactions, what may not be true for a total group may be true for certain subjects in the population. That is, if a study shows that for all fourth graders, together, it makes no difference whether they have homework assignments or not, an interaction might show that some low-ability students benefit greatly from homework compared to other low-ability students who receive no homework.

Interactions: Effect of independent variables together.

INTERNET CONNECTION

For further discussion of factorial designs, with additional examples, see **www.socialresearchmethods.net/kb.expfact.htm.**

FIGURE 9.3   Diagrams of 2 × 2 design.

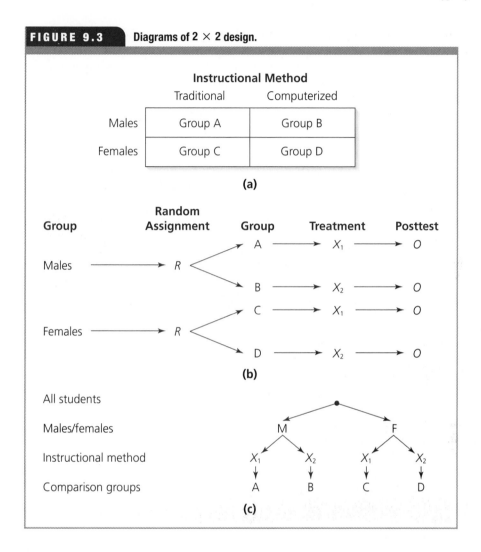

(a)

(b)

(c)

CONSUMER TIPS: *Criteria for Evaluating Experimental Research*

1. **The primary purpose is to test causal hypotheses.** Experimental research should be designed to investigate cause-and-effect relationships that are anticipated with clear research hypotheses. There should almost always be a research hypothesis in an experiment. If there is no research hypothesis there may be insufficient descriptive or relationship evidence to justify conducting an experiment, or the researcher may be uninformed about the need for a hypothesis.

2. **There should be direct control of the intervention.** An essential feature of an experiment is that the researcher controls and manipulates the intervention that subjects will receive. If it is not clear that such manipulation has occurred, the ability to make causal interpretations will be limited.

3. The experimental design should be clearly identified. Although it is not necessary for the researcher to use the specific language in this chapter to identify a design (e.g., randomized-to-groups posttest-only), it is important that sufficient details about the design are provided to enable you to understand what was done to which subjects and the sequence of measurement and interventions. In fact, there should be enough detail so that you could replicate the study. As noted, the threats you need to focus on to evaluate the study depend to a certain extent on the design. If you cannot understand the design, the researcher may not have understood it either!

4. The design should provide maximum control of extraneous/confounded variables. The researcher should indicate how specific aspects of the design control possible extraneous and confounding variables. Obvious threats, such as selection in the nonequivalent-groups designs, need to be addressed. If obvious threats are not controlled by the design, the researcher should present a rationale for why a particular threat is not a plausible alternative explanation for the results. Failure to provide such a rationale may indicate that the researcher does not fully understand how such variables can influence results.

Use Table 9.4 to systematically evaluate the possibility and plausibility of threats to internal validity. For any given study or design, check first whether the threat is possible, then identify any of those that would be plausible. Finally, depending on the specifics of the design, indicate whether any of the plausible threats would be considered "fatal flaws."

TABLE 9.4	Evaluating Threats to Internal Validity		
Threat	**Possible?**	**Plausible?**	**Fatal Flaw?**
History	____	____	____
Selection	____	____	____
Maturation	____	____	____
Pretesting	____	____	____
Instrumentation	____	____	____
Treatment replications	____	____	____
Subject attrition	____	____	____
Statistical regression	____	____	____
Diffusion of treatment	____	____	____
Experimenter effects	____	____	____
Subject effects	____	____	____

FIGURE 9.4   Results of *A–B–A* single-subject design.

One limitation of the *A–B–A* design is the difficulty in interpreting a positive change that is not altered during the second baseline. In this situation the intervention may be so strong that its effect lasts a long time, or something else may have occurred with the intervention that affected the behavior and did not stop when the intervention did.

Multiple-Baseline Designs. In a single-subject **multiple-baseline design,** observations are made on several subjects, different target behaviors of one or more subjects, or different situations. Thus, multiple baselines are conducted across subjects, behaviors, or settings. A design that has more than one subject may implement the intervention with each subject or use one or more subjects as a control condition. Different behaviors are studied when an intervention is applied to more than one target behavior. For example, the effectiveness of using time-out for institutionalized individuals with mental retardation can be observed for several types of behavior, including taking food from others and hitting others. If a study examines the effect of the same procedure on behaviors in several different settings or situations, such as different classes, a multiple-baseline across-settings design is employed. For instance, an investigator may be interested in whether a particular type of praise is as effective with an individual in math class as it is in science class.

Multiple-baseline design: More than one subject, behavior, or setting.

CONSUMER TIPS: *Criteria for Evaluating Single-Subject Research*

1. There should be reliable measurement of the target behavior. It is important for the measurement to be standardized and consistent. Evidence for reliability should be presented in the procedures section of the study. If more than one observer is used, interobserver reliability should be reported.

2. The target behavior should be clearly defined operationally. There should be a detailed definition of the dependent variable, described operationally in terms of how it is measured.

3. Sufficient measures are needed to establish stability in behavior. There should be enough measures to establish stability in the behavior that is measured. Typically a minimum of three or four observations is needed in each phase of the study to provide measures that do not show more than a small degree of variability. This step is especially important for the baseline condition since this is the level of behavior against which behaviors occurring during the treatment are compared, but it is also necessary for the intervention condition. Usually there is the same number of measures during each phase of the study.

4. Procedures, subjects, and settings should be fully described. Since the external validity of single-subject designs is relatively weak, the usefulness of the results depends to a great extent on the match between the procedures, characteristics of the subjects, and settings in the study with other subjects and settings. The best judgments of the extent of this match are made when there is a detailed description of what was done, to whom, and where.

5. A single, standardized intervention should be used. The procedures for administering the intervention should be standardized so that precisely the same procedure is given each time. Only one or one combination of interventions should be changed from the baseline to treatment phases of the study.

6. Experimenter or observer effects should be controlled. Because of the heavy reliance on a single observer, who in many cases is the same person as the experimenter, it is important to indicate how bias is controlled, that is, how bias is not a potential threat to internal validity. Judging the credibility of the researcher may not be easy, although you will find hints of bias in many parts of the research report or article.

7. Results should be practically significant. The results of most single-subject studies are analyzed by inspecting their graphic presentation and judging whether the patterns of behavior in different phases of the study appear to be different. This judgment should be based on graphs that do not distort differences by artificially increasing the intervals used to describe the behaviors. Clear differences should be evident, and they should be significant in practical terms, showing enough of a difference to clearly affect the behavior of the subject. Some single-subject studies use a statistical analysis of the results, but a "statistically significant" difference still needs to be practically significant.

Author Reflection *Is it really worth it to conduct experimental research? Sometimes it seems that there are so many possible and plausible threats to the design that it would be nearly impossible to say that there is strong internal validity, especially for field experiments. My perspective on this issue is that yes, field experiments can be very helpful, even with limitations. As long as the researcher is aware* *of possible threats before conducting the experiment, the design can be sufficiently strong to be able to make valid causal conclusions. What is most problematic is when the results show no difference. Then it is hard to know whether some limitation in the design led to the result or whether, in fact, the intervention was not effective. We'll explore this aspect of research in the next chapter.*

ANATOMY *of an* EXPERIMENTAL RESEARCH STUDY

The following article is an example of how an experimental study is designed and reported. This particular investigation is quasi-experimental.

EXHIBIT 9.1   Using Tests as an Incentive to Motivate Procrastinators to Study

Bruce W. Tuckman
Florida State University

Abstract. The purposes of this study were to compare two approaches for enhancing the recall and understanding of text and to compare the effectiveness of the two approaches for students differing in procrastination tendency. The first approach was to provide incentive motivation by giving a test on each text chapter; the second approach was to provide a learning strategy by requiring students to outline each chapter as a homework assignment. Eighty-two students were classified by level of procrastination based on scores on the Procrastination Scale. Half of the students experienced the test condition; the other half experienced the homework condition. Although the test condition produced significantly higher scores overall on a final achievement examination than the outline condition did, a significant interaction between condition and student procrastination level reflected an almost 12% advantage for the test condition among high procrastinators. There was virtually no difference between conditions for medium and low procrastinators.

MANY OF THE TASKS AND ENTERPRISES that individuals undertake are done voluntarily. Tuckman and Sexton (1990) labeled *self-regulated performance* acts that require the exercise of influence over one's own behavior, such as studying, dieting, or cleaning up after oneself. Self-regulated performance is particularly important in school. . . .

The absence of self-regulated performance has been labeled *procrastination*—the tendency to put off or avoid an activity under one's control (Tuckman & Sexton, 1989). Procrastination may result from a combination of (a) disbelieving in one's own capability to perform a task (Bandura, 1986), (b) being unable to postpone gratification, and (c) assigning blame for one's own "predicament" to external sources (Ellis & Knaus, 1977; Tuckman, 1989). To accurately measure and predict the tendency to procrastinate, Tuckman (1991) developed the Procrastination Scale.

> Introduction, background, significance

As a student proceeds through school, the responsibility for controlling performance shifts progressively from parents and teachers to the student, reaching a high point during the college years. The inability to overcome procrastination tendencies may be related to problems encountered by many college students, leading some researchers to be on the lookout for effective strategies that may help such students regulate their own learning (see, e.g., Tuckman, 1990; Zimmerman, 1989). In the present study, I investigated one such strategy: using tests to motivate procrastinators to study on a timely basis.

> General research problem

Incentives, or goal objects that individuals desire to attain or avoid, have figured prominently in a number of theories of motivation (e.g., Atkinson, 1964; Rotter, Chance, & Phares, 1972; Vroom, 1964). In these theories, the

(continued)

EXHIBIT 9.1   (continued)

Theoretical basis

degree to which the object is desired is referred to as its *incentive or reward value.* These incentive theories of motivation suggest that people will perform an act when its performance is likely to result in some outcome they desire. Behavior that is motivated or prompted by the desire to attain or avoid an incentive can be said to be the result of *incentive motivation* (Petri, 1996). Overmier and Lawry (1979) theorized that incentive motivation can be regarded as a mediator between the stimulus characteristics of a situation containing a goal object and the responses directed toward that object. . . .

Pintrich and Schrauben (1992) reviewed a large body of research that suggests that (a) the value of an outcome to a student affects that student's motivation and (b) motivation leads to cognitive engagement, with such engagement manifesting itself in the use or application of various learning strategies. . . . A technique for enhancing incentive value is to provide a situation that can be linked to performance incentives, or what Bandura (1986) referred to as *competency-contingent incentives.* Again, a test would seem to provide the very performance incentives that a procrastinator requires to overcome procrastination. . . .

Manipulated independent variable

In the present study, I compared two approaches for enhancing the recall and understanding of information. The *incentive approach* focused exclusively on will as a function of incentive motivation, and the *strategy approach* focused on skill, or effective strategy use. For the incentive approach, I used a semiweekly spot quiz on the information to be covered. I theorized that studying voluntarily on a semiweekly basis for the tests would reflect the desire to obtain a high grade or avoid a low one (the incentive), thus representing incentive motivation. The degree and nature of text processing would depend on the value of the incentive to the student. For the strategy approach, I used a text-processing homework assignment on that same information to ensure, at a minimum, a comparable degree of cognitive engagement across conditions. In the homework condition, processing of the text by the students would be guaranteed because it was assigned. It would not depend on motivation.

Research hypothesis

Tuckman (1996) showed that the incentive-motivation approach with spot quizzes has a greater impact on subsequent achievement than the homework approach does, particularly among college students with low grade point averages (GPAs). Based on that result, I hypothesized that the students in the test condition would outperform the students in the homework condition, primarily because the test condition would be more likely to motivate procrastinators to study on a timely basis.

METHOD

Suggests a quasi-experiment; no random assignment

Shows similarity between groups to rule out selection as a threat

Possible bias

Description of interventions

Eighty-two college juniors and seniors, preparing to be teachers, participated in the study. The average age of the students was 21, and two thirds of the group were women. They were enrolled in two sections of a 6-week, summer educational psychology course required for teacher certification. A comparison of the two classes on age, gender, and self-reports of scores on the combined verbal and mathematics portion of the College Level Academic Skills Test (CLAST), prior semester's GPA, and grade expectation showed them to be equivalent. Correlations between CLAST scores and achievement in this course have been found to be about .5 (Tuckman, 1993). Both sections met twice a week (at the same time of day), covered the same content (learning theories), and used the same textbook. The same instructor taught both courses.

At the beginning of each class period, one class was given a seven-completion item spot quiz (SQ) that covered the textbook chapter assigned for that week. The quiz was projected via an overhead projector. The instructor allowed 15 min. for its completion. At the time of the spot quiz, no instruction had yet been given on the chapter covered by the quiz. The only informational resource was the textbook itself. Following the spot quiz, the students exchanged papers and the instructor went over the answers so that the students could grade one another's tests. The students were informed that the average of their spot-quiz grades would count as much as the final achievement test toward their final grade.

The other class was given the homework assignment of preparing an outline of the assigned chapter that was arranged hierarchically and that covered major terms and their meanings. This approach is considered to be a cognitive strategy for extracting meaning from text (Gagne, Weidemann, Bell, & Anders, 1984; King, 1992). The students turned in their outlines, were given written feedback comparable to the feedback given following the spot quizzes, and were graded on the quality of the outlines. These grades were averaged and counted as the equivalent of the final achievement test, the same as in the spot-quiz condition.

Description of interventions

The students completed the 32-item Procrastination Scale (Tuckman, 1991) and were divided into high (≥ 79), medium (68–78), and low (≤ 67) groups. I selected cutoffs to produce groups of approximately equal size. Items on the scale include "I needlessly delay finishing jobs, even when they're important"; "I postpone starting in on things I don't like to do"; and "When I have a deadline, I wait till the last minute." The reliability of the scale (Cronbach's alpha) was .86. Construct validity was based on a correlation of $-.54$ between scores on the scale and performance on a voluntary task that reflected the motivational tendency to self-regulate (Tuckman, 1991). Concurrent validity was based on (a) a correlation between scores on the scale and on the General Self-Efficacy Scale of $-.47$ (Tuckman) and (b) a significant path coefficient linking scale scores and student ratings of course demands (Abry, 1997). The relative independence of the measure of procrastination from scores reflecting general achievement is shown by correlations of $-.19$ and $-.22$ between the procrastination scores and the students' self-reported expected grade and GPA, respectively (Abry).

Measures of attribute independent variables

The final achievement test contained 65 multiple-choice items, most of which measured conceptual, rather than factual, knowledge. The general content domain of the test corresponded equally to the content domain of the spot quizzes and the outlines. However, the nature of the items on the test was quite different from the nature of those on the spot quizzes. The reliability of the test (Kuder-Richardson) was .77. The students were also required to keep a log of time spent either preparing for spot quizzes or completing outlines and to turn the log in on a weekly basis.

Description of dependent variable

Check on the manipulation

RESULTS

I conducted a two-way analysis of variance (ANOVA) on scores on the final achievement test with condition (spot quiz vs. outline) and procrastination score (high, medium, low) as the independent variables. The results of the ANOVA are shown in Table 1, and the means and standard deviations are shown in Table 2. The main effect for condition was significant at the .01 level with the spot-quiz students outperforming the outline students on the achievement test (76.8% to 71.7%). The main effect of procrastination was not significant. The interaction of condition and procrastination level was significant at the .05 level. A comparison of means using the least significant difference approach revealed that although low and medium procrastinators differed only slightly on achievement across the two conditions (75.2% to 72.9% in favor of SQ for lows; 75.9% to 74.8% in favor of SQ for mediums), high procrastinators differed significantly in achievement across the two conditions, $t(26) = 3.54, p < .01$ (79.2% to 67.3% in favor of SQ). In other words, high procrastinators who took spot quizzes on each chapter obtained significantly higher achievement test scores on the final exam than those who completed outlines on each chapter did. No such advantage based on spot quizzes was found for low procrastinators.

Two independent variables, one with two levels, the second with three levels.

Time-log scores for class preparation by the students in the two conditions showed no significant differences. The students in both conditions reported an average of approximately 2 hr of preparation time per week. The relative independence of procrastination, by itself, and achievement was reflected in a correlation of $-.05$.

DISCUSSION

In the present study, the students who were given spot quizzes on each chapter outperformed the students who completed chapter outlines on a test of achievement; the difference between the conditions was based primarily on the performance of procrastinators, who profited most from the quizzes. . . .

Summary of results

(continued)

EXHIBIT 9.1 (continued)

TABLE 1 ANOVA of Achievement Test Score, by Condition and Procrastination Level

Source	df	SS	MS	F
Condition	1	527.27	527.27	6.05**
Procrastination level	2	63.28	31.64	0.70
Interaction	2	540.50	270.25	3.10*
Error	76	6,625.53	87.18	

*$p < .05$. **$p < .01$.

TABLE 2 Mean Achievement Test Scores and Standard Deviations for the Two Intervention Groups, by Procrastination Level

	Procrastination Level			
Treatment	Low	Middle	High	Combined
Spot quiz				
M	75.2	75.9	79.2*	76.8*
SD	8.7	9.2	7.5	8.4
Outline				
M	72.9	74.8	67.3*	71.7*
SD	8.4	7.2	10.2	10.3
Combined				
M	74.0	75.3	72.8	
SD	8.5	8.1	12.3	

*Significantly different from mean for other intervention ($p < .01$).

Explanation of results

Spot quizzes, as an instructional intervention, motivated procrastinators to study continually over an entire course. They induced students to study on a daily or weekly basis, rather than postponing studying until the middle or end of the course. Moreover, completing homework assignments did not have the same impact on procrastinators as weekly spot quizzes did, despite students' reports that they spent an equivalent amount of time completing assignments as studying for quizzes.

Relationship of results to theory

For procrastinators, incentive motivation may provide the needed inducement to self-regulate. Regular testing of assigned material appears to be a necessary stimulus for causing timely studying by procrastinators. Current thinking on instruction promotes the reduction of formal course requirements and the use of evaluation strategies other than testing, but teachers may be favoring the more motivated students by following that approach. Procrastinators may have difficulty acquiring new knowledge if steps are not taken to enhance their motivation. Frequent testing, therefore, may be thought of as a motivational "equalizer." Additional research should be undertaken to examine the long-term effects of this approach, especially in regard to transfer.

REFERENCES

Abry, D. (1997). *The relationships among procrastination, perceived course demands, and course satisfaction.* Unpublished manuscript, Florida State University, Tallahassee.

Atkinson, J. W. (1964). *An introduction to motivation.* Princeton, NJ: Van Nostrand.

Bandura, A. (1986). *Social foundations of thought and action: A social-cognitive theory.* Englewood Cliffs, NJ: Prentice-Hall.

Cook, L. K., & Mayer, R. E. (1983). Reading strategies training for meaningful learning from prose. In M. Pressley & J. R. Levin (Eds.), *Cognitive strategy research: Educational implications* (pp. 87–131). New York: Springer-Verlag.

Ellis, A., & Knaus, W. J. (1977). *Overcoming procrastination.* New York: New American Library.

Gagne, E. D., Weidemann, C., Bell, M. S., & Anders, T. D. (1984). Training thirteen-year-olds to elaborate while studying text. *Human Learning, 3,* 281–294.

King, A. (1992). Facilitating elaborate learning through guided student-generated questioning. *Educational Psychologist, 27,* 111–126.

Mayer, R. E. (1987). *Educational psychology: A cognitive approach.* Boston: Little, Brown.

Overmier, J. B., & Lawry, J. A. (1979). Conditioning and the mediation of behavior. In G. H. Bower (Ed.), *The psychology of learning and motivation* (Vol. 13, pp. 1–55). New York: Academic Press.

Petri, H. L. (1996). *Motivation: Theory, research, and applications* (4th ed.). Pacific Grove, CA: Brooks/Cole.

[References continue.]

STUDY QUESTIONS

1. What are the essential characteristics of experiments with groups of subjects? How are experiments different from relationship studies?
2. Why is internal validity important in interpreting experiments?
3. Give an example of how extraneous events (history) can threaten the internal validity of an experiment.
4. In what experimental designs is selection a serious threat to internal validity? Why?
5. How is selection "controlled" in the nonequivalent-groups pretest-posttest design?
6. Under what circumstances are so-called "preexperimental" designs valid?
7. What are potential threats to the internal validity of any type of experimental design? Why?
8. What does it mean to say that the number of subjects in a study is equal to the number of replications of the intervention?
9. Give an example of a factorial design.
10. Why is an interaction important in research?
11. What characteristics would you look for in a good single-subject design?
12. What are the advantages of a multiple-baseline single-subject design?
13. How are the results of a single-subject design analyzed? What does it mean to have "practical" significance?

@WWW SAMPLE TEST QUESTIONS

See this text's Companion Website at **www.ablongman.com/mcmillan5e** for sample test questions and answers.

mylabschool
RESEARCH NAVIGATOR™ ACTIVITIES

1. Read the article in the Research Navigator™ that illustrates an experimental study investigating the effect of reciprocal peer counseling on student self-concept (AN 20707534). Is this a true or quasi-experimental study? What threats to internal validity would be possible? What threats to internal validity would be probable? Overall, is this a strong study? Why or why not?

2. The study found by accessing AN 6411043 in the Research Navigator is an experiment. Is it a true or quasi-experimental study? What threats to internal validity are possible (hint: consider selection and experimenter effects)?

Chapter 10

Understanding Statistical Inferences

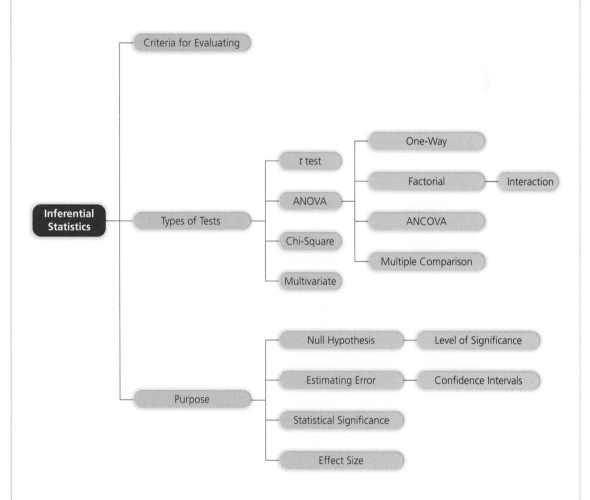

CHAPTER ROAD MAP

It may not be much of an understatement to say that you probably were not particularly eager to get to this chapter! There is usually a perception that complex mathematics are involved in understanding statistical principles and that the strange symbols and letters encountered are of little practical value. Although it is true that most statistical procedures require complex calculations, the computer handles these very efficiently. We will focus on the logic and meaning of the procedures, which will not require sophisticated mathematics, and on understanding and evaluating the use of the procedures in research reports and articles.

As a result of reading and studying this chapter, you will:

- Understand the need for using inferential statistics to estimate likely conclusions
- Understand hypothesis testing and types of errors that may be made
- Be able to interpret the results of specific statistical tests
- Understand limitations of inferential statistics
- Understand and apply estimates of practical significance
- Understand the difference between parametric and nonparametric statistical procedures
- Be able to evaluate the utility of inferential statistics as reported in specific studies

The PURPOSE *and* NATURE *of* INFERENTIAL STATISTICS

As indicated in Chapter 6, statistics are mathematical procedures used to summarize and analyze numerical data. In this chapter we will concentrate on procedures that use descriptive statistics to estimate from a sample what is true for a population, or what is likely to be true given the inexact nature of measurement. These procedures, called **inferential statistics**, are necessary to understand the precise nature of descriptions, relationships, and differences based on the data collected in a study.

Inferential statistics: Infers
characteristics of a
population.

Degree of Certainty

It would be nice (not to mention profitable) if we could be certain about our predictions. How certain is a principal that a particular kind of evaluation procedure will provide credible information on which to base merit salary increases? Are you confident in your ability to predict who will win a race or an election? If we know that a sample of sixth graders will pass a minimum competency test, how certain can we be that all sixth-graders will pass it? The degree to which we can be certain in each of these circumstances, and in others, will vary. There is some degree of uncertainty in the questions addressed in educational research, and inferential statistics indicate in a precise way what we can, for the most part, be confident about. The degree of confidence depends on the amount of error in sampling and measurement.

Estimating Errors in Sampling and Measurement

Sampling was discussed in Chapter 5 as a procedure for studying a portion of a larger population. Subjects in the sample are measured to obtain *descriptive statistics for the sample*. Inferential statistics are then used to *infer* to the entire population. Suppose a researcher is interested in the attitudes of seventh-graders toward learning and school. The population is large, say 1,000 seventh-graders, so a sample of 100 seventh-graders is selected randomly and these students respond to the attitude questionnaire. The researcher then uses the results from the sample to infer the attitudes of all 1,000 seventh-graders. Since there is some degree of error in sampling, this error must be taken into account in making the inference to the population. That is, even with a random sample, the mean attitude of the sample drawn is not exactly the same as that for the entire population. A second or third random sample of 100 students would result in a somewhat different mean.

If a researcher does take three random samples, which one is most correct? Which one can we be most certain will provide the most accurate estimation of the population? The answer is that we do not know because we have not measured the entire population. But we can estimate, on the basis of one sample, the error that should be considered in inferring the attitudes of the population. So if the mean attitude of the sample was 25, on a scale of 10 to 35, and there was little error, we might estimate the population attitude to be somewhere between, say, 23 and 27. If there was a large error, the estimate might be between 21 and 29. We use inferential statistics to indicate the precise range in which the actual mean attitude for the 1,000 students lies. Thus, we would conclude that the attitude of the population is probably between two values. This is what national polls indicate when the results are summarized as a number plus or minus some value (e.g., for 46% $\pm$ 3%, the value for the total population is probably between 43% and 49%).

Suppose a researcher uses the entire population. Would the measure be the "real" or "actual" value of the trait for the population? Although in this circumstance there is no sampling error, there is measurement error, which also needs to be taken into consideration. We infer a real or true value on a trait from imperfect measurement. Just as in sampling error, each time you measure a group the result will be somewhat different, depending on the reliability of the instrument. If the instrument is highly reliable, there will be little error, but if the reliability is low, the results could vary considerably each time especially for small samples. Thus, we take this error into account with inferential statistics by indicating the range in which true scores are likely to lie. The estimates of the true values of the population are then used to compare two or more values to see if significant differences exist between the groups that are being compared.

The Null Hypothesis

In a study that compares two groups on a measure of achievement, the question that is investigated is the likelihood that there is a difference between the groups.

Since we know there is error, it is more accurate to conclude that there probably is or is not a real difference. In most social science and educational research, the procedure for making the decision about whether there is or is not a difference begins with a **null hypothesis.** As indicated in Chapter 2, the null hypothesis is a statement that no difference exists between the populations that are being compared. In a relationship study, the null hypothesis would indicate that there is no relationship. The researcher uses inferential statistics to determine the probability that the null hypothesis is untrue, or false. If the null is probably untrue, the researcher concludes that there probably *is* a relationship or difference between groups. Thus, if we reject the null hypothesis, the chances are good that we are not wrong in saying that there is a difference.

> **Null hypothesis:** Statement of no difference or relationship.

INTERNET CONNECTION

To review further explanations and examples of hypothesis testing, try this Website and links to additional information: **http://davidmlane.com/hyperstat/ch9_contents.html**.

Inferential statistics tell us the probability of being wrong in rejecting the null hypothesis. This probability is called the **level of significance,** which is indicated with the small letter p (probability) and is reported as $p = x$ or $p < x$ (e.g., the level of significance is .05 or less than .05). The value of p indicates how often the results would be obtained because of chance (rather than a "real" difference). Thus, if $p = .20$, there is a 20% probability that the difference is due to a chance variation, that is, error in sampling and measurement. This is too great a chance to accept in research. Typically, researchers will not conclude that there is an actual difference in the populations unless the probability of obtaining the difference by chance is less than 5% ($p < .05$). This is a convention that is translated to mean a "statistically significant" difference. If the level of significance is .001, there is only 1 chance out of 1,000 that the difference obtained is due to chance. This would be a stronger result than a p value of .01 (1 chance out of 100). If the decision is to reject the null hypothesis when it is in fact true (no difference in the populations), the researcher has made what is called a **Type I error.** The probability of making this type of error is equal to the level of significance. It is also possible to fail to reject the null hypothesis when it is in fact not true and should have been rejected. This is called a **Type II error.**

> **Level of significance:** Probability of being wrong in rejecting the null hypothesis.

> **Type I error:** Rejecting the null hypothesis when it is true.

> **Type II error:** Not rejecting the null hypothesis when it is not true.

In most studies the researcher will indicate the level of significance of rejecting each null hypothesis. In some studies the level of significance is set prior to data collection as a criterion for rejecting the null hypothesis. This value is called the *alpha level* (α). Since there is no absolute rule in what constitutes statistical significance, it is necessary to interpret summary narrative statements in the context of the actual p values. Sometimes a p value between .10 and .05 is called "marginally" significant. In exploratory studies a p value of .10 may be judged sufficient to conclude that a significant difference exists. In medicine, where the probability of being wrong has serious consequences, a significant difference may require a p value of .0001.

The level of significance is affected by three factors. The first is the difference between the groups being compared. The greater the difference, the smaller the p value. The second is the degree of sampling and measurement error. The lower the error, the smaller the p value. The third factor is the size of the sample. If a very large sample is used, the p value will be smaller than if the sample size is small. In fact, in some studies a seemingly small difference may be reported as "significant," because of the large number of subjects. (If you increase the sample size enough almost any result will be "statistically significant.")

The level of significance helps us make a *statistical* decision related to the null hypothesis but it does not tell us anything about *why* there was a difference. When the null hypothesis is rejected, we examine the design of the study to see if there are extraneous variables that may explain the results. If the null hypothesis is not rejected, we are tempted to conclude that there is, in reality, no difference or no relationship. In a well-designed study, failure to reject the null hypothesis is just as important, scientifically, as rejecting it. The problem is that in many studies that find "no significant differences," there are usually factors in the design that may have contributed to the finding, for example, low reliability, sampling error, low number of subjects, diffusion of treatment, and other threats to internal validity. We simply do not know if there is really no difference or if the study as designed fails to show a difference that in fact exists.

BEYOND SIGNIFICANCE TESTING

There is a long-standing debate among researchers about the value of null hypothesis statistical significance testing. Some have argued, in fact, that such tests should be banned (which might make your student life a little easier!). Essentially, many believe that making a simple dichotomous decision based on an arbitrary level of significance (e.g., the *magical* $p < .05$ is completely arbitrary) is fundamentally flawed. This is because in many studies assumptions for using a specific statistical test may not be met due to the heavy influence of sample size, and because rejecting the null hypothesis does not tell us anything about the importance of the result.

Of course, as you know from reading quantitative research articles and reports, null hypothesis testing is still ubiquitous. Clearly, it is not going away any time soon. However, it is important to understand the limitations of this kind of reasoning, and to supplement inferential significance testing with other analyses that can ameliorate these limitations. There are three primary ways of doing this: using (1) descriptive statistics, (2) confidence intervals, and (3) effect size. Descriptive statistics have already been presented. Simple descriptive statistics, in the same metric that was used in the measurement of variables, is absolutely essential to be able to understand a statistically significant result. Scatterplots and graphs are also very helpful. We'll consider the other two procedures here in greater detail.

Confidence Intervals

Confidence intervals provide a range of values in which the population or "real" trait value lies with specific probabilities. It is calculated with the same data used

Confidence interval: Interval in which the true value of a trait lies.

for significance tests, but there is no *p* value or a specific cutoff point. This is how it works. Taking the sample data, the researcher calculates a measure of variability called the *standard error of the mean* (SE_M). This value is then used to create intervals around the sample mean that correspond to the probability of obtaining a population value in that interval. For example, if a sample mean is 60, a researcher might have a 95% confidence interval of 48–72. This means that there is a 95% chance that the population or "true" mean is somewhere in this interval. By presenting confidence intervals researchers utilize variability in reporting results. Without these intervals variance is used as part of the statistical test but is not reported separately. Confidence intervals are also used when comparing groups to show how much the intervals overlap. This gives you a sense of the likely difference(s) between two or more groups.

Effect Size

Chapter 8 pointed out that there is an important difference between statistical significance and practical significance. Practical significance is related to the importance and usefulness of the results. The null hypothesis and level of significance refer *only* to statistical significance. It is up to each consumer to judge the practical importance of what may be, in a scientific sense, statistically significant. This judgment is made by examining the actual differences or relationships that are called statistically significant and considering the context in which the results are used. A very small but statistically significant difference in the reading achievement of students may not justify changing the method of instruction if teachers' attitudes toward the new approach are negative. In the end, only the reader can determine what is practical and meaningful in using the results. In this sense, your conclusions are more important than those stated by the researchers.

There are several procedures that are used to quantify the practical significance of results. In correlational studies, the coefficient of determination is used. In studies that compare different groups, as with experiments, a procedure called *effect size* is often reported. The **effect size** is a way of quantifying the degree of difference between two groups. Some researchers use effect size to refer to any of several procedures for determining the magnitude, importance, or practicality of a difference or relationship. Other terms that are used include *effect magnitude*, *magnitude effect*, or even *magnitude of effect*. For our purpose here, effect size will be restricted to the comparison of two groups.

The logic of effect size is that the difference between means is contextualized by including the variance. This point is illustrated in Figure 10.1. It shows how the means of two groups can be the same but the amount of overlap, or variance, is quite different. When there is little overlap, as illustrated in the top half of Figure 10.1, the effect size is greater or more significant.

A simple formula, called Cohen's *d*, is often used with two groups, where $\overline{X}_1$ is the mean of one group, $\overline{X}_2$ is the mean of a second group, and *SD* is a measure of variance:

$$d = \frac{\overline{X}_1 - \overline{X}_2}{SD}$$

Effect size: Measure of practical significance.

FIGURE 10.1 Effect size estimates.

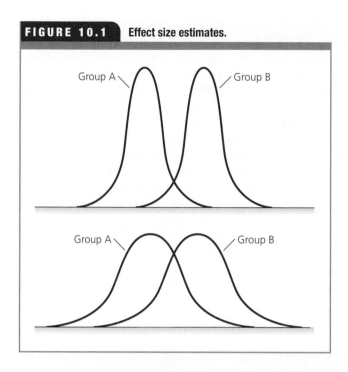

With this formula, *d* represents the difference between two groups as a function of variance. In other words, *d* expresses the difference in terms of standard deviation units. Thus, if the difference is 3 and the standard deviation is 3, $d = 0$. If the difference is 4 and the standard deviation is 2, then $d = .5$. A rule of thumb used in education to relate calculated *d* to practical significance is that $d = .2$ is a small effect, $d = .5$ is a moderate effect, and $d \geq .75$ is a large effect. However, this is only a rule of thumb. The determination of practical significance always depends on the context. It is best applied in situations when the effect can be stated as a measure that has direct practical application. For example, if an experiment shows that students in one group averaged a grade equivalency score of 9.3 while a comparison group was 9.0, and the *d* effect size estimate was 1.25, the approximate three-month difference would have high practical significance. If the *d* was .05, the same difference would have little practical significance.

It is important to remember that the meaning of a specific effect size is ultimately a matter of professional judgment, depending on circumstances, context, costs, and benefits. For example, finding that students who fail a high-stakes test and participate in a new computerized individualized instructional approach increase the likelihood of their passing the retest by 30% may be very important, even though it is likely that there would not be a statistically significant result. Waiting to obtain a $p < .05$ result could be unfair to these students. The following two excerpts illustrate the use of effect size using two different statistics. In the first example Cohen's *d* is used. In the second example a statistic called *eta* is used. Eta is often used to indicate the effect size when more than two groups are compared.

EXAMPLE | Reporting Effect Size

"More optimistically, a recent meta-analysis by Cooper, Charlton, Valentine, and Muhlenbruck (2000) identified 93 studies of summer school that were amenable to quantitative synthesis, and indicated that the average effect size for remedial summer programs was equal to approximately one-fifth of a standard deviation ($d = 0.19$). However, this review also concluded that among students who attended summer school, middle-class children benefited more than disadvantaged children. That is, summer school can widen the achievement gap when programs are offered to all children." (Borman, G. D., & Dowling, N. M. (2006). Longitudinal achievement effects of multiyear summer school: Evidence from the teach Baltimore randomized field trial. *Educational Evaluation and Policy Analysis, 28*(1), pp. 26–27)

"The effect size for the main effect for relevance instructions equaled .12 as measured by eta squared. . . . This approximates the value for a large effect size using the guidelines proposed by Olejnik and Algina (2000) in which values of .01, .06, and .14 indicate small, medium, and large effect sizes, respectively, when measured by eta squared." (McCrudden, M. T., Schraw, G., & Hartley, K. (2006). The effect of general relevance instructions on shallow and deeper learning and reading time. *The Journal of Experimental Education, 74*(4), p. 307)

INTERNET CONNECTION

For more information and examples of effect size estimates, search Bruce Thompson's extensive Website: **www.coe.tamu.edu/~bthompson/index/htm**.

INTERPRETING RESULTS *of* SPECIFIC INFERENTIAL TESTS

Parametric: Statistical procedures based on certain assumptions.

Nonparametric: Used when assumptions for parametric tests are not met.

Inferential statistics are procedures used to obtain a level of significance for rejecting a null hypothesis. There are many different inferential procedures. Each is used to analyze the results of particular research designs. Thus, depending on the design, a specific statistical formula is used to obtain a level of significance appropriate to the null hypothesis. Most of the procedures you will read about are **parametric** statistics. These statistics are used when certain assumptions can be made about the data, such as having a population that is normally distributed, equal variances of each group, and interval-level measures. If these assumptions cannot be met, researchers use **nonparametric** statistics. The interpretation of the results is the same with both types of statistics, but parametric statistics have greater power to detect significant differences. The computational equations are different, but both test a null hypothesis and report a level of significance. Parametric tests are sometimes used even when all needed assumptions are not clearly met. We will consider commonly used parametric and nonparametric procedures.

The *t* Test

The **t test,** a parametric statistical equation, is most often used to test the null hypothesis that the means of two groups are the same. The *t* test is also used to see if a correlation coefficient is significantly different from zero (no correlation) and to compare a mean to a set value. In comparing two means, the researcher uses the two sample means, the group variances, and the sample size with a formula that generates a number, called the *t* value or *t* statistic. This *t* value is then used to obtain a level of significance for rejecting the null hypothesis that the population means are the same. In most studies the researcher will report the *t* value for each *t* test, with corresponding *p* values. The *t* values may be in a table or in the narrative of the results section. Often there will be a table of the means of each group, with accompanying *t* values.

There are two forms of the *t* test. One, the *independent-samples t* test, is used in designs in which there are different subjects in each group, for example, two randomly assigned groups on a posttest of achievement. If the subjects in the groups are paired or matched in some way, a second form of the *t* test is used. This may be called a *dependent-samples, correlated,* or *matched t* test. It is most commonly used in the single-group pretest-posttest design when the same group of subjects is given both the pretest and posttest. Following is an example of the *t* test in published studies:

t test: Compares two means.

EXAMPLE | *t* Test

"Teachers who reported that their current teaching assignment was special education ($n = 38$) were compared to teachers who reported that their current teaching assignment was general education ($n = 275$). Only one of the measures' *p* values fell below .05: individual achievement tests ($t = 2.24$, $df = 299$, $p = .026$). Special education teachers rated individual achievements higher than general education teachers ($M = 4.05$, $SD = 1.48$ for general education teachers, $M = 4.63$, $SD = 1.55$ for special education teachers). However, with the large number of writing variables measured, a corrected alpha does not allow a positive determination of statistical significance to be made." (Gansle, K. A., Gilbertson, D. N., & VanDerHeyden, A. M. (2006). *Practical Assessment, Research & Evaluation, 11*(5), retrieved August 12, 2006, from **http://pareonline.net/pdf/v11n5.pdf.**)

The *df* in the example refers to "degrees of freedom." This number is used to calculate the level of significance and is approximately equal to the number of subjects in the study. It may be indicated in parentheses after the *t* without the letters *df.* In other articles the degrees of freedom may be implied or indicated in a table of results, not in the narrative.

Simple Analysis of Variance

Analysis of variance (abbreviated **ANOVA**) is a parametric procedure that has the same basic purpose as the *t* test: to compare group means to determine the

Analysis of variance (ANOVA): Compares two or more means.

probability of being wrong in rejecting the null hypothesis. Whereas the *t* test compares two means, ANOVA compares two or more means. In effect, ANOVA is an extension of the *t* test that allows the researcher to test the differences between more than two group means. In *simple* ANOVA (also called *one-way* ANOVA) a single independent variable is analyzed with a single dependent variable. For instance, if a researcher compares three types of students—high, medium, and low socioeconomic status (SES)—on a measure of locus of control, there are three levels of the independent variable. ANOVA would test the null hypothesis that there is no difference among the means of all three groups. It would be referred to as a 1 × 3 ANOVA (one independent variable with three levels). The ANOVA equation uses the variances of the groups to calculate a value, called the *F* statistic (or *F* ratio). The *F*, analogous to the *t* value, is a three- or four-digit number employed to obtain the level of significance that the researcher uses to reject or fail to reject the null hypothesis. If the *F* value is large enough, the null hypothesis can be rejected with confidence that at least two of the population means are not the same.

In the preceding example, let us assume that the locus of control means for each group are as follows: high SES, 30; medium SES, 23; low SES, 22. The null hypothesis that is tested is that 30 = 23 = 22. If the *F* statistic calculated with ANOVA is 4.76 and the *p* value is .01, the null would be rejected. However, this analysis does not indicate *which* pair or pairs of means are different. In some studies the results are such that the different pairs are obvious (as in this example), but in most studies there is a need for further statistical tests to indicate those means that are significantly different from other means. These tests are called **multiple comparison procedures** (or post hoc comparisons). There are several types of multiple comparison procedures, including Bonferroni, Fisher's LSD, Duncan's new multiple range test, the Newman-Keuls, Tukey's HSD, and Scheffe's test.

Multiple comparison procedures: Indicate which pairs of means are different.

The results of a simple 1 × 3 ANOVA are summarized in the following example.

EXAMPLE | **One-Way ANOVA and Multiple Comparison Test**

"Results of a one-way analysis of variance indicated significant differences among the groups in their mean ratings of the difficulty of the middle school transition, $F(2,260) = 6.77$, $p < .001$. Post-hoc comparisons at the .05 level using Tukey's HSD test indicated that both students ($M = 2.00$, $SD = 0.96$) and parents ($M = 2.00$, $SD = 0.87$) rated the middle school transition as "somewhat easy" and significantly easier than teachers ($M = 3.00$, $SD = 0.60$) did." Akos, P., & Galassi, J. P. (2004). Middle and high school transitions as viewed by students, parents, and teachers. *Professional School Counseling, 7*(4), p. 216)

Factorial Analysis of Variance

As stated in Chapter 9, factorial designs have more than one independent variable and allow the investigation of interactions among the independent variables.

The statistical analysis of such designs requires the use of **factorial analysis of variance.** The most common factorial ANOVA has two independent variables and is therefore referred to as a *two-way* ANOVA. In a two-way ANOVA three null hypotheses are tested: one for each independent variable and one for the interaction between the two independent variables. Consequently, there are three F ratios, one for each null hypothesis. The test for each independent variable, sometimes called a *main effect*, is similar to a one-way ANOVA for that variable by itself. Thus, there will be an F ratio and corresponding p value for each independent variable. If one variable in a factorial design has two levels and another variable has three levels, the analysis would be a 2 × 3 ANOVA. A 3 × 3 × 4 ANOVA would mean that there are three independent variables, two with three levels and one with four levels.

In interpreting factorial ANOVA studies, you will find that significant interactions are often presented in a graph. The graph is constructed to show how the means of all the groups compare. The values of the dependent variable are placed along the vertical axis of the graph, and levels of one of the independent variables are on the horizontal axis. The means of all the groups are then indicated in the graph by reference to the second independent variable. For example, Figure 10.2 illustrates a significant interaction. The two independent variables are student effort (high or low) and type of reward (intrinsic or extrinsic). The results of the 2 × 2 ANOVA indicate that, overall, high-effort students did better on achievement, a main effect for effort, and that there was a significant interaction—high-effort students who received an intrinsic reward did better than high-effort students who received an extrinsic

Factorial analysis of variance: Two or more independent variables analyzed together.

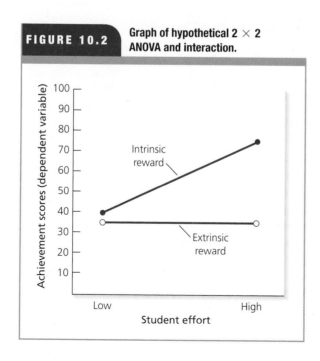

FIGURE 10.2 Graph of hypothetical 2 × 2 ANOVA and interaction.

reward. For low-effort students it did not matter if they received intrinsic or extrinsic rewards.

There are many variations of factorial designs and many terms are used to describe specific types of analyses. You may read such terms as *split plot, randomized block, within subjects,* or *repeated measures* in the results sections of articles. Regardless of the language, the results are interpreted in basically the same manner. There is some type of null hypothesis that needs to be tested, and the *F* ratios are used to see whether there were statistically significant differences.

EXAMPLE | Factorial Analysis of Variance

Results

Means, standard deviations, and sample sizes for the achievement and motivation levels by treatment group are reported in Table 1. The results of the ANOVA in which achievement level was the dependent variable and test anxiety and evaluative threat were the independent variables are given in Table 2. The main effect for test anxiety was not significant. $F(1,57) = 3.49$. $p < .05$. Students with high test anxiety did not obtain a significantly lower mean score ($M = 90.00$, $SD = 4.40$) in achievement than did students with low test anxiety ($M = 91.77$, $SD = 3.09$). However, there was a significant main effect for evaluative threat, $F(1,57) = 6.39$, $p > .05$. Individuals in the high evaluative threat group demonstrated a significantly lower average level of achievement ($M = 89.71$, $SD = 4.14$) than did their peers in the low evaluative threat group ($M = 92.07$, $SD = 3.26$). The magnitude of difference or effect size between the high and low evaluative threat groups as calculated with Cohen's *d* (Hedges & Olkin, 1985) was 0.57.

TABLE 1 Means, Standard Deviations, and Sample Sizes of Achievement and Motivation Levels

| | Threat of Evaluation | | | | | | | | |
| | Low | | | High | | | Overall | | |
Treatment Group	**M**	**SD**	**n**	**M**	**SD**	**n**	**M**	**SD**	**n**
Achievement									
Low test anxiety	91.3	2.52	15	91.60	3.67	15	91.77	3.09	30
High text anxiety	92.20	3.95	15	87.94	3.86	16	90.00	4.40	31
Overall	92.07	3.26	30	89.71	4.14	31	90.87	3.89	61
Motivation									
Low text anxiety	17.33	1.99	15	17.00	2.27	15	17.17	2.10	30
High test anxiety	17.73	2.12	15	14.63	3.16	16	16.13	2.63	31
Overall	17.53	3.03	30	15.77	2.49	31	16.64	2.43	61

TABLE 2 2 × 2 Analysis of Variance of Effects of Test Anxiety and Threat of Evaluation on Achievement

Variable	SS	df	MS	F
Test anxiety (TA)	43.93	1	43.93	3.49
Threat of evaluation (TE)	80.46	1	80.16	6.39*
TA × TE	58.18	1	58.18	4.67*
Residual	717.871	57	12.59	

*$p < .05$.

Furthermore, there was a statistically significant interaction, $F(1, 57) = 4.67, p < .05$ (see Figure 10.3), revealing an effect on students' achievement of the combination of independent variables. Specifically, high test anxiety students in the high evaluative threat condition obtained a significantly lower mean score ($M = 87.94$, $SD = 3.86$) in achievement than did high test anxiety students in the low evaluative threat condition ($M = 92.20$, $SD = 3.95$; ($t = 3.04, p < .05$) and low test anxiety students in both the high evaluative threat condition ($M = 91.60$, $SD = 3.67$; $t = 2.71, p < .05$) and the low evaluative threat condition ($M = 91.93$, $SD = 2.52$, $t = 3.39, p < .05$). (Hancock, D. R. (2001). Effects of text anxiety and evaluative threat on students' achievement and motivation. *The Journal of Educational Research, 94*(5), pp. 287–288)

FIGURE 10.3 Test anxiety (TA) and threat of evaluation on achievement.

FIGURE 10.4 Test anxiety (TA) and threat of evaluation on motivation.

Analysis of Covariance

Analysis of covariance (ANCOVA) is a variation of ANOVA. It is used to adjust for pretest differences that may exist between two or more groups. For instance, suppose in an experiment that one group has a mean value on the pretest of 15 and the other group has a pretest mean of 18. ANCOVA is used to adjust the posttest scores statistically to compensate for the 3-point difference between the groups. This adjustment results in more accurate posttest comparisons. The pretest used for the adjustment is called the *covariate*. Several other types of covariates can also be used in a study, such as socioeconomic status, aptitude, attitudes, and previous achievement. Sometimes a covariate other than the pretest is used with the pretest covariate, and sometimes covariates are used when there is no pretest in the design of the study. Covariates are helpful only if they are related to the dependent variable. ANCOVA is used with both one-way and factorial designs.

A good example of using ANCOVA is illustrated in a study that examined the effect of regular classroom-based social skills training on peer acceptance of first graders (Choi & Heckenlaible-Gotto, 1998). There was a control group at one school and a treatment group at a second school, so there could not be random assignment of subjects. In the description of the analyses the authors indicate why ANCOVA was appropriate:[1]

> **EXAMPLE** | **Analysis of Covariance**
>
> "We used one-way analysis of covariance (ANCOVA) to control for any initial differences that might have existed between the control group and the treatment group. The covariate was the pretest scores; the adjusted posttest scores were analyzed to compare the treatment and control groups." (Choi, H., & Heckenlaible-Gotto, M. J. (1998). Classroom-based social skills training: Impact on peer acceptance of first-grade students. *Journal of Educational Research, 91*, p. 211)

Multivariate Statistics

Each of the preceding parametric statistical procedures represents what is termed a **univariate** analysis because a single dependent variable is used. However, in many complex social settings, such as schools, there is often a need to study two or more dependent variables simultaneously. For example, a teacher may be interested in comparing two teaching methods on attitudes toward learning and school. A principal may want to determine the effect of a new homework policy on parent involvement, student confidence, and achievement in each of several different subject areas. In such situations it would be a mistake to analyze each dependent variable separately, with a different ANOVA or *t* test. The correct approach is to use a **multivariate** statistical procedure. Multivariate statistics analyze

Analysis of covariance (ANCOVA): Adjusts for pretest differences between groups.

Univariate: One dependent variable analyzed.

Multivariate: Two or more dependent variables analyzed together.

[1]Some researchers insist that ANCOVA should only be used with true experiments.

all the dependent variables in a single procedure, which is important in accounting for the relationships between the dependent variables. For each of the univariate statistical procedures, there is a multivariate analog (e.g., Hotelling's T for the t test, and MANCOVA for ANCOVA).

Multivariate procedures are now commonly reported in the literature. Although the computations and interpretation of multivariate tests are complex, they employ the same basic principles for rejecting the null hypotheses. It should also be pointed out that some researchers have a somewhat different definition of the term *multivariate*, which may refer to any study that has more than one variable, either independent or dependent. With this definition, multiple correlation would be considered a multivariate procedure.

EXAMPLE | **Multivariate Analysis of Variance**

"For each domain, a multivariate analysis of variance (MANOVA) was conducted with cluster membership as the independent variable and competency beliefs and achievement values as the dependent variables. When the results of an omnibus MANOVA were statistically significant, we used multivariate follow-up procedures to determine the source of significance." (Buehl, M. M., & Alexander, P. A. (2005). Motivation and performance differences in students' domain-specific epistemological beliefs profiles. *American Educational Research Journal, 42*(4), p. 715)

Chi-Square

When researchers are interested in the number of responses or cases in different categories, they use a procedure called **chi-square** to analyze the results. The null hypothesis is that there is no difference between an observed number and an expected number of responses or cases that fall in each category. The expected number is usually that which would be expected by chance alone. Suppose an administrator wanted to see if there is a difference between the number of male and female students who take advanced placement courses. The expected number by chance alone would be an equal number of males and females in advanced placement courses. The administrator would use the chi-square test to determine if the actual number of male students taking advanced placement courses was significantly different from the number of female students taking advanced placement courses.

Chi-square: Tests frequency counts in different categories.

The chi-square test (represented by χ^2) can also examine questions of relationship between two independent variables that report frequencies of responses or cases. For example, a researcher may be interested in investigating the relationship between gender and choices of books for a book report. There may be several types of books, such as romantic, adventure, mystery, and biography. The researcher would count the number of males and females who choose each type of book and analyze the results with a chi-square to determine if the null hypothesis, that there is no relationship between gender and book choice, can be rejected. This type of chi-square may be referred to as a *contingency table*, in this example a 2 × 4 table. The result is often reported with a single measure of relationship called a *contingency coefficient*, which is interpreted in the same way as a correlation coefficient.

The results of a chi-square will usually be reported in a table that shows either the number or percentage of responses or cases in each category. If the number is less than five in any single category, the chi-square test needs to be "corrected" with what is called *Yates's correction*. This correction statistically adjusts the numbers to get a more valid result. Another approach when a small number of observations is observed is to use a procedure called *Fisher's exact test*. The results will indicate the value of the chi-square (χ^2) and the level of significance with the χ^2.

In a study of student reflections on parent involvement with homework, Balli (1998) used chi-square to analyze the results. In the article, the author points out how the frequency of responses in different categories changes:

EXAMPLE | **Chi-Square Test**

"Answers to Question 1 indicated that a significant number of students (48) experienced parental involvement with the 20 homework assignments at least some of the time (chi-square = 49.28, *df* = 2, *p* < .01) . Seventeen students reported that they always worked with their parent(s) on the assignments. Two students reported that they never worked with their parent(s) on the assignments." (Balli, S. J. (1998). When mom and dad help: Student reflections on parent involvement with homework. *Journal of Research and Development in Education, 31*(3), p. 143)

The chi-square is a nonparametric statistical procedure because the data that are analyzed are nominal-level data, and assumptions of normal distribution and equal variances may not be met. There are nonparametric analyses that can be used instead of a particular parametric analysis. Some of these are summarized in Table 10.1.

TABLE 10.1 Parametric and Analogous Nonparametric Procedures

Parametric	Nonparametric
Pearson product-moment correlation coefficient	Spearman rank-order correlation coefficient
Independent samples *t* test	Median test
	Mann–Whitney *U* test
Dependent samples *t* test	Sign test
	Wilcoxon test
One-way ANOVA	Median test
	Kruskal–Wallis ANOVA

INTERNET CONNECTION

See this Website to find links within the WWW that are concerned with inferential statistics:
http://methods.fullerton.edu/chapter13.html.

CONSUMER TIPS: *Criteria for Evaluating Inferential Statistics*

1. Basic descriptive statistics are needed to evaluate the results of inferential statistics. Remember that the results of an inferential test rely on the descriptive data that were gathered—the means, variances, frequencies, and percentages. Although inferential statistics provide important information about the probability that conclusions about populations, or "true" values, are correct, the interpretation of the results depends on the descriptive statistical results. It may be misleading to rely solely on the conclusions of the inferential test results. *You should always look at the more basic descriptive data to derive meaning from the results.*

2. Inferential analyses refer to statistical, not practical, significance. It is easy to confuse statistical with practical significance. The results of inferential analyses should not be the sole criteria for conclusions about changing a practice or other decisions. The use of inferential tests should be kept in balance with other considerations relative to the use of the results.

3. Inferential analyses do not indicate external validity. Although we use inferential statistics to infer population values from sample values, generalizability to other subjects and settings depends on whether the subjects were randomly selected, the characteristics of the subjects, and the design of the study.

4. Inferential analyses do not indicate internal validity. The extent to which a result shows a causal relationship depends on how the data were gathered and what happened to the subjects. The inferential test is used to conclude that there is a high probability that the null hypothesis is not true, that is, that there is a difference or relationship. This is the first and necessary step to conclude that one variable caused a change in another variable. Once the statistics show that there is a relationship or difference, you need to analyze the design and procedures to determine if there is adequate internal validity.

5. The results of inferential tests depend on the number of subjects. An important factor in determining the level of significance for a statistical test is the number of subjects. If there are many subjects, a very small difference or relationship can be statistically significant; if only a few subjects are used, what appears to be a large difference or relationship may not be statistically significant. This phenomenon is especially important in experimental studies in which there is a difference between the number of subjects and replications of the treatment. If a researcher uses number of subjects when it is clear that the number of independent replications of the treatment is much smaller, the inferential test that leads to a conclusion to reject the null hypothesis may be invalid.

6. The appropriate statistical test should be used. It is important for researchers to use a statistical test that is appropriate to the design and questions of a study. Most journal reviewers and editors evaluate studies to be certain that the appropriate tests were employed. However, it is likely that many studies are published that use the wrong statistical test. The most likely mistakes are to use a parametric procedure when the assumptions for using such a test are not met and to use many univariate tests when a multivariate test would be more appropriate.

7. The level of significance should be interpreted correctly. Remember that the level of significance indicates the probability that the difference or relationship is not due to chance. It is not a definitive statement that there either is or is not a difference or relationship. A high level of significance (e.g., .20 or .40) does not necessarily mean that there is no difference or relationship in the population or in reality. Nonsignificant findings may result from inadequate design and measurement.

8. Be wary of statistical tests with small numbers of subjects in one or more groups or categories. Whenever there is a small number of subjects in a group, there is a good chance that the statistical test may provide spurious results. When only a few numbers are used to calculate a mean or variance, one atypical number may significantly affect the results. It is best to have at least 10 subjects in each comparison group and 30 subjects in calculating a correlation. The results of studies that use a small number of subjects also have less generalizability.

Author Reflection *I hope that you will not be intimidated by inferential statistics. They are only used to make estimates about statistical significance. The more important information is provided by simple descriptive statistics and carefully constructed figures that represent score distributions. Further, there is far too much reliance on statistical significance and not enough emphasis on practical significance. While some journals require magnitude-of-effect statistics, the use of these estimates is spotty at best, with little discussion of what effect size statistics, such as Cohen's d, really mean. As with so many topics in this book, you, as an informed consumer, will need to make your own evaluations.*

STUDY QUESTIONS

1. Why is it necessary to use inferential statistics?
2. What is the relationship between inferential and descriptive statistics?
3. What is the difference between sampling error and measurement error?
4. How is the null hypothesis used in inferential statistics?
5. Why is it important to understand what "level of significance" means?
6. What is the difference between Type I and Type II errors?
7. Does it matter whether the null hypothesis is rejected?

8. Why is it important to distinguish between "statistical" and "practical" significance?
9. What is "effect size" used for?
10. Under what circumstances would it be appropriate to use nonparametric statistical tests?
11. Give an example of a study that would use an independent sample *t* test.
12. Give an example of a study that would use simple ANOVA.
13. Give an example of a study that would use factorial ANOVA.
14. What does a factorial ANOVA tell us that a simple ANOVA does not?
15. Why would it be helpful to use ANCOVA rather than ANOVA?
16. Why are multivariate statistics used?
17. Give an example of a study that would use a chi-square statistical analysis.

@WWW SAMPLE TEST QUESTIONS

See this text's Companion Website at **www.ablongman.com/mcmillan5e.** for sample test questions and answers.

RESEARCH NAVIGATOR™ ACTIVITIES

1. Read studies found in AN 20707534 and AN 6411043 and identify the statistical procedures for determining results. Are the statistical analyses sections clear? Are the statistical procedures aligned with the research questions?
2. Effect size is discussed in further detail in Research Navigator AN 21984694. What are three main points in the article that would be important for educational researchers?

Chapter 11

Qualitative Research Designs *and* Analysis

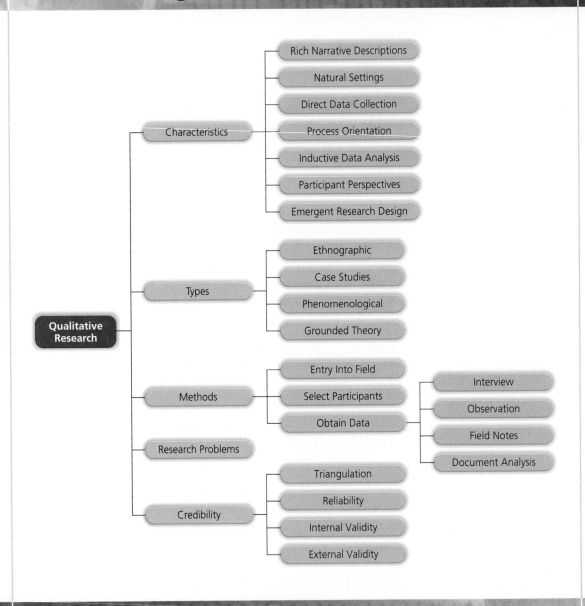

CHAPTER ROAD MAP

This chapter is a rather abrupt change from the previous four, not only in research methods and data analysis but also philosophical assumptions about how it is best to understand what is being studied. We begin by reviewing characteristics that are common to most qualitative studies, then review in greater detail methods of four types of qualitative research that have different perspectives about how to gather and interpret the data. The chapter concludes with a discussion of criteria that should be used to judge the credibility of qualitative studies.

After reading and studying this chapter, you will:

- Describe how qualitative studies differ from quantitative studies
- Understand key characteristics of qualitative studies
- Be able to differentiate between major types of qualitative studies
- Identify methods of conducting ethnographic, case study, phenomenological, and grounded theory approaches
- Understand the role of triangulation, reliability, and internal validity in judging the quality of qualitative studies
- Be able to read, understand, and critique qualitative studies

INTRODUCTION *to* QUALITATIVE RESEARCH

Although the vast majority of studies use quantitative techniques, you will also read research based on a different set of assumptions and methods. It is important to remember that these methods are no less "scientific" than quantitative methods. Indeed, most qualitative researchers would maintain that their approach is scientific with respect to being systematic and rigorous. What is most different for qualitative studies are epistemological assumptions about the nature of the information that is needed to arrive at credible findings and conclusions. Researchers using a qualitative approach believe that there are multiple realities represented in participant perspectives, and that context is critical in providing an understanding of the phenomenon being investigated. In contrast, a quantitative study assumes that there is a single, objective reality that can be measured. Qualitative approaches are characterized by the assumption that the researcher's biases and perspectives must be understood and used in interpreting findings, whereas in a quantitative study researcher bias is a threat to internal validity. One approach is not necessarily better than another. Each has advantages and disadvantages, strengths and weaknesses. Most educational researchers would agree that problems are best investigated by using whatever methods are most appropriate, separately or in combination; that is, we begin with a research question or problem and *then* select the methods that will provide the most credible answers.

CHARACTERISTICS *of* QUALITATIVE RESEARCH

In Chapter 1, qualitative research was described as a tradition of research techniques, as well as a philosophy of knowing. The term *qualitative* refers to a number of approaches that share some common characteristics. Before examining the four qualitative approaches covered in this chapter in greater detail, we will review these characteristics (summarized in Table 11.1). Finally, it is also helpful to remember that there are many terms associated with qualitative research, such as *field research, naturalistic, participant observation, ecological, constructivist, ethnomethodology*, and *case study*. The exact definition and use of these terms, as well as "qualitative," vary according to their disciplinary roots (anthropology, sociology, psychology, political science, and philosophy). Educational researchers are likely to use qualitative in a generic sense, as a methodology that has some or all of the following characteristics.

Natural Settings

A distinguishing characteristic of most qualitative research is that behavior is studied as it occurs naturally. There is no manipulation or control of behavior or settings, nor are there any externally imposed constraints. Rather, the setting for some qualitative research is an actual classroom, school, playground, clinic, or neighborhood. This is why qualitative research is often described as *field research;* much of it takes place out in the field or setting. For example, a qualitative approach to studying beginning teachers would be to conduct the research in a few schools and classrooms in which these individuals were teaching. In contrast, a quantitative approach might use a questionnaire to gather the perceptions, beliefs, and practices of a sample of beginning teachers. There are two reasons for conducting research in the field. Qualitative researchers believe that

TABLE 11.1	**Key Characteristics of Qualitative Research**
Characteristic	**Description**
Natural setting	Study of behavior as it occurs naturally.
Direct data collection	Researcher collects data directly from source.
Rich narrative descriptions	Detailed narratives that provide in-depth understanding of contexts and behaviors.
Process orientation	Focus on why and how behaviors occur.
Inductive data analysis	Generalizations induced from synthesizing gathered information.
Participant perspectives	Focus on participants' understanding and meaning.
Emergent research design	Research design evolves and changes as the study takes place.

(1) behavior is best understood as it occurs without external constraints and control, and (2) the situational **context** is very important in understanding the behavior. The setting influences the way humans behave and, therefore, it is not possible to understand the behavior without taking into account the situational characteristics.

Context: Environment in which behavior occurs.

Direct Data Collection

In qualitative studies the investigator has a direct role in obtaining information, as either the interviewer, an observer, or as the person who studies artifacts and documents. Qualitative researchers want to obtain information directly from the source. They do this by spending a considerable amount of time in direct interaction with the settings, participants, and documents they are studying. They tend to be reluctant to use other observers or quantitative measuring techniques because the researchers are then not as "close" to the data as they need to be for a full understanding.

Rich Narrative Descriptions

Qualitative researchers approach a situation with the assumption that nothing is trivial or unimportant. Every detail that is recorded is thought to contribute to a better understanding of behavior. The descriptions are in the form of words or pictures rather than numbers, although simple numerical summaries are used in some qualitative studies and in investigations that use both qualitative and quantitative methods. The intent is to provide rich descriptions that cannot be achieved by reducing pages of narration to numbers. Rather, the descriptions capture what has been observed in the same form in which it occurred naturally. Nothing escapes scrutiny or is taken for granted. The detailed approach to description is necessary to obtain a complete understanding of the setting and to accurately reflect the complexity of human behavior. To accomplish these goals the studies may extend over a long period of time and require intense involvement, and they typically culminate in extensive written reports.

Process Orientation

Qualitative researchers want to know how and why behavior occurs. In contrast with most quantitative studies, qualitative methods look for the *process* through which behavior occurs, not just the outcomes or products. For example, while quantitative research can document the effect of teachers' expectations on student achievement, qualitative studies would be appropriate for understanding *how* teachers' expectations affect students' achievement and behavior. The emphasis would be on how expectations are formed and how they are played out in the nature of teacher interactions with students. The emphasis on process allows for conclusions that explain the reasons for results. For instance, suppose a state is interested in how staff development affects student achievement. A quantitative approach would be to simply record student behavior following the staff development, whereas a qualitative inquiry would focus on how the teachers changed as a result of the staff development and how this change affected student achievement. This approach would provide a greater understanding of what it was about the staff development that was most important.

Inductive Data Analysis

Qualitative researchers do not formulate hypotheses and gather data to prove or disprove them (deduction). Rather, the data are gathered first and then synthesized inductively to generate generalizations, models, or frameworks. Conclusions are developed from the "ground up," or "bottom up," from the detailed particulars, rather than from the "top down." This approach is important because the qualitative researcher wants to be open to new ways of understanding. Predetermined hypotheses limit what data will be collected and may cause bias. The process of qualitative research is like an upside down funnel (see Figure 11.1). In the beginning, the data may seem unconnected and too extensive to make much sense, but as the researcher works with the data, progressively more specific findings are generated.

FIGURE 11.1 Steps in inductive data analysis.

Step 6
Conclusion, Model, Framework, or Structures

Step 5
Reduce Categories to Eliminate Redundancy

Step 4
Create Categories from Codes

Step 3
Code and Verify Data

Step 2
Close Reading of Text or Notes

Step 1
Gather Extensive Detailed Data

Synthesis

Synthesis

Participant Perspectives

Qualitative researchers try to reconstruct reality *as the participants they are study-ing see it.* They do not apply predetermined definitions or ideas about how people will think or react. For example, a quantitative researcher may assume that a teacher's praise is interpreted by students in a certain way, whereas a qualitative researcher would be interested in how the participants (students) interpreted the praise. The goal in qualitative research is to understand participants from their point of view. In other words, the focus is on the *meaning* of events and actions as expressed by the participants. With this approach there are multiple "realities" as different people construct subjective meaning from the same event. As a result, much of what is reported in qualitative studies is participants' perspectives. Thus, in a qualitative study of what motivates students, it would be important to focus on what the students said and did, to describe motivation using the words and actions of the students, not the researcher.

Emergent Research Design

As in quantitative research, qualitative researchers have a plan or design for con-ducting the research. The difference is that in a qualitative study researchers enter the investigation "as if they know very little about the people and places they will visit. They attempt to loosen themselves from their preconceptions" (Bogdan & Biklen, 2007, p. 54). Because of this perspective, they do not know enough to begin the study with a precise research design. As they learn about the setting, people, and other sources of information, they discover what needs to be done to fully describe and understand the phenomena being studied. Thus, a qualitative researcher will begin the study with *some* idea about what data will be collected and the procedures that will be employed, but a full ac-count of the methods is given *retrospectively*, after all the data have been collected. The design is emergent in that it remains flexible and evolves during the study.

Before going on to more specific types of qualitative designs, I want to stress again that the above characteristics are typically present *to some degree* in any sin-gle qualitative investigation. The extent to which each characteristic is included depends on the particular design and the orientation of the researcher. In "pure" qualitative studies each of these characteristics is present, whereas in other qual-itative studies only some of them are present.

We will now examine the nature of four specific qualitative approaches in greater detail. We will begin with ethnography, which typically contains all of the characteristics described, and summarize important aspects of formulating the research problem, selecting participants, obtaining data, and data analysis. We will then consider the three other approaches, with a focus on how their design features differ from ethnography. You will find that, while most of the discussion focuses on ethnography, there is much overlap in many aspects of the four designs.

studied. When reading qualitative research you should look for the justification used in selecting participants. It is important that you understand how and why the participants were selected because the findings are based on the data collected from a relatively low number of participants.

Obtaining Data

There are three common methods of collecting data for ethnographic studies—observation, interviews, and analysis of documents. In fact, these three methods are most common for all types of qualitative designs. We will begin with observation, which is essential in most ethnographies.

Observation. In ethnographic observations the researcher spends an extended period of time in the setting. By observing naturally occurring behavior over many hours or days, the researcher hopes to obtain a rich understanding of the phenomenon being studied. The nature of the observation is *comprehensive* in that it is continuous and total. When reading the methods section of an ethnographic article, you should look for information on the amount of time the researcher spent in the setting. The quality of the results is often directly related to the length of the observations. It is unlikely that valid and credible data will result from a few hours of observation.

An important aspect of the observation is the extent to which the researcher is an active participant with the subjects. If the researcher is a genuine participant in the activity being studied, he or she is called a **participant observer.** For example, to study the life of a college freshman, the participant observer would become a college freshman, directly experiencing everything other freshmen experience. This is essentially what an anthropologist would do in conducting ethnographic research on a culture. The anthropologist would virtually become a member of the group and live just as others in the group live.

In educational research, it is rare for the investigator literally to adopt the same role as the individuals who are being studied. There may be some participation in some of the activities, but it is usually limited. The researcher interacts with the participants to establish a rapport and a relationship but does not become a member of the group. When participation is limited, the researcher is called an *observer participant.*

As illustrated in Table 11.2, you can think of the degree of participation and involvement as a continuum, ranging from a *complete participant* on one end to a *complete observer* on the other end. A **complete observer** is totally detached from the behavior of the participants who are being studied. Of course, the mere presence of an observer, whether involved or detached, may affect the behavior of those observed.

The extent of participation by an ethnographic observer often changes during a study. In the beginning, the researcher may limit participation to become accepted. As the group being studied becomes comfortable with the researcher, participation increases. Another variable that affects the extent of participation is the nature of the research question. If, for example, the study is focused on the

Participant observer: Observer involved as a participant.

Complete observer: Observer detached from participants.

Document Analysis. The third primary method of collecting data for ethnographic studies is by reviewing documents. **Documents** are written records. They can be virtually anything written or printed, such as yearbooks, school budgets, dropout rates, committee minutes, memos, letters, newspapers, diaries, test scores, and books. Nonprint materials, such as pictures, videotapes, memorabilia, and films can also be used. If the documents provide firsthand information, they are *primary* sources. In a primary source the document is written in first person. It is written by someone who has had direct experience with the phenomenon, organization, or group being studied. *Secondary* sources are secondhand documents, such as descriptions of an event on the basis of what is heard from others, or a summary of more extensive primary information.

> **Documents:** Written records.

In ethnographic studies the most common use of documents is to verify or support data obtained from interviews or observations. For example, teacher notes taken at the end of the school day that reflect on the successes and obstacles in using a new curriculum could be used to supplement researcher observations about the new curriculum. Student essays could also be examined if written as part of the curriculum. The researcher usually finds existing documents that have been produced, but occasionally a researcher will ask participants to keep records or narratives as a way of producing documents. It should be clear, however, that a document is written or created as a natural outgrowth of the situation, and not in response to some kind of predetermined structure imposed by the researcher.

Data Analysis and Interpretation

Observation, interview, and document analysis techniques result in a great amount of data that must be summarized and interpreted. Pages of field notes or interview transcripts must be critically examined and synthesized. The analysis is done during data collection as well as after all the data have been gathered. In many qualitative studies data collection and analysis are interwoven, influencing one another. The goal of the analysis is to discover patterns, ideas, explanations, and "understandings." Specific data elements have to be organized and then synthesized to derive the patterns and ideas that will form the basis of the conclusions. A thorough analysis requires three steps: organization of the data, summarizing the data, and then interpreting the data.

Data Organization. The first step in data analysis is to organize the data, separating it into workable units or segments. With many pages of data, simply organizing the data is quite a task. Fortunately, several computer software programs are available to record and analyze the data more efficiently.

Most studies organize the data according to their source. **Emic** data contain information provided by the participants, in their own words. By capturing language, actions, expressions, terms, and explanations as communicated by the participants, the richness and depth of the findings can be summarized. **Etic** data are representations of the researcher. These representations are the researcher's interpretation of emic data. This is usually illustrated with themes or conclusions that explain trends and findings. For example, in a study of teachers' reasons for

> **Emic:** Participant wording.

> **Etic:** Researcher representations of emic data.

using particular grading practices, the participants might say something like "I use objective tests to show parents how grades were determined" and "I use tests that have the same type of items as the high-stakes test given at the end of the semester." These statements represent emic data. The researcher might synthesize these and call them "external pressures," which would be etic data.

The most common approach to organizing both emic and etic data is to read through the narratives and researcher comments look for words, phrases, or events that seem to stand out; and then create **codes** for these topics and patterns. The codes are then used as categories to organize the data. "Families" of codes can be applied to most studies. The families include codes related to setting and context, subjects' definitions of a setting, subjects' perspectives about other people and aspects of a setting, process changes over time, activities, events, techniques subjects use to accomplish things, and relationships and social structures. Typically, 30 to 50 codes are used in an ethnographic study. Some may be *major* codes, which tend to be broad, general categories, while others may be *subcodes*, which are divisions among the major codes. For example, in an ethnographic study of the effect of a new testing program, major codes might be time of testing, effect on teacher, effect on student, effect on school climate, effect on teacher relationships. Subcodes under effect on students could include motivational effects, effort, student preparation, student reactions after testing, student reactions after receiving scores.

Because the creation of codes is up to each researcher and is critical to the study, it is important to know something about how the codes were created. The key is for the data to suggest codes, not vice versa. Look for some kind of systematic process in the development of the codes, such as using general research questions that are stated prior to the research and that are generated during the study. Regular review of field notes to plan next steps keeps a researcher close to the data and familiar with major themes. Ethnographers should write many observer comments as they are interviewing or observing or reviewing documents because these comments form the basis of important insights and categories. Sometimes playing with analogies and metaphors will provide an overview of organization of ideas.

An example of coded field notes is illustrated in Figure 11.2.

Codes: Words or phrases to signify units of data.

Data Summary. Organized data then need to be summarized into a much smaller number of categories or themes. This step can be arduous. Before computers, it would not be unusual to have each piece of information written on cards and sorted into piles according to different codes. Imagine a room with 30 piles of cards, each pile having 10 to 50 data elements. For example, in the aforementioned study on the effect of testing, one code is effect on students. In this pile there would be many cards that indicate observations or interview responses pertaining to effect on students. This could be something as simple as "the students moaned when testing was mentioned" to more complicated entries such as "One student came up after class and asked the teacher for more details about the testing. The student wanted to know about the difficulty of the test in comparison to classroom tests, and whether it would help to study for the test." The researcher's job in

FIGURE 11.2 **Example of coded field notes.**

teachers' work	Then I went down to the teachers' lounge to see if anybody might happen to be there. I was in luck. Jill Martin sat at the first table, <u>correcting papers;</u> Kathy Thomas was also there, walking around and smoking. I said, "Hi Jill, hi Kathy. Okay if I join you?" "Sure," Jill said. "You and your husband have been to China, right?" I said, "Yes. Why?" Jill then turned to Kathy and said, "Have you studied China yet? Sari has slides that she can show." <u>Kathy said</u> to me that she was going to study
authority	<u>world communities, even though "they" had taken them out of the sixth-grade social studies curriculum. "Now can you tell me who 'they' are?"</u> I asked her. She said, "You know, 'them': 'they.'"
autonomy	Both Jill and Kathy were upset at how "they" had mandated what the teachers could teach in their rooms. "They" turned out to be the central office who had communicated the state's revised sixth-grade social studies curriculum. The state has "taken out all the things that we think are important" from the curriculum and have substituted the theme of "economic geography" for the sixth-graders to study.
doing your own thing	Both Jill and Kathy think that "sixth-graders can't comprehend economic geography well," and think world communities of Africa and Asia are more important. They said they planned to teach what they wanted to anyway. Kathy said, "They'll come around one of these days." "Oh, Kathy, are you a rebel?" I asked. "No," she replied, "I'm just doing my own thing."
parents	After we chatted for a little while, Jill turned to me: "<u>You're interested in what concerns us. I guess one thing is parents.</u>" She proceeded to describe a parent conference she had participated in yesterday
parents	afternoon with a child's parents and a child's psychiatrist. She said, "What really upsets me is how much responsibility they placed on me to change the child's behavior." They seemed to give lip service, she reported, to have "controls" come from the child when they said, "It's so difficult for parents to see that kids need to take responsibility for their actions."

Source: Bogdan, Robert C. and Biklen, Sari Knopp. (2007). Qualitative research for education: An introduction to theories and methods (5th ed., p. 188). Published by Allyn and Bacon, Boston, MA. Copyright © 2007 by Pearson Education. Reprinted by permission of the publisher.

summarizing is to examine all the entries that have the same code and write a sentence or two that captures the essence of the information.

A **category,** then, is formed from coded data as a more general and abstract idea that represents the meaning of similarly coded information. Some codes will be used in more than one category.

Category: Idea that represents coded data.

Data Interpretation. Once the data have been coded and summarized, the researcher looks for relationships among the categories and patterns that suggest generalizations, models, and conclusions. At this point the researcher interprets the findings inductively, synthesizes the information, and draws inferences.

The researcher essentially tells what he or she has found and what it means. Because so much of the analysis depends on the researcher, it is best to know the researcher's perspectives, background, and theoretical orientation. For each major finding and interpretation it is common for the researcher to use actual quotes from participants, field notes, or documents to illustrate the point and enliven the results. It also gives the reader an opportunity to see how the researcher has been thinking and the basis for conclusions.

A recent study of adult self-disclosure about having a learning disability presented five themes to organize the interview data the researchers obtained. Here is an excerpt from one theme to show how exact quotes are used. The second excerpt is from a study on the use of higher-level thinking to enhance student self-regulation. Interviews were conducted with seven teachers.

EXAMPLE | **Use of Participant Quotes**

"In fact, 15 of the 18 interviewees offered responses that specifically referred to the stigma of their disability. For example, one adult said, 'you feel terrible stupid. . . . I'm hesitant . . . the word *disability* . . . there's so many stigmas out there.' A second explained, 'It [disclosed learning disability] can be damaging to you.' A third told us 'The biggest thing I'm afraid of is people thinking I'm stupid and treating me differently, like my boyfriend's family does.'" (Price, L. A., Gerber, P. J., Mulligan, R., & Williams, P. (2005). To be or not to be learning disabled: A preliminary report on self-disclosure and adults with learning disabilities. *Thalamus, 23*(2), p. 22)

"Six of seven teachers interviewed for the study found writing higher-order thinking questions for reading assignments and quizzes to be initially challenging in that they had been used to prepare questions on the literal level of comprehension. As one teacher noted, 'The greatest challenge I faced was maintaining the higher-order thinking skills notion when writing the questions. We've become so accustomed to asking literal questions and emphasizing the meaning of certain vocabulary words.' Teachers regress just as well as students. Since students are more successful and comfortable with the literal interpretation of readings, teachers have become comfortable in asking literal questions." (Cooper, J. E., Horn, S., & Strahan, D. B. (2005). If only they would do their homework: Promoting self-regulation in high school classes. *High School Journal, 88*(3), p. 19)

The process of pattern-seeking begins with the researcher's informed hunches and ideas as data are being collected and interpreted. Once tentative patterns are identified, additional data are examined to determine if they are consistent with that pattern. It is also common to have different researchers independently review data to see if they come up with the same patterns. This is a more deductive process, one in which there is a search for negative or discrepant data that would not support the pattern. Such a finding modifies the pattern. Pattern-seeking is also characterized by enlarging, combining, subsuming, and creating new categories that make sense logically. It is not uncommon to derive overarching models that show the relationships among several patterns in the findings visually, in

FIGURE 11.3 A model of teacher assessment in decision making.

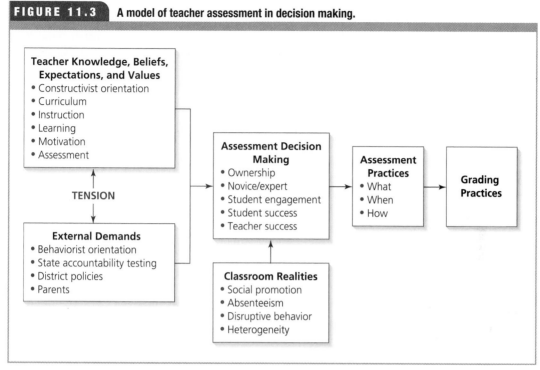

Source: Adapted from McMillan, 2002.

the form of a diagram or chart. For example, a recent qualitative study of teachers' classroom assessment and grading decision making found that there were six major categories with subcategories that explained the data. Figure 11.3 identifies some of the data, codes, and categories from this study. Note how some data are used in more than one category.

The following ethnographic study illustrates the comprehensive, in-depth nature of data collection. This investigation examined racial messages and lessons from parents and teachers in a suburban school.

EXAMPLE | Ethnographic Data Collection

"Data were collected during the 1997–1998 school year. I spent 2 days a week conducting participant observation in a fourth- to fifth-grade classroom (and on the school yard, in the staff lunch room, in the main office, and other parts of the school grounds) and attended multiple staff meetings, Parent-Teacher Association (PTA) meetings, and other school events. In addition, I conducted formal and informal interviews with parents and students. . . . Over the course of the year I informally interviewed most students in the class. . . . I deliberately interviewed students who were in one way or another on the racial margins of the class. . . . Whenever possible I also interviewed their parents. . . . I interviewed a random selection of

> white students. . . . I also conducted formal and informal interviews with staff and teachers and collected numerous site documents and school materials." (Lewis, A. E. (2001). There is not "race" in the school-yard: Color-blind ideology in an (almost) all-white school. *American Educational Research Journal, 38*(4), pp. 784–785)

CASE STUDIES

Case study: In-depth analysis of a single experience or entity.

A **case study** is an in-depth analysis of one or more events, settings, programs, social groups, communities, individuals, or other "bounded systems" in their natural context. The case study is an investigation of one entity, which is carefully defined and characterized by time and place. The single entity could be a single school, for example, which would be a *within-site* study, or a number of schools (*multisite*). Also, in a single study there may be one or multiple cases.

Note in the following example how the researchers justified their use of a case study design of two student-initiated retention programs to meet the needs of underrepresented students of color.

EXAMPLE | **Case Study Methodology**

"We chose case study as a research method for the obvious reason that we needed to develop a holistic understanding of SIRPs [Student Initiated Retention Project]. Yin (1989) described case study research as a flexible form of inquiry best suited for studying a particular phenomenon within its natural context. Such studies, . . . through the use of interviews and observations, seek to develop 'thick descriptions' of the setting or phenomenon in question. . . . Accordingly, we relied on formal structured interviews, informal interviews (with key informants), observations, and key documents." (Maldonado, D. E. Z., Rhoads, R., & Buenavista, T. L. (2005). The student-initiated retention project: Theoretical contributions and role of self-empowerment. *American Educational Research Journal, 42*(4), p. 615)

Though the term *case study* has become identified as a type of qualitative research, this is typically because in-depth studies of a single entity use qualitative methods to gather data. Case studies can also be conducted with quantitative approaches. Often, both qualitative and quantitative methods are used in the same case study. In our discussion here, however, we will restrict usage of case study to qualitative research.

Once a researcher has decided on using a case study approach, the type of case study needs to be specified to determine appropriate research questions and methods. Table 11.3 summarizes several types of case studies. Each is targeted for a unique need.

Because the primary purpose of a case study is to obtain a detailed description and gain an understanding of the case, generalizability of the findings is a concern. Sometimes, researchers will try to identify a "typical" case to study. If

TABLE 11.3	Types of Case Studies

Type	Description
Historical organizational	Focus is on a specific organization over time, often tracing the organization's development.
Observational	Participant observation is the primary method of gathering data to study a particular entity or some aspect of the entity (such as a school or classes within a school).
Life history	A first-person narrative that is completed with one person; also referred to as an *oral history*.
Situation analysis	A specific event (e.g., how students deal with the death of a parent) is studied from different perspectives.
Multicase	Several different independent entities are studied.
Multisite	Many sites or participants are used to, in the main, develop theory.

so, they are concerned with at least some generalization to a larger group or other situations as traditionally defined. However, this is difficult in education since it is not very feasible to find a single exemplar that is representative of others. For example, doing a case study of a single classroom to investigate how a beginning teacher functions will provide in-depth descriptions of that classroom and teacher, but it is unlikely that other classrooms or teachers will be the same. The best to hope for is that the readers will come to their own conclusions regarding generalizability.

Research Problem Statement

Research problem statements in case studies are written to focus on an in-depth description and understanding. Often there is a single central question, followed by several subquestions. For example, the following questions were used in a recent study that examined how three middle school teachers integrated the use of laptop computers for instruction. Note how the authors emphasized the need to reconstruct the questions as the study was undertaken.

EXAMPLE | **Case Study Research Questions**

"Before we defined specific boundaries for the study, broad areas of investigation were identified with the understanding that they would serve as guidelines for collection of data about the school community and that research questions, along with their data collection strategies, would be developed over time. After several months, two questions emerged that we felt captured the complexity of how the teachers were learning to use laptop technology in the classrooms:

> 1. How do participants' personal histories and beliefs about learners and learning play out within the institutional culture to influence their technology-related instructional practices?
> 2. How do teachers construct technology-related norms and practices with peers and students through their participation in various activity settings?" (Winidschitl, M., Schendel, J. M., & Ulman, J. E. (2002). Tracing teachers' use of technology in a laptop computer school: The interplay of teacher beliefs, social dynamics, and institutional culture. *American Educational Research Journal, 39*(1), p. 172)

Entering the Research Site

Entry into the research site is essentially the same as in an ethnography. A site should be selected after visiting several possibilities. This gives the researcher a better idea about which site will provide the needed information. It is important that the site be fully accessible for the researcher, and that the individuals at the site cooperate fully. Usually the site is one in which the same people are involved over time.

Selecting Participants

In a case study, a "group" of participants is usually identified. The group is a collection of individuals who interact with each other, share the same space, and identify with each other. Typical groups in educational case studies would be students in a classroom, athletes on a team, teachers in the same grade level or department, and learning-disabled students in a mainstreamed class. One consideration in selecting the group is size. Other factors being equal, the smaller the group the greater the chance that the researcher's presence will change their behavior. For example, in a case study of teenage same-sex friendships in which the researcher stayed with two or three pairs of participants, it is likely that the researcher's involvement would affect the friendships. A larger number of participants makes it easier to remain unobtrusive and relatively anonymous. Of course, a larger number of participants makes it more difficult to keep detailed records on everyone; depth is sacrificed for less intrusion.

Internal sampling: Selection of participants, times, and documents at a site.

Many case studies employ what is called *internal sampling*. **Internal sampling** is concerned with the people, times, and documents that will be selected once the site is determined. The researcher selects those individuals, times, and documents that will provide the greatest amount of information. Key informants are identified and used in groups where all cannot be studied. Certain documents deserve more attention than others because they are richer. Remember, the goal of any qualitative study is to generate depth of description and understanding. Consequently, it is better to select a few entities for in-depth study rather than a large number that would be studied only superficially.

Purposive sampling for a case study is illustrated in the following study that investigated economically disadvantaged, high achieving urban high school students.

EXAMPLE | **Purposive Sampling in a Case Study Investigation**

"For the purpose of this study, high ability students were defined as those demonstrating well above average potential as measured by a score above the 90th percentile using local norms on standardized intelligence or achievement tests during his or her school career. . . .
The participants were recommended by the high school's guidance counselors for the study as achievers when three of the following four criteria were met: (1) identified and enrolled in an academically gifted elementary or middle school program, (2) achieved at a superior level academically as evidence by high grades, (3) nominated for the study by a teacher/counselor and (4) received various academic awards and honors." (Reis, S. M., Colbert, R. D., & Jebert, T. P. (2005). Understanding resilience in diverse, talented students in an urban high school. *Roeper Review, 27*(2), p. 113)

Obtaining Data

The primary means of data collection in case studies is similar to what would be used in an ethnography, mostly observation and interview with some document analysis. A complete and detailed description of the case is necessary. Because a case study is concerned with a single entity, using two or more forms of data collection for the same study provides greater depth. It is also more likely that the data collection in case studies is more intrusive because of the high degree of immersion into the programs or events. Otherwise, the methods summarized for ethnography are applicable for case studies as well.

Data Analysis

Data analysis in case studies is also much the same as for an ethnography. Transcripts and field notes need to be organized, transcribed, coded, summarized, and interpreted. Stake (1995) outlines four kinds of data analysis, in addition to description, that are used in case studies. The first is called *categorical aggregation*, in which the researcher codes data and collects instances from which meanings will emerge. *Direct interpretation* uses a single example to illustrate meaning. *Drawing patterns* is needed to examine the correspondence between two or more categories or codes. Finally, *naturalistic generalizations* are culled from the data that suggest what others can take from the research to apply to other situations.

PHENOMENOLOGICAL STUDIES

The purpose of conducting a **phenomenological** study is to describe and interpret the experiences of participants in order to understand the "essence" of the experience *as perceived by the participants*. The basis of phenomenology is that there are multiple ways of interpreting the same experience, and that the meaning of the experience to each participant is what constitutes reality. This is akin to the previously mentioned characteristic of *participant perspectives*. Though all qualitative studies have this orientation, a phenomenological study focuses much

Phenomenological:
Understanding the essence of experiences.

selected first, one in which each individual has had a similar experience. Once the theory is developed, a heterogeneous sample, individuals who have had different experiences, may be selected to confirm or disconfirm tenets of the theory. Typically, 20 to 30 interviews are needed with a homogeneous sample to reach a point where no new important information related to the theory is obtained (this is referred to as *saturation*).

As in phenomenological studies, the individual interview is the primary method of data collection. The interviews are open-ended and searching. The researcher needs to learn as much as possible from the participants about their perceptions of the nature and impact of the experiences as related to a possible theory.

Data analysis in grounded theory studies is fairly well prescribed and standard. The goal is to engage in a process called *constant comparison*, in which information is obtained through interviews and constantly compared to emerging themes as part of a more encompassing theory. *Theoretical sampling* is also used, in which additional cases are used to expand and refine theory. The systematic process of data analysis consists of the following steps:

1. Initial categories are formed from the information, with subcategories and descriptions of extreme possibilities on a continuum.
2. Following initial coding, the data are assembled in new ways. A coding paradigm is used in which the central tenets are described with causal conditions, resultant actions, contextual conditions, and consequences.
3. Selective coding is used to write a story that integrates the codes that have been established. Conditional propositions or hypotheses may be presented.
4. The theory is developed using constant comparison and theoretical sampling.

The final theory can be presented in a variety of ways. Grounded theory studies may formulate hypotheses, use a visual model or diagram, use stories, or use some combination of hypotheses, visuals, and stories.

The following excerpt is taken from a grounded theory study that examined which cognitive strategies students use, how often the strategies are used, and how they are acquired. Forty-two open-ended audio-recorded interviews and some observations were conducted over a nine-week period to collect data.

EXAMPLE | **Grounded Theory Study**

"This research study used grounded theory in an attempt to explain how 10th grade public school students in average and advanced classes used strategies to learn material in their high school social studies classes. This study sought to understand the strategies that students used to learn information, the frequency of their strategy use, and the students' method of acquiring these strategies. The results suggested that cognitive strategy use involves the students' knowledge of cognitive strategies, a need to use the strategies, and a motivation by the students to use the strategies." (Martin, L. (2005). Use of cognitive strategies by high school social studies students. *Action in Teacher Education, 26*(4), p. 63)

TABLE 11.4	Comparison of Different Types of Qualitative Studies			
	Purpose	**Data Collection**	**Data Analysis**	**Reporting of Results**
Ethnography	Describing a cultural group	Primarily observations and interviews	Description, analysis, interpretation	Description of cultural behavior
Case Study	In-depth analysis of single or multiple cases	Use of multiple sources of data	Descriptions, themes, assertions	In-depth description of case(s)
Phenomenology	Understanding the essence of experiences	Extended interviews with up to 10 participants	Statements, meanings, themes, general description	Description of essence of the experience from participants' perspectives
Grounded Theory	Developing a theory from field data	Interviews with 20–30 participants	Coding to constantly compare findings to themes	As a set of propositions, hypotheses, or theories

Source: Adapted from Creswell, 2005.

The four traditions or approaches to qualitative studies presented in this chapter are summarized and compared in Table 11.4. Remember that the different types of qualitative studies will overlap in many respects to some degree, and that the general characteristics summarized at the beginning of the chapter will apply to each type. We now move on to issues that are important in judging the quality of qualitative studies. For this purpose, all four will be considered together since the principles are pertinent to all types.

INTERNET CONNECTIONS

The following Websites offer excellent resources in qualitative research that will expand on what is presented in this chapter and offer opportunities for more involvement.

www.aera.net/—Go to Special Interest Group (SIG) #82, Qualitative Research, to keep in touch with people and resources.

www.qualitativeresearch.vga.edu/QualPage/8da.html—QualPage lists resources for qualitative research, including announcements, forums, methods, papers, and other information.

CREDIBILITY *of* QUALITATIVE RESEARCH

An important aspect of reading qualitative studies is to judge the overall credibility and usefulness of the results. In quantitative research the criteria for credibility are based primarily on the validity and reliability of the scores and on internal validity. In qualitative research somewhat different criteria are necessary because its approach, design, and data are different.

The primary criterion for evaluating qualitative studies is the *credibility* of the study. **Credibility** is defined as the extent to which the data, data analysis, and conclusions are believable and trustworthy. Are the themes and the patterns that emerge from the data plausible? Are they accurate, consistent, and meaningful? How much confidence do you have in the results and conclusions? Qualitative researchers judge the credibility of a study from a holistic perspective. Although it is difficult to identify single factors or design flaws in the overall judgment, the following principles relate to the credibility of most qualitative studies.

Credibility: Believability and trustworthiness.

Triangulation

One of the most common analytical techniques to enhance the credibility of a qualitative study is **triangulation,** the use of different methods of gathering data—or collecting data with different samples, at different times, or in different places—to compare different approaches to the same thing. For example, a researcher might observe what appears to be a pattern and then see if the same pattern is repeated in interviews and in written documents or if the pattern was the same at different times. If the results of several methods of collecting data agree, the finding is judged to be credible.

Triangulation: Compares the findings of different techniques.

EXAMPLE | **Triangulation**

"The credibility of the findings was verified through data triangulation . . . by using several sources: field notes by two persons, verbatim transcripts, multiple raters, moderator, observer, second rater, member checks the accuracy of notes, and stakeholder reviews." (Gallagher, P. A., Rhodes, C. A., & Darling, S. M. (2004). Parents as professionals in early intervention: A parent educator model. *Topics in Early Childhood Special Education, 24*(1), p. 9)

"Trustworthiness was established by first triangulating the data using multiple data sources, including teacher questionnaires, teacher interviews, and student interviews. Second, the teachers reviewed the transcribed interviews. This member-checking procedure (Creswell & Miller, 2000) permitted teachers to verify the content of the interviews and offer any clarification of points, if needed. . . . Finally, the data were examined by and discussed with a peer debriefer trained in qualitative research." (Xiang, P., Solomon, M. A., & BcBride, R. E. (2006). Teachers' and students' conceptions of ability in elementary physical education. *Research Quarterly for Exercise and Sport, 77*(2), p. 190)

Reliability

The definition of *reliability* in qualitative research is somewhat different from the quantitative definition. Rather than looking for consistency of behavior, qualitative researchers are interested in the accuracy and comprehensiveness of their observations and inferences. Hence **reliability** is the extent to which what is recorded as data is what actually occurred in the setting that was studied, as well as whether interpretations and conclusions are accurate. Reliability is enhanced by detailed field notes, teams of researchers to ensure better comprehensiveness and accuracy, the review of field notes for accuracy by participants, use of tape recorders, photographs and videotapes, use of participant quotations and literal descriptions, and an active search for discrepant data or cases. A useful method of enhancing reliability is called *member checking*. With this technique, the researcher gives his or her notes to the participant so that the participant can verify that the recording was accurate.

> **Reliability:** Extent to which what has been recorded is what actually occurred.

More generally, it is important to obtain an accurate match between the researcher's categories and interpretations and what is actually true. That is, do the meanings, categories, and interpretations of the researcher reflect reality? Is a pattern actual or have limitations in the data gathering or situation distorted the pattern?

Since the researcher is the medium through which the data are collected and interpreted, any opinions, biases, or expectations that the researcher has may be reflected in the results, diminishing accuracy. Good qualitative researchers are aware that their subjectivity and potential bias may threaten the credibility of the research and they take steps to avoid it. For example, long, intensive study is needed to establish credibility, so if it looks like the researcher took some shortcuts or examined the phenomena superficially, it is more likely that bias and expectations will affect the results. Furthermore, detailed field notes diminish the effect of the researcher's subjective opinions.

It is also possible for the presence of an observer to change the behavior of the participants. These changes are called *observer effects*. Again, there are procedures for diminishing the possibility of this limitation. As previously mentioned, when there are many participants an observer is less likely to have an effect, and a good observer does everything possible to be unobtrusive, to literally blend into the background. My experience in educational settings is that students, in the main, are not affected much by an observer, especially after the first few meetings. Adults, on the other hand, seem more susceptible to observer influences.

Accuracy is strengthened if enough time is taken to obtain a valid judgment of what is being observed. A long and intense period of study allows triangulation and in-depth analyses of the data *during* data collection. Reliability is also enhanced by abundant use of detail. For example, details of conversations and observations can illustrate patterns and interpretations. This detailed description should include as much verbatim language from the participants as possible. Detail should also be provided concerning the process that was used in the research and the setting. This provides a framework from which you can understand context.

Note in the following example how multiple methods of data collection are utilized to ensure trustworthiness and reliability (accuracy). This study took three years to complete, which surely meets the criteria of having sufficient length!

> **EXAMPLE** | **Establishing Reliability**
>
> "In this study, the accuracy of the observations and the trustworthiness of this investigation were enhanced by the use of tape-recorded interviews and field notes that enabled the researcher to examine and clarify information; photography that was used to document and study specific situations and/or settings that required more than a single view; triangulation between methods; depth of detail; and continuous cross-checking for accuracy. The methods, procedures, and strategies used to ensure accuracy included: observations of informants in various settings; interviews with informants, teachers, relatives, and others; document review; and photography." (Reis, S. M., Colbert, R. D., & Jebert, T. P. (2005). Understanding resilience in diverse, talented students in an urban high school. *Roeper Review, 27* (2), p. 113)

External Validity

External validity in qualitative studies is similar to that in quantitative studies, referring to the generalizability of the findings. Generalizability is often weak in qualitative studies because the purpose of the research is to increase an understanding of a phenomenon, not to represent a larger population, and the methods used in any single qualitative study are unique to that study. There is little or no emphasis on replications. Qualitative researchers use terms such as *translatability* and *comparability* as concepts related to external validity. The emphasis is on how well the data, categories, analyses, and patterns are described and how well other researchers can understand the findings so that they can be used in other settings.

CONSUMER TIPS: *Criteria for Evaluating Qualitative Research*

1. **The researcher's background, interests, and possible bias should be clear.** Because a qualitative study is influenced greatly by the researcher's perspective, it is necessary to know the researcher's background—previous experiences, motivations for the research, and characteristics that may affect the recording or interpretation of data. Good qualitative researchers acknowledge how their expectations and preconceived ideas affect what they observe, interpret, and conclude.

2. **The conceptual and theoretical frameworks for the study should be clear.** The frameworks selected by the researcher guide the study and affect the results. You should look for an explanation of such frameworks early in the study, along with other thoughts and perceptions of the researcher.

3. **The method of selecting participants should be clear.** Qualitative studies research a few persons in depth rather than many subjects more superficially. Consequently, the choice of subjects is critical to the results of the study. The researcher should indicate how and why the participants were selected and the extent to which they are representative of others in the setting.

4. The degree of researcher involvement in the setting should be indicated. You need to know how involved the researcher was in the setting that was studied. Although the researcher hopes to be as unobtrusive as possible, it is unrealistic to expect that he or she will not affect the setting and behaviors of the participants to some degree. Any distortion in the data can be more easily recognized if the researcher has had prolonged engagement with the participants. If the researcher is not very involved in the setting, it is more difficult to understand how his or her presence or other research procedures may have affected the participants.

5. Field notes should contain detailed objective descriptions of just about everything. This goal may seem impossible, but it is one for which qualitative researchers strive. They should give detailed descriptions of behaviors and indicate the place, time, date, and physical setting of the observations. The descriptions should avoid using interpretive words such as *effective, positive attitude,* and *hostile.* Field notes that are not detailed suggest that the researcher may have missed important behaviors or may have biases that anticipated the results.

6. Researchers should be trained to conduct data collection. Because the researchers are directly involved in collecting data, either as observers, interviewers, or reviewers of documents, they should be trained in the procedures they use. Although adequate training is not easy to determine, you should look for some indication of previous experience that has been checked for adequacy. Untrained researchers are tempted to conduct qualitative research because it sounds so promising and interesting (and does not involve statistics). What happens is that there is usually a cursory level of involvement, without evidence for reliability.

7. The credibility of the research should be addressed. Researchers should summarize their procedures to enhance the credibility of the findings. They should analyze reliability and external validity and indicate limitations.

8. Descriptions should be separate from interpretations. In the core of a qualitative article or you will find specific and general descriptions of what was observed or recorded and interpretations of the data. The descriptions are the basis for the researcher's analyses and interpretations. If these descriptions are not clearly separate from the analyses and interpretations, it is difficult for you to judge the reasonableness of the researcher's claims (e.g., if there was selective presentation of data or if inductive processes seem reasonable on the basis of the data presented). It is also difficult to know if the researcher was objective in recording or observing behavior.

9. The researcher should use multiple methods of data collection. The quality of qualitative research is greatly enhanced by multiple methods of collecting data. If only one method is used, the findings may be significantly influenced by the limitations of the technique. Multiple methods allow for triangulation, which is the strongest type of evidence for the credibility of the findings. If the study is limited to one method, its limitations should be addressed.

10. The study must be long enough. Accurate and credible qualitative research requires the researcher to become intimately involved with what is being studied, to know it completely. It usually takes a long time to achieve this intense level of involvement. It cannot be done in interviews of 20 minutes or observations that last a few hours. You need to know how much time the researcher spent with the participants. Sufficient time will be reflected in the detailed data and in the researcher's depth of understanding.

ANATOMY *of a* QUALITATIVE RESEARCH STUDY

The following case study uses a variety of ethnographic techniques to collect qualitative data.

EXHIBIT 11.1   Learning on the Job: An Analysis of the Aquisition of a Teacher's Knowledge

Paul G. Schempp
The University of Georgia

This study analyzed the criteria used by an experienced teacher to acquire the knowledge necessary to teach. An interpretive analytic framework and case study methodology were used in this yearlong project with a midcareer high school teacher. Data were collected using a variety of ethnographic techniques including: nonparticipant observations, artifact and document analysis, stimulated recall from videotapes, and formal and informal interviews. Data analysis followed the conventions described by Glaser and Strauss (1967). Five distinct knowledge categories were identified each with unique selection criteria. These knowledge forms included: class organization and operation, teaching behavior, subject matter, pedagogical content knowledge (Shulman, 1986), and external conditions. In matters of class organization and operation, Bob (the teacher) looked to his experience for those things that worked (i.e., insured classroom order). The acquisition of instructional behavior came largely from observations of other teachers (e.g., cooperating teacher, peers) or from experience. Bob selected subject matter knowledge based upon previous knowledge, current personal interests, resource availability, and student interest. Pedagogical content knowledge was comprised in three phases: demonstrations, drills, and activities. External conditions were influences outside the classroom (e.g., laws, school policy). Years of occupational service have left Bob with a well developed set of criteria upon which he acquires the knowledge to teach.

Case study of a single teacher

A distinguishing characteristic of any profession is the body of knowledge for practicing that profession. Professionals are called into service because they bring a unique undestanding and critical insight to a situation that is inaccessible to the uninitiated. It is the body of professional knowledge that explains what those in a particular occupation do and why (Schon, 1983). The body of knowledge currently used in a profession is, therefore, of major concern to those practicing the profession and preparing future practitioners. . . .

Related literature

Within the last decade, educational researchers have studied rules and principles used in teacher thinking (Elbaz, 1983), teachers' classroom images (Clandinin, 1985), the experience of classroom cycles and rhythms (Clandinin & Connelly, 1986), subject matter expertise (Leinhardt & Smith, 1985), and pedagogical content knowledge (Grossman 1989; Gudmundsdottir & Kristjansdottir, 1989). These studies, and other similar work, represent the start of a growing trend in research into what teachers know and how they use that knowledge in their classrooms. This study continues that line of inquiry by offering a glimpse into the world of an experienced high school teacher. Specifically, this case study examines the criteria one teacher employed in acquiring the knowledge he found necessary for his professional practice.

> Research problem statement

METHOD

Teacher

Robert Halstop has taught high school physical education for the past 14 years at Hillcrest High School (HHS). Over those years, Bob has coached many sports and been involved in numerous school clubs, groups, and projects. At the time of this study, he was coaching the girls' varsity basketball team. Besides teaching and coaching, he performed normal student counseling activities and other school duties assigned by the administrators. Bob worked at a local lumber mill during the summers, but did not work outside the school during the academic year. Bob's school day officially began at 7:30 a.m. and ended at 3:30 p.m., but he was usually in school much earlier and it was common for him to stay later. There were seven instructional periods in the day. Bob was assigned six classes, one planning period, and had a 30-minute lunch break. . . .

> Detailed description of the teacher

Setting

Hillcrest is a small, rural community in the Pacific Northwest. Education was held in high esteem as evidenced by the town having one of the highest tax bases in the state. Hillcrest High School enrolled approximately 470 students. Two years before this study, HHS received an educational excellence award from the United States Department of Education. All first-year students were required to take physical education for one year and could elect physical education after that. The freshman physical education classes were separated by gender and were taught as a survey course to cover many subject areas. The other physical education classes were coeducational and defined by student interest (e.g., recreational sports, weight training). HHS had two physical education teachers: one for boys (Bob) and one for girls (Kathy).

> Description of context

Data Collection

Data were collected and analyzed using a variety of qualitative techniques. Among these techniques were non-participant observation, artifact and document analyses, stimulated recall using videotaped classes, and both formal and informal interviews. Besides Bob, Kathy and other school personnel (e.g., students, teachers, administrators) were also interviewed. Field notes were recorded during and after observations and a summary statement was made off site after each day of data collection. Data collection began 2 days before the start of school and officially ended just before the Christmas break. I was present in the school on a daily basis for the first month of the study and made field trips twice a week on average after that.

Data Analyses

Data analysis began on the first day of the study and ended approximately I year later. Concurrently collecting and analyzing data allowed me to develop data summary themes and check the emerging themes against recurring field activities. Analyzing data during the study also allowed data collection techniques to be tailored to gather data that were amenable to testing and understanding the emerging themes. Specific strategies employed to insure data trustworthiness included triangulation of methods, member checks (particularly the use of key informants and the constant use of follow-up interviews to check consistency of responses), disconfirming case

> Emergent research design

> Triangulation

(continued)

EXHIBIT 11.1 (continued)

[Enhances credibility]

analyses (the investigation of responses and/or occurrences that were incompatible with emerging themes), and cultivating reactions from the case-study teacher to the themes, categories, and events to be included in the final report.

My key informant was Bob's teaching colleague, Kathy. At the time of this study, Kathy and Bob had been teaching physical education together at Hillcrest for 3 years. Kathy was particularly helpful in cross-checking stories and events described by Bob. In cases where discrepant information occurred (e.g., differences between what Bob told me and what I observed) Kathy often provided valuable insights.

[Data analysis procedures]

Data analysis involved summarizing data into themes and categories using procedures recommended by Miles and Huberman (1984), Goetz and LeCompte (1984), and Patton (1980). The construction of these categories was influenced by Shulman's (1987) theory of a knowledge base for teaching. He identified seven categories of teachers' knowledge: subject matter, general pedagogical, curriculum, pedagogical content, learners, contexts, and purposes. As themes emerged and clustered into categories, these categories were checked against Shulman's propositions. Four of Shulman's seven categories were ultimately used to describe the forms of knowledge Bob acquired in pursuit of his professional practice: subject matter, general pedagogical (renamed teaching behavior), pedagogical content, and context (renamed external conditions). Classroom organization and operation was a category constructed independent of Shulman's theory as it appeared to better describe a dominant form of Bob's knowledge.

[Data analysis procedures (categories and coding)]

The themes and categories identified forms of knowledge as well as the criteria Bob used in acquiring pedagogical knowledge. The categories allowed the data to be summarized and reported in a succinct, yet accurate, manner. The first step was to review the collected data to determine tentative categories. Next, the data were coded using the tentative scheme. The category scheme underwent revisions until the data were able to be classified within the scheme with no redundancy of categories. The constant comparison method of analysis (Glaser & Strauss, 1967) was used to identify these patterns and relationships.

[Credibility established]

The final step of the analytic procedure was to present a copy of the report to Bob for his comments and reactions. The findings were brought back to the case study teacher so that he could: (a) check the accuracy of the data (reliability), and (b) validate the findings of the report. This procedure was considered a critical component for establishing the validity and trustworthiness of the study's findings (Lather, 1916). Additional revisions were then made based on the responses and reactions from the teacher. Events contained in the report seen by Bob as either inaccurate or threatening to confidentiality were rechecked and eliminated where appropriate. Bob's comments and additional supporting evidence were incorporated into the final draft of the report to lend strength to the propositions put forth.

FINDINGS

From years of contact with many sources of occupationally useful information, Bob had constructed a comfortable set of criteria for evaluating and selecting knowledge necessary for his day-to-day classroom operation. He seemed to have a clear sense of both the expectations others held for him and his own purpose for being in the school. These criteria formed a screen through which all potential pedagogical knowledge passed. Bob's knowledge acquisition represented an intersection between the demands of his day-to-day practice and the knowledge available to meet those demands. Thus, Bob appropriated knowledge based upon his perception of the power and quality of its source, and his perception of its potential to solve a recurring problem or improve a current practice.

[Categories emerged from the data]

In analyzing the data, five knowledge categories emerged: (a) classroom organization and operation, (b) teaching behavior, (c) subject matter, (d) pedagogical content knowledge, and (e) external conditions. Each category was unique in terms of the problems it addressed, the sources from which it came, and the criteria that determined knowledge selection and rejection.

Class Organization and Operation

Like many teachers (West, 1975; Yinger, 1980), classroom order and control were predominant concerns for Bob. The concern for classroom organization and controlled operation rose from Bob's belief that, if order was not established and the classroom not operated in the manner he needed, little could be accomplished. In his own words,

I'm going to get across more to kids in a structured setting. Otherwise kids are pretty much allowed to go where they want to and pick and choose what they want to take and what they don't want to take. . . . I have more kids working at a higher level than I would otherwise.

> Direct quote to illustrate findings

. . . Bob, like many teachers (Clandinin, 1985; Clandinin & Connelly, 1986), relied on practical rules and principles, routines, and habits to guide classroom operation rather than inflexible standards or absolute rules.

> Relationship to literature

Bob perceived the ability to organize and operate a class to be a fundamental and critical responsibility of a teacher. When asked "What would you look for in a high school teacher to determine if they were a good teacher?" he responded with a list of criteria heavily skewed toward organizational and operational concerns. His list included: (a) the kids are paying attention; (b) gives directions clearly and the kids respond to directions showing that they heard; (c) what he said made good sense; (d) organized drills, organized calisthenics, lesson didn't get bogged down; (e) didn't let a few kids take over the lesson; and (f) didn't get distracted from where he wanted to go.

[Discussion of findings continues.]

Teaching Behavior

A significant portion of Bob's everyday actions and activities were devoted to the task of instructing students. Knowledge for meeting these demands was classified by Shulman (1987) as general pedagogical knowledge, for this knowledge transcended a particular subject content. Much of Bob's teaching behavior was characterized by well-rehearsed, time-worn rituals. Every class began with student-led exercises while Bob took attendance. Then Bob informed the students of the day's activities. A brief skill demonstration or explanation was followed by a drill. Most classes closed with a game or culminating activity. Sometimes, a game was played for the entire class period. The practices that defined Bob's teaching behavior were largely composed of comfortable habits and familiar routines. In crafting a teaching style, comfort does not appear to be an uncommon criterion among teachers (Lange & Burroughs-Lange, 1994; Russell & Johnston, 1988).

Bob did not actively pursue knowledge that directly affected his instructional practices. The roots of this perspective can be traced to his undergraduate days. "When I was going through college," he said, "they didn't have any methods classes. None. Zero." The fundamental criterion used to determine the success of a lesson was, therefore, not so much what students learned, but rather their level of enjoyment. During one interview Bob told me that "they really seem to enjoy it (the activity). They develop certain skills. The more skill they develop, the more they seem to enjoy it."

> Importance of participant perspectives

[Discussion of findings continues.]

Although student learning was a concern in Bob's occupational activity, it was not the driving force behind his pedagogical practices. He harbored a stronger concern for maintaining control over the collective social behavior of the students. He showed far greater frustration when there was a breach of order than when students failed to make significant learning gains. The concern for classroom control over educational substance has been a consistent finding in research on physical education teachers' conceptions of their occupational duties and responsibilities (Placek, 1983; Schempp, 1985, 1986).

> Relationship to literature

(continued)

EXHIBIT 11.1 **(continued)**

The immediate and multiple demands placed on Bob's time in school often relegated the learning of his approximately 130 students to the back burner of his priorities. During one observation, Bob and I were in his office between classes and I remarked, "I can't believe all the things you have to attend to." His comment was

Illustrative quote

Yeah, there's a lot going on. Right now I'm trying to get a test set up, get the equipment I need for that, worry about the two kids who are on their way to the counselors' office to drop the class, answer kids' questions about what we're doing today, think about that indoor soccer ball for next period, I have two home counseling visits coming up, remember to read the announcements this period, and I have an executive school meeting.

Detailed observation

He rose out of his chair, picked up his roster book, glanced over a tardy note pushed into his hand by a late student, and was on his way to take roll and begin another class.

Subject Matter

The content of Bob's classes was described and detailed in a curriculum guide he had compiled. Objectives for each program were identified and the policies used to conduct the program were also described. The largest portion of the guide was composed of the specific subject-matter units. When asked about the resources used to complete the guide, Bob told me that most of the units came from an undergraduate curriculum course assignment. He has added to the guide materials and resources gathered at in-service programs.

In-depth anecdotal observation

Although the guide was a 148-page document and included an outline of each subject taught, it was used sparingly. Over the course of my time with Bob, I observed him using the guide perhaps a half dozen times, mostly to review teaching points for an upcoming lesson or remind himself of game rules. The guide did not hold the majority of subject matter Bob taught, for experience has taught him that he must "keep most of the (subject matter) knowledge organized in my head and I can't write it down because everything is situation specific."

Bob acquired new subject-matter knowledge based upon these criteria: (a) perceptions of his own competence in teaching the subject, (b) personal interest in the subject matter, (c) perceptions of student interest, (d) actual student demand as demonstrated by elective class enrollments, (e) time investment necessary to teach or prepare to teach the subject, (f) the novelty of the subject, and (g) facility and equipment constraints.

Importance of detailed description

Bob reported that gymnastics and outdoor education were two content areas recently dropped. Gymnastics was no longer offered because Bob did not like teaching it and had a concern for liability. Outdoor education was no longer part of the curriculum because the individual who taught the course had left the school and Bob did not want to give up his weekends for the activities. Weight training was a new subject added to the course offerings because of student demand, Bob's personal interest in teaching the subject, and the availability of an adequate facility. Personal understanding and meaning of subject matter plays an important role in Bob's acquisition and use of content knowledge. Teachers in other subject areas also appear to rely on personal understanding in selecting content (Wilson & Wineburg, 1988).

By his own admission, Bob is not an expert in many of the areas he teaches. Rather, he knows enough to teach a 10-day unit in the selected subject. He would draw from the subject areas in which he had expertise to bolster areas that were unfamiliar. For example, soccer drills were structured very much like basketball drills. Bob was required to teach over 23 different units in any given year. It would be difficult for any teacher to be knowledgeable in so many different subjects.

[Discussion of findings continues.]

Pedagogical Content Knowledge

Shulman (1986) defines pedagogical content knowledge as content knowledge "which goes beyond knowledge of subject matter per se to the dimension of subject matter for teaching" (p. 9). Years of experience have forged a mode of operation, a routine, which frames the knowledge Bob imparts to his students. Bob seeks curricular content that fits his teaching style. In pedagogical practice, he teaches an activity in terms of its essential skills by giving brief explanations and sometimes demonstrations, then has students practice these skills through drills, and after varying amounts of practice the students are then given the rules and play the game. These procedures have been used for years by Bob with all varieties of subject matter. He is, therefore, more inclined to select new activities that fit his mode of operation than he is to look for new ways to teach old subject matter. Further, Bob was less likely to teach subject matter in depth and more likely to teach many activities at the introductory level. The more new information conveniently fits into familiar routines, the more likely it would be incorporated.

    Bob's content knowledge appeared to not only influence what he teaches, but how he teaches. Activities, particularly skill drills, were borrowed from better-known subject lessons and adapted and applied in lesser-known subject areas. In concept explanations, metaphors and images were drawn from parallel concepts in better-known subjects and used to help explain subject concepts that he did not know well. Bob does not appear unique in this regard. Teachers of mathematics (Leinhardt & Smith, 1985; Marks, 1990), social studies (Gudmundsdottir & Shulman, 1987), and English (Grossman, 1989, 1990; Gudmundsdottir, 1991) all seem to follow this process in acquiring and developing pedagogical content knowledge.

> Findings compared to literature

    As Bob screened new content knowledge for his pedagogical practice, he used the term practical to identify acceptable pedagogical content knowledge. For example, in explaining why he takes few university courses, he stated he had "a great deal of difficulty finding coursework of relevance for a teacher in my situation. A lot of philosophy, theory, etc., but not many practical, time-proven methods which I can use in my class." Another time, he identified coaching clinics as more worthwhile than teaching workshops because the clinics "offer practical information that can be directly implemented into our program." Content that could be incorporated into the existing classroom routines and rituals was highly valued. Previous research reveals that Bob is not alone in his regard for knowledge that is easily imported into existing classroom practices (Alexander, Muir, & Chant, 1992; Elbaz, 1983).

> Importance of participant's wording of explanations

External Conditions

    Conditions originating outside the classroom, and removed from Bob's immediate control, came to bear on several pedagogical decisions. These conditions include local regulations and requirements that were imposed by the administration and school board as well as regulations and laws handed down from state and federal agencies. Therefore, the wishes and demands of administrators, students, parents, and state agencies factored into Bob's procurement of knowledge. The influence of administrators, parents, and students on Bob's knowledge was discussed above. School and state regulations also influenced him, but to a far lesser degree.
[Discussion of findings continues.]

CONCLUSION

    After years of service, Bob had a well developed set of criteria to guide his acquisition of occupational knowledge. These criteria allowed Bob to identify gaps in his knowledge and to assess new knowledge in light of its potential contribution to his teaching. Contrary to the belief of many students, administrators, and colleagues, Bob continually reviewed and screened new information and then made attempts to integrate this knowledge into his professional practice. Because the criteria used in acquiring new knowledge were primarily comprised of experiences, interests, values, beliefs, and orientations, Bob's professional knowledge appeared personal and idiosyncratic (Carter, 1990; Zeichner, Tabachnick, & Densmore, 1987). Bob was, by his own admission, set in his ways. Therefore, the changes and alterations he did make were neither dramatic nor overtly visible. In short, little changed in the observable practices of Bob's day-to-day activities as a teacher and he became fairly predictable in his course of action.

(continued)

EXHIBIT 11.1 (continued)

Classroom order and operation held the highest priority in Bob's pedagogical knowledge. Subject matter that fit his personal interests, workplace conditions, and would result in student enjoyment had the greatest chance of penetrating the curriculum. New knowledge that conformed to his well-worn classroom practices passed Bob's test of valued professional knowledge. He acknowledged a lack of information regarding effective teaching behavior, and given his workplace conditions, this situation appears to have little chance to change. Will Bob ever change? He is, in fact, always changing as new information comes to him and is incorporated into his professional knowledge base. In the final analysis, however, Bob's time in service has made him well aware of who he is, what he does, why he does it, and what knowledge is required for him to meet the demands of teaching in a public school.

REFERENCES

Alexander, D., Muir, D., & Chant, D. (1992). Interrogating stories: How teachers think they learn to teach. *Teaching and Teacher Education, 8,* 59–68.

Carter, K. (1990). Teachers' knowledge and learning to teach. In W. R. Houston (Ed.) *Handbook of Research on Teacher Education* (pp. 291–330). New York: Macmillan.

Clandinin, D. J. (1985). Personal practical knowledge: A study of teachers' classroom images. *Curriculum Inquiry, 15,* 361–385.

Clandinin, D. J., & Connelly, F. M. (1986). Rhythms in teaching: The narrative study of teachers' personal practical knowledge of classrooms. *Teaching and Teacher Education, 2,* 377–387.

Doyle, W. (1986). Classroom organization and management (pp. 392–431). In M. Wittrock (Ed.) *Handbook of Research on Teaching* (3rd ed.). New York: Macmillan.

[References continue.]

Author Reflection *Heed this warning if you want to do qualitative research: Patience and extensive periods of time are needed for gathering, analyzing, synthesizing, and interpreting the data. The amount of time needed to do good qualitative research almost always surprises people. At first it seems so simple—just do some interviewing or observation—but if it remains simple the results will not be very credible. I learned this lesson well in one of the first qualitative studies I directed, on the resilience of at-risk students. I continually miscalculated the amount of time needed to do the study, always thinking that it should take less time. Plan accordingly when carrying out (or reading) qualitative studies so you won't be frustrated in this electronic age of immediacy. You will likely be rewarded with a depth of understanding that will have lasting and positive impacts.*

STUDY QUESTIONS

1. What are the major characteristics of qualitative research?
2. What is the difference between qualitative research and ethnography?
3. In what ways are qualitative research problems different from quantitative research problems?

4. How are participants usually selected for a qualitative study?
5. What types of roles may a qualitative observer assume in a study?
6. Why is it necessary to have detailed field notes?
7. What are different ways to conduct qualitative interviews?
8. How are ethnographic and case study data analyzed?
9. What is the fundamental difference between ethnographies and case studies, phenomenological studies, and grounded theory?
10. What are some approaches for establishing the credibility of qualitative studies?
11. What is triangulation? How is it related to reliability?

@WWW SAMPLE TEST QUESTIONS

See this text's Companion Website at **www.ablongman.com/mcmillan5e** for sample test questions and answers.

mylabschool RESEARCH NAVIGATOR™ ACTIVITIES

1. Use the ResearchNavigator™ to access AN 10614572. This is an article that discusses two methods of conducting qualitative observations—participant observer and the use of video. What are the advantages and disadvantages of using each type of observation? In what circumstances would it be desirable to use video recording rather than in-person observation?

2. By accessing AN 21701245 in the Research Navigator you will find a qualitative study on the success of African American high school students in mathematics. Read the article and identify the qualitative design used. What sources of data are triangulated? Using the Criteria for Evaluating Qualitative Research in the book, what is the overall credibility of the findings?

2005). Authors may use terms like *multiple methods* and *mixed-methodology*; however, *mixed-method* as a formal research design, refers to mixing or combining quantitative and qualitative research techniques at multiple stages from the formulation of research questions through the collection, analysis, and interpretation of data (Creswell, 2005; Greene, Caracelli, & Graham, 1989; Onwuegbuzie & Slate, 2006; Tashakkori & Teddlie, 1998). This usage is in contrast to authors who use the term *multimethod* to refer to the use of multiple quantitative or qualitative techniques (e.g., collecting quantitative data using both opinion surveys and achievement tests, or collecting qualitative data through both observation and semistructured interviews).

Previous chapters have covered a variety of quantitative and qualitative research designs, highlighting the types of research problems and questions most appropriately addressed with each design, along with their specific characteristics and procedures. Based on what you have learned to this point, it might seem that quantitative and qualitative research designs are like apples and oranges (or maybe apples and onions), particularly with regard to paradigm or "worldview" that underlies each. Recall that quantitative research methods are grounded in the scientific method, are deductive, and rely on objectivity on the part of the researcher and a belief that there is a single reality everyone experiences in similar ways. In contrast, qualitative research methods focus are inductive and grounded in subjectivity or the belief that individuals experience and interpret the world differently, so rather than a single reality, multiple realities exist. These divergent perspectives initially led many researchers to criticize mixed-method research on the basis that the perspectives are essentially incompatible.

However, given the right context, apples and oranges or even apples and onions can be mixed together to create something that is more appealing and satisfying than any one alone (e.g., a traditional fruit or Waldorf salad). Such is the case with mixed-method research designs—the research problem/research questions under investigation provide the context. The end results are answers to research questions that are more robust and provide a more thorough explanation of the problem than either quantitative or qualitative research procedures could alone. Advocates of mixed-method designs suggest adopting a pragmatic, or "what works," worldview that values both objective and subjective understanding, and relies on diverse approaches to research problems (Creswell & Plano Clark, 2006; Onwuegbuzie & Slate, 2006; Tashakkori & Teddlie, 2003). As Johnson and Onwuegbuzie (2004) note, "What is most fundamental is the research question—research methods should *follow* research questions in a way that offers the best chance to obtain useful [and the most thorough] answers" (pp. 17–18).

Advantages and Disadvantages of Using Mixed-Method Designs

There are several advantages to using mixed-method designs when conducting research (Table 12.1). Of these, the two biggest advantages are (1) the ability to provide more a thorough understanding of a research problem because of the opportunity to examine multiple forms of data that are more comprehensive than data that might be collected via either quantitative or qualitative methods geometric shapes—see Creswell & Plano Clark, 2006, for examples) to illustrate the design for readers:

- Uppercase letters (e.g., *QUAN* or *QUAL*) to indicate the method given *priority* (primary method used) in the study
- Lowercase letters (e.g., *qual* or *quan*) to indicate if a method was given a lower priority (less emphasis) in the study
- Arrows (→) to indicate that methods occur in a sequence;
- Pluses (+) to indicate that methods occur simultaneously.

Explanatory. In an *explanatory* design, quantitative data are collected first, and, depending on the results, qualitative data are gathered afterward. This design involves two phases—the collection and analysis of quantitative data followed by the collection and analysis of qualitative data.

$$\text{QUANT} \longrightarrow \quad \text{qual}$$

Explanatory designs are used when the purpose of the study is to elucidate, elaborate on, or explain quantitative findings. Typically, the qualitative phase receives less emphasis or priority, while the quantitative component makes up the main focus of the study. Often qualitative data are used to analyze outliers or other extreme cases.

A two-stage study by McMillan (2000) is a good example of an explanatory design. In this study a large sample of teachers (850) was surveyed to determine the extent to which different factors were used in classroom assessment and grading. This provided a general overview of the teachers' practices. In the second phase teachers were selected who represented extremely high or low scores on the factors in the survey. These teachers were interviewed using a qualitative method to determine reasons why certain practices were used. Thus, the qualitative phase was used to augment the statistical data to provide explanations for the practices. This same approach was taken by another recent study that examined the impact of teacher preparation programs on teaching competence. As illustrated in the following example, the researchers first gathered survey data from a large number of teachers over four years, then employed interviews and observations.

EXAMPLE | **Explanatory Study**

"In this study, we sought not only descriptions but also explanations of results, in this case teacher education outcomes. . . . The challenge in deciding on the design of the study was to reduce the complexity of the research object without . . . unjustifiable simplifications. . . . We faced the "breadth-depth" problem. . . . Written questionnaires were the chief instruments used to survey the whole sample. . . . We selected from all of the respondents a smaller number to form a representative subset . . . which was studied by . . . qualitative methods." (Browwer, N., & Korthagen, F. (2005). Can teacher education make a difference? *American Educational Research Journal, 42*(1), pp. 167, 171.)

Exploratory. An *exploratory* mixed-method design is another two-phase or sequential design in which the qualitative data are gathered first, followed by a quantitative phase. In these designs, results from the qualitative data analysis are used to help determine the focus and type of data collection in the quantitative phase. The purpose of this design is typically to use the initial qualitative phase with a few individuals to identify themes, ideas, perspectives, and beliefs that came from the larger scale quantitative part of the study. The premise is that exploration is needed because "measures or instruments are not available, the variables are unknown, or there is no guiding framework or theory" (Creswell & Plano Clark, 2006, p. 75).

Often, this kind of design is used to develop a survey. By first using a qualitative component, researchers are able to use the language and emphasis of the subjects in the wording of items for the survey. This increases the validity of the scores because they are well matched to how the subjects, rather than the researchers, think about, conceptualize, and respond to the phenomena being studied. It could be represented as follows:

$$\text{Qual} \longrightarrow \text{QUANT}$$

For example, in a study by Rue, Dingley, and Bush (2002), the researchers utilized qualitative interviews and language from many participants with varied chronic health conditions to develop an instrument to measure "inner strength." This study relied heavily on participant language and experiences with chronic conditions to develop items for a survey that could then be used to quantitatively assess inner strength. Here the major emphasis is the quantitative measure, and qualitative interviews helped to form the survey. If the quantitative portion of the study is used to confirm, determine, or expand on qualitative findings, the qualitative part of the study will be emphasized:

$$\text{QUAL} \longrightarrow \text{Qant}$$

Triangulation. Of the mixed-method designs discussed, *triangulation* designs are the most commonly used. In this design, the researcher simultaneously implements both quantitative and qualitative methods—collecting and analyzing data concurrently. At each stage of research, the researcher employs the most appropriate quantitative or qualitative techniques, merging results together to facilitate a single interpretation. Sometimes researchers may choose to transform qualitative data to a more quantitative format to facilitate merging data and interpretation. Triangulation designs are typically used when researchers are interested in validating and expanding on the quantitative findings through the use of qualitative methods. The purpose is to develop a more thorough understanding of a single phenomenon. A special subtype of triangulation designs, called *nested designs*, involves using different methods to gather information from individuals or groups at different levels within a system (Tashakkori & Teddlie, 1998). For example, a researcher might use observations of students, interviews with teachers, surveys with administrators, and focus groups with parents. The general purpose is the same, but the interest is in gaining multiple perspectives from individuals or groups who have different roles within a system.

Approximately equal emphasis is given to each method, even though one can follow the other:

$$\text{QUAL} \longrightarrow \text{QUANT} \quad \text{or} \quad \text{QUANT} \longrightarrow \text{QUAL}$$

If conducted at the same time the study could be represented by:

$$\begin{array}{ccc} \text{QUANT} & & \text{QUAL} \\ + & \text{or} & + \\ \text{QUAL} & & \text{QUANT} \end{array}$$

An example of a triangulation design is a hypothetical study on school culture. A quantitative school culture survey could be used in conjunction with some focus groups of students, teachers, and administrators. To the extent that that survey results match focus group results, the greater is the validity of the conclusion that a certain type of culture exists in the school. The advantage of the survey is that a large number of students, teachers, and administrators can be represented, while the focus group would provide descriptions in voices specific to each group. In the following excerpt the researcher explains how both quantitative and qualitative data are obtained. In this study, a survey was used prior to selecting the students for interviews, and then an additional survey and interviews were conducted.

EXAMPLE | **Triangulation Design**

"The participants responded to a prestudy measurement of their attitude toward computers. . . . I used the Sense of Classroom Community Index (SCCI) . . . to evaluate the sense of classroom community. . . . To collect qualitative data, I used semistructured interviews with follow-up questions to probe for additional information." (Wighting, M.J. (2006). Effects of computer use on high school students' sense of community. *Journal of Educational Research, 99*(6), pp. 373–374.)

The advantages and challenges of each type of design are presented in Table 12.2. A good source for discussion and comparisons of additional types of mixed-method designs is *Designing and Conducting Mixed-Methods Research* (Creswell & Plano Clark, 2006).

Characteristics and Procedural Considerations for Mixed-Method Designs

Regardless of the research questions and type of design chosen, all mixed method studies should include the following characteristics: an explicit rationale for the type of design chosen, both quantitative and qualitative types of data, discussions of priority/weighting, sequence/timing, and data mixing.

Rationale. It is important to clearly identify and explain your reasons for mixing quantitative and qualitative methods. Readers should have enough information about why you have chosen a mixed-method design to be able to determine for

TABLE 12.2	Advantages and Challenges of Different Mixed-Method Designs	
Type of Design	**Advantages**	**Challenges**
Explanatory	• The two-phase structure makes its implementation straightforward. • The two-phase structure makes writing the report straightforward because it can be completed in two phases. • The focus on quantitative methods in the first phase often appeals to researchers whose primary expertise is quantitative methods.	• The two-phase structure requires additional time for implementation and data collection. • Researchers need to make a decision whether to collect data from the individuals, the same sample, or separate samples from the same population in both phases. • Because the researcher cannot identify how participants will be selected for the qualitative phase until after initial quantitative results have been explored, it can be more difficult to obtain institutional review board (IRB) approval.
Exploratory	• Separate phases make implementation straightforward. • The inclusion of the quantitative component in a design that generally emphasizes qualitative methods is likely to make this design attractive to research whose primary expertise is quantitative method.	• The two-phase structure requires additional time for implementation and data collection. • Researchers need to make a decision whether the same individuals will serve as participants in both phases. • It is difficult to specify the quantitative procedures to be implemented. • Prior analysis of qualitative data can create issues with obtaining institutional review boards (IRBs).
Triangulation	• The design is intuitive making it the first choice of researchers new to mixed methods. • In terms of time for implementation data collection it is an efficient design as both types of data are collected and analyzed at the same time. • Because the quantitative and qualitative data can be collected and analyzed independent of one another, these designs are well-suited to collaborations or research teams.	• Because of the concurrent nature of data collection, additional effort and expertise in each method are required if researchers are working alone on a study. • Researchers may encounter situations in which the results of the quantitative and qualitative data analyses diverge (do not agree or appear to tell different "stories"). • This may require additional data collection to determine the nature of the inconsistencies.

Note: Adapted from Creswell & Plano Clark (2006).

themselves if your methods are justified. Creswell and Plano Clark (2006) suggest researchers devote a paragraph at the start of the methods section to an overview of the study design that includes four topics: (1) identification of the type of design, (2) defining characteristics of the design, (3) the overall purpose or reason for using the type of design (this is distinct from the study's stated purpose), and (4) references to mixed-method literature.

Priority/Weighting. *Priority* refers to the weight or emphasis the quantitative and qualitative methods receive within a study (Creswell, 2005). Depending on the type of design and purpose for the study, researchers have three choices in terms of weighting: (1) quantitative and qualitative data can be given equal weight (i.e., triangulation designs); (2) qualitative data can be weighted more heavily than quantitative data (i.e., exploratory designs); or (3) quantitative data can be weighted more heavily than qualitative data (i.e., explanatory designs). In terms of notation, priority/weighting is depicted by upper- or lowercase letters.

Choosing how to weight the quantitative and qualitative methods in a study is dependent primarily on the purpose of the study; and which data collection and analysis methods are most well-suited to answering the research questions. Additional considerations include the availability of resources and time constraints, relative expertise of the researcher(s) in implementing quantitative and qualitative methods, and the intended audience. Limitations in terms of time and resources may force the researcher to prioritize and focus more on one method than the other. If researchers are uncomfortable or lack the expertise to implement either quantitative or qualitative methods effectively, they may rely more on methods that are within their realm of expertise. Finally, if the intended audience is more familiar with or expects a certain method to be employed, researchers may choose to emphasize that method.

Sequence/Timing. *Sequence* refers to the both the timing of implementation of the quantitative and qualitative methods and the order in which data are used (Creswell & Plano Clark, 2006). Concurrent studies are those in which both the quantitative and qualitative methods are implemented simultaneously (i.e., triangulation designs). In contrast, sequential studies are those in which either the quantitative methods are implemented before the qualitative methods (i.e., explanatory), or the qualitative methods are implemented before the quantitative methods (i.e., exploratory). In terms of notation, sequence is indicated by (+) for concurrent designs or (→) for sequential designs.

Data Mixing. *Data mixing* refers to how the quantitative and qualitative data are combined and the types of data that are mixed (Creswell & Plano Clark, 2006). Researchers can employ different strategies to mix data during research studies. One involves merging the two types of data into a single data set, usually during the interpretation phase (discussion). In this case, quantitative and qualitative data are analyzed and reported separately within the results section. Researchers might also choose to merge data sets during analysis by transforming data of one type into another. Triangulation designs typically employ this strategy and involve a single phase. Another option is to connect data of one type to data of another type by using the analysis of one type of data to inform the data collection of the other type. Explanatory and exploratory designs employ this strategy. In explanatory designs, the quantitative data analyses influence the qualitative data that are collected; for exploratory designs, the qualitative data analyses influence the quantitative data that are collected.

Table 12.3 presents some examples of types of data collection procedures and their uses broken down by each type of design; as well as the sequence of implementation.

TABLE 12.3	Data Collection, Design, and Analytic Procedures in Mixed-Method Studies	
Sequence of Data Collection	**Type of Mixed-Method Design**	**Examples of Analytic Procedures**
Concurrent (QUAN and QUAL data collected simultaneously)	Triangulation QUAN + QUAL	• Quantifying qualitative data: Code qualitative data, assign numbers to codes, and record the number of times codes appear as numeric data. Descriptively analyze quantitative data for frequency of occurrence. Compare the two data sets. • Qualifying quantitative data: Factor-analyze the quantitative data from questionnaires. These factors then become themes. Compare these themes to themes analyzed from qualitative data. • Comparing results: Directly compare the results from qualitative data collection to the results from quantitative data collection. Support statistical trends by qualitative themes or vice versa. • Consolidating data: Combine qualitative and quantitative data to form new variables. Compare original quantitative variables to qualitative themes to form new quantitative variables.
	Nested (QUAN and QUAL data collected from participants at multiple levels at the same time)	• Examining multilevels: Conduct a survey at the student level. Gather qualitative data through interviews at the class level. Survey the entire school at the school level. Collect qualitative data at the district level. Information from each level builds to the next level (Tashakkori & Teddlie, 1998).
Sequential	Explanatory (QUAN followed by qual) QUAN → qual	• Following up on outliers or extreme cases: Gather quantitative data and identify outlier or residual cases. Collect qualitative data to explore the characteristics of these cases. • Explaining results: Conduct a quantitative survey to identify how two or more groups compare on a variable. Follow up with qualitative interviews to explore the reasons why these differences were found. • Using a typology: Conduct a quantitative survey and develop factors through a factor analysis. Use these factors as a typology to identify themes in qualitative data, such as observations or interviews.
	Exploratory (QUAL followed by quan) QUAL → quan	• Locating an instrument: Collect qualitative data and identify themes. Use these themes as a basis for locating instruments that use parallel concepts to the qualitative themes. • Developing an instrument: Obtain themes and specific statements from individuals that support the themes. During the next phase, use these themes and statements to create scales and items in a questionnaire. Alternatively, look for existing instruments that can be modified to fit the themes and statements found in the qualitative exploratory phase of the study. After developing the instrument, test it out with a sample of a population. • Forming categorical data: Site-level characteristics (e.g., different ethnic groups) gathered in an ethnography during the first phase of a study become a categorical variable during a second-phase correlational or regression study. • Using extreme qualitative cases: Qualitative data cases that are extreme in a comparative analysis are followed by quantitative surveys during a second phase.

Note: Adapted from Creswell et al. (2003) and Creswell (2005).

Steps in Conducting a Mixed-Method Study

Creswell (2005) has identified seven steps to conducting mixed-method studies, regardless of their design specifications (see Figure 12.1).

1. Determine the feasibility of conducting a mixed-method study. Feasibility is a function of the level of training and expertise of the researcher(s) or team, and resources and time available for data collection and analysis. If any of these are less than adequate, the likelihood of successfully implementing a mixed-method design is reduced.

2. Identify the rationale. As previously discussed it is important to identify the reasons for conducting a mixed-method study prior to the actual start of the research. If you are unable to clearly identify why you are conducting a mixed-method study, you are unlikely to be able to clearly justify your purpose to readers.

3. Determine the design, types of data, and a strategy for how you will collect data. Determining the type of mixed-method design (triangulation, explanatory, or exploratory), the priority and sequence of data collection, and the specific forms of information to be gathered is essential to planning the specific procedures to be followed. It is also useful at this point to map out the design using the notation system and diagramming methods presented earlier in the chapter.

4. Establish specific quantitative and qualitative research questions. Although Creswell suggests identifying questions at this step, the authors would argue that research questions need to be established in advance in order to determine whether a mixed-method study is warranted. At this stage questions should be refined to ensure they clearly reflect the design and can be answered by the identified data collection methods. In the case of explanatory designs, it may be difficult to define the qualitative questions prior to analysis of the quantitative data. Typically, researchers develop separate quantitative and qualitative research questions to incorporate into a single study. In developing your research

FIGURE 12.1 Steps in conducting mixed-method studies.

questions, be sure to follow the guidelines for each type of research question presented earlier in the text. Creswell and Plano Clark (2006) present examples of mixed-method research questions based on the type of research design.

5. Collect the data. The sequence of data analysis should already be identified by the type of design that was chosen. In terms of the research process, this stage is likely to be lengthy and time-consuming. It is important that conventional procedures for each type of data are followed to ensure the appropriateness of data collection.

6. Analyze the data. Depending on the type of design, quantitative and qualitative data will be analyzed separately and independently; or might involve the integration of quantitative and qualitative data into single analytic strategy.

7. Write the report. As with many aspects of mixed-method studies, writing up the results of a study in a research report with depend on the type of design employed. Regardless of the design, the procedures employed in both the quantitative and qualitative components of the study need to be clearly explained in detail, and are usually reported separately within the method section of the report. In explanatory and exploratory designs, results for quantitative and qualitative analyses may be reported in a separate section for each phase of the study. In contrast, reports of triangulation designs are most likely to integrate the quantitative and qualitative results structured around the research questions in a single results section of the report.

CONSUMER TIPS: *Evaluating Mixed-Method Studies*

As we have seen, not all research studies are created equal. In critically evaluating mixed-method research studies, there are several considerations that must be considered in addition to the criteria used to evaluate entirely quantitative or qualitative studies. First and foremost, what sets mixed-method studies apart from other research designs is the intentional and substantial collection of both quantitative and qualitative data. This is the primary way to evaluate the rigor of mixed-method designs (Creswell and Plano Clark, 2006). For example, a study that collected data via quantitative surveys employing Likert scales and that included a few open-ended questions at the end of the survey, as the "qualitative" component, is not a true mixed-method design. Similarly, a study that employs random sampling as the only quantitative component of the study is not a mixed-method design because of insufficient use of quantitative methods. For the most part, mixed-method studies should be able to "hold their own weight" with regard to standards of rigor and quality checks for both quantitative and qualitative methods.

Mertens (2005, p. 304) presents eight questions that can be applied to the evaluation of mixed-method studies:

1. What are the multiple purposes and questions that justify the use of a mixed-method design?
2. Has the researcher matched the purposed and questions to appropriate methods?

3. To what extent has the researcher adhered to the criteria that define quality for the quantitative portion of the study?
4. To what extent has the researcher adhered to the criteria that define quality for the qualitative portion of the study?
5. How has the researcher addressed the tension between potentially conflicting demands of paradigms in the design and implementation of the study?
6. Has the researcher appropriately acknowledged the limitations associated with data that were collected to supplement the main data collection of the study?
7. How has the researcher integrated the results from the mixed methods? If necessary, how has the researcher explained conflicting findings that resulted from different methods?
8. What evidence is there that the researcher developed the design to be responsive to the practical and cultural needs of specific subgroups on the basis of such dimensions as disability, culture, language, reading levels, gender, class, and race or ethnicity?

Anatomy of a Mixed-Method Research Study

The following article is an example of how a mixed-method study is designed and reported. This particular study involves a triangulation design.

EXHIBIT 12.1 | Student Perceptions of the Transition from Elementary to Middle School

Patrick Akos
University of North Carolina

    Transitions are often a difficult time of life. The stress and challenge inherent in adjustment can create developmental crises for even the heartiest individuals. Helping students in transition is similarly challenging. To facilitate successful transitions, helping professionals such as school counselors should consider the developmental tasks of various stages, the coping abilities and flexibility of individuals, and the potent systemic and contextual factors of influence. — General research problem

    School personnel recognize the difficult transition students undertake when moving from one level of schooling to another. The transition from elementary to middle school may be especially challenging because it often involves significant school and personal change. One consideration is that most middle school environments differ significantly from the elementary environment (Perkins & Gelfer, 1995). Contextual transitions commonly include additional and unfamiliar students and school staff, and multiple sets of behavioral and classroom rules and expectations.

    This contextual change during the transition to middle school is heightened by personal change. Physical, emotional, and social changes that occur in puberty have been associated with heightened emotionality, conflict, and defiance of adults (Berk, 1993). Although pubertal changes have been viewed more as an opportunity than a crisis (Papalia, Olds, & Feldman, 2001), the varied timing of preadolescent development is difficult for students (Berk, 1993). Pubertal changes occur at different times and at different rates for students in the same grade. Therefore, as students transition to middle school, they confront both external contextual changes and internal pubertal changes.

    Research has highlighted the developmental and academic difficulties often associated with the transition from elementary to middle school. Both boys and girls show a significant increase in psychological distress across the transition to middle school (Chung, Elias, & Schneider, 1998; Crockett et al., 1989). Even though declines in — Review of literature

(continued)

EXHIBIT 12.1 (continued)

Review of literature

achievement and increased distress are not gender exclusive, boys tend to show a significant drop in academic achievement, while girls seem to experience a greater level of psychological distress after the transition (Chung et al., 1998). Also, during the transition, girls find peer relationships most stressful, whereas boys find peer relationships, conflict with authority, and academic pressures as equal stressors (Elias, Ubriaco, Reese, Gars, Rothbaum, & Haviland, 1992).

Along with psychological and academic outcomes, studies have shown that student motivation and attitudes toward school tend to decline during the transition to middle school (Anderman, 1996; Harter, 1981; Simmons & Blyth, 1987). Eccles et al. (1993) used "stage-environment fit" to describe the poor fit between the developmental needs of preadolescents and the environment of middle school or junior high school (e.g., academic tracking, increasing competition, and awareness of personal peer group status). Declining student motivation and attitude were highlighted by Simmons and Blyth, who found more negative consequences for students in the transition from elementary to middle school as compared to students making the same grade transition in K–8 schools.

Analysis of literature

While most of the research describes the negative outcomes associated with the transition to middle school, several authors also suggested interventions to reduce negative outcomes. Schumacher (1998) identified social, organizational, and motivational factors as important aspects of successful interventions. Eccles et al. (1993) suggested strategies designed to create a school context appropriate to developmental levels of preadolescents. These included building smaller communities within the school, using teaming and cooperative learning, eliminating tracking, empowering teachers, and improving student/teacher relationships. Similarly, Felner et al. (1993) found teaching teams and advisory programs as important preventative interventions for students in transition.

Review of literature

Although much of the research has either noted the detrimental effects of the school transition or suggested interventions, few investigations have sought student perceptions during the transition to middle school. Arowosafe and Irvin (1992) interviewed students about the transition at the end of the sixth-grade year. They asked students about stressors, school safety, perceptions of school, and what people told them about middle school. Students reported heightened levels of stress related to safety concerns in the school. They also noted that students report friends and the information they received from others as critical factors that affect the transition experience.

The purpose of the current investigation was to learn more about student perceptions during the transition from elementary to middle school. The research questions were:

Specific research questions

- What questions do students have about middle school?
- What specific concerns do students have about middle school?
- What aspects of middle school do students see as positive?
- What do students think middle school will be like?
- Whom do students turn to for help during the transition into middle school?
- What is important for students to know about coming to middle school?

METHOD

Participants

Description of sample

The research was conducted in four phases. For phases I and II, participants included all 331 fifth-grade students in a large, rural, Southeastern public school district. Participants included students from three different elementary schools that were scheduled to enter one large middle school (sixth to eighth grade). The mean age was 11.8 years, with a range of 10 to 13 years old. Racial composition of the participants included 59% white students ($n = 195$), 37% black students ($n = 122$), and 4% other ($n = 14$). There were 175 females (53%) and 156 males (47%). Approximately 45% ($n = 149$) were on free or reduced lunch during the fifth-grade year.

Random selection (quantitative)

At the start of the sixth-grade year (phase III), 103 students (four home-base classrooms) were randomly selected from the 331 fifth-grade students. Demographic information mirrored that of the first sample. Phase IV included a purposeful sample of participants ($n = 97$), again from the 331 fifth-grade students, who experienced success at the middle school. The sample was selected in December of the sixth-grade year. Success was defined by average or better grades (no grade lower than a C), appropriate behavior (no more than one behavior referral), and regular attendance (no more than two unexcused absences) during the first academic marking period (9 weeks) of sixth grade. The researcher felt that perceptions and insight from students with generally positive records, rather than a random or complete sample, would be valuable for understanding student perceptions of the transition. The phase IV sample included students with similar demographics as compared to the participants for the earlier phases.

> Purposeful sampling (qualitative)

> Rationale for qualitative methods

Setting

Due to the contextual influence on this research (i.e., the significance of elementary school and middle school context), it is important to provide data about the setting. In the participating elementary schools, students attend neighborhood schools that use self-contained classrooms. This middle school is centrally located in the large rural county. The middle school uses teaching teams, four teachers per team that cover primary subjects, and each student has one of those teachers for a home base. As with most middle schools, students move between four to six teachers and are introduced to lockers, showering in gym class, and more responsibility than in elementary school. Students from this district can also travel for up to one and one-half hours each way on a bus to and from their middle school. Although middle school students commute to school on a bus with students from similar geographic areas, students also ride with all students in grades 6 to 12 in the school district.

> Importance of context

Procedure

A longitudinal analysis of student perceptions occurred in four phases, starting in January of fifth grade and concluded in December of sixth grade. In phase I (January of the fifth-grade year), the participants submitted questions about middle school. In phase II (May of the fifth-grade year), the participants completed a questionnaire designed to discover more information about student perspectives. In phase III (in August—the start of the sixth-grade year in middle school), students completed a questionnaire similar to the one used in phase II. The phase III questionnaire was administered in home base at the conclusion of the first two weeks of school. In the last phase, phase IV (December of the sixth-grade year), a purposeful sample of selected successful students completed a questionnaire that repeated questions from phases II and III. The phase IV questionnaire was administered at a meeting of selected students led by the school counselor to assist in planning for the upcoming year.

Data Collection

One writing assignment and three questionnaires were used to elicit student perspectives during the transition. In phase I, participants were asked to write any questions they had about middle school. In phase II, the participants completed a five-item questionnaire. One item of the questionnaire asked students to select concerns from a list of 13 themes. A second item consisting of the same 13 themes, asked students to select positive aspects. The checklist items were generated from themes written by students in phase I, and each checklist included an open-ended response. The checklists were identical and included items such as changing classes, using your locker, getting good grades, older students, and making friends. The questionnaire also assessed general feelings about coming to middle school. One question asked students to indicate how they feel about coming to middle school (worried, a little worried, a little excited, or excited). Additionally, an open-ended question was included to assess perceptions of what middle school would be like. Finally, one question asked students to select the person or persons they felt were most helpful to them during the transition to middle school (teachers, counselors, parents, friends, or someone else).

> Questionnaires that include both quantitative and qualitative questions

(continued)

EXHIBIT 12.1 (continued)

> Questionnaires that include both quantitative and qualitative questions

During phase III, students completed a second questionnaire in home base. This seven-item questionnaire inquired about academic strategies and goals for sixth grade. Included in the questionnaire were items replicated from previous phases. Students were asked what, if any, questions they had about middle school and what concerns they had about middle school.

The third questionnaire again replicated previous questions. This six-item questionnaire included open-ended questions about concerns and best aspects of middle school. The questionnaire also replicated the question about the person or persons who helped students during the transition to middle school. These questions were worded as reflections over the past transition year (e.g., "What were the best aspects about coming to middle school?"). The questionnaire also included an open-ended question to seek students' recommendations for helping fifth-grade students in the transition to middle school for the next academic year. Finally, the questionnaire concluded with one question about class schedule and one about team membership.

Data Analysis

> Shows qualitative emphasis

The open-ended writing assignment and series of questionnaire responses were analyzed for content and qualitative themes concerning the transition. Data were subjected to content analysis to identify emergent themes in the responses. Because categories in a content analysis should be completely exhaustive and mutually exclusive, a step classification system (Holsti, 1969) was used. First, each participant's response was categorized into a meaning unit. Meaning units are described as perceived shifts in attitude or a shift in the emotional quality of a response (Giorgo, 1985). These units are not meant to be independent, but rather expressions of aspects of the whole response. For the writing assignment, each question listed by students was coded as a meaning unit. In questionnaires, individual question responses were also coded as meaning units. Open-ended questions on the questionnaires were analyzed for meaning shifts and coded accordingly. For example, a response such as "both scary and fun" would be coded as two separate meaning units. The data, divided into meaning units, describe meaningful aspects of the response, with minimal inferences from the researcher (Seidman, 1991).

After meaning units were coded and tabulated for all data, the researcher examined the coding for their thematic meaning and collapsed coded content into larger themes. Larger themes were identified from the most frequent responses emerging from the initial coding. For example, one student wrote eight separate questions. Although all eight questions were distinct meaning units, the first five focused on rules and procedures, while the last three listed concerns about bullies and older students. Additionally, several responses did not collapse into larger categories and were judged atypical. These responses represented less than 3% of the total responses.

Researcher and Researcher Bias

> Possible threat to internal validity

The researcher is a white male who at the time of the study was a practicing school counselor at the middle school. Although student perceptions formed the base of all conclusions, the researcher also had assumptions that may have influenced the results. As a school counselor, research bias included an increased focus on personal/social adjustment during the transition. The researcher also assumed a level of anxiety concerning the transition to middle school.

RESULTS

Phase I—January of Fifth-Grade Year

What questions do students have about going to middle school? Three hundred thirty-one participants submitted a total of 555 questions. Most students submitted 3 to 5 questions, with a range from 1 to 15. Twenty-eight percent ($n = 156$) of the questions focused on rules and procedures (e.g., "What's the consequence for being late?"), 16% ($n = 90$) on class ˉschedules in sixth grade (e.g., "Do sixth graders get to do chorus?"), 11%

($n = 60$) on PE or gym class (e.g., "Do you get to play basketball in gym class?"), 9% ($n = 52$) on expectations for sixth graders (e.g., "Do you have a lot of work to do?"), and 9% ($n = 52$) on lunch (e.g., "if you have last lunch, do you always have pizza?"). The remaining questions (27%) addressed topics (each one comprised less than 5% of the total) that included lockers, extracurricular programs, recess, teachers, and sports. Of particular note and consistent with current events in schools today, a few of the questions concerned school violence or safety. For example, two questions included "What happens if you threaten to hurt a teacher?" and "Do people kill people in middle school?"

Phase II—May of Fifth-Grade Year

What specific concerns do students have about coming to middle school? A total of 735 concerns were selected by the 331 participants. The frequency of selected concerns was spread somewhat evenly over the 13 choices provided in the questionnaire. In fact, no one response comprised more than 15% of the total selections. The most frequent responses included older students, 14% ($n = 102$); homework, 13% ($n = 98$); using one's locker, 12% ($n = 88$); and getting good grades, 12% ($n = 85$). Only lunchroom, bathrooms, and the open-ended choice received little attention (comprised less than 1%).

Which aspects of middle school do students see as positive? A total of 808 items were selected by the 331 participants. Parallel to the worries of fifth-grade students, students selected a variety of potential positive aspects of middle school. The most mentioned aspects included making friends, 16% ($n = 130$); gym/PE class, 15% ($n = 124$); using your locker, 11% ($n = 90$); and both changing classes and getting good grades, 10% ($n = 82$ for each). Only the open choice received less than 1% ($n = 10$).

What do students think middle school will be like? A total of 329 meaning units were coded from the responses by the 331 participants. Forty-five percent of the responses listed that middle school will be "fun" ($n = 148$), 14% of the responses mentioned that middle school will be "exciting" ($n = 46$), 11% of responses suggested it will be "cool" ($n = 36$), while 9% of the responses listed "hard" or "scary" ($n = 31$). A variety of other responses (each category represented less than 5% of the total) included "weird," "tight," "good," "awesome," and "like a maze."

Whom do students turn to for help during the transition to middle school? A total of 480 choices were selected by the 331 participants. Thirty-five percent of the responses specified friends ($n = 166$), 22% parents ($n = 105$), 21% teachers ($n = 103$), 14% school counselor ($n = 68$), while 8% mentioned other sources including "cousins," "siblings," and "other family" ($n = 38$).

Mix of quantitative and qualitative data

Phase III—August of the Sixth-Grade Year

What questions do students have about middle school? A total of 91 responses were reported by 103 randomly selected participants from phases I and II. Thirty-four percent of the responses indicated no questions about middle school ($n = 31$), 16% of responses centered on rules and procedures ($n = 15$; e.g., "Can I have one more minute extra to change classes?"), 15% of the responses focused on homework ($n = 14$; e.g., "How much homework do we get?"), and 7% of the responses focused on classes ($n = 6$; e.g., "Do I have to take an elective?"). The remaining responses ($n = 31$) were varied, and each category accounted for less than 5% of the total.

What specific concerns do students have about middle school? A total of 115 responses were tabulated from the 103 randomly selected participants from phases I and II. Twenty-four percent of the responses focused on bullies or older students ($n = 28$; e.g., "Being picked on on the bus with the older kids"), 19% about getting lost in the building ($n = 22$; e.g., "Getting lost"), and 19% about doing well in classes ($n = 22$; e.g., "I am worried that I might not do as well as I have in the past years"). Fourteen percent of the responses suggested there were no

(continued)

EXHIBIT 12.1 **(continued)**

concerns ($n = 16$) and 7% of the responses centered on being tardy to class ($n = 8$; e.g., "What happens if I am a minute late to class?"). The remaining responses ($n = 27$) were varied, and each category accounted for less than 5% of the total responses.

Phase IV-December of Sixth-Grade Year

What were the most difficult aspects of middle school? A total of 152 responses were listed by the 97 participants from a purposeful sample of successful students in phases I and II. Twenty-six percent of the responses focused on getting lost ($n = 40$; e.g., "Fear of getting lost"), 13% on making friends ($n = 19$; e.g., "Getting to know people"), 11% on learning the class schedule ($n = 17$; e.g., "Knowing how to change classes"), 10% on lockers ($n = 16$; e.g., "Opening your locker"), 8% on getting to class on time ($n = 12$; e.g., "Tardies, all of them you can get"), and 5% of responses indicated there were no difficulties. The remaining responses ($n = 50$) were varied, and no category accounted for more than 5% of the total.

What were the best aspects of being in middle school? A total of 118 responses were reported from 97 participants of a purposeful sample of successful students from phases I and II. Forty-three percent centered on freedom/choices ($n = 51$; e.g., "You get more freedom, like not having to walk in lines"), 18% focused on friends ($n = 21$; e.g., "Get more time to talk to friends"), 16% on classes ($n = 19$; e.g., "Different and better classes"), and 13% on lockers ($n = 15$; e.g., "You get your own space and can put stuff in your locker"). The remaining responses ($n = 12$) were varied, and each category accounted for less than 5% of the total.

Who helped students the most with the transition to middle school? A total of 131 choices represented the people most helpful to the 97 participants. Forty percent of the responses selected friends ($n = 52$), 23% chose teachers ($n = 30$), 19% selected parents ($n = 25$), 11% selected other family (($n = 14$); e.g., "brothers," "cousins"), while 8% selected the school counselor ($n = 10$).

What is important to tell fifth-grade students about coming to middle school? Of the 158 responses from the 97 participants, 23% felt it was most important to tell fifth-grade students about rules ($n = 36$; e.g., "You can't chew gum"), 18% reported expectations/responsibilities ($n = 29$; e.g., "You have to do your homework to go to incentive day"), 10% where classes and other items are located ($n = 16$; e.g., "Art is on the eighth-grade hall"), 9% that it is fun ($n = 14$; e.g., "It is more fun than elementary school"), 8% there are nice teachers ($n = 12$; e.g., "Teachers are pretty nice"), and 6% that it is not hard ($n = 9$; e.g., "Most of the classes are easy, except social studies"). The remaining responses ($n = 69$) accounted for categories represented by less than 5% of the total.

DISCUSSION

Students' questions about middle school were dominated by rules and procedures throughout the transition from fifth to sixth grade. Although school rules may be a typical part of orientation programs, being explicit and thorough about rules and procedures seems crucial. The data suggest that students are keenly aware of the contextual change in the transition. Although sixth-grade students at times may exhibit adolescent characteristics, it seems important to remember that these students need an "elementary" orientation concerning rules and procedures. Rules such as walking in the halls or keeping one's hands to oneself, or procedures such as reporting to class before the tardy bell seem simplistic, but these rules and procedures are what students asked about the most. In fact, students 9 weeks into the sixth grade still reflected that expectations and responsibilities were most important to tell fifth-grade students. Although class scheduling is often the start and focus of the orientation process for students in fifth grade, these data suggest that rules/procedures and expectations are most important to students.

Student worries about middle school include a wide variety of topics. Although orientation programming attempts to minimize these concerns, these data indicate that it is important to address a variety of worries involved in the transition. In fact, the spread and frequency of reported worries suggest that there is a generalized or overall persistent level of worry for most students in transition. This conclusion is similar to research suggesting the difficulty of school transitions (Chung et al., 1998; Crockett et al., 1989).

It is also noteworthy both in the fifth grade and at the start of the sixth-grade year that older students or bullies were a particular concern. This echoes findings from Arowosafe and Irvin's (1992) study in which students reported safety as a concern because of rumors about older students. Orientation programming could address this persistent concern by including older students as tour guides or peer mentors in the school to ease the transition. Alternatively, schoolwide bullying programs may help alleviate student concerns about school safety. It is also important to note that homework and doing well in classes seem to be of particular concern to students in both fifth grade and the start of sixth grade. Students' academic concerns may suggest that it is important to build students' confidence in the "classroom by teaching homework and study skills. In light of research (Anderman, 1996; Harter, 1981; Simmons & Blyth, 1987) that suggests academic and motivational declines in the transition, addressing these concerns seems especially important. Additionally, getting lost in middle school is a main concern of students upon reflection in December of the sixth-grade year. This fear could be addressed by providing school tours or comprehensive class schedule-based orientations.

Although intervention or orientation programming can be useful to address questions and worries, designing orientation programs that facilitate and build upon student enthusiasm and confidence might provide encouragement to overcome worries and build motivation during the transition. Students recorded more entries for positive aspects than concerns and indicated excitement about a variety of aspects of middle school. In fact, 70% of the student responses were positive to the open-ended question, "What will middle school be like?" During the transition, orientation leaders should highlight aspects of middle school that students seem to enjoy, including increased freedom and choices, the opportunity to change classes, and having their own lockers. Also, it is important to note that students mentioned friends as the top source of help during the transition. This finding supports the need to include peers in transition interventions and orientation programming. Upon reflecting about the transition, sixth-grade students suggest it is important to tell fifth graders that middle school is fun and there are nice teachers.

Although a few studies have found students that thrive in the transition (Crockett et al., 1989; Hirsch & Rapkin, 1987), these data contradict most of the previous research reporting the transition as a rather negative event for students (Anderman, 1996; Chung et al., 1998; Crockett et al., 1989; Elias, Gara, & Ubriaco, 1985; Harter, 1981; Simmons & Blyth, 1987). This study suggests that there are equal, if not more positive, aspects related to the transition to middle school from the student perspective.

This study revealed the importance of including a variety of people in the transition or orientation program. Although school counselors are often responsible for transition planning, students reported that friends, parents, and teachers are all sources of help in the transition. Again, friends and peers are reported as the most frequent resource for students in transition. However, some peers may not provide accurate or helpful information. In this way, it may be useful to identify role-model students who exhibit a desire and skill set that would make them good candidates to help students in transition. An ambassador or peer-helping program may be extremely helpful in the transition (Arowosafe & Irvin, 1992). In fact, Mittman and Packer (1982) found that students attribute a good start frequently to the presence of old friends and the making of new friends. This type of peer support has a strong relationship with adolescent mental health (Hirsch & DeBois, 1992).

Similarly, including teachers and parents in programming is important. Although teachers often provide an orientation to their individual classrooms, integrating teachers in a systemic way may be useful. For example, teachers may have unique classroom rules of procedures, but perhaps a combined orientation can be presented by teachers about general topics such as hall passes or discipline referrals. Arowosafe and Irvin (1992) suggested that teachers can be integrated in advisor/advisee activities. Similarly, although parents are included in open house and class scheduling in most cases, it seems important that parents are informed about rules/proceedings and expectations in the middle school.

Current study related to literature

Implication of results

Implication

Conclusion

Implication for practice

(continued)

EXHIBIT 12.1 (continued)

Arowosafe and Irvin (1992) also suggested it is important to provide parent consultation on the transition to middle school, as they found most parents tended to provide warnings rather than positive information about middle school. In this way, parent orientation can strengthen and support student orientation to the middle school. Students look for help from parents during the fifth-grade year, while teachers replace parents to become more important during the sixth-grade year. This shift in adult influence fits developmentally as preadolescents struggle to form an identity independent of family. Interestingly, students still continue to desire adult assistance throughout the transition.

Limitations

With only one primary researcher, qualitative data coding is limited. No researcher can enter into a study without bias (Rowan, 1981). With only one researcher involved with data analysis and only one school district, this study requires replication. Interviews, rather than questionnaires, with students may also elicit richer information about difficulties and positive aspects of the transition. All of the data are self-report, which has inherent limitations.

IMPLICATIONS FOR SCHOOL COUNSELORS

Data from this research and the research to date (e.g., Arowosafe & Irvin, 1992; Crockett et al., 1989; Eccles & Midgley, 1989) on school transition suggest that preventive or proactive programming is needed to assist students with the elementary to middle school transition. The transition provides both a challenge and opportunity for school counselors. This research suggests the following guidelines for school counselors coordinating transition programs: (a) rules, expectations, and responsibilities are the primary concern of students and should be presented early in fifth grade and infused throughout the transition year (this is also an excellent opportunity to include administrators and teachers in transition programming), (b) school counselors have an opportunity both to address concerns and stressors and to promote positive aspects of the transition to middle school, (c) transition programs should include peers, family, and teachers as students look to significant others for help, and (d) transition programs should evolve throughout the transition year as student perceptions and needs change.

REFERENCES

Anderman, L. (1996). The middle school experience: Effects on the math and science achievment of adolescents with L. D. *Journal of Learning Disabilities, 31*, 128–138.

Arowosafe, D., & Irvin, J. (1992). Transition to a middle level school: What kids say. *Middle School Journal, 24*(2), 15–19.

Berk, L. (1993). *Infants, children, and adolescents.* Needham Heights, MA: Allyn & Bacon.

Chung, H., Elias, M., & Schneider, K. (1998). Patterns of individual adjustment changes during the middle school transition. *Journal of School Psychology, 36,* 83–101.

Crockett, L., Peterson, A., Graber, J., Schulenburg. J., & Ebata, A. (1989). School transitions and adjustment during early adolescence. *Journal of Early Adolescence, 9,* 181–210.

Eccles, J., & Midgley, C. (1989). Stage/environment fit: Developmentally appropriate classrooms for early adolescents. In R. Ames & C. Ames (Eds.), *Research on motivation in education* (Vol. 3, pp. 139–186). New York: Academic.

Eccles, J., Wigfield, A., Midgley, C., Reuman, D., MacIver, D., & Feldlaufer, H. (1993). Negative effects of traditional middle schools on students' motivation. *The Elementary School Journal, 93,* 553–574.

Elias, M., Gara, M., & Ubriaco, M. (1985). Sources of stress and support in children's transition to middle school: An empirical analysis. *Journal of Clinical Child Psychology, 14,* 112–118.

Elias, M., Ubriaco, M., Reese, A., Gara, M., Rothbaum, P., & Haviland, M. (1992). A measure of adaptation to problematic academic and interpersonal tasks of middle school. *Journal of School Psychology, 30,* 41–57.

Felner, R., Brand, S., Adan, A., Mulhall, P., Flowers, N., Sartain, H., & DuBois, D. (1993). Restructuring the ecology of the school as an approach to prevention during school transitions: Longitudinal follow-ups and extensions of the School Transition Environment Project (STEP). *Prevention in Human Services, 10*(2), 103–136.

Giorgo, A. (1985). *Phenomenology and psychological research.* Pittsburgh. PA: Duquesne University.

Harter, S. (1981). A new self-report scale of intrinsic versus extrinsic orientation in the classroom: Motivational and informational components. *Developmental Psychology, 17,* 300–312.

Hirsch, B., & DuBois, D. (1992). The relation of peer support and psychological symptomatology during the transition to junior high school: A two-year longitudinal analysis. *American Journal of Community Psychology, 20,* 333–347.

Hirsch, B., & Rapkin, B. (1987). The transition to junior high school: A longitudinal study of self-esteem, psychological symptomatology, school life, and social support. *Child Development, 58,* 1235–1243.

Holsti, O. (1969). *Content analysis for the social sciences and humanities.* Reading, MA: Addison-Wesley.

Mittman, A., & Packer, M. (1982). Concerns of seventh graders about their transition to junior high school. *Journal of Early Adolescence, 2,* 319–338.

Papalia, D., Olds, S., & Feldman, R. (2001). *Human development* (8th ed.). New York: McGraw-Hill.

Perkins, P., & Gelfer, J. (1995). Elementary to middle school: Planning for transition. *The Clearing House, 68,* 171–173.

Rowan, J. (1981). A dialectical paradigm for research. In P. Reason & J. Rowan (Eds.), *Human inquiry* (pp. 93–112). New York: John Wiley.

Schumacher, D. (1998). *The transition to middle school* (Report No. EDO-PS-98-6). Washington, DC: Clearinghouse on Elementary and Early Childhood Education. (ERIC Document Reproduction Service No. ED 422 119)

Seidman, I. (1991). *Interviewing as qualitative research: A guide for researchers in education and the social sciences.* New York: Columbia Teachers Press.

Simmons, R., & Blyth, D. (1987). *Moving into adolescence: The impact of pubertal change and school context.* Hawthorne, NY: Aldine de Gruyter.

Acknowledgment: This research was sponsored by the American School Counselor Association Practitioner Grant.

ACTION RESEARCH

What Is Action Research?

OK, now it's time to plan and conduct your own study! This will be accomplished with what is called *action research*. **Action research** is a systematic investigation conducted by practitioners to provide information to immediately improve teaching and learning. The emphasis is on teachers, counselors, and administrators designing, carrying out, and using the results of a study in their immediate work environment.

Action research: Conducted by and for practitioners.

With the recent emphasis on "data-driven" decision making in the schools, these studies have become commonplace and very important. The emphasis on action research is exciting because it brings together characteristics of systematic inquiry and practice, making it highly relevant and useful. The emphasis is on practical value, not publication in journals (though many action research studies are published).

Here are some definitions of action research to give you a better idea of what it is all about. Action research is

- An investigation conducted by the person or the people empowered to action concerning their own actions, for the purpose of improving their future actions (Sagor, 2005, p. 4)
- Any systematic inquiry conducted by teacher researchers, principals, school counselors, or other stakeholders in the teaching/learning environment to gather information about how their particular schools operate, how they teach, and how well their students learn . . . [it] is done by teachers for themselves (Mills, 2007, p. 5)
- A constructive inquiry, during which the researcher constructs his or her knowledge of specific issues through planning, acting, evaluating, refining and learning from the experience . . . a continuous learning process in which the researcher learns and also shares the newly generated knowledge with those who may benefit from it (Koshy, 2005, p. 9)

Clearly the word *action* signifies a significant departure from traditional research. The intent is to do something different in teaching, to change instruction, based on more than personal experience or suggestions from others. There is an application of systematic inquiry into a teacher's classroom. By being directly relevant and because of the investment of effort, the results are often very persuasive. Knowledge is generated from within the school, rather than from outside sources. Table 12.4 is a summary of how action research differs from traditional research.

Because so much of the emphasis of action research is on teachers, you may find the terms *teacher researchers* or *teachers-as-researchers* in such studies. Other terms used to indicate a type of action research include *classroom research, teacher research, teacher action research, classroom action research, school research, school action research,* and *collaborative action research.*

Benefits of Action Research

Action research has a number of benefits. In the process of conducting action research, teachers, counselors, and administrators collaborate with others and reflect meaningfully on why the results were obtained and what the results mean as related to their teaching or counseling. This not only empowers teachers, it also helps them understand the benefits of existing literature in an area as well as evidence-based systematic inquiry. Action research engages individuals and acts as a powerful professional development activity. It models a way of thinking for students, and changes the professional dispositions of teachers. Finally, action research changes the climate of a school to a more open atmosphere in which it is standard practice to openly ponder teaching methods, take risks, and depend on others to design studies and to understand the usefulness of results. Glanz (2003, p. 19) lists the following benefits of action research:

TABLE 12.4	Characteristics of Action Research Versus Traditional Research	
Characteristic	**Action Research**	**Traditional Research**
Goal	New knowledge relevant to the local setting	New knowledge that contributes to the field of study
Who determines the research question and carries out the study?	Practitioners: teachers, principals, counselors	Trained researchers: university professors, scholars, graduate students
Setting in which research is carried out	Schools and classrooms where the practice is implemented	Any setting in which appropriate control is achieved
Literature review	Brief, with a focus on secondary sources	Extensive, with an emphasis on primary sources
Instrumentation	Measures are often locally developed and are convenient and easy to administer and score	Measures typically off-the-shelf, selected on the basis of technical adequacy
Sampling	Convenience, purposeful sampling of teachers and students in the targeted setting	Tends to be random or representative
Design	Tends to be nonexperimental or quasi-experimental	Whatever design is needed
Data analysis	Descriptive	Descriptive and inferential
Dissemination of results	To specific individual or school	To the field through presentations and publications

- Creates a systemwide mind-set for school improvement—a professional problem-solving ethos.
- Enhances decision making—provides greater feelings of competence in solving problems and making instructional decisions. In other words, action research provides for an intelligent way of making decisions.
- Promotes reflection and self-assessment.
- Instills a commitment to continuous improvement.
- Creates a more positive school climate in which teaching and learning are foremost concerns.
- Impacts directly on practice.
- Empowers those who participate in the process. For instance, educational leaders who undertake action research may no longer uncritically accept theories, innovations, and programs at face value.

There is one additional benefit that I think is very important. Implementing action research gives practitioners tools to think more systematically about the effectiveness of the practices. The tools are principles of research, such as how to present and summarize data, construct graphs, and consider threats to internal validity. Through the process of action research these skills are strengthened and subsequently applied to reading published studies and critically analyzing conclusions. The approach to learning about research is relevant and meaningful, something that may be missing in a class or workshop on traditional research.

Conducting Action Research

As illustrated in Figure 12.2, the steps in conducting action research are cyclical, indicating an ongoing series of studies to address a research problem, coupled with action and critical reflection. As such, it is an emergent process that modifies research based on the results of action. This is important because it increases the relevance and application of the results, promotes collaboration, and stresses the recursive nature of the process. Essentially it is a continuing process of research → action → reflection → research → action → reflection → research → action → reflection. Note in the following example the reference to this cyclical process.

EXAMPLE | **Cyclical Process in Action Research**

"This study was conducted in three phases over a two-year period and involved students and staff from three faculties. . . . An action research process based on cycles of action and reflection . . . was used to develop peer assessment procedures that were responsive to the student and staff needs and concerns. This process was participatory, collaborative, and reflexive." (Ballantyne, R., Highes, K., & Mylonas, A. (2002). Developing procedures for implementing peer assessment in large classes using an action research process. *Assessment and Evaluation in Higher Education, 27*(5), p. 427)

FIGURE 12.2 Steps in conducting action research.

Selecting a Focus, Topic, or Issue to Study. Selecting a focus area is the initial step in any kind of research. Most importantly, you need to identify a practical problem that can be systematically investigated. There are five criteria to use to when identifying an area. The area of study should:

1. Involve some aspect of teaching/learning
2. Be something that is a part of your own teaching, classroom, or school
3. Be something that you can control or have influence on
4. Be something that you can change or improve
5. Be something you feel passionate about, something that you are motivated to learn more about

Once an area is identified, it is helpful to reflect on the area through a process termed *reconnaissance*. **Reconnaissance** occurs as you take time to self-reflect on the area from the perspective of your own beliefs and from the context of the classroom or school. This time of self-reflection allows you to enhance your understanding of the area from the perspective of theories, values, beliefs, knowledge, the larger context of your school, and relevant historical contexts. Essentially, reconnaissance is self-reflection that solidifies the significance of your area of focus.

Reconnaissance:
Self-reflection of focus

There are several practical approaches to take in identifying the area of focus. One technique is to write down some reflections about what has and has not worked in your area of interest, or to keep a journal of thoughts. Note in the following example how this teacher simply lets her thoughts flow, without trying to identify a specific area.

> **EXAMPLE** | **Teacher Written Self-Reflection**
>
> "Teaching social studies to eighth-graders had become such a battle for me. Over the years, I became used to seeing the same pattern: My students came to class on Day 1 expecting to hate it. They saw no purpose in studying government and were sure that this was going to be the most boring material they would ever have to endure.... What was even worse was dealing with their cynicism. Truthfully, I was starting to dread the start of each new class. I once read where at the beginning of each term, the students and the teacher negotiate a treaty." (Sagor, R. (2005). *The action research guidebook: A four-step process for educators and school teams.* Thousand Oaks, CA: p. 13)

Eventually, you will want to focus on *who, what, where,* and *when.* Answering these questions will help you identify more specific research questions from a general area of focus. For example, a teacher could ask the following about the general area of teaching grammar:

- Which students are having the most difficulty with grammar?
- What is the nature of the evidence used to confirm that this is, indeed, a problem?
- Are students having difficulty during class or with homework?
- How much time do students spend on grammar in class and with homework?

Addressing these questions, the teacher might decide to focus on grammar homework and identify students who are having the most difficulty. Alternatively, the teacher could decide to use a new instructional approach in her classroom that purportedly maintains better student engagement and motivation.

Another approach to reconnaissance is to simply talk with others. Not only will your own thoughts be clarified by articulating them to others, but through the discussions you will get different perspectives, ideas, and suggestions about the nature of interventions, measurement of variables, and data analysis. Involving others helps establish a team mentality and keeps individual perspectives in context. Administrators need to talk with teachers, and teachers need to talk with administrators.

It is always helpful to do some reading on the topic. This can be accomplished through a brief review of literature, which is easily done by accessing ERIC on the Internet. The Internet can be searched more generally as well. Chances are very good that other practitioners have written and thought about the same topic. Professional journals that come to the school can be reviewed, and professional organizations have many good ideas and resources. The important part of doing a literature review is to *keep it brief.* There is so much out there that it's easy to keep reading and reading. Action research is primarily intended to inform practice, so the literature needs to be reviewed with that purpose in mind. Practitioners have limited time, which is why secondary sources are excellent. Trying to understand primary studies may simply take too long for this type of research. That being said, it is always helpful to read the literature!

As a result of reconnaissance, specific research questions can be generated. If data collection involves quantitative methods, independent and dependent variables should be identified. If qualitative, then the questions will be more general. At this point it's also helpful to indicate if there is a need for descriptive, comparative, relationship, or causal conclusions. This will help direct the nature of the design for collecting data.

Notice in the following excerpt the informal, conversational tone of the author describing how the area of focus was identified for her study. This style of writing is typical.

EXAMPLE | **Identifying an Area of Focus**

"While I was teaching, I was concurrently enrolled in a master's degree program where I learned new strategies for middle school students and involved them in action research pilot projects. I experienced some success in my classroom and offered to share the approached I'd learned with Lydia and Jane. . . . I just wanted to help struggling students and teachers. . . . I came to realize that changing just a few aspects of the reading program would not be enough; the entire program needed to be overhauled." (Ahrens, B. C. (2005). Finding a new way: Reinventing a sixth-grade reading program. *Journal of Adolescent and Adult Literacy, 48*(8), p. 645)

Determine Design and Data Collection. The second step in doing action research is to determine what kind of design will be employed, the nature of the data that need to be gathered, and how that data will be collected. Decisions need to be made about whether the design is qualitative, experimental, or nonexperimental; what type or types of data need to be collected; and the sample from which the data will be collected. Initially, both quantitative and qualitative methods should be considered. Using both approaches and a variety of data collection strategies strengthens the study by providing multiple perspectives.

The first important design issue is whether it is primarily qualitative, quantitative, or mixed-method. All of these can be effectively employed. The determination should be made after the important questions and area of focus are identified. With the emphasis on *action* in action research, it is often recommended that teachers do a small-scale experiment by using an intervention and then seeing the effect of it on student outcomes such as achievement and attitudes. With these experiments it is difficult, to say the least, to have a within-class control or comparison group, and to randomly assign students to an intervention and control group. This means that most experimental action research is, at best, quasi-experimental. Often it is a simple pretest-posttest design in which students complete a pretest, experience an intervention, and then take the posttest. Here the most significant threat to internal validity is history, but that can usually be addressed because the teacher is intimately involved in the situation and will know what other influences have occurred. It's as though the teacher is an anthropologist, from a qualitative perspective, in knowing very well what has transpired during the experiment. This is a great supplement to an experiment. Of course, there is also a greater potential for the teacher to be biased, to have an experimenter effect. This threat can be lessened by the use of a detailed protocol for the intervention.

The most typical qualitative design is a case study. When there is a need to understand something within the context of a specific class or school, it is essentially a signal entity that is studied. The nature of the case is defined as a single group of students in the case of a classroom, or teachers if the focus is on the school. The purpose is to gain a detailed description and understanding of the area of focus. The research question is general, rather than specific. The results are used to determine possible actions in the setting, rather than to study the effect of an intervention *as* action. Different qualitative data collection techniques can be used, with the greatest emphasis on interviewing and observation.

The sample is usually a given—whoever is in the class or school being studied. What you need to think about is which students or teachers in the school should be included in data collection. Sometimes it is best to use all students in a class, especially when the inquiry has clear implications for all of them. Sometimes it's better to select a sample from a larger group, as when investigating certain types of students or when conducting a small-scale experiment in which there is a control or comparison group. A factor in determining the sample will be what is needed for human subjects' protection. You have a responsibility to follow accepted ethical guidelines. That will probably mean obtaining permission from parents to conduct research with their children, and quite possibly permission from the students. This means that your sample may be smaller than you'd like! It also means that if many students don't participate, you'll need to be careful about bias in the sample.

A recently completed study illustrates sampling by targeting specific students. The area of focus is on the motivation of high-ability students, and a single-subject design is used, much like an experiment with only two subjects.

EXAMPLE | **Purposeful Sampling in Action Research**

"After nearly a full year in the second-grade class, both students have shown varying degrees of interest in learning and self-discipline. There was an apparent discrepancy between their scores on standardized tests their actual performance on daily work in the classroom. They quite often seemed to coast and attempt to get by with the barest minimum of effort." (Hargrove, K. (2005). What's a teacher to do? *Gifted Child Today, 28*(4), p. 38)

In selecting measurement tools and approaches it's a challenge to select the right one or ones, primarily because there is so much to choose from (see Figure 12.3). A good starting point is to decide whether quantitative or qualitative measures will be used by themselves or in some combination. Whatever the approach, measures typically are locally developed and targeted to the class or school, rather than being standardized. The quality of the measures, then, depends heavily on judgments of items and instruments related to reliability and validity. Here indi-

FIGURE 12.3 Examples of different types of action research.

viduals need to have others review intended measures for clarity and credibility, making sure that researcher bias is minimized. Another important principle about instrumentation for action research is to use more than one measure of the dependent variable or outcome of interest. This allows for triangulation to support credibility and trustworthiness.

Mills (2007) suggests that it is helpful to think about qualitative data collection techniques in one of three categories: experiencing, enquiring, or examining. These categories are especially relevant to the nature of action research. *Experiencing* refers to the use of direct observation of participants. Teachers constantly observe, so it is relatively easy and convenient for them to formalize their observations to be more systematic and rigorous. As an active participant in the class, the teacher often takes on the role of *participant observer.* With this role in qualitative data collection, the teacher needs to find a way to record what is or has occurred. Since teaching requires full immersion, the recording of observations needs to be somewhat formal. This can be done by allowing a few minutes after a lesson or classroom activity to write notes, at the end of the day, and at breaks during the day. Discipline is required! From a qualitative perspective you might want to record "everything" going on, but it is more realistic to try to be more focused. Keep your recording of what has happened separate from your opinions about what it means. That helps to control personal bias and allows others to more easily check what might be inferred.

Enquiring in qualitative approaches means interviewing students, teachers, parents, or whoever would be most appropriate, to obtain information. It is best to have a semistructured format so that, as in observing, there is some degree of focus. A completely unstructured interview is simply too broad and has less probability of eliciting important information. Also, unstructured interviews require greater training. By asking a few questions to prompt open-ended responses, you will have the best chance of getting the data you need. Plan on taking notes during the interview, whether it is with an individual or with a small group. Notes should be brief and completed as soon as possible after the interview. While tape-recording interviews can be very helpful, it can be time-consuming to listen and/or do written transcriptions.

There are two key features of successful interviews in action research. The first is to make sure that you are interviewing the right students or parents. Interviews are effective as a way to gather in-depth data from just a few individuals, so those selected to be interviewed are critical. You want to select individuals who (1) will answer the questions with more than just a few words, and (2) will not be influenced by their "subordinate" position to you. This second issue is a difficult one. If you don't get honest, thoughtful answers the study will not be productive. Ensuring confidentiality is helpful, but most important is your ability to set participants at ease and take the time necessary to establish a positive relationship in the interview. Often a combination of small group and individual interviews is effective, though in some groups there might be a reluctance for participants to be honest and/or for a few participants to dominate. Again, the best approach is to use more than one method of collecting information so that you are not entirely dependent on what is obtained from the interview.

Examining refers to the use of existing documents, records, and other artifacts that are already available or will become available. Examples include minutes of meetings, archival data, attendance, discipline referrals, test scores, and student participation in co-curricular activities. Student journals and responses to open-ended questions and prompts can also be used. For example, if you did a study to enhance students' interest in reading, an artifact that could be used would be the number of books taken from the school library. In the following example the authors used student written and verbal reactions related to assignments to better understand how students acted on them.

EXAMPLE | **Qualitative Data Collection**

"Because we were interested in how students understood and acted on these assignments, we focused considerable attention on each student's verbal and written reactions to the social and community inquiry assignments. Using standard qualitative data analysis techniques for developing themes through coding, we examined these data sources to learn how our students understood broad systems of oppression and how that understanding was in turn associated with their role as teachers." (Hyland, E., & Noffke, S. E. (2005). Understanding diversity through social and community inquiry: An action-research study. *Journal of Teacher Education, 56*(4), p. 372)

Quantitative data collection can be divided into tests, quizzes, papers, and projects designed to assess student knowledge and understanding (cognitive) and questionnaires that measure student or teacher perceptions. Teacher-made tests are used most frequently, though in our current climate of accountability there are often district tests that can provide a more "external" assessment of knowledge, understanding, and skills. It is very important for teachers to have colleagues review tests, both before giving them and after students' open-ended answers and products, such as papers, projects, and presentations, are graded. These judgments will provide validity evidence to support the accuracy of the evaluations. While "objective" tests reduce the potential influence of researcher bias, remember that professional judgments are involved in both the development of questions and scoring of responses.

Noncognitive quantitative assessment occurs as students self-report their attitudes, values, and beliefs on questionnaires. These instruments are very helpful, especially if they can be administered in a way that ensures students' anonymity. It is best to use short questionnaires, and better to use several short ones rather than a long one. Questionnaires are relatively easy to prepare, administer, and score, and provide a very helpful supplement to qualitative methods.

Summarizing and Interpreting Data. When quantitative measures are used, the best kind of summary and interpretation is descriptive, using calculations such as mean, range, and standard deviation. The data need to be cleaned to remove any outliers or any obviously inaccurate numbers. The summary presents what you found; the interpretation focuses on what the summary means, how it should be interpreted. Graphs of results are commonly used, including bar graphs and histograms, and provide an effective summary. Descriptive statistics should be interpreted on the basis of practical, not statistical, significance. With the small number of subjects used in action research it is very difficult to obtain statistical significance, and many teachers are not well versed in what statistical significance means. What is most important is a descriptive summary that best informs the practice of education within the specific context.

INTERNET CONNECTION

Action Research Resources is an excellent, substantial Website for action research that contains many links to additional resources, such as recent books, mailing lists, and work in progress. Go to **http://scu.edu.au/schools/gcm/ar/arhome.html**.

CONSUMER TIPS: *Criteria for Evaluating Action Research*

1. Determine the motivation and involvement of the researcher. Good action research is conducted by individuals who have a vested interest in the study, but at the same time this motivation should not result in experimenter bias. The more the researcher is involved in doing an intervention and obtaining information, the greater the opportunity for experimenter bias.

2. Look for consistency between the research question and your methodology. Action research uses whatever methodology is most appropriate, so the determining factor is nature of the question. Much, if not most, action research has some kind of qualitative component. That approach is best when the emphasis is on deeper understanding of a practice or effect on learning.

3. Look for whether multiple methods of data collection have been utilized. There are many advantages to using multiple methods of data collection, especially in action research where there may not be sophisticated psychometric properties of the measures.

4. Confirm that there has been an emergent, cyclical process of research—action—reflection. The cyclical nature of action research is essential to being effective. It's not simply a matter of doing a single study, there needs to be a continual spiral of action based on research that is reflected on and followed by more research, action, and reflection.

5. Is there any external monitoring or feedback? In the best of circumstances teachers and administrators who are conducting action research receive some kind of "external" review of their methodology, results, and reflection. This can be accomplished by another professional in the school or district. It's an important step to maintain quality control and give feedback that will facilitate further good research which provides credible information that can be used to change practice.

Anatomy of an Action Research Study

EXHIBIT 12.2 Improving Student Understanding and Motivation of Multiplication Facts

> Fourth-grade teacher (teacher-researcher)

> Abstract

Alyson Maryland

This action research project focuses on promoting student understanding and motivation while teaching the basic multiplication facts (0–9). The study examined the effectiveness of teaching methods with an emphasis on rote memorization, compared to those focusing on problem solving. Research advocates the use of problem solving when introducing and teaching basic facts, and holding off on drill and practice methods until after they've developed an understanding. The participants in the study consist of thirty-five fourth-grade students. The students participated in lessons on arrays and multiplication games, and they discussed efficient versus inefficient counting strategies. Data were collected from their old timed tests, state math scores, interviews, and worksheets. The results of the study suggest a positive relationship between balancing conceptual under-standing and procedural skills, and student success with basic facts. The results also show a positive relationship between playing games and student motivation for studying the basic facts.

> Research problem focused on instructional strategies

INTRODUCTION

Research suggests that for every time you do something wrong, you have to do it right seventeen times be-fore your brain gets used to doing it correctly. These findings are startling when you consider the vast amount of drill and practice methods used in the classroom to teach students their basic math facts. The purpose of my ac-tion research project was to seek out and examine effective and efficient methods for teaching the basic facts. My second objective for this project was to develop effective strategies for increasing student motivation in terms of studying their multiplication facts. Students are often frustrated and bored studying things they don't understand, or when using tedious study methods.

> Review of literature

BACKGROUND

According to the 2004–2005 Oregon State Standards, by the end of fourth grade students are expected to have developed efficient strategies for solving multiplication problems. They should be fluent with these strate-gies and able to solve all basic fact problems mentally within three seconds. Unfortunately, researchers have found that an alarming number of eighth grade students still resort to finger counting and other inefficient strategies when solving simple problems (Isaacs, Carroll, & Bell, 2001). These strategies are inefficient because they take too much time and are not done mentally.

One promising practice is to reduce the use of drill and practice methods (Jones, 1995). These methods in-clude timed tests, flash cards, and worksheets with rows of basic facts. One reason researchers advise educa-tors to stay away from drill and practice methods is because they don't aid in students' conceptual understanding of multiplication. These methods provide students with procedural skills that they are taught to mimic. Teaching in this way makes it hard for students to apply multiplication concepts to word problems or real-life situations.

> Significance

Effective strategies for teaching basic facts include balancing procedural skills and conceptual knowledge. Teaching with balance includes the use of word problems, arrays, and open-ended problem-solving assignments. Isaacs et al. (2001) recommend practicing multiplication in a variety of contexts and situations to increase the stu-dents' ability to transfer the skill/concept.

Other promising practices suggest three components to use when teaching basic facts. The first component is developing a strong understanding of the operations of number relationships. The second focuses on trading inefficient strategies for efficient ones, and the third component is providing students with drill and practice as-signments. Van de Walle (2003) stresses the importance of not moving to step three until after the students have developed efficient strategies. If you introduce drill before the students have mastered one or more efficient strategies, the practice will only reinforce the inefficient strategies. Inefficient strategies include counting on fin-gers, adding the numbers instead of multiplying them, using manipulatives, drawing pictures, etc. Inefficient methods are inefficient because they take a long time and cannot be done mentally. Efficient methods include skip counting, simplifying the problem, and ultimately, memorization.

INTERVENTION

Suggests experimental study

My planned intervention to address students' understanding of, and motivation to learn, basic number facts included the following:

Note informal first person style of writing

- Lessons focused on building students' conceptual understanding of the multiplication process.
- Teaching students efficient strategies for solving basic facts.
- Introducing students to fun games they could play while studying their basic number facts.

DATA COLLECTION

The data collection tools I used were:

1. Students' scores on state math tests
2. Results of timed tests
3. Informal interviews
4. Students' written work

Very brief; suggests mixed-methods.

DATA ANALYSIS

The data I collected from the students' state math test was surprising. I was shocked to find that eleven students (about thirty-five percent of the class) did not meet the state standards in math. The students who did not meet state standards were consistent with the students who were not passing their timed tests. I decided I would need to spend some extra time working with these eleven students.

Experiencing

The data I collected from students' timed tests were by far the most helpful in planning my intervention and understanding where students were having the most trouble. The data I collected from the timed tests focused on the types of errors students were making. Edelman, Abdit, and Valentin (1995) describe four types of errors humans make when multiplying; they include operand, table, operation, and non-table errors. Operand errors occur when the incorrect answer given is correct for another problem that shares an operand (e.g., $4 \times 2 = 16$, when 16 is the correct answer for 4×4). Table errors occur when the incorrect answer given does not share an operand with the correct answer, but the answer given does reside in the multiplication table (e.g., $6 \times 9 = 56$). Humans make operation errors when they perform a different operation, such as adding or subtracting, when solving a multiplication problem (e.g., $9 \times 0 = 9$). The final error is a non-table error, and it occurs when the incorrect answer is not an answer to any problem in the multiplication table (e.g., $5 \times 6 = 31$). Operand errors were by far the most common error made by the students, They accounted for fifty-five percent of the error total. This data told me that students were associating the incorrect answer with one of the operands, and the early emphasis on drill and practice has reinforced these wrong answers. Non-table errors accounted for twenty-three percent of the errors. I believe students are making a high amount of non-table errors, because they are miscounting on their fingers. Solving 6×7 on your fingers is both hard and confusing, so I assumed students who rely on their fingers make the majority of the table errors. Operation errors occur mostly in problems containing an operand of zero or one. The students often switch to addition and solve the problem by adding zero or one to the other number. This error occurs mostly when the zero or one is on the bottom. I didn't feel the error occurred consistently enough to be considered a problem, so I decided not to focus on it during my intervention.

Examining

Researcher interpretation

I also used the students' timed tests to identify which multiplication facts they were having the most trouble with. The problems I found gave students the most trouble were 6×7, 7×6, 7×4, 7×7, 8×8, 8×7, 6×6, 8×6, and 6×8. In general, though, any problem including an operand of six, seven, eight, and/or nine was answered incorrectly by the majority of students. This data was especially helpful in adjusting my interventions, because it allowed me to focus on the problems with which students were having the most trouble.

Shows direct involvement with the intervention

(continued)

EXHIBIT 12.2 (continued)

Qualitative; enquiring

The informal interviews provided me with insight into what the students thought about timed tests, what strategies they used to solve basic fact problems, and how well they could transfer their skills to real-world situations. I was surprised to find that very student answered "yes" to the question about whether or not they felt timed tests were helpful. The majority of students supported their answer stating that timed tests gave them a chance to practice their multiplication facts. The interviews also allowed me to discover which strategy each student relied on when solving multiplication facts.

DISCUSSION

Restatement of purpose

Direct benefits for the teacher-researcher

Implications for others

Reflection

The purpose of my action research project was to seek out and examine effective and efficient methods for teaching basic math facts. Upon completion of my action research project, I feel confident that I will be able to effectively and efficiently teach basic facts to any grade, first through sixth. I am now aware of the common misconceptions regarding rote memorization and the premature use of timed tests.

My results tell me that timed tests can be beneficial when used as a form of practice. Students should be able to correct their own tests, allowing for immediate feedback on which problems they got wrong and what the correct answer should have been. Teachers should also consider not grading the tests so students can focus on improving their skills and not on a grade.

From my research, experience, and results I was also able to infer that effective teaching strategies center around balancing conceptual understanding and procedural skills. To provide this balance, educators should emphasize problem-solving strategies at an early age. Problem-solving methods provide students with flexibility in their learning, making it easier for them to transfer their knowledge to various math problems and real-life situations. Also, teachers should teach one concept at a time, and teach it to master before moving on.

Conclusions and implications for others

Cyclical process

To motivate their students, educators must first develop their understanding of the multiplication procedure and concept. This understanding will boost the students' self-esteem, giving them confidence and motivating them intrinsically. The second step in motivating students is introducing fun ways for them to learn, study, and memorize the basic facts. In my experience, students preferred competitive games, especially when playing against the teacher. The participants in my study were really excited about having a "multiplication bowl," where the two fourth-grade classes would face off in a multiplication competition. I am excited to continue to test these teaching strategies in the next cycle of my action research journey.

REFERENCES

Not APA format

Edelman, B., Abdit, H., & Valentin, D. (1995). Multiplication number facts: Modeling human performance with connections networks. *Psychologica Belgica*. 1–23.

Isaacs, A., Carroll, W., & Bell, M. (2001). UCSMP everyday mathematics curriculum. *Everyday Mathematics*. 2–5.

Jones, S. C. (1995). Review of cognitive research. *Educational Memory Aids*. 57–60.

Van de Walle, J. A. (2003). Elementary and middle school mathematics: Teaching developmentally. *Pearson*. 156–176.

STUDY QUESTIONS

1. What is mixed-method research?
2. What are the advantages and disadvantages of mixed-method research designs?
3. When are mixed-method designs useful?

4. How do explanatory, exploratory, and triangulation designs differ in terms of their purposes and procedures?
5. What are the key advantages and disadvantages of each type of mixed-method design?
6. Why is it important for researchers to clearly explain their rationale for conducting a mixed-method study?
7. What is the difference between *priority* and *sequence* in mixed-method designs?
8. How do explanatory, exploratory, and triangulation designs differ in terms of priority and sequence?
9. What are some strategies for mixing quantitative and qualitative data in mixed-method designs?
10. How do explanatory, exploratory, and triangulation designs differ in terms of data mixing?
11. What are some key considerations when evaluating mixed-method studies?
12. What makes action research more relevant to practitioners than other types of research?
13. Why does action research use both qualitative and quantitative methods?
14. What is the sequence of steps in conducting action research?
15. How is action research reported?
16. How is the credibility of action research determined?

@WWW SAMPLE TEST QUESTIONS

See this text's Companion Website at www.ablongman.com/mcmillan5e for sample test questions and answers.

RESEARCH NAVIGATOR™ ACTIVITIES

1. A mixed-method study of the effect of high school student's friendship is reported in the Research Navigator, AN 12670776. What type of mixed-method study is illustrated? What are the more specific quantitative and qualitative designs? To what extent do results from each method contribute to the finding and conclusions?
2. Action research is illustrated in a study of student engagement of exceptional children (AN 14315340). Read the study and identify principles of action research presented in this chapter. In particular, what role did teacher reflection play in the study? Do you think these results would be helpful to other teachers? Why or why not?

Chapter 13

Discussion *and* Conclusions

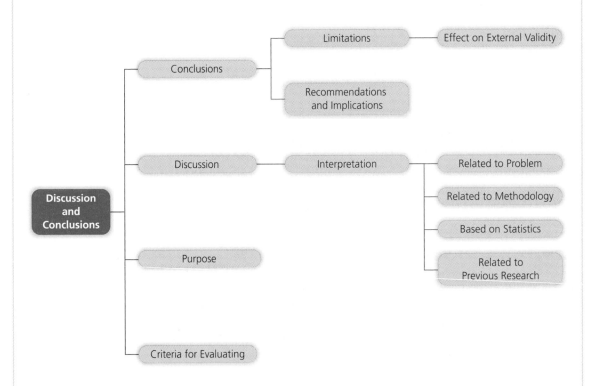

CHAPTER ROAD MAP

We have come to the final section of research reports. Once the results of a study have been summarized, the researcher will present a nontechnical discussion of their meaning. This section of an article may be identified as *Conclusions, Conclusions and Recommendations, Discussion, Summary,* or *Discussion and Conclusions.*

We will first consider why interpretations of the results are needed and the nature of interpretations, then turn to conclusions. As a result of studying this chapter, you will:

- Understand the difference between interpretations and conclusions
- Be able to identify interpretations based on the research problem, methodology, statistical procedures, and effect size
- Understand the difference between population and ecological external validity
- Be able to describe limitations based on subject characteristics and methodology
- Distinguish among different aspects of the methodology that may limit external validity
- Understand the nature of recommendations for future research and implications for practice

PURPOSE *and* NATURE *of the* DISCUSSION

The purpose of the discussion is to present an interpretation of the results, the conclusions, and recommendations for further study. Authors use the discussion to explain the meaning of the results and to speculate about their implications. The discussion is more than a summary of the study; it is an evaluation of the methodology and results to help readers understand what the results mean and how they can be used. It is essentially a synthesis of the study reflecting the professional judgment of the researcher. The synthesis integrates the research problem and review of literature with the results. The professional judgment of the researcher is reflected in the nature of the synthesis and the implications suggested in the form of conclusions and recommendations.

You will find that discussion sections are the least structured parts of an article and that authors differ about content and organization. Some authors begin the discussion with conclusions and then analyze the conclusions, whereas others will explain why they obtained the results, the limitations of the study, and then present the conclusions. Some authors may even combine results with discussion and conclusions. We will consider each of the major aspects of the discussion section, even though the order in which these are found in articles will vary.

INTERPRETATION *of the* RESULTS

Once the results are presented it is necessary to analyze and interpret them. This analysis consists of reasoned speculation to answer these kinds of questions: Why did the results turn out as they did? What may have affected the results? Are there any limitations that should be noted? To what extent were hypotheses supported? What is the meaning of the findings? How do the results relate to previous research findings? Interpretation of the results may be related to the research problem and/or hypothesis, theory, statistical procedures, the methodology of the study, and previous research on the problem.

Interpretation Related to the Problem and/or Hypothesis

Discussion sections often begin with a restatement of the problem or hypothesis, followed by some indication of the answer to the problem or degree of support for the hypothesis. There may be an evaluation that the findings provided a strong or clear answer or the hypothesis was strongly or marginally supported. Unexpected findings may be summarized as surprising. In this type of interpretation, the authors indicate their professional opinion about how well the data answer the questions. It is important when reading these interpretations to think about how experimenter bias may have influenced the opinions that are expressed. Your judgment about the relationship between the questions and the findings may be quite different from that of the researcher. Sometimes researchers will focus only on findings that support their expectations.

Interpretation Based on Theory

When research has a clear theoretical basis it is helpful to interpret results in light of that theory. Sometimes competing theories are examined, which would also result in a discussion of how the results are related to the contradictory theories and the extent to which the study contributed to a resolution. Note in the following excerpt how the authors address theoretical implications of their findings.

EXAMPLE | **Interpretation Based on Theory**

"Theoretically, the results generally support instructional practices based on a dual coding theory of reading (Sadoski & Paivio, 2001, 2004), and specifically the VV program of Bell (1986) designed to develop reading comprehension consistent with dual coding theory principles. . . . Other aspects of the LBLP program that are consistent with dual coding theory . . . also received support." (Sadoski, M., & Willson, V. L. (2006). Effects of a theoretically based large-scale reading intervention in a multicultural urban school district. *American Educational Research Journal, 43*(1), p. 151)

Interpretation Related to Methodology

As stressed throughout this book, methodology is very important in understanding and analyzing results. Often methods are used as a reason for obtaining certain results and also suggest specific limitations. Consequently, when researchers interpret the results, they refer to specific aspects of the methodology. Even if the researchers do not do so, you should! You may find significant weaknesses that are not addressed by the researcher in explaining the results. This may suggest that the researcher is unaware of the weakness or chooses to ignore its implications.

For example, suppose a researcher uses a general measure of locus of control, Rotter's I-E (internal-external) scale, and expects to find that the locus of control as measured by Rotter's scale will be related to the reasons students give for cheating. The hypothesis may be that students who cheat believe that their performance is out of their control (external), whereas students who do not cheat believe that their performance is largely dependent on themselves (internal). If the results fail to show this relationship, a possible interpretation may be that the instrument, since it was a generalized measure, was not specific to the situation and therefore failed to show a relationship with cheating. If the researcher is unaware of the generalized nature of the measure, and does not understand that locus of control is situation-specific, then this lack of knowledge may be reflected in the failure to mention these points in the discussion.

Interpretation Related to Selection of Subjects. One aspect of the methodology that may affect the results is the selection of subjects. As noted in Chapter 5, volunteer and available samples may give unique and limited results. Often there is a tendency to ignore the effects of specially selected subjects. In the following example, the authors appropriately point out limitations in the results because of sampling.

EXAMPLE | **Interpretation Based on Subject Selection**

"This study has several limitations. Therefore, these limitations should be considered when results are interpreted. First of all, sample size seems too small. Although the current study is titled as Turkish mothers, results should not be generalized to all Turkish mothers or culture. . . . Secondly, almost all participant mothers had little education and all were housewives. This aspect should be carefully taken into account while interpreting the results." (Diken, I. H. (2006). Turkish mothers' interpretations of the disability of their children with mental retardation. *International Journal of Special Education, 21*(2), p. 16)

Interpretation Related to Measurement of Variables. A second type of interpretation is to examine how the measurement of variables may affect the results. Many of the points in Chapters 6 and 7 are relevant:

- Instruments should show evidence of validity and reliability.
- Procedures for administering an instrument can be important.
- Possible effects of observers and interviewers need to be documented.

- There is the possibility of response set and faking in noncognitive measurement.
- Norms may not be appropriate.

Sometimes results of two studies of the same phenomenon will differ if different types of instruments are used. Discussion sections tend to refer to measurement of variables when the results do not meet expectations or when no significant differences are found.

EXAMPLE | **Interpretation Based on Measurement of Variables**

"Certainly, the present results confirm the value of independent assessment of both intrinsic and extrinsic motivations. Our modified version of Harter's (1980, 1981) scale is an initial step toward this end. Indeed, intrinsic and extrinsic motivations were assessed independently in the present with instruments that have been shown to be both reliable and valid. . . . Thus, our decomposed version of Harter's original scale provides the first independent measure of extrinsic motivation for elementary and middle school children. . . . A second advantage of our measures of intrinsic and extrinsic motivation related to the removal of several items from Harter's original scale that were either psychometrically or conceptually problematic in the new format." (Lepper, M. R., Corpus, J. H., & Iyengar, S. S. (2005). Intrinsic and extrinsic motivational orientations in the classroom: Age differences and academic correlates. *Journal of Educational Psychology, 97*(2), p. 191)

Interpretation Related to Experimental Intervention. A third category of factors in interpreting results concerns experimental intervention. The specific nature of some aspect of an intervention or the manner in which treatments are administered may influence the results.

EXAMPLE | **Interpretation Based on the Nature of the Intervention**

"Another potential limitation of the study is the use of only one manipulation of grade distributions and one of grading procedures. In actuality, students' perceptions of distributive fairness may be influenced not only by comparison between their grades and expectations, but also by comparisons between their grades and others' grades." (Tata, J. (1999). Grade distributions, grading procedures, and students' evaluations of instructors: A justice perspective. *The Journal of Psychology, 133*(3), p. 268)

Interpretation Based on Statistical Procedures

An important factor in a discussion is an analysis of the statistical procedures used in the study. Although a complete discussion of statistical problems is beyond the scope of this book, a few basic statistical principles need to be considered.

The first thing a reader should do is check for any apparent errors in reporting statistical results. This is done by looking for consistency and agreement between numbers reported in tables and graphs and the statements written in narrative form in the article. Errors will inevitably appear despite proofreading because of the frequent transfer of data (from answer sheets to coding sheets to computers to manuscript to typeset copy).

A second concern is whether statistical procedures have violated important assumptions. A *t* test or analysis of variance, for instance, assumes a population that has a normal distribution, about the same variance for each group, and interval-level measurement. In studies in which violation of the assumptions could have important implications, the researcher should indicate whether the assumptions have been met. In many educational studies there is a question about the appropriate unit of analysis. Because students influence each other in a class and treatments given to classes are not replicated for each individual student, most statisticians believe that the classroom, not the individual student, is the appropriate unit of analysis (the unit of analysis determines the level of significance of the statistical test).

Some researchers assume that the failure to find a statistically significant difference should be interpreted to mean that there is in reality no difference. As noted in Chapter 9, there are many reasons why researchers fail to find a significant difference or relationship, only one of which is that there really is no difference or relationship. Researchers also confuse statistical differences with practical or meaningful differences. That is, there is confusion between what is statistically significant and what is educationally significant. Meaningfulness should be judged by examining the difference between means, or the correlation coefficient, and by considering the specifics of the situation in which the results will be used. Often, what are summarized as significant differences turn out to be very small actual differences with little practical value.

With the increasing use of effect size statistics, researchers often include this measure of the practicality of the findings in the interpretation part of the article. Good examples are the following:

EXAMPLE | **Interpretation Based on Effect Size**

"To evaluate the practical importance of the $4\frac{1}{2}$-year findings, we compared the effect sizes that were associated with child care with effects associated with two other well-recognized influences on young children's development: parenting quality and poverty. The obtained quantity effects on caregivers' reports of child behavior problems were larger than the effects on behavior problems that were associated with parenting ($d = .38$ versus $.23$) and almost as large as the effects associated with poverty ($d = .43$ versus $.47$)." (NICHD Early Child Care Research Network. (2002). Early child care and children's development prior to school entry: Results from the NICHD study of early child care. *American Educational Research Journal*, *39*(1), p. 157)

"Moderate to large effect sizes were also found for many components when analyzed by ability level and subject matter. Clear patterns emerged with ability level of the class, indicating that this is an important variable related to assessment and grading practices and cognitive levels of assessments. This is illustrated by the magnitude of positive relationships among ability level of the class and use of academic achievement ($d = .78$), use of constructed-response assessments ($d = .41$), and assessment of higher-order thinking (.89)." (McMillan, J. H. (2001, April). *Teachers' classroom assessment and grading practices decision making.* Paper presented at the Annual Meeting of the National Council of Measurement in Education, New Orleans, p. 31)

Interpretation Related to Previous Research

The purpose of a review of previous research is to place the study in the context of other investigations. Once the study is completed, the results should be discussed in light of the reviewed literature to help explain the reasons for the results and the meaningfulness of the study. Although the style of relating results to previous studies will vary, there is usually an indication of whether the current findings are consistent or inconsistent with previous research. When the results are inconsistent or contradictory, the authors should provide explanations, usually in terms of the research design. For example, suppose it is found, contrary to previous research, that principals with autocratic leadership styles communicate more effectively with teachers than do principals who use participatory leadership. An explanation might be found in different samples, different instruments of leadership style, or administration of instruments at different times of the year.

Interpretation as related to previous studies and other literature is the most common feature of discussion sections. Such an interpretation is important because it places the results more directly and explicitly in the context of other research, thereby enhancing the contribution of the new research to a recognized body of knowledge. It also demonstrates that the authors have a good understanding of the literature, which increases their credibility.

The following are examples of how results are interpreted by relating them to other studies or literature.

EXAMPLE | **Interpretation Based on Previous Research**

"The results of the analyses, consistent with earlier research by Brookhart (1994) and Cizek et al. (1995), show that most elementary teachers use a multitude of factors in grading students. The hodgepodge of factors considered when grading appear to be organized into six distinct components. Academic performance is clearly the most important factor in grading students, as also reported by Stiggins and Conklin (1992), but the results of the present study show that nontest performance and behavior, such as effort, participation, and extra credit work, also are very important for many teachers, consistent with the Gullickson (1985) study." (McMillan, J. H., Myran, S., & Workman, D. (2002). Elementary teachers' classroom assessment and grading practices. *The Journal of Educational Research, 95*(4), p. 211)

"The results suggest that children are more self-regulated learners in small-group and seat work. However, the results do not imply that teacher-directed instruction is not *an effective means of teaching.* On the contrary, we agree with Weinert and Helmke (1995) that some strategies are more effectively taught and enhanced through *teachers' direct instruction* and modeling. Teachers' direct or explicit instruction of learning strategies can promote children's regulatory performance (Cardell-Elawar, 1992; King, 1991; Meloth & Derring, 1994). However, in order for children to truly become self-regulated learners, the classroom should include all three contexts to provide direct instruction, independent practice, and the opportunity to practice metacognitive skills in a social situation." (Stright, A. D., & Supplee, L. H. (2002). Children's self-regulatory behaviors during teacher-directed seat-work and small-group instructional contexts. *The Journal of Education Research, 95*(4), p. 242)

"As in previous research (DiBattista et al., 2004; Epstein & Brosvic, 2002), students had favorable responses to the IFAT, with more than three quarters indicating that they would like to use the IFAT in all of their courses having multiple-choice tests. It is not surprising that almost all students liked having the opportunity to obtain partial credit on multiple-choice items . . . students may also prefer the IFAT because they believe that it is fairer than other types of multiple-choice response techniques, lets them learn more, and makes the test feel a bit like a game (DiBattista et al.). . . . Our findings agree with previous research that has consistently shown test anxiety to be inversely related to test performance in a variety of settings (Clark et al., 1998; Hembree, 1988; Musch & Bröder, 1999; Powers, 2001). We found inverse associations among RTAS scores and various measures of test performance, including overall test scores and scores on the multiple-choice and nonmultiple-choice portions of the test. In contrast, trait anxiety was not associated with any of these measures of test performance, and, furthermore, the associations between RTAS scores and test performance were not statistically significantly diminished when trait anxiety was statistically controlled. These findings are consistent with the notion that test anxiety is related to, yet distinct from, trait anxiety (Spielberger et al., 1978)." (DiBattista, D., & Gosse, L. (2006). Test anxiety and the immediate feedback assessment technique. *The Journal of Experimental Education 74*(4), p. 309)

CONCLUSIONS

One of the final parts of a research article is a statement of the conclusions. Conclusions are summary statements of the results as they pertain to the research problem, often presented as answers to the questions, hypotheses, or purposes of the research. Sometimes conclusions simply repeat a technical, statistical presentation of the results in short summary sentences in nontechnical language. In other studies, the conclusions will be based on the interpretation of the results, reflecting the professional judgment of the investigators. Usually the major or most significant findings are summarized as conclusions.

if a study of fourth-grade students shows that cooperative learning strategies are better than individualized approaches, the results are limited to other fourth-graders with similar characteristics. Similarly, research conducted with high school students is limited to other high school students; research done with males should not be generalized to females; what may be true for one type of student may not be true for other types of students; and so forth.

One key to understanding the extent to which results should be limited to subject characteristics is to know the characteristics. That may seem rather obvious, but you will find in some studies that the subjects are not described adequately enough to allow you to judge generalizability. Another important aspect of the study is whether probability sampling was used. If representative sampling was used, then the limitations apply to the population rather than to the sample. If available samples were used, you need to examine the procedures to see if limitations are suggested, for example, as with paid or volunteer samples. Results may be internally valid but limited to subjects who volunteer.

A second limitation is to be careful not to generalize what is true for a group of subjects to individuals or subgroups. For example, if you determine that teachers' expectations of students seem to be affected by reviewing test scores from the previous year, the overall finding is true for the group as a whole and may not be true for any individual teacher or for certain groups of teachers. In other words, expectations may be influenced in some types of teachers but not in other types of teachers, even though when all types of teachers are analyzed together there are significant results. It is similar to saying that although in the entire group of 12th-grade students there is a positive relationship between attendance and achievement, the relationship may be more or less positive for particular groups of 12th-graders.

The following examples show how results may be limited because of how subjects were selected.

EXAMPLE | **Limitation Based on Subject Selection**

"In fact, generalizing the present study's findings to younger or less-advanced music students should be done with caution. The musicians who served as subjects in this study are in many ways quite different than the learners who populate school music programs. It is possible that the acquisition of expressive performance skills is best accomplished by other means (not reflected in this report), depending on the learners' developmental level. Additional research with younger musicians would provide needed insight into this." (Woody, R. H. (2006). The effect of various instructional conditions on expressive music performance, *Journal of Research in Music Education, 54*(1), p. 34)

"This study was limited in the fact that one, sixth-grade class was examined. Participants were chosen based solely on the convenience method (the researcher's students were used). Students and their parents from this class only were surveyed and tested and in this way results are not generalizable." (Hawes, C. A., & Plourde, A. (2005). Parental involvement and its influence on the reading achievement of 6th grade students. *Reading Improvement, 42*(1), p. 56)

> "The current sample, although random, represented juvenile delinquents from a geographically restricted region. Thus, the extent to which these findings generalize to juvenile offenders from other geographic regions is not clear." (Caley, C. E., & Onwuegbuzie, A. J. (2004). Attributions toward violence of male juvenile delinquents: A concurrent mixed-methodological analysis, *The Journal of Social Psychology, 144*(6), p. 567)

Limitations Related to Situational Characteristics. Situational characteristics are specifics of the setting and context in which the study is conducted. They include the place of the study—whether in a classroom, laboratory, playground, home, and so on—and what is present in this setting—for example, the type of equipment in a playground or the objects in a classroom. If research on prosocial behavior is studied in a day-care center, for example, the results may not be generalizable to unstructured play in a neighborhood. What may occur in one school may not occur in another because of differences in their structure and specific features. Limitations because of settings are part of the conditions of conducting the research. (Other conditions are considered below.) Together they may be referred to as factors affecting the **ecological validity** of the research. Ecological validity is strong when the results can be generalized to different settings. This is obviously a limitation in studies that occur in a single classroom or school. As with subject characteristics, your judgment of generalizability will depend on how well the setting is described. If your situation is similar in most respects, the findings may be useful. On the other hand, if your situation is quite different, for example, an inner-city school compared to a suburban school, the results may not be useful.

Ecological validity: Generalizability to other settings, times, treatments, and measures.

Limitations Related to Methodology. One of the most common limitations is related to the nature of the methodology that was used. Often studies that are nonexperimental and examine relationships will indicate that causal conclusions should not be reached. Similarly, caution is often suggested in making causal conclusions for quasi-experiments or for studies in which internal validity is weak. Notice in the first example how the researcher makes it very clear that causal conclusions are not appropriate:

EXAMPLE | **Limitation Based on Methodology**

> "Because this was an observational study, it cannot prove causality. It does, however, add to our knowledge of the differences between schools and classrooms whose students are attaining higher than expected levels of literacy achievement, and those who are not, across a very diverse range of schools and student populations." (Langer, J. A. (2001). Beating the odds: Teaching middle and high school students to read and write well. *American Educational Research Journal, 38*(4), p. 877)

> "The present study is of course not without limitations. Principal among these is the fact that it employed a retrospective, cross-sectional design. With this type of design, the participants' pretransition recollections could have been influenced either by their post-transition experiences or by forgetting given that they were surveyed in October, approximately two months after the students had entered their new school." (Akos, P., & Galassi, J. P. (2004). Middle and high school transitions as viewed by students, parents, and teachers. *Professional School Counseling, 7* (4), p. 218)

Limitations Related to When the Research Is Conducted. There are several ways in which time is related to limitations. The first is that treatments may be effective at one time but not at another. What may work in the morning may not work in the afternoon, and what may be effective in the fall may be ineffective in the winter. Responses of subjects to treatments and measures also vary according to time. Students' responses may be much more accurate in the morning than in late afternoon. Measures of self-concept will be affected by when the students respond, as will attitudinal measures. From a broader perspective, the sociohistorical context in which the research is carried out may limit the findings. That is, how students respond will be affected by the cultural values at the time the research is conducted.

Limitations Related to Interventions. In experimental research generalizability is limited by the nature of the intervention. It is necessary to know how an intervention is defined and carried out to know whether it will be useful to you in your situation. For example, there has been a great amount of research recently on what is termed "active teaching or instruction," but its definition may vary from study to study. The same would be true for such practices as cooperative learning, homogeneous and heterogeneous grouping, individualization, praise, and reinforcement. You need to look at what is sometimes the fine print in the methodology section to know precisely how an intervention is defined and implemented. Results and conclusions are, of course, limited to this operational definition and the procedures for implementing the treatment.

One aspect of many interventions that limits generalizability is the individuals' knowledge that they are subjects in a study. In this case the treatment is confounded with the subjects' awareness of being studied. Because some people then act differently, the results are generalizable only to other people who know they are in a study. In other words, the intervention may work only when it is implemented as part of a study. As noted in Chapter 9, this is termed the **Hawthorne effect**. Also, if a new treatment disrupts a normal routine, the novelty or disruption is confounded with the treatment and limits the generalizability to other new or novel situations.

Hawthorne effect:
Individuals' realization that they are subjects in a study.

Limitations Related to Measures. Research is limited by the manner in which the variables, independent or dependent, are measured. For example, an independent variable may be "on-task behavior" and the dependent variable "attitudes toward learning." Both of these variables can be measured in several ways. Results of research are generalized to other situations in which the variables are measured, or at least conceptualized, in the same manner. Thus, it is necessary to understand in some detail how the variables are defined and measured.

EXAMPLE | **Limitations Related to Measures**

"In spite of our attempt to model all the channels for a class size effect, a caveat is in order: The curriculum and instructional measures available in the TIMSS are very crude. The number of math topics taught indicates the breadth but not the depth of the curriculum. In TIMSS, there are many variables on teacher-reported instructional practices. Virtually all indicate how often teachers use certain instructional methods. Clearly, to use a method more or less does not necessarily tell us how well teachers use a particular method." (Pong, S., & Pallas, A. (2001). Class size and eighth-grade math achievement in the United States and abroad. *Educational Evaluation and Policy Analysis, 23*(3), p. 269)

"Another factor to consider in these analyses is the limitations created by other measures used in our studies. For example, reliabilities for the social desirability scale were lower than we would have liked." (Polan, S. A., & Aguilar, T. E. (2001). Measuring educator's beliefs about diversity in personal and professional context. *American Educational Research Journal, 38*(1), p. 175)

Reasonable Limitations. There is a tendency to be too strict in analyzing the limitations of research. If we are overly strict, the results of studies would be useful only in a few situations and to other individuals who are just like those in the study. It is better to use our best, reasonable, professional judgment. The situation may be somewhat different, as may be the measures or subjects, but the differences may not be great enough to affect the usefulness of the findings. For example, suppose you read a study that examines the effect of advance organizers on a lesson (advance organizers are broad conceptual frameworks to structure and organize the material). The study is conducted with a biology unit, using seventh-graders as subjects, and finds that students who use advance organizers show better learning and retention. Your class is sixth grade and you need to teach a social studies unit. Should you simply dismiss the implications of the study because your situation is not exactly the same? In a case like this the limitations of the study may suggest some caution in using advance organizers in your class, but overall there is sufficient overlap to conclude that what worked in the study would probably work for your social studies unit as well.

Recommendations and Implications

Toward the end of the discussion section you will usually find statements that suggest future research or practice as a result of the study. These statements are called *recommendations* and *implications*. In journals primarily intended for other researchers, the recommendations tend to be oriented toward changes in specific methods in the study, such as instruments, sampling, or procedures. Recommendations and implications in journals that consumers are likely to read tend to be related to practice. It is important for researchers to be specific in their recommendations and implications. It is inadequate for researchers to say, simply, "Further research is needed in this area." What is needed is an indication of what types of research are necessary.

Following are examples of recommendations and implications that have adequate specificity.

EXAMPLE | **Recommendations for Further Research**

"Our initial comparisons of the direct and indirect writing formats support the continued refinement and use of performance-based writing assessments for school accountability purposes. Further research should be directed at determining how student agility and background may interact with the content and format of the writing tests developed, the correspondence and divergence in cognitive domains that each format assesses, and the optimum number of content tasks in writing that might be needed to generalize about the overall performance." (Heck, R. H., & Cripslip, M. (2001). Direct and indirect writing assessments: Examining issues of equity and utility. *Educational Evaluation and Policy Analysis, 23*, p. 32)

"Future studies should consider the extent to which other aspects of language besides vocabulary can be increased (e.g., syntax, phonological processing). In addition, more work is needed to understand the factors that affect the degree to which Head Start teachers implement language-enhancing strategies in their classrooms." (Wasik, B. A., Bond, M. A., & Hindman, A. (2006). The effects of a language and literacy intervention on head start children and teachers. *Journal of Educational Psychology, 98*(1), pp. 72–73)

EXAMPLE | **Implications for Practice**

"Findings like these could suggest to teachers where their practices might inadvertently steer students towards some genres and not others. The findings can also inform teachers about what students may feel more familiar and comfortable with in their writing and therefore which genres offer more of a challenge for them. It would allow teachers to choose the examples of novel openings with gender representations in mind and plan discussion that considers this." (Murphy, P., & Ivinson, G. (2005). Gender, assessment and students' literacy learning: Implications for formative assessment. *Teacher Development, 9*(2), p. 198)

"This finding suggests the efficacy of reciprocal teaching as a viable method for Chapter 1 high school students. Furthermore, in this study, the self-monitoring intervention was effective in large groups, which shows reciprocal teaching as a more economically efficient form of intervention than demonstrated in previous studies." (Alfassi, M. (1998). Reading for meaning: The efficacy of reciprocal teaching in fostering reading comprehension in high school students in remedial reading class. *American Educational Research Journal, 35*(2), p. 322)

CONSUMER TIPS: *Criteria for Evaluating Discussion and Conclusion Sections*

1. **The results should be interpreted.** It is important that the researcher do more than repeat the major findings of the study. The discussion should include interpretations of the research problem, methodology, and previous research. It should include a detailed analysis of how imperfections in the design and extraneous variables may have affected the results and how the results are integrated with other literature on the topic. All major findings should be addressed in the discussion, including those that are unexpected, surprising, and conflicting. There should not be an analysis of every specific result, but important findings should not be ignored or overlooked.

2. **Conclusions should answer research problems.** Each problem or research question should be clearly answered by the conclusions. The answers should accurately reflect the results and interpretations of the data.

3. **Conclusions should be limited by subject characteristics and selection.** The discussion should include an analysis of how the characteristics of the subjects, such as age, gender, and socioeconomic status, limit the generalizability of the conclusions. Researchers should not overgeneralize either in terms of subject characteristics or by suggesting that what may be true for the group of subjects as a whole is true for individuals or subgroups.

4. **Conclusions should be limited by the nature of interventions and measures.** Researchers should indicate how specific aspects of interventions and measures should be considered in interpreting conclusions. They should point out, when appropriate, how different operational definitions of treatments and measures might lead to different conclusions.

5. **Statistical significance should not be confused with practical significance.** Researchers should not interpret statistically significant results to mean that they have practical value or importance. Statistical significance does not necessarily mean that the results will have important practical implications.

6. **Failure to show statistical significance does not necessarily mean that there is no relationship or difference.** Researchers need to be careful in interpreting results that fail to show statistical significance. Most studies do not provide an adequate test of whether the statistical insignificance reflects no relationship, nor whether weaknesses in the design account for the findings.

7. **Limitations of findings should be reasonable.** Researchers should find a middle ground between being overly strict or too confining and completely ignoring obviously important limitations. There are shortcomings to all research, but there is no need to dwell on every possible specific limitation. Important limitations should be mentioned even though the results support a hypothesis.

8. **Recommendations and implications should be specific.** Recommendations and implications for future research should be included in the discussion

and should specifically describe the changes in methodology that would be desirable in subsequent studies. Recommendations and implications for practice should be made only when the data and design support such inferences.

> **Author Reflection** *Now that you have read some research articles, have you noticed how many qualifiers are used to limit, restrict, or otherwise provide a basis for caution? While on the one hand it seems like such language simply allows the researchers to avoid stating in clear terms what was found, it also is very much needed to help consumers of research draw accurate conclusions so that possible influences on practice are not overgeneralized. In my experience, in fact, most authors do not give sufficient attention to limitations and often reach untenable conclusions. Also, when you write up a study you will find that the interpretation section is quite challenging because of the need to incorporate previous studies when explaining why the results were obtained. While there is a need for analysis of the results, in light of different kinds of limitations, it is also important to bring in other studies to shed light on the interpretations, conclusions, and implications and recommendations.*

STUDY QUESTIONS

1. What is the purpose of a discussion section in an article?
2. What are the major components of a discussion section?
3. Why is it important to relate findings to previous research?
4. What aspects of the methodology of a study may have implications in interpreting the results?
5. Give an example of a specific feature of the design of a study that would be important in interpretation.
6. What is the purpose of the conclusions?
7. What is the difference between limitations based on generalizing to other people and generalizing to individual subjects?
8. In what ways should conclusions be limited to the timing of the research and to the nature of treatments and measures?
9. What is wrong with recommending that "further studies need to be done"?
10. Is it a mistake to conclude that no statistical significance means that there is no relationship? Why?

 SAMPLE TEST QUESTIONS

See this text's Companion Website at **www.ablongman.com/mcmillan5e** for sample test questions and answers.

Chapter 14

The *Intelligent* Consumer: Putting It All Together

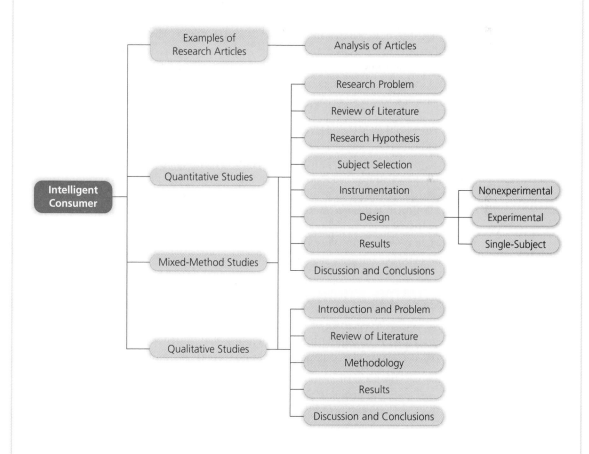

M y aim in this book has been to present and explain fundamental principles of educational research that you will be able to use in evaluating research. As a consumer of educational research, you need to be able to locate, read, critically analyze, and then use, when appropriate, the results of research to enhance teaching and learning. Throughout the book there has been an emphasis on how knowledge derived from research can enhance your role as a professional who will constantly make decisions and judgments.

Research on educational problems can provide information that will improve your judgments, but the quality of published research varies greatly. In fact, there is evidence that a substantial percentage of published studies have serious flaws. It is essential that you have the knowledge and skills to evaluate critically the research you read. A consumer of educational research may use the information provided in studies, but you must be an *intelligent* consumer. Intelligent consumers can make their own judgments about the credibility and usefulness of research. By being able to understand the researcher's intent, the type of design used, the deficiencies in sampling and measuring, the results, and the conclusions, the intelligent consumer can judge the quality and usefulness of the study.

Throughout the book key points for analyzing and evaluating different aspects of research reports have been summarized as Consumer Tips. In this chapter these tips are rephrased as questions that you will want to ask yourself when reading a study. The intent is to gather, in one place, the most important questions that should guide your evaluation. If you remember that every study will contain some deficiencies, the answers to these questions, when considered as a whole, will provide an overall impression of the credibility and usefulness of the findings. You may also find what could be called "fatal flaws." These deficiencies are so serious that they render the results useless.

Following the outlines of questions there are three complete research studies. Each article is critically analyzed on the book Website by answering the appropriate questions in these outlines.

QUESTIONS *for* QUANTITATIVE STUDIES

1.0 Research Problem
 1.1 Is the problem researchable?
 1.2 Is the problem significant? Will the results have practical or theoretical importance?
 1.3 Is the problem stated clearly and succinctly?
 1.4 Does the problem communicate whether the study is descriptive, experimental, or nonexperimental?
 1.5 Does the problem indicate the variables and population studied?

2.0 Review of the Literature
 2.1 Does the review of literature seem comprehensive? Are all important previous studies included?
 2.2 Are primary sources emphasized?

2.3 Is the review up to date?

2.4 Have studies been critically reviewed, and flaws noted, and have the results been summarized?

2.5 Does the review emphasize studies directly related to the problem?

2.6 Does the review explicitly relate previous studies to the problem?

2.7 If appropriate, does the review establish a basis for research hypotheses?

2.8 Does the review establish a theoretical framework for the significance of the study?

2.9 Is the review well organized?

3.0 Research Hypothesis

3.1 Is the hypothesis stated in declarative form?

3.2 Does the hypothesis follow from the literature?

3.3 Does the hypothesis state expected relationships or differences?

3.4 Is the hypothesis testable?

3.5 Is the hypothesis clear and concise?

4.0 Selection of Subjects

4.1 Are the subjects clearly described?

4.2 Is the population clearly defined?

4.3 Is the method of sampling clearly described?

4.4 Is probability sampling used? If so, is it proportional or disproportional?

4.5 What is the return rate in a survey study?

4.6 Are volunteers used?

4.7 Is there an adequate number of subjects?

5.0 Instrumentation

5.1 Is evidence for validity and reliability clearly stated and adequate? Is the instrument appropriate for the subjects?

5.2 Are the instruments clearly described? If an instrument is designed for a study by the researchers, is there a description of its development?

5.3 Are the procedures for gathering data clearly described?

5.4 Do the scores distort the reality of the findings?

5.5 Do response set or faking influence the results?

5.6 Are observers and interviewers adequately trained?

5.7 Are there observer or interviewer effects?

6.0 Design

6.1 Nonexperimental

6.1a If descriptive, are relationships inferred?

6.1b If comparative, are criteria for identifying different groups clear?

6.1c Are causal conclusions reached from correlational findings?

6.1d Is the correlation affected by restriction in the range and reliability of the instruments?

6.1e If causal-comparative, has the causal condition already occurred? How comparable are the subjects in the groups being compared?

  6.2 Experimental

    6.2a Is there direct manipulation of an independent variable?

    6.2b Is the design and procedure clearly described?

    6.2c What extraneous/confounding variables are not controlled in the design?

    6.2d Is each replication of the intervention independent of other replications? Is the number of subjects equal to the number of intervention replications?

  6.3 Single-Subject

    6.3a Is the measurement of the target behavior reliable?

    6.3b Is the target behavior clearly defined?

    6.3c Are there enough measures of the behavior to establish stability?

    6.3d Are procedures, subjects, and settings described in detail?

    6.3e Is there a single intervention?

    6.3f Are there experimenter or observer effects?

7.0 Results and Analysis

  7.1 Is there an appropriate descriptive statistical summary?

  7.2 Is statistical significance confused with practical significance?

  7.3 Is statistical significance confused with internal or external validity?

  7.4 Are appropriate statistical tests used?

  7.5 Are levels of significance interpreted correctly?

  7.6 How clearly are the results presented?

  7.7 Are data clearly and accurately presented in graphs and tables?

8.0 Discussion and Conclusions

  8.1 Is interpretation of the results separate from reporting of the results?

  8.2 Are the results discussed in relation to previous research, methodology, and the research problem?

  8.3 Do the conclusions follow from the interpretation of the results?

  8.4 Are the conclusions appropriately limited by the nature of the subjects, treatments, and measures?

  8.5 Is lack of statistical significance properly interpreted?

  8.6 Are the limitations of the findings reasonable?

  8.7 Are the recommendations and implications specific?

QUESTIONS *for* QUALITATIVE STUDIES

1.0 Introduction and Problem

  1.1 Are the researcher's background, interests, and potential biases clear from the outset?

  1.2 Does the researcher have the skill and training needed to conduct the study?

1.3 Is the problem feasible?

1.4 Is the problem significant?

1.5 Is there a clear conceptual and theoretical framework for the problem?

1.6 Does the introduction include an overview of the design of the study?

1.7 Is the purpose of the study clearly stated?

2.0 Review of the Literature

2.1 Is the review preliminary? Does it indicate that the researcher is knowledgeable about previous work in the area?

2.2 Is the review up to date?

2.3 Does the review establish an adequate background and theoretical framework for the study?

2.4 Is the review well organized?

2.5 Is the literature analyzed as well as summarized?

3.0 Methodology

3.1 Is the method of selecting participants clear?

3.2 Is the selection of participants biased?

3.3 Will the participants selected provide a credible answer to the research question?

3.4 How involved is the researcher in the setting? Will the researcher's involvement affect the findings?

3.5 Are data collectors trained?

3.6 Are multiple methods of data collection used?

4.0 Results and Analysis

4.1 Is there adequate detail in presenting results?

4.2 Are direct quotes from participants?

4.3 Is there adequate immersion in the field to develop a deep understanding of what is being studied?

4.4 Is there an analysis of triangulation?

4.5 Is there consideration of researcher bias or perspective in interpreting the results?

5.0 Discussion and Conclusions

5.1 Are descriptions clearly separate from interpretations and researchers' opinions?

5.2 Is the credibility of the findings addressed in terms of reliability, credibility, and trustworthiness?

5.3 Are the results discussed in relation to previous research?

5.4 Do the conclusions follow from the interpretation of the results? Are the conclusions consistent with what is known from previous research?

5.5 Are appropriate limitations indicated?

5.6 Are appropriate recommendations and implications indicated?

QUESTIONS *for* MIXED-METHOD STUDIES

1.0 Introduction and Problem
    1.1 Is the problem feasible and researchable?
    1.2 Is the problem significant? Will it have practical and/or theoretical importance?
    1.3 Is the problem stated clearly and succinctly?
    1.4 Are separate research questions asked for the quantitative and qualitative aspects of the study?
    1.5 Is it clear if the study is primarily quantitative or primarily qualitative?
    1.6 Does the quantitative research question indicate the variables, population, and logic of the design?
    1.7 If there is a research hypothesis, is it clear, concise, and testable? Does it follow from the literature?

2.0 Review of the Literature
    2.1 Is the review primarily preliminary or comprehensive?
    2.2 Are primary sources emphasized?
    2.3 Is the review up-to-date?
    2.4 Are studies analyzed as well as summarized, and related to the research questions?
    2.5 Does the review establish an adequate background and theoretical framework for the study?
    2.6 Is the review well organized?

3.0 Selection of Participants
    3.1 Is the selection of the participants clear?
    3.2 Are the participants well described?
    3.3 Is it likely that the participants will provide credible data?
    3.4 Are the participants likely to be biased?
    3.5 If sampling was used, what was the return rate? Is it adequate?

4.0 Instrumentation
    4.1 Is there adequate evidence of reliability and validity?
    4.2 Are instruments clearly described?
    4.3 Are procedures for data collection clearly described and adequate?
    4.4 Are interviewers and/or observers adequately trained?
    4.5 Is there likely to bias from participants, interviewers, and/or observers?
    4.6 Are multiple methods of data collection used?

5.0 Design
    5.1 Is the design explanatory, exploratory, or a triangulation?
    5.2 If nonexperimental quantitative, is the study descriptive, comparative, causal-comparative, ex post facto, or correlational?
    5.2 If experimental, is the intervention clearly described?

5.3 If experimental, are possible extraneous/confounding variables accounted for?

5.4 Is it clear how the researcher gained entry into the field and the role of the researcher in data collection?

5.5 Are there multiple settings and contexts from which data are gathered?

5.6 Is the design likely to provide credible information to answer the research questions?

6.0 Results

6.1 Are data clearly and adequately described, including the use of tables and figures?

6.2 Is there adequate discussion of practical significance? Is it distinguished from statistical significance?

6.3 Are field notes and interviewer notes adequately detailed?

6.4 Are verbatim transcriptions and quotations used?

6.5 Is there triangulation?

6.6 Are codes and categories adequately described?

6.7 Are results clearly separate from researcher opinion?

7.0 Discussion and Conclusions

7.1 Are the results discussed in terms of previous research, methodology, and research question?

7.2 Is the credibility of the results addressed in terms of reliability, internal validity, credibility, and trustworthiness?

7.3 Are there conclusions? Do they follow logically from the results and interpretation?

7.4 Are limitations to the findings indicated?

7.5 Are appropriate recommendations and limitations indicated?

EXAMPLES *of* RESEARCH ARTICLES

EXHIBIT 14.1   Investigating High School Students' Science Experiences and Mechanics Understanding

Katherine A. Phillips   Lloyd H. Barrow
University of Missouri–Columbia

ABSTRACT

This research study was designed to provide an introductory examination of how high school students' out-of-school science experiences, particularly those relevant to the physical sciences, relate to their learning of Newtonian mechanics. A factor analysis of the modified Science Experiences Survey ("SES," Mason & Kahle, 1988) was performed, leading to three factors: Learning Attributes Related to Science, Physical Science Experiences, Nature Experiences. The students' learning of Newtonian mechanics was measured by their gain score from a pre-instruction/post-instruction administration of the Force Concept Inventory (FCI; Hestenes, Wells, & Swackhamer, 1992). An analysis of variance showed that females and males in honors physics courses demonstrated

(continued)

EXHIBIT 14.1 (continued)

similar gain scores, while males in non-honors courses demonstrated larger gains ($p < 0.05$) than the females. When the students' total SES and SES factor scores were correlated with their FCI pretest and gain scores, the SES Physical Science Experience score was found to be significantly related to the FCI pretest score ($p = 0.0$). No other correlations were significant.

In attempts to assess the effectiveness of various methods of physics instruction in promoting student learning of mechanics, many researchers have used the Force Concept Inventory (FCI; Hestenes, Wells, & Swackhamer, 1992). The FCI has been administered primarily at the introductory college and university physics level (Hake, 1998; Morote & Pritchard, 2002; Royuk & Brooks, 2003; Van Domelen & Van Heuvelen, 2002; Willson, Ackerman, & Malave, 2000; Yamamoto, 1998), but has also been used to assess high school age students (Adams & Chiappetta, 1998; Hake, 1998; Jauhiainen, Koponen, & Lavonen, 2001; Savinainen & Scott, 2002) and preservice teachers (Grim, 1999).

The original developers of the FCI stated that "every student begins physics with a well-established system of common-sense beliefs about how the physical world works derived from years of personal experience" (Hestenes, et al., 1992, p. 141). Differences in the quality and quantity of personal experience, then, may impact the development of physics "common sense" and also the development of Newtonian mechanics beliefs.

Many researchers have documented the differences in everyday science experiences between female and male students. In examining the National Assessment of Educational Progress in science data from more than 25 years ago, Kahle and Lakes (1983) found that females ages 9, 13, and 17 reported significantly fewer hands-on experiences with physical science materials, such as magnets, mirrors, and electricity than did same age males. They further found that females ages 13 and 17 were far below the national averages for their respective ages when reporting how often they had performed electrical and mechanical fixing tasks. More 13- and 17-year-old females than males reported participating in activities attempting to diagnose unhealthy plants and animals. These researchers found similar results when studying the extracurricular science experiences of high school students in schools across the Midwest and South (Kahle, Matyas, & Cho, 1985). Similarly, Hanson (1996) reported data from the Longitudinal Study of American Youth from the late 1980s showing that seventh-grade boys are more likely to have talked to scientists and have science related equipment (e.g., telescopes) at home.

These out-of-school gender differences have persisted through time and over a generation. Tamir's (1990) study of high school students found that males participated in more physics and technology-related hobbies than did females. Ten years later, Jones, Howe, and Rua (2000) reported that female students in Grade 6 had more experiences with biological science related activities and males had more physical science related experiences.

In an effort to link outside experiences with science achievement, Tracy (1990) conducted a study with elementary school-aged students to determine if the toys the students played with were related to their science achievement scores. No significant relationships were found between playing with physical-science-related toys (e.g., rockets, chemistry sets) or moving target toys (e.g., ball-throwing) and overall science achievement for either females or males. In another study of elementary school-aged students, it was determined that males significantly outperformed females on science achievement items that covered material not taught in the students' classrooms (Zuzovsky, Chen, & Tamir, 1990). The researchers proposed that males' extracurricular activities were a contributing factor in their superior achievement scores.

In an interpretive study by Erickson and Farkas (1991), students were asked to identify their source of science knowledge based on their responses to a standardized science examination. Females relied on knowledge gained from school experiences, while males reported that their knowledge was derived from out-of-school experiences and a category of nonspecific responses the authors termed common knowledge. In explaining males' higher scores on the science achievement examination, Erickson and Farkas suggested that males' greater outside knowledge gives them an advantage on such tests.

A study of seventh-grade German students (Dresel, Zeigler, Broome, & Heller, 1998) determined that boys had a greater amount of prior knowledge in physics, but that experience-based prior knowledge, because it is often flawed, was not predictive of future physics achievement. The researchers asserted that self-related cognitions, instead of experience factors, were more likely the contributors to gender differences in physics achievement. However, Tamir (1990) found strong association between involvement in informal/nonformal science and intentions for further study and career aspirations, factors tied to self-related cognition. It is not so simple to disassociate the role of extracurricular physics experiences and the cognitions which they may help promote.

The present study was designed to provide an introductory examination of how high school students' out-of-school science experiences, particularly those relevant to the physical sciences, relate to their learning of Newtonian mechanics. Specifically, the following research questions were investigated:

1. When administered to high school students, can the Science Experiences Survey (SES; Mason & Kahle, 1988) be separated into distinct subscales, one of which measures physical science experiences?
2. Does gender and/or level of physics class enrollment (honors versus regular) affect Newtonian mechanics understanding as measured by the FCI?
3. How strong is the relationship between out-of-school science experience as measured by the SES, and Newtonian mechanics understanding, as measured by the FCI?

METHODOLOGY

Population and Setting

The site for this study was a midwestern high school with a total enrollment of just over 900 students. The data were collected from students enrolled in four physics classes, all taught by the same physics teacher, a male who had been teaching more than 20 years and who has served as a Physics Teaching Resource Agent of the American Association of Physics Teachers. The teacher has a doctor of philosophy degree in science education and regularly attends local and national professional society meetings.

The only prerequisite for physics enrollment at this school was completion of algebra and trigonometry courses. Students were allowed to choose either regular or honors physics courses. To register for the honors class, students self-selected based on their mathematics courses completed. Typically, students enrolled in advanced mathematics courses (e.g., pre-calculus) selected the honors class, and the remaining students selected the regular physics course. This school used A/B block scheduling, with each physics course meeting every other day for 100-minute periods.

A total of 59 students completed the data collection process. The honors group was composed of 16 females and 21 males, and the regular group was composed of 14 females and 8 males. All students were in the 11th or 12th grade of high school.

All classes were taught using the same learning cycle based methodology, with activities divided between exploration, development, and application lessons. Many of the activities were adopted from the PRISMS physics curriculum (University of Northern Iowa, 1997) and were supplemented with computer-based mechanics investigations. The curriculum of both the honors and regular physics courses was comprised primarily of mechanics topics, with the honors courses covering more in-depth topics, such as circular motion, gravitational forces, satellite motion, and rotational motion. The honors course also placed more emphasis on physics computations. Traditional written laboratory reports and grading procedures were employed.

Instruments

Force Concept Inventory. The FCI was used to assess the students' ideas about Newtonian mechanics. The FCI was developed from the Mechanics Diagnostic Test (MDT; Halloun & Hestenes, 1985), an instrument which

(continued)

EXHIBIT 14.1 (continued)

underwent extensive validity and reliability testing. Since approximately half of the questions on the FCI are the same as the MDT, the developers of the test stated that "formal procedures to [establish reliability and validity of the FCI] are unnecessary because the test designs are so similar" (Hestenes et al., 1992, p. 148). The test developers also conducted extensive interviews to verify student responses and other reliability-related investigations.

The FCI consists of 30 questions on the mechanics topics of kinematics, laws of motion, the superposition principle, and various kinds of force. Each question has five possible responses, with one representing the Newtonian belief and the others representing common alternative conceptions.

Science Experiences Survey. A modified version of the SES (Mason & Kahle, 1988) was administered to determine students' out-of-school science-related experiences. The SES was modified by Farenga and Joyce for use with elementary-age students (Farenga, 1995). The reliability coefficient for the modified version, using the Spearman-Brown split-half formula, was $r = .86$ (Joyce & Farenga, 1999). That version was then edited for use in this study to tailor the questions to the likely experiences of primarily rural high school students in the Midwest. For example, a question about the frequency of visiting the seashore was changed to the frequency of visiting a cave, mine, or rock quarry. The resultant 31-item SES was scored on a 1- to 4-point Likert scale (1 = never, 2 = seldom, 3 = fairly often, 4 = frequently). A student's total score was determined by summing the responses on the 31 items, for a scale range of 31 to 124.

Previous research using the SES has been aimed at relating elementary students' science experiences with science attitudes and future career choices (Joyce & Farenga, 1999). Greenfield (1997) expanded the use of the SES to measure elementary, middle, and high school students' extracurricular experiences.

Data Collection and Analysis

The SES and the FCI pretest were administered at the start of the school year to the students in honors physics (two classes) and regular physics (two classes). The instruments were given before any physics instruction had occurred. Students were given written consent forms and were allowed to decline to participate in the study with no negative repercussions. As a part of the consent process students were told that the data was being collected for a study that would help determine how science students could benefit from enrolling in physics courses. Students were given part of one class period to complete the SES. The FCI was administered during another class period. The FCI was scored by the physics teacher.

The curricular emphasis in all of the classes for the first three academic quarters was mechanics, and the FCI posttest was administered at the end of the study of mechanics in each class. The FCI was not used as a part of the students' course grades.

The FCI gain score was computed by using the following method:

Gain = (Posttest Score-Pretest Score)/(100-Pretest Score) This method of computing individual gain scores is recommend by Hestenes and Halloun (1995) for a pre/post administration of the FCI.

A principal component analysis of the items on the SES was performed using Varimax rotation. Three components (factors) were extracted, explaining a total of 34% of the variance of the scores. Items having factor loadings of greater than 0.4 were included in each factor. The three factors correspond to items on the SES relating to general Learning Attributes Related to Science, Physical Science Experiences, and Nature Experiences.

Results

Table 1 contains the FCI pretest, posttest, and gain scores for the students by gender and class level. Table 2 contains the results of the factor analysis of the SES. In order to determine if there were any differences in learning of the Newtonian mechanics concepts (as measured by the FCI) between groups in this study, an analysis of variance was performed on the gain scores. Table 3 shows the results. There was a significant interaction effect of gender by class type, with $F = 6.18$ $p = 0.02$) and [eta] = 0.1. This effect size is below the average effect size of 0.31 reported by Lipsey and Wilson (1993) for effects on achievement in science and mathematics instruction. The male students in the regular classes had significantly higher ($p < 0.05$) gain scores than did the females in the regular classes. The females and males in the honors classes did not have significantly different gain scores (female, $M = 0.58$, $SD = 0.20$; male, $M = 0.57$, $SD = 0.18$).

TABLE 1 Mean FCI Scores by Gender and Class Type

Class Type	N	FCI Pretest		FCI Posttest		Gain	
		M	*SD*	*M*	*SD*	*M*	*SD*
Female							
Regular	14	7.1	3.4	17.7	2.6	0.45	0.13
Honors	16	5.7	2.2	19.7	5.2	0.58	0.20
All	30	6.3	2.8	18.8	4.2	0.52	0.18
Male							
Regular	8	8.5	2.9	23.6	3.4	0.69	0.19
Honors	21	9.0	4.0	20.9	4.2	0.57	0.18
All	29	8.9	3.7	21.6	4.1	0.61	0.18
All							
Regular	22	7.6	3.2	19.9	4.1	0.54	0.19
Honors	37	7.6	3.7	20.4	4.6	0.58	0.18
All Students	59	7.6	3.5	20.2	4.4	0.56	0.18

TABLE 2 Factor Analysis of Items on the Science Experiences Scale

Scale Item	Factor Loading
Factor 1: Learning Attributes Related to Science	
Talked about science topocs with friends	0.84
Listened to science/medical reports on news	0.76
Read science articles in newspapers	0.64
Worked with science-related hobbies	0.61
Read science articles in magazines	0.57
Read books about science/scientists	0.51
Viewed a solar or lunar eclipse	0.43
Factor 2: Physical Science Experiences	
Helped someone work on a car	0.82
Fixed something mechanical	0.82
Taken something apart to see how it works	0.75
Fixed something electrical	0.75
Made model rockets, cars or airplanes	0.41
Factor 3: Nature Experiences	
Visited a national park/preserve or wildlife refuge	0.75
Played with objects found in nature	0.73
Visited a cave, mine or rock quarry	0.63
Found a fossil	0.58
Read books about science/scientists	0.51
Visited a nature center or science center	0.42

(continued)

EXHIBIT 14.1   (continued)

TABLE 3 Analysis of Variance of Gain Scores

	df	Sum of Squares	Mean Square	F	Effect Size
Gender	1	0.17	0.17	5.4*	[eta] = .09
Class Type	1	0.001	0.001	0.03	
Gender x Class Type	1	0.19	0.19	6.2*	[eta] = .1
Within-group Error	55	1.7	0.03		

*$p < .05$

The SES total score and the three factor scores were compared to the FCI pretest scores and the gain score for all students and for females and males separately. The correlations between the scores for all students in the study are shown in Table 4. As expected, the SES Total score and the individual subscales are highly correlated ($p = 0.01$) with each other. The only other significant ($p = 0.01$) correlation is between the SES Physical Science score and the FCI pretest score for all students. When disaggregated by gender group, none of the correlations were significant; it is interesting to note, however, that all correlations between the SES and the FCI pretest and gain for females were negative.

TABLE 4 Correlation Between Subscales of the SES and the FCI Pretest Score Gain

	SES Total	SES Learning Attributes (LA)	SES Physical Science (PS)
SES Total	—	.83**	.75**
SES LA		—	.48**
SES PS			—
SES N			
FCI Pretest			
Gain			

	SES Nature (N)	FCI Pretest	Gain
SES Total	.81**	.17	−.12
SES LA	.61**	.17	.04
SES PS	.45**	.34**	.04
SES N	—	.00	−.15
FCI Pretest		—	.07
Gain			—

**$p = 0.01$

DISCUSSION

The first research question was answered in the affirmative: The SES can be separated into subscales, one of which measures physical science experiences. The results of the factor analysis of the SES were similar to those found by Farenga and Joyce (1997). They termed their factors Life Science-Related Experience, Physical Science-Related Experience, and General Learning Attributes Related to Science. Of particular importance to this study was the similarity of the items that loaded onto Farenga and Joyce's Physical Science-Related Experience factor and the Physical Science Experiences factor in this study. The items were identical, with the exception of two additional items that were included in Farenga and Joyce's factor, but did not load onto the Physical Science Experiences factor in this study: (a) performed a chemical experiment and (b) used Lego equipment. In this study, the chemical experiment question had a loading value of 0.36, just below the 0.4 level for inclusion in the factor. The Lego question is likely more applicable to the elementary students in Farenga and Joyce's study; it may be that even those high school students who scored highly on the other physical science-related items did not consider their Lego experiences recent enough to indicate a high frequency of participation. With the modifications for age and geography, the authors believe that the SES is a useful tool for studying out-of-school science experiences with secondary students.

In answer to the second research question, the analysis of variance for the FCI gain scores showed a significant effect for gender, depending on the class enrolled ($F = 6.18$, $p = 0.02$, [eta] $= 0.1$). Females and males in the honors courses showed essentially equal gain scores over the course of the study. Males in the regular physics classes, however, earned significantly higher ($p < 0.05$) gain scores than did females in the regular classes. Hakenes (1998) defined high gain scores to be greater than 0.7 and low gain scores to be less than 0.3. In his study, traditional physics instruction resulted in gains of 0.23 and interactive engagement instruction in gains of 0.48. All subgroups in this study demonstrated midrange gains, with the males in the regular physics classes at the upper end of that range with $g = 0.69$. The overall gain of 0.56 is similar to the gain of 0.57 found by Savinainen and Scott (2002) in their study of 16-year-old Finnish students.

It is interesting to note the dissimilar FCI gain scores for females and males in the regular physics courses. In the honors physics courses, females achieved gain scores of 0.58 and males achieved scores of 0.57. Similar gains such as these might be expected among students enrolled in the same course. However, females in the regular classes achieved gains of only 0.45, while the males achieved scores of 0.69. These students, too, were enrolled in the same courses, but clearly different learning patterns occurred. The unexplained disparate pattern of achievement mirrors that found by Dresel, et al. (1998), who found that neither prior knowledge in physics, nor inherent mental talent could explain higher physics course grades for males.

In addressing the third research question, the correlation data indicate that there is a significant positive correlation ($r = .34$, $p = 0.01$) between a student's score on the SES Physical Science subscale and score on the FCI pretest. When those data are analyzed by gender, however, no significant correlation emerges for either group in this study, likely due to low sample sizes. This finding differs from that of Tracy (1990), who found that physical science related play was not significantly related to science achievement. However, Tracy was measuring a general science achievement score, not one as specific as the FCI.

The significant correlation value seems to indicate that the more out-of-school experiences related to physical sciences a student has had, the higher that student will score on the FCI before formal instruction. Findings from the disaggregated data indicate that this assertion holds true only for the males in this study. The female scores had a weak correlation in the opposite direction; the more out-of-school experiences related to physical science, or all sciences, the lower a female student will score on the FCI before formal instruction (for SES Total $r = -.20$; for SES Physical Science, $r = -.07$) and the lower her gain score will be after instruction (for SES Total $r = -.32$; for SES Physical Science, $r = -.32$). It would not be particularly surprising to discover that out-of-school experiences lead students to develop non-Newtonian concepts in physics (see Dresel et al., 1998); however, further research is needed to determine why this might be the case for females and not males. A partial answer may lie in the findings of Erickson and Farkas (1991) that females rely more heavily on in-school science knowledge to answer achievement test items than do males.

(continued)

EXHIBIT 14.1 **(continued)**

Recommendations for Further Study

The correlation results presented lead to many questions for further investigation. Are there differences in the quality of out-of-school physical science experiences that would lead to positive correlations with FCI scores for males and negative correlations for females? What aspects of these experiences might promote or inhibit further incorporation of Newtonian mechanics concepts that differ by gender? Perhaps a more focused, **mixed-method study** of the out-of-school experiences of female students exhibiting high FCI gain scores would illuminate the findings from this study. Conducting interviews with the students to determine their solution strategies and knowledge basis for their solution methods could lead to further explanation.

A theoretical model of the relationship between gender and science in schools (Kahle, Parker, Rennie, & Riley, 1993) suggested that previous science experiences affect observable student outcomes such as achievement scores through mediating factors like the perception of the relevance of science, student confidence, and student interest in science. Including data measuring these mediating factors would be a useful addition to the examination of this complicated relationship.

To further investigate the gender differences in FCI gain scores found in the study, it would be instructive to analyze the data by individual FCI item. Such an analysis would give insight into patterns of learning and continued misunderstanding of Newtonian concepts. Further, since students' prior belief systems are based on contextual experiences, the scores of items based on similar contexts (e.g., playing hockey) could be compared to the scores of an instrument that assesses experiences in those contexts. A study such as the building on the assessment context research of Rennie and Parker (1996, 1998), could help determine the context dependency of physics beliefs and ways context might interact with the development of Newtonian understanding.

Author Note: Correspondence concerning this article should be addressed Katherine A. Phillips, Science Education Consultant, 3728 Morningside Dr., Fairfax, VA 22031.

Electronic mail may be sent via Internet to kathyphysics@cox.net.

REFERENCES

Adams, A. D., & Chiappetta, E. L. (1998, April). Students' beliefs, attitudes, and conceptual change in a traditional high school physics classroom. Paper presented at the annual meeting of the American Educational Research Association, San Diego, CA.

Dresel, M., Ziegler, A., Broome, P., & Heller, K. A. (1998). Gender differences in science education: The double-edged role of prior knowledge in physics. *Roeper Review, 21*(2), 101–06.

Erickson, G., & Farkas, S. (1991). Prior experience and gender differences in science achievement. *The Alberta Journal of Educational Research, 37*(3), 225–39.

Farenga, S. J. (1995). Out-of-school science-related experiences, science attitudes, and selection of science mini-courses in high ability, upper elementary students (Doctoral dissertation, Columbia University Teachers College, 1995). *Dissertation Abstracts International, 56,* A1242.

Farenga, S. J., & Joyce, Beverly A. (1997). What children bring to the classroom: Learning science from experience. *School Science and Mathematics, 97*(5), 248–52.

Greenfield, T. A. (1997). Gender- and grade-level differences in science interest and participation. *Science Education, 81,* 259–76.

Grim, N. C. (1999). A force concept correlation study with instructional methods, anxiety, perceptions of difficulty and student background variables. Chicago, IL: Chicago State University. (ERIC Document Reproduction Service No. ED 438 164)

Hake, R. R. (1998). Interactive-engagement vs. traditional methods: A six-thousand-student survey of mechanics test data for introductory physics courses. Bloomington, IN: Indiana University. (ERIC Document Reproduction Service No. ED 441 679)

Halloun, I., & Hestenes, D. (1985). The initial knowledge state of college physics students. *American Journal of Physics, 553,* 1043–55.

Hanson, S. L. (1996). Lost talent: Women in the sciences. Philadelphia: Temple University Press.

Hestenes, D. H., & Halloun, I. (1995). Interpreting the Force Concept Inventory: A response to March 1995 critique by Huffman and Heller. *Physics Teacher, 33*(8), 502, 504–06.

Hestenes, D., Wells, M., & Swackhamer, G. (1992). Force concept inventory. *Physics Teacher, 30*(3), 141–58.

Jauhiainen, J., Koponen, I. T., & Lavonen, J. (2001). The Force Concept Inventory in diagnosing the conceptual understanding of Newtonian mechanics in Finnish upper secondary schools. In M. Ahtee, O. Bjorkqvist, E. Pehkonen, & V. Vatanen (Eds.), *Research on mathematics and science education: From beliefs to cognition, from problem solving to understanding* (pp. 101–14). Jyvaskyla, Finland: Institute for Educational Research.

Jones, M. G., Howe, A., & Rua, M. J. (2000). Gender differences in student experiences, interests, and attitudes toward science and scientists. *Science Education, 84*(2), 180–92.

Joyce, B. A., & Farenga, S. J. (1999). Informal science experience, attitudes, future interest in science, and gender of high-ability students: An exploratory study. *School Science and Mathematics, 99*(8), 431–7.

Kahle, J. B., & Lakes, M. K. (1983). The myth of equality in science classrooms. *Journal of Research in Science Teaching, 20*(2), 131–40.

Kahle, J. B., Matyas, M. L., & Cho, H.-H. (1985). An assessment of the impact of science experiences on the career choices of male and female biology students. *Journal of Research in Science Teaching, 22*(5), 385–94.

Kahle, J. B., Parker, L. H., Rennie, L. J., & Riley, D. (1993). Gender differences in science education: Building a model. *Educational Psychology, 28*(4), 379–404.

Lipsey, M. W., & Wilson, D. B. (1993). The efficacy of psychological, educational, and behavioral treatment: Confirmation from meta-analysis. *American Psychologist, 48*(12), 1181–1209.

Mason, C. L., & Kahle, J. B. (1988). Student attitudes toward science and science-related careers: A program designed to promote a stimulating gender-free learning environment. *Journal of Research in Science Teaching, 26*(1), 25–39.

Morote, E. S., & Pritchard, D. E. (2002, April). What course elements correlate with improvement on tests in introductory Newtonian mechanics? Paper presented at the annual meeting of the National Association for Research in Science Teaching, New Orleans, LA.

Rennie, L. J., & Parker, L. H. (1996). Placing physics problems in real-life context: Students' reactions and performance. *Australian Science Teachers Journal, 42*(1), 55–9.

Rennie, L. J., & Parker, L. H. (1998). Equitable measurement of achievement in physics: High school students' responses to assessment tasks in different formats and contexts. *Journal of Women and Minorities in Science and Engineering, 4,* 113–27.

Royuk, B., & Brooks, D. W. (2003). Cookbook procedures in MBL physics exercises. *Journal of Science Education and Technology, 12*(3), 317–24.

Savinainen, A., & Scott, P. (2002). Using the Force Concept Inventory to monitor student learning and to plan teaching. *Physics Education, 37*(1), 53–8.

Tamir, P. (1990). Factors associated with the relationship between formal, informal, and nonformal science learning. *Journal of Environmental Education, 22*(2), 34–42.

Tracy, D. M. (1990). Toy-playing behavior, sex-role orientation, spatial ability, and science achievement. *Journal of Research in Science Teaching, 27*(7), 637–49.

University of Northern Iowa. (1997). PRISMS: Physics resources and instructional strategies for motivating students [online]. Available at http://www.prisms.uni.edu

Van Domelen, D. J., & Van Heuvelen, A. (2002). The effects of a concept-construction lab course on FCI performance. *American Journal of Physics, 70*(7), 779–80.

(continued)

EXHIBIT 14.1 (continued)

Willson, V. L., Ackerman, C., & Malave, C. (2000). Cross-time attitudes, concept formation, and achievement in college freshman physics. *Journal of Research in Science Teaching, 37*(10), 1112–20.

Yamamoto, T. (1998). A comparison of the quality of integrated freshman-year curriculum for science, engineering and mathematics with a conventional curriculum. Terre Haute, IN: Rose-Hulman Institute of Technology. (ERIC Document Reproduction Service No. ED 436 359)

Zuzovsky, R., Chen, D., & Tamir, P. (1990). Science knowledge acquired within and outside the school. *Studies in Educational Evaluation, 16,* 399–420.

EXHIBIT 14.2 How Elementary School Counselors Can Meet the Needs of Students with Disabilities

Helen Nicole Frye

ABSTRACT

This article presents the results of an ethnographic study that examined how three elementary school counselors meet the personal/social needs of students with disabilities. For this study, the term "students with disabilities" included any student with a disability who was receiving special education services in each counselor's school. Counselor strategies, reliance on theories, and use of the ASCA National Model[R] are explored. Critical themes to emerge out of this study included the influence of the ASCA National Model, advocacy, the variety of counseling strategies, collaboration and teaming, and leadership. Implications for school counselors are presented.

In 1993, the American School Counselor Association (ASCA) issued position statements on school counselor involvement with students with disabilities and suggested the following school counselor roles in working with students with disabilities: (a) advocacy, (b) transition planning, (c) behavior modification, (d) counseling parents, (e) making referrals to specialists, (f) improving self-esteem, (g) working as part of the school multidisciplinary team, (h) teaching social skills, and (i) serving as consultants to parents and school staff (ASCA, 1993). The most recent education and counseling reform movements—No Child Left Behind (U.S. Department of Education, 2002), the ASCA National Standards (ASCA, 2003), and the ASCA National Model (ASCA, 2003)—have further increased the focus of meeting the needs of all students, including students with disabilities (ASCA, 1993, 2003; Baumberger & Harper, 1999; Milsom, 2002; U.S. Department of Education). These new national standards call for school counselors to "change their emphasis from service-centered for some of the students, to program-centered for every student" (ASCA, 2003, p. 18).

School counselors do not have much training in working with students with disabilities, despite the fact that reform movements call for increasing their involvement with these students (Astigarra & McEachern, 2000; Deck, Scarborough, Sferrazza, & Estill, 1999; Helms & Katsiyannis, 1992; Milsom, 2002). With pressure to change their role in schools to ensure that all students' needs are being met, school counselors will quickly need to focus their efforts on changing the services they provide to all students, including those with disabilities, and to provide evidence and data to support that their school counseling activities are effective.

PERSONAL/SOCIAL DEVELOPMENT

Many young children with disabilities have unique personal/social needs in addition to academic issues related to their disability. Current research suggests a number of personal/social difficulties that come with a diagnosis of a physical disability, emotional disorder, or learning disability. Some of these issues include higher levels of stress and anxiety (Margalit, 1992), poor social skills (Okolo & Sitlington, 1986; Voeller, 1993), and learned helplessness and low self-esteem (Barton & Fuhrmann, 1994; Bender & Wall, 1994; Bowen & Glenn, 1998; Glenn & Smith, 1998). Students with disabilities often have negative school experiences (Kottman, Robert, & Baker, 1995), maintain an external locus of control (Bender & Wall; Omizo & Omizo, 1994; Tabassam & Grainger, 2002), and demonstrate ineffective anger management strategies (Baker, 2000; Garcia, Krankowski, & Jones, 1998).

There is also an increased risk of suffering from depression, conduct disorders, and substance abuse, related to a diagnosis of a disability (Brumback & Weinberg, 1990; Larson, 1998; Rodis, Garrod, & Boscardin, 2001; Spreen, 1988). It now appears that students with disabilities develop low self-concepts in more areas than just academics alone (Kloomok & Cosden, 1994). Kish (1991) maintained that students with disabilities become more handicapped by their lack of personal/social skills than by their academic skill deficits, and research indicates that strong personal/social skills are necessary for future success as an adult and that these skills can be learned (Schumaker, 1992).

PURPOSE OF THE STUDY

This study examined how three elementary school counselors meet the personal/social needs of students with disabilities, through the use of the ethnographic interview method of qualitative inquiry (Spradley, 1979). Qualitative methodology was chosen to obtain an in-depth account of the experience of elementary school counselors working with students with disabilities. The following questions were the main focus of this study: (a) Are these three professional school counselors using the ASCA National Model to guide them in their work with students with disabilities? (b) What strategies do these three professional school counselors use in their work with students with disabilities and how are they implemented? (c) What theories guide these three professional school counselors in their work with students with disabilities? And, (d) how do these three professional school counselors make a difference in the lives of students with disabilities? These four subquestions help to answer the main research question of the study, "How do these three professional school counselors meet the personal/social needs of students with disabilities?"

METHODS

Participants

The three school counselor participants all worked in a large metropolitan school system on the East Coast of the United States. There were two female participants who described themselves as Caucasian and one male who described himself as African American. Each of the school counselors had been a school counselor for at least 4 years and only one counselor had worked in the field of education before becoming a school counselor. Each of the school counselors held a master's degree and one was enrolled part-time in a doctoral program. All of the school counselors had a minimum of 440 students on their caseload, which included students with a variety of disabilities. None of their students was diagnosed with traumatic brain injury and that was the only disability qualifying for special education that was not represented among their students.

Procedure

Because of the newness of the ASCA National Model, it was important to choose a school system where school counselors had already received some training in using it as a guide. The three school counselor participants were chosen by reputational case selection through a joint decision between two of their county supervisors of guidance. Patton (1990) has described this type of sampling as sampling extreme or deviant cases to shed

(continued)

EXHIBIT 14.2 (continued)

light on an issue, and Merriam (1998) has described this as the best approach to use when the sample is of interest because it is so unique or different. The supervisors had been informed of the purpose of the study and chose these school counselors because they felt they were actively involved in meeting the needs of students with disabilities, they were fully licensed school counselors, and they had received ASCA National Model training, thus meeting the criteria for involvement in the study. Dunn, Wood, and Baker (2002) indicated that not all school counselors actively work with students with disabilities, so it was very important for this study to examine school counselors who actively worked with students with disabilities.

The ethnographic interview method was employed over a 12-week period at the start of the school year and focused on gathering information from each school counselor through the use of an open-ended survey with vignette, three in-depth interviews, and journals that allowed the school counselor to reflect upon and provide important, relevant examples of issues (Spradley, 1979). This procedure allowed the collection of rich data to gain an understanding of how school counselors meet the personal/social needs of students with disabilities and how they view their involvement with these students. Survey and interview questions were developed after a literature review as a multistep process and originally piloted with school counselors working in another school system before this study took place. Following the pilot study, an additional literature review was conducted; at this time, questions regarding the ASCA National Model were incorporated into the interviews and survey.

Data Measures

The school counselor survey was conducted along with the first interview in September at the start of the school year. The survey included demographic information from the school counselors along with information regarding their training and counseling activities and required a response to a vignette that focused on how they would work with a student diagnosed with Asperger syndrome (considered a higher-functioning form of autism) who was having difficulty at school.

Interviews were held during the 1st, 6th, and 12th week of the 12-week study. They were recorded and transcribed verbatim, which allowed for documentation and reflection upon the school counselor's native language (using the exact terminology that the school counselors used to describe their experience) (Spradley, 1979). Multiple reviews of the tapes ensured that transcripts were correct. School counselors were encouraged to provide a "full and accurate report that gave detailed, concrete material, rather than generalizations" (Weiss, 1994, p. 212). They were reminded of the purpose of the study before each interview and were given final copies of the product, per Spradley's recommendations for ethnographic interviewing. A definition of a "student with a disability" and a copy of the Executive Summary of the ASCA National Model were given to the school counselors to assist in answering questions and to ensure that all involved in the study would share a common understanding of terms discussed.

Following Spradley's (1979) research recommendations, the interviews asked descriptive, structural, and contrast questions to discover the cultural themes and native language (counseling terminology, such as using the term "personal/social skills" versus "social-emotional skills") that the school counselors used. Spradley has provided a "Taxonomy of Ethnographic Questions" (p. 223), which was used to develop the interview questions throughout the research process. An example of descriptive questions from the interview was, "Can you tell me about the last time you worked with a student with a disability? What kind of issues did they present? Describe for me what the counseling process looked like?" The following structural question was asked in one interview: "What words would school counselors use to describe these students?" Contrast questions were the last type of question and an example from the interview was, "Special educators often try to meet the personal/social needs of students with disabilities by giving them work from a social skills training program. How do school counselors meet the personal/social needs of students with disabilities?"

The counselors' journals provided additional data during the weeks that there were no interviews and they provided a way to triangulate the data that school counselors described in the survey and interviews. Writing down their thoughts and experiences during the weeks they were not interviewed assisted the school counselors in recalling counseling activities for upcoming interviews, and this reflection helped to provide more in-depth answers to interview questions (LeCompte & Pressle, 1993). The school counselors recorded their work with students with disabilities in journals each week; the journal was an opportunity to document their work and reflect upon their effectiveness and was an outlet for discussing frustrations and expectations as well as brainstorming new ideas.

Data Analysis and Interpretation

Each of the interviews was transcribed, coded, and then merged using a qualitative data analysis software program, NVivo (QSR International, 2003), which assisted with the development of themes and categories. The comparison and analysis of survey, interview, and journal data was ongoing to identify themes and patterns and to create additional questions per Spradley's (1979) guidelines for ethnographic inquiry, and coding matrices were developed and refined through ongoing interaction with the data. The constant comparative method of data analysis (Glaser & Strauss, 1967) was used in this study to review all data sources and to systematically code examples into as many categories as possible.

Through ongoing interaction with the data, additional categories were developed and defined. Developing codes were analyzed to determine how the data relate to one another. The analysis of information was "issue focused," to describe what has been learned from all of the respondents about people in their situation and to achieve both local and inclusive integration (Weiss, 1994, p. 153). Categorical examples and non-examples also were analyzed and interpreted, and the researcher checked for alternative explanations and negative evidence and compared the results with existing theory. The researcher also shared the results with the school counselors in the study and with experts in the field. These methods enabled the researcher to effectively deal with the major validity threats to the study, which included bias in the selection of counselors and self-report bias.

RESULTS

As found in prior research, these school counselors all described personal/social difficulties in their students with disabilities that included difficulties with social skills (Okolo & Sitlington, 1986: Voeller, 1993), behavior (Bender & Wall, 1994; Garcia et al., 1998; Omizo, Cubberly, & Longano, 1984; Tabassam & Grainger, 2002), and low self-esteem (Barton & Fuhrmann, 1994; Bender & Wall, 1994; Bowen & Glenn, 1998; Glenn & Smith, 1998). The school counselors in this study found similar difficulties in their students in the areas of high stress and anxiety levels and ineffective anger management skills (Garcia et al., 1998; Margalit, 1992). School counselors observed how the deficits these students had in social skills resulted in rejection from their peers and less involvement in social activities (Gresham, 1992; LaGreca & Vaughn, 1992; Schumaker, 1992; Swanson & Malone, 1992; Tabassam & Grainger, 2002; Vaughn & Hager, 1994).

Previous research indicated that there was great variation in whether students with disabilities received counseling services (Deck et al., 1999; Helms & Katsiyannis, 1992) or whether school counselors had time to focus on the personal/social difficulties of students with disabilities (Dunn et al., 2002). However, the school counselors in this study considered students with disabilities "on their caseload" and actively sought out ways that these students could participate in counseling activities that would be helpful to them. Unlike Grigsby's (1990) evaluation of school counselors as having limited involvement and desire to work with students with disabilities, these school counselors felt they were important in meeting the personal/social needs of students with disabilities. The school counselors in this study did not defer the responsibility of meeting the personal/social needs of students with disabilities to other school personnel, as has been indicated by previous research studies (Deck et al.; Glenn, 1998).

(continued)

EXHIBIT 14.2 (continued)

Influence of the ASCA National Model

In the review of the data obtained from this study, several themes related to the ASCA National Model emerged (ASCA, 2003). Findings revealed that school counselors felt they were doing many of the things suggested by the ASCA National Model and were encouraging other school counselors to utilize the model. Themes that emerged from this study included the influence of the ASCA National Model, advocacy, the variety of counseling strategies, collaboration and teaming, and leadership. While this study examined school counselors' work toward meeting the personal/social needs of students with disabilities, it was apparent that the three school counselors were focusing on activities that supported all three domains suggested by the Foundation portion of the ASCA National Model (ASCA, 2003, pp. 27–37). School counselors were using collaboration with other school staff to meet students' personal/social needs. They reflected on their efforts in working with students with disabilities to constantly monitor what was working, and they also were trying to find the best ways to collect and use data to monitor students' progress.

Under the Delivery System component of the ASCA National Model, school counselors were teaching the guidance curriculum, planning individually with and for students, providing responsive services, and using consultation and collaboration with others (ASCA, 2003, pp. 3944). The Management System portion of the ASCA National Model was used by the school counselors as they were monitoring student progress and using data to support action plans (ASCA, 2003, pp. 45–58). The school counselors felt they were being held more accountable for their work with students and they used data to demonstrate their success, although each one had his or her own way of documenting successes. They also had a few suggestions on ways to use data to demonstrate progress. Some of the ways they demonstrated success were using journals to record their work, gaining pre- and post-measures of skills, having students complete self-report measures, and using parent and/or teacher feedback forms.

The county school system currently is reviewing the Accountability portion of the ASCA National Model (ASCA, 2003, pp. 59–66). The school counselors have been collecting their own information, knowing that they are held more accountable than they were in the past, to demonstrate to their county supervisors the work they are doing with students. At this point, however, the school system has not told counselors what to collect and they are just collecting data on their own. The school counselors feel that they are holding themselves more accountable to all of their students, and their conscious effort to meet the needs of students with disabilities is more a result of holding themselves accountable than of having a supervisor tell them they are accountable.

These particular counselors have been collecting data to measure their own effectiveness. They felt that the biggest areas of change since the ASCA National Model have involved measuring effectiveness and collecting data. One of the counselors described the model as an "extra focus on what they are already doing." The counselor further explained that they already used data to demonstrate that their activities were effective, instead of using data solely to demonstrate how often they did a particular counseling activity. Now they would be sharing their data with their supervisors instead of using it for their own self-reflection. They felt they were prepared to demonstrate their effectiveness to others because they were already measuring it for themselves through their self-evaluations, counselor checklists, observations, and parent/teacher checklists or interviews.

After the data were examined, it was apparent that school counselors were beginning to feel the influence of the ASCA National Model in their work with students with disabilities. While many of the different aspects of the ASCA National Model have not taken full effect in their school system (e.g., a change in the evaluation of school counselors, the management system, and a mandated school system-level collection of specific data), the school counselors seemed to agree that there is an increased demand for demonstrating effectiveness and using data and that they are held more accountable for their work with all students than they were in the past.

Advocacy

The next theme that emerged from the study was advocacy. Advocacy is one of the ASCA National Model's main themes and the use of advocacy was indicated as a strategy that counselors employ to meet the personal/social needs of their students with disabilities. Advocacy was demonstrated when the school counselors focused on looking at the individual needs of students with disabilities and used individual planning to create personal goals to meet their needs. Therefore, school counselors viewed students with disabilities as individuals and as part of the larger school group. Advocacy also was demonstrated when counselors made sure to include students with disabilities in all of their counseling program activities, not just ones they created for groups of students with disabilities. Counselors also made certain that students with disabilities were included in school-wide activities, not just those activities that were counselor created.

Counselors were proactive in that they were very cognizant of the unique personal/social needs of these students and they watched out for areas of concern. They sought out ways they could collaborate with other professionals to increase their own training to better work with these students and they actively found additional school staff and professionals to assist them in meeting the needs of their students with disabilities. These counselors reinforced the belief that it was their job to meet the personal/social needs of students with disabilities and they encouraged other school counselors to focus on meeting the personal/social needs of their students with disabilities.

Variety of Counseling Strategies

All data sources provided examples of counseling strategies that the three school counselors used to meet the personal/social needs of students with disabilities. These strategies included (a) individual planning and individual counseling; (b) goal setting for students; (c) actively making sure students with disabilities are included in activities; (d) refusing to accept the "duplication of services" idea (the idea that students with disabilities already get help from special education, so they are not on a counselor's caseload); (e) modifying classroom guidance lessons; (f) developing behavior management plans; (g) providing specific skills training (e.g., social skills, behavior management, anger management); (h) collaborative counseling; (i) counseling with art, books, and play; (j) counseling with social stories; (k) leading groups (e.g., social skills, anger management, coping with divorce, lunch bunches for friendship); (l) developing connections with students; (m) doing active collaboration; (n) training parents and teachers; and (o) participating in Independent Evaluation Plan meetings.

While the school counselors seemed to have an eclectic approach to choosing strategies for working with students with disabilities, each of the three counselors provided examples in which they (a) served as an advocate, (b) provided training, (c) collaborated, (d) used group counseling, and (e) communicated with others. Each of the school counselors indicated that he or she worked with students with disabilities every week through classroom guidance, group counseling, or individual counseling when necessary. It is important to note that none of these counseling strategies or activities was specifically designed to be used only with students with disabilities. The counselors all explained that whether or not they would implement the strategies was based on their personal exposure to, experience with, and ease of comfort in using each of the strategies.

The school counselors all described learning and using more strategies the longer they were a school counselor. The counselors learned two of the strategies (sensory box and social stories) from collaborating with other school personnel (occupational therapist and special education teacher). The sensory box was a school box that had been filled with items (gel bags, rice bags, silly-putty, etc.) that students could use that may help them reduce overstimulation from the classroom environment and calm down. Social stories, which often are used with students with autism, are easy-to-read stories that help students to learn routines or deal with upsetting situations.

(continued)

EXHIBIT 14.2   (continued)

Counseling Theories

All of the school counselors had difficulty responding to questions regarding how counseling theories influenced their choice of activities with students with disabilities, for two reasons: (a) They were not looking at theories specifically for students with disabilities, and (b) they tended to look at specific counseling strategies in their work with students rather than relying on specific counseling theories to guide their practice. During the first round of interviews, school counselors made comments such as, "There may be theories guiding it, but it would be subconsciously," and, "I wouldn't have a clue as to what a counseling theory regarding counseling special ed students would even entail." When struggling to find helpful activities for a student with a disability, they would collaborate with other school personnel or "use trial and error."

The counselors indicated that they could pull activities from any of the counseling theories, such as Adlerian/play (Corey, 1996; Seligman, 2001), brief/solution focused (Amatea, 1989; Thompson & Littrell, 1998), person-centered (Goor, McKnab, & Davison-Aviles, 1995; Williams & Lair, 1991), or reality choice theories (Garcia et al., 1998), but they maintained that they were choosing counseling activities based on the activity, and not based on reliance on a particular counseling theory. The school counselors each advocated using an eclectic approach when working with students with disabilities.

Collaboration and Teaming

Collaboration and teaming is an important theme in the ASCA National Model and one that was demonstrated in each of the data measures in this study. The school counselors collaborated with other school counselors and staff to plan, participate in collaborative counseling, and obtain new ideas and strategies. They communicated with doctors and outside therapists to coordinate services for their students and connected parents who needed assistance to outside sources. When asked to describe their work with students with disabilities, one counselor said, "Collaborative, because almost nothing you do with special ed kids are you doing on your own. There are a lot of other professionals helping, so you have to keep the lines of communication open. So it's a collaborative process." Each of the school counselors described collaboration as "very effective" at meeting the needs of students with disabilities, especially in developing goals for students and in monitoring student progress.

The following is a list of individuals with whom the school counselors could collaborate: (a) regular education teacher, (b) special education teacher, (c) gifted education teacher, (d) parents, (e) other school counselors, (f) behavior specialist, (g) special education counselor, (h) supervisor of counseling, (i) school administrator, (j) occupational therapist, (k) speech teacher, (l) physical therapist, and (m) school psychologist.

As the school counselors spoke about the need for collaboration, they mentioned that collaboration was the best advice they could give to other counselors who were interested in developing their skills in working with students with disabilities. These counselors suggested collaborating to develop their own support system for the following reasons: (a) "It is very difficult working with students with disabilities, because you don't always see the positive results and sometimes they are hard to find"; (b) "there will always be things or issues that come up that you don't know how to help and the important thing to do is to keep trying until you find the fight person to ask"; and (c) collaboration helps one to "continue to grow professionally."

One counselor described how her initial attempts to collaborate have led to increased collaboration with school staff as they hear about her collaborative efforts. She suggested collaboration with special education teachers to learn more strategies for counseling students with disabilities and gave the example of using social stories with nondisabled students:

> All the different special ed strategies, you can use in all aspects of your job. You can use them in a group that nobody has labeled special ed, but [where] they could all benefit from a social story, especially kindergarteners. They don't have to have Asperger's to benefit, because it's pictures. And that is what is going to work for any kindergartener who is trying to learn a routine.

In the review of the information obtained from the school counselors, collaboration served two purposes. Collaboration helped to better meet the personal/social needs of students with disabilities, through having other staff brainstorm and work on the same goals. Collaboration also served to provide school counselors with additional strategies they could use in working with their students.

Leadership

The last theme that emerged from this study, leadership, is yet another theme encompassed in the ASCA National Model. These school counselors were chosen to participate in this study based on their reputation of leadership, of actively working to meet the personal/social needs of students with disabilities in their schools when not all school counselors focus on working with these students. These school counselors described working with students with disabilities as challenging and unclear, and even though they felt undertrained, they continued to focus on working with these students and took the initiative to learn more about the students and their disabilities.

The fact that these school counselors have been moving their counseling programs toward an increased focus on students with diverse needs demonstrates in itself the excellent leadership skills of the school counselors. These counselors also have been taking steps to implement the recommendations of the ASCA National Model into their counseling programs even though they had not been mandated to do so, had not received much training on the ASCA National Model, and had not been given specifics on how to do this at the time.

These school counselors have been serving in leadership roles within their schools. They actively made certain that students with disabilities were included in all school activities, not just in counseling activities. They went against the status quo and attempted to make improvements in how these students' needs were best served. They assisted in training school staff and parents in how to work with these students. Through the influence of their data collection and reflection, they consistently tried to improve their school's counseling programs.

Additional Factors That Influence Working with Students with Disabilities

Several issues that surfaced during the study illustrated additional challenges faced by school counselors working with students with disabilities. One major issue was in counselors describing how some school principals place a greater emphasis on the school counselor working on academic improvement over personal/social issues in students. If a school counselor was working for a principal who was more focused on academic success, it may be more difficult for that counselor to spend time focusing on the personal/social needs of students.

Another issue discussed in the study was time. School counselors found it difficult to schedule groups around guidance counseling activities because students with disabilities were already being pulled out of the classroom for additional supportive services such as speech and occupational therapies.

The overabundance of reform initiatives was the next issue. At the time of this study, the state was in the process of creating its own set of guidance standards. Counselors were distracted by the recent development of the state guidance standards that were currently in draft form. While these were closely aligned with the ASCA National Model, the counselors had to remind themselves which one they were talking about during the study because they were receiving information on both at the same time, along with information on No Child Left Behind. School counselors seemed to be inundated with new guidelines and materials at this time as the school system was attempting to sort out the school counselor's role in working with students and in response to recent legislation.

The fourth issue of "duplication of services" was described by the school counselors as an issue that they reject but one that many counselors consider. The idea of "duplication of services" suggests that students with disabilities who are involved in counseling activities are getting double services, once from special education and another time from the counselor. One counselor mentioned that some school counselors make it a point not to actively counsel students with disabilities because they feel that they are already getting services from special

(continued)

EXHIBIT 14.2 (continued)

education and that special education students are not on their caseload. While the counselors involved in this study disagreed with this idea, they felt that some students may not be served if their counselor agrees with the idea of "duplication of services."

DISCUSSION

The ASCA National Model asks school counselors to examine "how students are different because of school counseling" (ASCA, 2003, p. 17). The school counselors involved in this study stated that students with disabilities are different because of school counseling for several reasons. These students make a connection with the school counselor and have someone who will advocate for them when necessary to make sure that the student is included and involved in all school activities. Students with disabilities can better deal with their personal/social difficulties because they are learning coping skills, such as improving self-esteem and behavior, from the school counselor. They learn to feel comfortable in who they are and to not see their disability as a limitation. Classroom guidance helps students with disabilities because it focuses on treating others with respect, fairness, and dignity and it incorporates anti-bullying lessons.

In summary, these school counselors meet the personal/social needs of students with disabilities through an eclectic counseling approach. They use classroom guidance and both individual and group counseling activities that focus on teaching students how to improve behavior and social skills and increase their self-esteem. These counselors help students by going against the status quo, providing activities that help the students feel better about themselves, and teaching students coping skills.

It is important to note that the school counselors do not see the counseling strategies they use as strategies that are specific to working only with students with disabilities, but rather as strategies that they have added to their repertoire for all students. This is advantageous for those who are concerned about becoming more skilled in working with students with disabilities. These school counselors are adapting their current counseling activities to meet the needs of these students, not having to acquire numerous new techniques and training that requires years of experience to develop skills. They are building on their professional expertise with other educational staff present in their own schools. They have found that through their desire to learn more about disabilities and through collaboration with other school professionals, they have gained additional counseling strategies that could be used with a variety of students.

Despite the newness of the ASCA National Model, it was interesting to note that many of the activities described by these school counselors as part of their repertoire of working with students with disabilities are those same activities encouraged and recommended by the model as part of ASCA's vision of successful and effective counseling and guidance programs.

Limitations

Limitations to this study include the small number of participants and the fact that the ethnographic interview method is designed only to provide information as to how these individual elementary school counselors meet the needs of the students with disabilities at their schools. The fact that these school counselors were chosen based on purposeful sampling and reputational case selection indicates that they were considered exemplary for their work with students with disabilities and that they do things differently than other school counselors. Therefore, these results most likely do not represent what other school counselors are doing to meet the needs of students with disabilities. The school counselor survey is another limitation as it was created by the researcher and is not a standardized measurement based on psychometrics. This study is unique and there is limited research on the ASCA National Model from which to compare this study's results.

The study and survey also could be criticized for looking at students with various disabilities, rather than looking at specific counseling strategies for particular disabilities. Another limitation comes from the use of self-report measures in the journal, vignette, survey, and interview questions. While efforts were made to triangulate the data through asking questions in different formats—that is, survey, journal, interview—and with different phrasing, the researcher was not present in any counseling session and did not observe the events that school counselors described.

Researcher bias is also a possible limitation to this study. While the researcher has experience with collaborative counseling and is enrolled in a counseling program, this researcher is a special educator. Efforts to control for this possible bias included receiving input from dissertation committee members on survey, interview, vignette, and journal question formats, including member checks throughout the process, and asking descriptive and contrast questions throughout the interviews. In fact, interview questions clearly focused on this issue and asked school counselors to describe their role compared to the roles of other school personnel in working with students with disabilities.

Implications for Practice

The school counselors in this study felt there was still more they would like to learn in regards to working with this population. Therefore, in-service training could be developed that would provide school counselors with counseling recommendations so they don't have to generate counseling strategies on their own. School counselors could develop in-service training to help principals and school staff better understand the counselor's role in working with all students, including those with disabilities, and assist in making certain their counselors had training in working with this population.

School counselor preparation programs could incorporate counseling internships that include more exposure to working with students with disabilities, specific counseling strategies and materials that are successful with students with disabilities, and strategies that encourage collaboration with other school personnel. An increased effort could be made within these courses to link counseling strategies for students with disabilities to specific counseling theories. In this way, school counselors could feel more comfortable in relation to counseling theory and their chosen interventions as well as be certain they were using counseling strategies that were supported by research.

Examining the existing beliefs and attitudes of school staff as well as counselor beliefs about their roles would be important in making certain that all involved in meeting the personal/social needs of students with disabilities were performing and doing so with specific awareness of their unique roles in meeting these needs. Additional training on the ASCA National Model and in strategies for working with students with disabilities also would help school counselors reluctant to work with students with disabilities to understand that these students are part of their caseload, thus refuting the "duplication of services" idea.

CONCLUSION

This study demonstrated that school counselors are providing activities to students with disabilities to meet their personal/social needs and that the activities they use with these students are in accordance with the ASCA National Model (ASCA, 2003). In order for schools to best meet all the needs of their students with disabilities, the academic, career, and personal/social needs of students with disabilities must be better recognized and addressed. When school counselors work with students with disabilities, they are following the ASCA National Model's guidelines for meeting the diverse needs of all of their students. The work that school counselors do to meet the needs of students with disabilities (collaboration, serving in leadership roles, advocating for students, and using a variety of strategies) is not a supplemental or discrete task required of school counselors. Rather, it is an example of school counselors using the ASCA National Model as it was intended—to guide forward the tasks of the counselor and to serve as a framework to help all students experience success.

(continued)

EXHIBIT 14.2 (continued)

REFERENCES

Amatea, E. S. (1989). *Brief strategic intervention for school problems.* San Francisco: Jossey-Bass.

American School Counselor Association. (1993). *Position statement: Students with disabilities.* Alexandria, VA: Author.

American School Counselor Association. (2003). *The ASCA national model: A framework for school counseling programs.* Alexandria, VA: Author.

Astigarra, J., & McEachern, A. G. (2000). Not broken, just different: Helping teachers work with children with attention-deficit/hyperactivity disorders. *CACD Journal, 20,* 27–33.

Baker, S. B. (2000). *School counseling for the 21st century.* Englewood Cliffs, NJ: Merrill.

Barton, S., & Fuhrmann, B. (1994). Counseling and psychotherapy for adults with learning disabilities. In P. Gerber & H. Reiff (Eds.), *Learning disabilities in adulthood: Persisting problems and evolving issues* (pp. 82–92). Boston: Andover Medical.

Baumberger, J. P., & Harper, R. E. (1999). *Assisting students with disabilities. What school counselors can and must do.* Thousand Oaks, CA: Corwin Press.

Bender, W. N., & Wall, M. E. (1994). Social-emotional development of students with learning disabilities. *Learning Disability Quarterly, 17,* 323–341.

Bowen, M. L., & Glenn, E. E. (1998). Counseling interventions for students who have mild disabilities. *Professional School Counseling, 2,* 16–25.

Brumback, R., & Weinberg, W. (1990). Pediatric behavioral neurology: An update on the neurological aspects of depression, hyperactivity, and learning disabilities. *Pediatric Neurology, 8,* 677–703.

Corey, G. (1996). *Theory and practice of counseling and psychotherapy* (5th ed.). Pacific Grove, CA: Brooks/Cole.

Deck, M., Scarborough, J. L., Sferrazza, M. S., & Estill, D. M. (1999). Serving students with disabilities: Perspectives of three school counselors. *Intervention in School and Clinic, 34,* 150–153.

Dunn, N., Wood, A., & Baker, S. A. (2002). Readiness to serve students with disabilities: A survey of elementary school counselors. *Professional School Counseling, 5,* 277–284.

Garcia, J. G., Krankowski, T., & Jones, L. L. (1998). Collaborative interventions for assisting students with acquired brain injuries in school. *Professional School Counseling, 2,* 33–39.

Glaser, B. B., & Strauss, A. L. (1967). *The discovery of grounded theory: Strategies for qualitative research.* Chicago: Aldine.

Glenn, E. E. (1998). Counseling children and adolescents with disabilities. *Professional School Counseling, 2,* iii–iv.

Glenn, E. E., & Smith, T. T. (1998). Building self-esteem of children and adolescents with communication disorders. *Professional School Counseling, 2,* 39–47.

Goor, M. B., McKnab, P. A., & Davison-Aviles, R. (1995). Counseling individuals with learning disabilities. In. A. F. Rotatori, J. O. Schween, & F. W. Litton (Eds.), *Advances in special education: Counseling in special populations: Research and practice perspectives* (Vol. 9, pp. 98–118). Greenwich, CT: JAI Press.

Gresham, F. M. (1992). Social skills and learning disabilities: Casual, concomitant, or correlational? *School Psychology Review, 21,* 348–360.

Grigsby, D. A. (1990). Dialogue: Cross cultural counseling for exceptional individuals and their families. *National Forum of Special Education Journal, 1,* 67–69.

Helms, N. E., & Katsiyannis, A. (1992). Counselors in elementary schools: Making it work for students with disabilities. *The School Counselor, 39,* 232–237.

Kish, M. (1991). Counseling adolescents with LD. *Intervention in School and Clinic, 27,* 20–24.

Kloomok, S., & Cosden, M. (1994). Self-concept in children with learning disabilities. The relationship between global self-concept, academic discounting, nonacademic self-concept, and perceived social support. *Learning Disability Quarterly, 17,* 104–153.

Kottman, T., Robert, R., & Baker, D. (1995). Parental perspectives on attention-deficit/hyperactivity disorder: How school counselors can help. *The School Counselor, 43,* 142–150.

Larson, K. A. (1998). A research review and alternative hypothesis explaining the link between learning disability and delinquency. *Journal of Learning Disabilities, 21,* 357–369.

LaGreca, A. M., & Vaughn, S. (1992). Social functioning of individuals with learning disabilities. *School Psychology Review, 21,* 423–427.

LeCompte, M. D., & Pressle, J. (1993). *Ethnography and qualitative design in educational research* (2nd ed.). San Diego, CA: Academic Press.

Margalit, M. (1992). Sense of coherence and families with a learning-disabled child. In B. Wong (Ed.), *Contemporary intervention research in learning disabilities* (pp. 134–145). New York: Springer-Verlag.

Merriam, S. B. (1998). *Qualitative research and case study applications in education.* San Francisco: John Wiley & Sons.

Milsom, A. (2002). Students with disabilities: School counselor involvement and preparation. *Professional School Counseling, 5,* 331–338.

Okolo, C. M., & Sitlington, R. (1986). The role of special education in LD adolescents' transition from school to work. *Learning Disability Quarterly, 9,* 141–155.

Omizo, M. M., Cubberly, W. E., & Longano, D. M. (1984). The effects of group counseling on self-concept and locus of control among learning disabled children. *Humanistic Education and Development, 23,* 69–79.

Omizo, M. M., & Omizo, S. A. (1994). Group counseling's effects on self-concept and social behavior among children with learning disabilities. *Journal of Humanistic Education and Development, 26,* 109–117.

Patton, M. Q. (1990). *Qualitative evaluation and research methods* (2nd ed.). Newbury Park, CA: Sage.

QSR International. (2003). *NVivo: New generation software for qualitative data analysis.* Doncaster Victoria, Australia: Author.

Rodis, P., Garrod, A., & Boscardin, M. L. (2001). *Learning disabilities and life stories.* Boston: Allyn and Bacon.

Schumaker, J. B. (1992). Social performance of individuals with learning disabilities: Through the looking glass of KUIRLD research. *School Psychology Review, 21,* 387–399.

Seligman, L. (2001). *Systems, strategies, and skills of counseling and psychotherapy.* Upper Saddle, NJ: Prentice Hall.

Spradley, J. P. (1979). *The ethnographic interview.* Orlando, FL: Harcourt.

Spreen, O. (1998). *Learning disabled children growing up: A follow-up into adulthood.* New York: Oxford University Press.

Swanson, H. L., & Malone, S. (1992). Social skills and learning disabilities: A meta-analysis of the literature. *School Psychology Review, 21,* 427–442.

Tabassam, W., & Grainger, J. (2002). Self-concept, attributional style, and self-efficacy beliefs of students with learning disabilities with and without attention deficit hyperactivity disorder. *Learning Disability Quarterly, 25,* 141–151.

Thompson, R., & Littrell, J. M. (1998). Brief counseling for students with learning disabilities. *Professional School Counseling, 2,* 60–68.

U.S. Department of Education. (2002). *No Child Left Behind.* Retrieved April 26, 2003, from http://www.ed.gov/nclb/landing.jhtml

Vaughn, S., & Hager, D. (1994). Social competence as a multifaceted construct: How do students with learning disabilities fare? *Learning Disability Quarterly, 17,* 253–266.

(continued)

EXHIBIT 14.2 **(continued)**

Voeller, K. (1993). Techniques for measuring social competence in children. In G. Lyon (Ed.), *Frames of reference for the assessment of learning disabilities* (pp. 523–554). Baltimore: Brookes.

Weiss, R. S. (1994). *Learning from strangers: The art and method of qualitative interview studies.* New York: First Free Press.

Williams, W. C., & Lair, G. S. (1991). Using a person-centered approach with children who have a disability. *Elementary School Guidance and Counseling, 25,* 194–204.

EXHIBIT 14.3 **The Effect of Reciprocal Peer Counseling in the Enhancement of Self-Concept Among Adolescents**

E. O. Egbochuku   J. J. Obiunu

INTRODUCTION

The desire for a positive evaluation of self affects a person's feelings, actions, and aspirations throughout life. School experiences play an important role in the development of self-perceptions in the course of childhood and adolescence and this can have powerful long-term effects on an individual's self concept; yet most proposals for school improvement and reform emphasize either teachers, administrators, parents, or class size, overlooking one of the most crucial change agents—the students. All of this is contrary to the peer principle, which believes that deep, lasting changes, individually and structurally, must ultimately come from sharing with like individuals.

The effectiveness of the use of peer counsellors within the school system has been well documented in foreign literature (Hsiao-Chen, 2003; Ladyshewsky 2001; Hoffman and Warner, 1976). Gartner and Riessman (1998) in their study proposed the application of the peer counseling principle in schools since research has shown that peer counselling and other peer support programmes are effective in improving attitudes and behavior and even have a ripple effect on the schools' overall dynamics. Shechtman (2002) reviewed the outcome of research on group psychotherapy with children and found a consensus on its effectiveness. Shechtman's review also found that in order to improve achievement, the social and emotional dimensions along with academic need must be addressed. Peer counsellors fall under the general rubric of paraprofessionals—that is those without professional training who are selected from the group to be served, trained and given on-going supervision to perform some key functions generally performed by professionals. Peer group counselling provides a non-judgemental acceptance, care and support; provides opportunities to give and receive from others and creates a non-competitive, empowering environment.

In the Nigerian society, the child in school is expected to receive instruction and guidance from the adults in the school. There is no evidence in literature about the use of peers as counsellors in Nigerian secondary schools. However, it is critical to note that young people are far more influenced by their peers than by parents, teachers or other adults (Gartner and Riessman, 1998). Peers have a profound effect on each other's fashions, social attitudes and decisions. For better or for worse, they model themselves on other young people. While there may be unquestionably much negativity in peer influence, there are lots of young people who are dedicated to their own advancement and that of their mates. These students, if trained can form the core of the peer counselling programmes, the essential idea being that people are influenced and can be helped best by others who share their problems or conditions.

Brigman and Campbell (2003) opined that one of the most promising interventions for school counsellors interested in making their impact felt on students' achievement and behaviour is peer group counselling. Peer group counselling is a mode of counselling which involves a relationship among three or more persons of relatively same age and status in which all mutually seek the goal of bringing about positive behavioural changes in group members. One of them acts as the facilitator. A modification of this mode of counselling is the reciprocal peer group counselling in which group members act as facilitators in turns. Such developmental programmes are proactive and preventive, helping students acquire the attitudes necessary for successful mastery of normal developmental tasks. But do our educational administrators understand fully the potentials and significance of peer programmes? Do they understand that peer influence can be positive? If a child is given the opportunity to participate in peer counselling as a counsellor having the opportunity to share a valuable and worthwhile experience, will he or she not gain in self worth? Will the experience not motivate him/her to reach out to others and to perfect his or her skills? In the same vein, if a child is a client to a peer counsellor after whom he or she can model himself or herself, will his or her feeling of self worth not be enhanced because he or she has a counsellor who truly understands? Will the similarity in experience not enhance the self-concept of both counselor and client?

It is therefore hoped that the results of the present study will draw the attention of school counsellors, educational planners, and administrators to the significance of the peer principle in relation to self-concept enhancement that will invariably influence the school improvement and reforms.

Hypotheses

The following null hypotheses were formulated to guide the study.

1. There will be no significant difference in the self-concept of adolescent students in the experimental and control group at post-test.
2. There will be no significant difference in the self-concept of males and females in the treatment groups.

Methodology

This study is experimental in nature. A pre-test/post-test control design was employed. The impetus of the study was to observe the effects of peer counselling on self-concept. The variables were peer counselling verse control (manipulated variables), and sex (intervening variable) on enhancement self-concept (criterion variable). The population of the study was all the senior secondary schools in Benin City, Edo State. There are about thirty-four senior secondary schools in Benin City. These are single sex and co-educational schools with population ranging from 5002,500 students. The choice of Benin City is based on its metropolitan nature. It is the state capital consisting of three out of the eighteen local government areas in the state. The inhabitants are of diverse socioeconomic status.

Stratified random sampling was employed to select three schools from the strata—Boys', Girls', and co-educational schools. The sample consisted of sixty-eight senior secondary school II students (males and females) from the three schools randomly selected. Simple random sampling was used to select one intact class each from the SS II classes in the three schools. The choice of SS II students for the study was made because SS I students are new in the senior secondary school system and are still settling down while SS III is the certificate class, preparing for an external examination.

The initial concept of the study was to select only subjects with low self-concept scores: However, on administration of the instrument (pre-test), it was found that there were no students with low self-concept. This could be as a result of parental involvement with the African child. Students were therefore randomly assigned to the treatment and control groups. The final selection of subjects was carried out at the point of analysis of data collected. Subjects with very high self-concept at the pre-test were dropped.

(continued)

EXHIBIT 14.3 (continued)

A 40-item self-concept scale was constructed, validated and used to measure the variable, self-concept. Peer counselling was employed to effect self-concept modification in the subjects, while a control group of students also received a non-specific treatment. Sixty-eight senior secondary school two students were involved in this study. One instrument was used in the study. The instrument, an Adolescent Self Concept Inventory (ASCI) was adapted from the Akinboye (1977) adolescent personal data inventory (self concept scale). The original version of the scale was made up of 30-items. Some items on the scale were modified in language and ten new items were added to make the present instrument a 40-item scale. In Akinboye (1977), APDI a nine-point scale ranging from least "like me" to "most like me" was used to rate each item, while the present instrument used a 5-point Likert scale ranging from "completely true of me" to "completely untrue of me."

Treatment Programs

The treatment programmes for the study included pre-treatment, treatment and post treatment sessions. There were two groups of subjects, the treatment and control groups. The treatment programme for the treatment group was designed to enhance the self-concept of the subjects. The treatment programme for the control group consisted of lessons in English language on the topic-spoken English, which was taught by the English teachers in the three schools.

The pre-treatment for all the subjects, involved, first, a pre-test of the instrument, and secondly, random assignment of subjects into the treatment groups. For the treatment group, besides the pre-test and random assignment of subjects into the group, peer counsellors were randomly selected and trained; research assistants were also trained. Eleven sessions were used for the training of the ten peer counsellor (on a one-to-one basis) and research assistants in each of the schools. The treatment programme involved 10 one (1) hour sessions in which the subjects in a peer group counselling encounter focussed on the topics: Leadership skills, self esteem, good study habits, skills for effective study habits, preparing for examinations, self awareness, self worth, body image, self acceptance and being yourself. For the control group, the treatment programme involved English lessons on spoken English, which focussed on consonant sounds. This also lasted for 10 sessions.

RESULTS

To determine the effects of treatment on the self-concept of the subjects, the following hypothesis was tested at .05 level of significances.

There will be no significant difference in the self-concept of adolescent students in the various treatment groups at post-test.

The data displayed on Table 1, reveal that the mean score for peer counseling ($M = 164.71$) is significantly higher than that of the control group ($M = 132.82$). This indicates a significant difference in the self-concept of adolescent students who participated in the various treatment programmes. Further analysis was carried out to determine if the mean score for the peer-counselling group was significantly higher than that of the control group.

TABLE 1 Distribution of Post-Test Mean Scores for Self-Concept

Groups	N	Mean	SD
Peer counselling	34	164.71	13.44
Control	34	132.82	26.63

Analysis on Table 2 reveals that the calculated t-value of 6.58 is greater than the critical t-value of 1.96 with $df = 66$ and alpha level of .05. The null hypothesis is therefore rejected at $p < .05$ and conclusion is reached that there is a significant difference in the self-concept of subjects in the treatment groups at post-test.

TABLE 2 Mean, Standard Deviation, and *t*-Test Data on the Effects of Treatment on Post-Test Self-Concept of Subjects

Treatment	N	X̄	SD	Mean Difference	t
Peer-counselling	34	164.71	13.45		
Control	34	132.82	24.86	31.88	6.58*

*Significant at .05 level.

There will be no significant difference in the self-concept of male and females in the treatment groups at post-test.

Figures in parentheses represent number of subjects in the subgroups.

The data displayed in Table 3 reveals that the mean score for males in the treatment groups as ($M = 148.25$) is not significantly different from the mean score for female ($M = 149.36$). Further analysis of the data shown on Table 4, also reveals that the calculated *t*-value of .17 is less than the critical *t*-value of 1.96 with degree of freedom, 66 and at level of .05.

TABLE 3 Distribution of Mean Post-Test Scores of Treatment Groups by Sex

Sex	Treatment		Total
	Peer Counselling	Control	
Male	165.5 (18)	132.8 (20)	148.28 (38)
Female	163.81 (16)	132.85 (14)	149.36 (30)
Total	164.71 (34)	132.82 (34)	68

Figures in parentheses represent number of subjects in the subgroups.

TABLE 4 Mean, Standard Deviation, and *t*-Test Data on the Effects of Sex on the Post-Test Self-Concept of Subjects

Sex	N	X̄	SD	Mean Difference	t
Female	30	149.37	26.62		
Male	38	148.29	24.96	1.08	.17*

*Not significant at $p > 0.05$.

The null hypothesis which states no significant difference in self-concept between male and female is therefore accepted at $p > 0.05$.

Discussion

The finding of this study indicates that reciprocal peer counselling has a significant positive effect on the self-concept of the adolescent students. This finding lend credence to the assertion made by (Hoffman and Warner 1976; Divers-Starnes 1991; and Ladyshewsky 2001; Hsiao-Chen, 2003) among others, that paraprofessionals, particularly peers can be as effective as professionals in counselling when given the required training. The findings are also in agreement with those of Oladele (2000) who reported positive effect in programme participants' self efficiency and behaviour as well as increased self-esteem, self-awareness and capacity for empathy. The researchers of the present study are not surprised at the outcome of the study. Peers have a profound influence on one another and peer-oriented interventions are designed to capitalize on the potentially positive influence of peers

(continued)

EXHIBIT 14.3 (continued)

in bringing about improvement in behaviour (Choudhury, 2001). Generally, studies have shown that children have certain advantages over adults in helping their peers. They understand their problems better because they are cognitively closer and this fact makes the peer counsellor present the issue in terms the group members will understand (Nwagwu and Nwaneri, 2002). The peer counsellors can effectively model study skills and habits, ask and answer questions posed by group members. It was based on the above assumptions that the present study set out to improve the self concept of adolescents through reciprocal peer group counselling in which many of the children had the opportunity of being models to others and these enhanced the self-concept of the students. As Patwardhan (2002) noted in his study, the similarity between model and learner increases with the influence of modelling. The findings of this study therefore give support to the use of peers in bringing about fundamental positive changes in students' behaviour, both academic and general.

The findings of the study indicate that there is no significant effect of sex on the self-concept of the students involved in the study. These findings are at variance with the findings of Fontana, (1981), and Obidigbo (2002) who reported that girls had a lower self-concept than boys. A possible explanation for this is that in the last few decades, women's career choices and social relations have been diversified and the distinction between jobs for men and women are becoming hazy. This has resulted in Nigerian adolescents, perceiving themselves positively irrespective of sex, age or socio-economic status. Moreover, models exist for both sexes in all spheres of life encouraging both sexes in all spheres of life encouraging both sexes to aspire high. The findings of the study are in consonance with those of Egbochuku, (1997) and Nwagwu and Nwaneri (2002) who studied the demographic difference in adolescent self-concept, and made findings, which indicated no significant difference in the way, Nigerian boys and girls perceive themselves.

CONCLUSION

The results of the study reveal that reciprocal peer counselling is effective in enhancing the self-concept of individuals; sex has no effect on the self-concept of the adolescents. It can be concluded that peer influence can be positive and that the peer group counselling encounter can be psychologically rewarding. Also there was no significant difference in the way males and females perceive themselves in the study. This shows that peer counselling is a technique that can be used for the enhancement of self-concept for both sexes. Since Reciprocal peer counselling therapy proved effective in the enhancement of self-concept, it follows therefore that the result of this study is valuable to the Nigerian educational system. The implementation of the results of this study will to a large extent bring about a change both to the individuals and the school and the society at large, which could lead to a reduction in cult activities; and wastage rates in the school system.

REFERENCES

Akinboye, J. O. (1977), Adolescent personal data inventory (self-concept scale), University Press Limited Ibadan.
Brigman, G., and Campbell, C. (2003) "Helping students improve academic achievement and school success behaviour". Professional school counselling. Dec. 2003. American School Counsellor Association.
Choudhury, I. (2001). Use of reciprocal peer tutoring technique in an environmental control systems course at an undergraduate level. ASC proceedings of the 37th Annual Conference, University of Denver, Colorado.
Diver-Starnes, A. C. (1991) "Assessing the effectiveness of an inner-city high school peer counselling program." *Urban Education 26,* 269–284.
Egbochuku, E. O. (1997). "Differential effectiveness of three guidance techniques to fostering maturity among secondary school adolescents." Unpublished Ph.D. Thesis. University of Benin-Benin City, Nigeria Coppersmith.
Fontana, D. (1981). *Psychology for teachers.* British Psychological Society and Macmillan Publishers, Ltd.

Hoffman, A. M., and Warner, R. M. (1976). "Paraprofessionals effectiveness." *Personnel and Guidance Journal, 54*(10).

Hsiao-Chen, H. (2003). "A research on career self concept and its relevant factors of high school students from single-parent family."

Ladyshewsky, R. (2001). *Reciprocal peer coaching: A strategy for training and development in professional discipline.* Jamison, ACT, Australia: Higher Education Research and Development Society of Australia Inc.

Nwagwu H. and Nwaneri, C. (2002). "The demographic differences on adolescent self-concept." *Nigerian Journal of Clinical and Counselling, 8*(2), 44–166.

Obidegbo, G. C. (2002). "The relationship between self concept and academic performance of Nigerian Students." *IFE Psychologia, 10*(2).

Oladele, J. O. (2000). *Fundamentals of guidance and counselling. A functional approach.* Johns-Lad Publishers. Lagos.

Patwardhan, V. (2002). Self-concept of Eritrean Students: Exploring self-concept of students' links with gender grade and future identity.

Shechtman, Z. (2002). "Child group psychotherapy in the school at the threshold of a new millennium." *Journal of Counselling and Development, 50,* 293–299.

Sisco, P. (2000). "Peer Counselling: An Overview." Independent Liong Institute Canada.

REFERENCES

Balli, S. J. (1998). When mom and dad help: Student reflections on parent involvement with homework. *Journal of Research and Development in Education, 31,* 142–147.

Bogdan, R. C., & Biklen, S. K. (2007). *Qualitative research in education: An introduction to theory and methods* (5th ed.). Boston: Allyn & Bacon.

Borich, G. D., & Madden, S. K. (1977). *Evaluating classroom instruction: A sourcebook of instruments.* Reading, MA: Addison-Wesley.

Borman, G. D., & Dowling, N. M. (2006). Longitudinal achievement effects of multiyear summer school: *Evidence from the teach Baltimore randomized field trial. Educational Evaluation and Policy Analysis, 28*(1), 25–48.

Bryman, A. (2006). Integrating quantitative and qualitative research: How is it done? *Qualitative Research, 6*(1), 97–113.

Calhoun, E. M. (1994). *How to use research in the self-renewing school.* Alexandria, VA: Association for Supervision and Curriculum Development.

Campbell, D. T., and Stanley, J. C. (1963). Experimental and quasi-experimental designs for research on teaching. In N. L. Gage (Ed.), *Handbook of research on teaching.* Chicago: Rand-McNally.

Case, R. E. (2004). Forging ahead into new social networks and looking back to past social identities: A case study of a foreign-born English as a second language teacher in the United States. *Urban Education, 39*(2), 125–148.

Certo, J., Cauley, K. M., & Chafin, C. (2002). Students' perspectives on their high school experience. Paper presented at the Annual Meeting of the American Educational Research Association, April, New Orleans.

Choi, H., & Heckenlaible–Gotto, M. J. (1998). Classroom-based social skills training: Impact on peer acceptance of first-grade students. *Journal of Educational Research, 91,* 209–214.

Chun, K. T., Cobb, S., & French, J. R. P., Jr. (1974). *Measures for psychological assessment: A guide to 3,000 original sources and their applications.* Ann Arbor: Institute for Social Research, University of Michigan.

Comrey, A. L., Backer, T. E., & Glaser, E. M. (1973). *A sourcebook of mental health measures.* Los Angeles: Human Interaction Research Institute.

Conger, D. (2005). Within-school segregation in an urban school district. *Educational Evaluation and Policy Analysis, 27*(3), 225–244.

Creswell, J. W. (2005). *Educational research: Planning, conducting, and evaluating quantitative and qualitative research* (2nd ed.). Upper Saddle River, NJ: Pearson Education.

Creswell, J. W., & Plano Clark, V. L. (2006). *Designing and conducting mixed methods research.* Thousand Oaks, CA: Sage.

Fabiano, E. (1989). *Index to tests used in educational dissertations.* Phoenix, AZ: Oryx Press.

Gall, M. D., Borg, W. R., & Gall, J. P. (2003). *Educational research: An introduction* (7th ed.). New York: Longman.

Gall, M. D., Gall, J. P., & Borg, W. R. (2007). *Educational research: An introduction* (8th ed.). Boston: Allyn & Bacon.

Giebelhaus, C. R., & Bowman, C. L. (2002). Teaching mentors: Is it worth the effort? *The Journal of Educational Research, 95,* 246–254.

Glanz, J. (2003). *Action research: An educational leader's guide to school improvement* (2nd ed.). Norwood MA: Christopher-Gordon.

Goldman, B., & Mitchell, D. (1997). *Directory of unpublished experimental mental measures* (Vol. 7). Washington, DC: American Psychological Association.

Goodwin, W. L., & Driscoll, L. (1980). *Handbook for measurement and evaluation in early childhood education: Issues, measures, and methods.* San Francisco: Jossey-Bass.

Greene, J. C., Caracelli, V. J., & Graham, W. F. (1989). Toward a conceptual framework for mixed-method evaluation designs. *Educational Evaluation and Policy Analysis, 11*(3), 255–274.

Hammill, D. D., Brown, L., & Bryant, B. (1992). *A consumer's guide to tests in print* (2nd ed.). Austin, TX: Pro-Ed.

Hanson, W. E., Creswell, J. W., Plano Clark, V. L., Petska, K. S., & Creswell, D. J. (2005). Mixed methods research designs in counseling psychology. *Journal of Counseling Psychology, 52*(2), 224–235.

Heck, R. H. & Crislip, M. (2001). Direct and indirect writing assessments: Examining issues of equity and utility. *Educational Evaluation and Policy Analysis, 23,* 19–36.

INDEX